Selling Out Education

The Knowledge Economy and Education

Volume 8

Scope:
The aim of this series is to provide a focus for writers and readers interested in exploring the relation between the knowledge economy and education or an aspect of that relation, for example, vocational and professional education theorised critically.

It seeks authors who are keen to question conceptually and empirically the causal link that policymakers globally assume exists between education and the knowledge economy by raising: (i) epistemological issues as regards the concepts and types of and the relations between knowledge, the knowledge economy and education; (ii) sociological and political economic issues as regards the changing nature of work, the role of learning in workplaces, the relation between work, formal and informal learning and competing and contending visions of what a knowledge economy/knowledge society might look like; and (iii) pedagogic issues as regards the relationship between knowledge and learning in educational, community and workplace contexts.

The series is particularly aimed at researchers, policymakers, practitioners and students who wish to read texts and engage with researchers who call into question the current conventional wisdom that the knowledge economy is a new global reality to which all individuals and societies must adjust, and that lifelong learning is the strategy to secure such an adjustment. The series hopes to stimulate debate amongst this diverse audience by publishing books that: (i) articulate alternative visions of the relation between education and the knowledge economy; (ii) offer new insights into the extent, modes, and effectiveness of people's acquisition of knowledge and skill in the new circumstances that they face in the developed and developing world, (iii) and suggest how changes in both work conditions and curriculum and pedagogy can led to new relations between work and education.

Selling Out Education

National Qualifications Frameworks and the Neglect of Knowledge

Stephanie Allais
University of the Witwatersrand, Johannesburg, South Africa

SENSE PUBLISHERS
ROTTERDAM/BOSTON/TAIPEI

A C.I.P. record for this book is available from the Library of Congress.

ISBN: 978-94-6209-576-2 (paperback)
ISBN: 978-94-6209-577-9 (hardback)
ISBN: 978-94-6209-578-6 (e-book)

Published by: Sense Publishers,
P.O. Box 21858,
3001 AW Rotterdam,
The Netherlands
https://www.sensepublishers.com/

Printed on acid-free paper

This book raises fundamental questions about National Qualifications Frameworks which have been adopted in many countries. This penetrating analysis raises fundamental questions about the relationships between these frameworks and the place of knowledge in the curriculum. The issues that Dr Allais raises should be of fundamental concern to all educational policy makers, academics and teachers. It is a book that should be read. - **Hugh Lauder, Professor of Education and Political Economy, University of Bath, Editor of *Journal of Education and Work* and co-author of *The Global Auction : The Broken Promises of Education, Jobs and Incomes.***

This book is original in both theoretical and policy terms and brings together an impressive range of data on qualifications reform in developed and developing countries. For researchers it offers a critical examination of the link between the misplaced focus on 'learning outcomes' and the totally unrealistic claims for National Qualification Frameworks. At the same time it is the first attempt to bring together a critical political economy and a realist sociology of knowledge in a broader based social theory. For policy makers, it not only provides a trenchant critique of qualification-led reforms, but provides a serious and practical alternative strategy based on 'institution building' and a knowledge-led approach to the curriculum of particular relevance to developing countries. - **Michael Young, Emeritus Professor of Education, Institute of Education, University of London**

To allow the market mechanism to be sole director of the fate of human beings and their natural environment, indeed, even of the amount and use of purchasing power, would result in the demolition of society. For the alleged commodity 'labour power' cannot be shoved about, used indiscriminately, or even left unused, without affecting also the human individual who happens to be the bearer of this peculiar commodity. In disposing of man's labour power the system would, incidentally, dispose of the physical, psychological, and moral entity 'man' attached to that tag. Robbed of the protective covering of cultural institutions, human beings would perish from the effects of social exposure; they would die as victims of acute social dislocation through vice, perversion, crime and starvation. Nature would be reduced to its elements, neighbourhoods and landscapes defiled, rivers polluted, military safety jeopardized, the power to produce food and raw materials destroyed. Finally, the market administration of purchasing power would periodically liquidate business enterprise, for shortages and surfeits of money would prove as disastrous to business as floods and droughts in primitive society.
Polanyi, The Great Transformation, p. 73

A Moderate
His Holiness the Pope says the sun goes around the earth
while the earth goes round the sun, say extremists in the north.
In a war of propaganda, no one says what he means
I think, the Truth, as usual, lies somewhere in between.

Michael Rosen. Mind the Gap. 1992.
Scholastic Publications. London

TABLE OF CONTENTS

LIST OF FIGURE AND BOXES

ACKNOWLEDGEMENTS

Many people assisted me in many different ways on the long journey towards writing this book. Foremost among them is Njogu Morgan, who was patient, kind, loving, caring, considerate, and indulgent. He read bits; listened to arguments, ideas, and rantings; and forced me to take much needed breaks. Of my colleagues, I would like to particularly mention Professor Michael Young from the Institute of Education at the University of London, Professor Yael Shalem from the School of Education at the University of the Witwatersrand, and Dr Christine Evans-Klock from the International Labour Organization. Michael supervised my doctoral research, on which this book draws substantially. He was an extraordinarily generous PhD supervisor, both with his time and ideas, and has remained as generous, supportive, and kind as a colleague. To work with such a knowledgeable and wise person is a great privilege. Yael is the best of mentors: encouraging, funny, and incisive. I will always be grateful for the amount of time she spends reading my work, and explaining what I need to do to make it make sense. Christine, whom I worked for when conducting some of the research that is discussed in this book, was the best boss a researcher could hope for: having commissioned a sensitive piece of research, she was supportive in every way to make it happen, rigorously reading and commenting on drafts, and never interfering with the conclusions even when they were difficult. It was a great pleasure to work for her. The ILO was a generative learning environment, and I appreciate the many debates and discussions with colleagues, many of whom disagreed with some of my analysis and conclusions.

Also deserving of special mention are Jeanne Gamble, Peliwe Lolwana, Carmel Marock, and Lynne Slonimsky, for support and generative advice over the years, and of course my parents, Jo and Marco Allais, whose constant support is invaluable. Many other colleagues, friends, and comrades have provided ideas, encouragement, advice, wisdom, and friendship. They include (in alphabetical order): Lucy Allais, Cecile Badenhorst, Patrick Bond, Franzette Bower, Karin Brodie, Deborah Byrne, Michel Carton, Borhene Chakroun, Linda Chisholm, Sue Cohen, Linda Cooper, Ben Fine, Sheri Hamilton, Lynn Hewlett, Edward French, Christine Hoffman, Kenneth King, Andrew Lawrence, Rosemary Lugg, Simon McGrath, Anne Mclennan, Ian Moll, John Pampallis, Devan Pillay, David Raffe, Fiona Tregenna, Ben Scully, Carola Steinberg, Volker Wedekind, Leesa Wheelahan, and Tessa Welch. Clara Pope did a painstakingly careful edit, proving once again to be a wonderful, intelligent, helpful, and humorous editor. The Faculty of Social Sciences and Humanities at Wits University contributed to covering the cost of having the draft edited, for which I am grateful.

Parts of this book were written during an ESRC Post-Doctoral Fellowship, award number PTA-026-27-2166. This enabled time spent at the Centre for Educational Sociology in the beautiful and inspirational city of Edinburgh, which was invaluable towards the completion of this book.

ACKNOWLEDGEMENTS

Chapters 1, 4, and 8 draw on the research published in 'The Impact and Implementation of National Qualifications Frameworks: a comparison of 16 countries', and 'The Changing Faces of the South African National Qualifications Framework', both published in the *Journal of Education and Work,* Vol 24, Nos 3 – 4, and chapter 6 draws to a more limited extent on material presented in the article 'Claims versus practicalities: lessons about using learning outcomes', from vol 25 (3). Chapter 5 draws on material published in 'Will skills save us? Rethinking the relationships between vocational education, skills development policies, and social policy in South Africa' in the *International Journal of Educational Development* 32 (2012). Chapter 7 draws on 'Economics imperialism, education policy, and educational theory', published in the *Journal of Education Policy,* 27(2). I thank the editors of these journals for kindly giving permission to draw on these articles for the purpose of this book.

I dedicate this book to my little ones, Emma Wamucii and Joanna Muthoni Morgan-Allais.

INTRODUCTION:
FIRST AS FARCE, THEN AS TRAGEDY....

Karl Marx famously said, "Hegel remarks somewhere that all great world-historic facts and personages appear, so to speak, twice. He forgot to add: the first time as tragedy, the second time as farce."[1]

Fads in education reform also repeat themselves, but sometimes, in a reversal of Marx's aphorism, first as farce, then as tragedy. In this book I argue that many reform fads start out in rich countries as farces. But they have tragic consequences when they are implemented in poorer countries, often with the assistance of 'experts' from the richer countries. This book examines a particular manifestation of this depressing cycle.

My object of analysis is the development of learning outcomes and national qualifications frameworks, a reform trend that has rapidly gained international momentum.

I demonstrate that, far from being beneficial, outcomes-based qualifications frameworks are at best a waste of time and resources, and at worst destructive of education systems. Whereas in developed countries strong education institutions, traditions, and professionals may mask the problems of outcomes-based qualifications, this masking does not take place in poor countries where education systems and institutions are weak, and so the problems are clearly exposed. The experiences of developing countries can thus shed light on the key practical and conceptual problems of outcomes-based qualifications frameworks in both developed and developing countries.

My primary aim in writing this book is not, however, to convince people that investing time and other resources in the creation of learning outcomes and national qualifications frameworks is misguided. My primary aim is to convince educationalists about the value of organized bodies of knowledge, and that a primary role of education is assisting learners to acquire this knowledge; consequently, bodies of knowledge should be the starting point of curriculum design. This argument needs to be made because many of us, in the past and present, have abandoned or neglected organized bodies of knowledge in education. We have aimed to recreate the everyday world in the curriculum in the hope of making education more accessible to learners; we have over-emphasized competence and skills at the expense of knowledge; we have over-emphasized the social construction of knowledge at the expense of any sense that there are bodies of knowledge that are worth acquiring and that give us real insight into the natural and social world; or we have over-emphasized the extent to which the curriculum expresses ruling class ideology. There have been, and continue to be, valid reasons for all of these stances of educational reformers. Traditional curricula *do* need to be reformed, they *do* reflect dominant ideologies in various ways—although exactly *how* they do this is not straightforward and is much neglected by educational researchers—and education systems *have* failed many young people. But, I suggest that while the aim of educationalists has been to empower learners, particularly those learners who have not succeeded in formal education, the marginalization of knowledge has had the opposite effect, and has had negative consequences for individuals and society, particularly for poor learners, and learners in poor countries.

My experiences in education in South Africa have offered a particularly clear lens on the conundrums of curriculum reform and debates about the role of knowledge.

The 1990s in South Africa were a heady time of possibility. We had overthrown apartheid, the most notorious system of racial oppression ever known, and we felt we could do anything. Many serious problems faced the new nation. Optimistic in what we believed to be a unique opportunity to create things anew, to build a new society, to make real and meaningful changes, we responded with a flurry of policy development.

I was a student activist in the early 1990s, before the democratic elections. As students we were involved in developing education policy in what was known as the mass democratic movement, broadly aligned to the African National Congress. There was excitement in the air, and a sense that we could develop new education policies that would unite our divided nation, overcome inequalities, and forge a prosperous new society. We were going to ensure redress for people who had been denied access to education. We would increase access to education, and improve education for the majority of the population. This meant transforming apartheid education institutions and apartheid curricula, which, particularly in the school system, had been authoritarian, prescriptive, and, obviously, had taught about the world from the perspective of the apartheid state and the perceived interests of the white population. We would ensure that workers could have their skills recognized, to open up possibilities for promotion, and we would ensure more training for workers.

The mass democratic movement had a tradition of robust and lively debate and discussion, and although many ideas for new education policies were brought back from study tours, visits, or the experiences of exiles, we believed that we were forging something unique and powerfully South African. After a brief stint teaching at a high school, I went to work for a trade union as the education officer. The union movement was also involved in education policy development, mainly focused on a system to recognize and improve workers' skills, which also promised to change our economy, and overturn the legacy of apartheid education. In particular the union movement was influenced by international counterparts who argued that a prosperous future could be achieved through an industrial compact between labour, the state and business, and that improving education of the workforce could increase productivity and therefore general prosperity, at the same time as increasing workers' autonomy in the workplace.

Some years later, first while working for a non-governmental organization in education and later for a government regulatory body, I started developing a profound sense that, despite our good intentions, we had somehow got things very wrong.

I was increasingly perturbed by the ideas of learning outcomes and the national qualifications framework, which, together, were key to the educational reform agenda. I started investigating the origins of these ideas more critically, and was surprised to find an unlikely alliance of trade union and business representatives, both of whom had brought ideas back from study tours of Australia and New Zealand. What could underlie this unusual friendship? Was it proof that we could build a society in everyone's interest, that the class and racial conflicts of the past could be overcome? This did not seem impossible at the time, given the powerful imagery of the rainbow nation, as well as the international influence of post-Fordist ideas and 'third way' politics. It seemed unlikely, however, and the more I investigated the education policies which emerged, the more it seemed to me that something valuable and important about education systems was being dismissed and undermined. I began to perceive that not just the national qualifications framework and outcomes-based education, but a whole approach to educational reform that styled itself as 'progressive', and claimed to be emancipatory, was likely to make things worse, not better, particularly for poor people.

I thought, though, that this was a problem peculiar to South Africa. Of course I read about similar problems in other countries, and noticed that in the United Kingdom and New Zealand these problems seemed very like our own. I never imagined, however, that ten years later, qualifications frameworks and learning outcomes would be spreading around the world like wildfire, into well over 100 countries. And until I conducted a comparative study of qualifications frameworks in 16 countries for the International Labour Organization, I did not imagine that in country after country, similar problems would manifest themselves. What intrigued me were the similar theoretical concerns about the relationships between knowledge, work, qualifications, and the economy, which surfaced in this study of qualifications frameworks (Allais, 2010b), cutting across national, educational, political, and economic debates.

In South Africa in the early 1990s, we who worked in education, as well as many who didn't, seemed to believe that education could work miracles in society. At the same time, we believed that almost everything about our existing education system was wrong, and needed to be completely changed. In this, we were not alone. Chapter 1 of this book looks at how, around the world, education has increasingly come to be seen as the solution to social and economic problems. At the same time, it is seen as the cause of many of these problems. This emphasis on the intertwining of education and economy explains the focus of policy makers on qualification reform and outcomes-based qualifications frameworks. Used in both education and work, qualifications are expected to provide a mechanism to mediate between these two spheres. Learning outcomes, it is claimed by their advocates, are the mechanism to ensure that qualifications improve relationships between education and work, make curricula better and more 'relevant' to the needs of the economy, provide learners with more choice and assist them to access education more easily, and increase the quality of education on offer. Learning outcomes are also presented as a key mechanism to make education systems more learner centred. At a time when more and more is expected of education systems, and at the same time more and more criticisms are leveled at them, outcomes-based qualifications frameworks seem to have captured the moment, appearing to be a policy which addresses almost everyone's concerns. There is, however, little evidence that outcomes-based qualifications frameworks have achieved the goals claimed for them.

Why has this idea been attractive to many educationalists, including many progressive educationalists, as well as to policy makers around the world? My exploration of this phenomenon derives from a detailed tracking of attempts to implement outcomes-based qualifications frameworks, located in an analytical framework that draws on political economy as well as the sociology of knowledge.

In Chapter 2 I consider the educational ideas which have been drawn into the justifications for qualifications frameworks, and show that many of the ideas which are claimed as part of a 'new learning paradigm' in contemporary policy documents have a long history in educational debates and reform. I trace ideas about learning outcomes as well as different interpretations of the idea of learner centredness from the early twentieth century to the present. The common ground which often emerges between these sets of ideas is a degree of hostility to the idea of the acquisition of bodies of knowledge (which in schools take the form of subject areas) as the basis of the curriculum, and as a key purpose of education. Both approaches tend towards an anti-subject stance even when they explicitly claim to value knowledge, because they tend to reject or take insufficient account of the ways in which subjects are internally structured based on the bodies of knowledge from which they are derived; the boundaries between subjects; and the boundaries between subjects and everyday knowledge.

Having considered the history of the idea of learning outcomes and learner centredness in Chapter 2, I turn, in Chapter 3, to examine how these ideas became institutionalized in the reform of qualifications in the United Kingdom, Australia, and New Zealand, in what became the models for many qualifications frameworks as well as competency-based approaches to vocational education throughout the world. The wider context in which this happened was the rise of neoliberalism in politics and the economy, affecting all areas of life and shaping policies in all fields. Neoliberal ideas about education (as well as other previous economistic approaches to education) express similar ideas about knowledge to those discussed above: that subjects as defined by teachers or disciplinary experts in universities are not the best starting point for curriculum design, as they are outdated and irrelevant, and a cause of a 'mismatch' between the skills produced by education and training systems and those required by the labour market.

I show that with the growing influence of neoliberalism, criticisms of education institutions and subject-based curricula were harnessed to push through the marketization of education provision. Learning outcomes were introduced in the belief that they could at the same time ensure that curricula were more transparent and responsive to the needs of employers and learners, and that education was provided through more competitive and market-like mechanisms. Neoliberal public sector reformers pushed for states to shift from providing public goods to regulating markets or quasi-markets through which services would be delivered. I show how outcomes-based qualifications frameworks fit with this logic as they are intended to operate as mechanisms for regulating and contracting provision of education. These reforms in Australia, the United Kingdom, and New Zealand were not particularly successful, either in achieving their stated goals, or in gaining widespread acceptance. But this lack of success did not prevent them from being exported to poor countries.

What happened when these policies became a focus for reform in many poor countries—how they have affected, and are likely to affect, countries with weak education systems—is discussed in Chapter 4. The chapter focuses in detail on South Africa, as the country with the most advanced and most researched qualifications framework among poor and middle-income countries, and extends the analysis to other poor and middle-income countries introducing qualifications frameworks. The patterns which emerge in these countries are, in the main, similar to those discussed in richer countries; however, the problems that arise are far more serious. Firstly, in most instances the main achievement of qualification reform has been to develop many paper qualifications that are recorded on a 'qualifications framework' but are in fact never used, despite the involvement of industry representatives and other stakeholders in their development. Secondly, there is no evidence that such qualifications improve the capacity of state institutions to evaluate the quality of educational provision, nor indeed is there evidence that a regulatory state which places emphasis on the 'quality assurance' of different providers has increased the quantity or quality of provision. In some cases (particularly in South Africa) it may have decreased it. The waste that this leads to is a tragedy not just because of the scarce resources used up when there are a number of competing priorities, but also because many more serious educational priorities (such as strengthening the capacity of schools, colleges, and universities) are neglected. It is assumed that the introduction of an outcomes-based qualifications framework will enable providers to develop appropriate curricula, and state organizations to check up on them, thereby ensuring educational quality. This chapter concludes the overview and analysis of the main empirical research in this area. The following three chapters explore in greater depth the issues raised by outcomes-based qualifications frameworks.

In Chapter 5, I focus on the chimera of employer-specified competencies, and why they have not succeeded in increasing the take-up of vocational qualifications or in improving education/labour market relationships. I argue that outcomes-based qualifications frameworks and competency-based training reforms are more likely to be a symptom of weak relationships between education and labour markets than a way of strengthening such relationships. Much current qualification reform attempts to change the relationship between education systems and labour markets by changing aspects of education such as curriculum and assessment without changing the labour market and the economy. This ignores the extent to which developments in education will always be affected by, and so must be understood within, the context in which they exist. Differences in industrial relations, welfare systems and social policy, income distribution, and production strategies are major factors in determining the shape of this development, and are a major factor in accounting for differences between national systems of vocational education and training. The chapter concludes with a brief critique of the claim that learning outcomes improve labour mobility.

In Chapter 6 I focus on the role that is claimed for learning outcomes in *curriculum* reform. The chapter starts by examining the explicit and implicit epistemological stance behind outcomes-based qualification frameworks. Outcomes-based qualification frameworks are premised on the idea that any 'bit' of knowledge can be selected, as long as it leads to the outcomes or competences required by employers. This resonates with much educational thinking, which argues that the selection of curriculum knowledge should primarily be driven by the interests of learners. Knowledge is viewed as information or facts—something that can be broken into little bits which can be selected and combined at will. This implicitly rejects or ignores the conceptual relations within and between bodies of knowledge. The bodies of knowledge which have formed the basis of most education systems, despite various efforts to change this, are not arbitrary selections of facts which can be acquired in arbitrary orders. They are organized in conceptual and hierarchical relationships. This is what gives them explanatory and conceptual power, enabling reflection and abstraction, and the transcending of the immediate contexts. The outcomes approach leads to curricula that are narrowly specified bits of information, making curriculum coherence impossible. I demonstrate further how these problems shed light on broader debates about the curriculum and the purpose of education. While many learners fail to master subject-based curricula, and the content of many syllabuses is influenced by dominant ideologies, the learning outcomes-approach does not offer a viable alternative.

Chapter 7 explores further the problem of starting with learning outcomes when thinking about education. It starts by demonstrating that outcomes-based qualifications frameworks have a similar logic to neoclassical economics—they are built on the notion of rational individuals making rational choices about investments in 'human capital', as well as notions of market imperfections due to information asymmetries. By specifying learning outcomes, qualifications frameworks are supposed to improve information in what policy makers see as the 'learning market', thereby improving individual choices, and making it easier for governments to regulate and support markets to supply education and training. Using the tools of neoclassical economics to analyze society, as if society were nothing but the market, ignores everything that other disciplines have learnt over time about what is specific to different spheres of society (to say nothing of the problems with neoclassical economics even when it is focused only on the market and the economy). What is particularly interesting is how the *educational* ideas like learner centredness and learner selected outcomes which are invoked in association with outcomes-based qualifications frameworks, and which have often been seen as progressive, empowering, or anti-elitist by educationalists, have commonalities with the tools of analysis of neoclassical economics.

Chapter 8 returns briefly to specific cases, looking at some developments in the design and implementation of qualifications frameworks, particularly in Europe, and considers whether they offer a way out of the problems discussed earlier in the book. Some researchers suggest that while there are problems with the competency-based training model, or a strong learning outcomes model, there may be other successful ways of designing qualifications frameworks. Considering available evidence for the achievements of qualifications frameworks, I argue that while some frameworks *seem* to have achieved *some* successes, or at least, to have not caused much conflict, this is mainly because they do not attempt to achieve the kinds of claims made by the advocates of qualifications frameworks. At most, they attempt to make very modest contributions to achieving these claims. In theory, qualifications frameworks could be modest reforms which describe existing education and training systems, and try to make the relationships between different sorts of qualifications a bit more explicit. There is some evidence that qualifications frameworks could play these roles. But if this is all they are, qualifications frameworks cannot be the grand solution to problems in education systems that they are claimed to be—advocates of qualifications frameworks suggest that they are radical reform mechanisms which can change curricula, the delivery of education, and the relationships between education systems and labour markets. The chapter speculates on the current trajectory of qualifications frameworks and suggests that while in some developed countries they may lead to modest educational reforms, the increasing spread of qualifications frameworks could be indicative of the growing liberalization of labour markets and economies, which may be detrimental to education systems in the long term.

Three main arguments are made across these eight chapters, drawn from my analysis of outcomes-based qualifications frameworks internationally.

The first is that the economy (and more specifically the market) has come to be seen as a model for education. Education is understood within a neoclassical economic framework in which individual free agents conduct sensible transactions with each other in their own self-interest. This affects how delivery of education and the curriculum are thought about, as well as notions of the role of education in society, particularly from a policy point of view. I argue that the goals claimed for education in much policy rhetoric today are misguided and unrealistic, and reflect a lack of willingness to tackle structural economic and political problems; at the same time, they have considerable negative consequences for individuals and education systems.

The second arguments follows from the first: increasingly education is seen as the solution to economic problems. Further, it is seen as something individuals must purchase, and institutions must sell. Both of these developments correspond with the rise of neoliberalism. The rolling back of welfare states in the developed world and the denial of welfare in poor countries has decreased public provision of education at the same time as positioning education as the only alternative to poverty. This has led, in many countries in the world, to individuals being seen as responsible for collective and individual welfare. This does not seem to be changing. While neoliberalism as a theory of economic growth has lost plausibility since the economic crisis of 2008, it seems to remain influential as an ideology that dominates education policy.

The third argument concerns the curious agreement between, on the one hand, ideas that have historically been influential in education reform, and which have generally been supported by those who see themselves as leftwing or progressive, and on the other hand, education policies that derive from neoliberalism. Specifically, much educational thinking has opposed the idea of the acquisition of bodies of knowledge as one of the main purposes of education and of subjects as the starting point of the curriculum. This has been associated with a conflation of curriculum and pedagogy which has run through much educational thought over the past century: many educationalists have confused *how* we teach with *what* we teach, and have suggested that it is learners who should decide what they should learn. This has had the effect making education seen as a malleable activity, open to be defined by anyone. If learners can choose what they should learn, so can employers, or other interest groups in society. Policy makers believe they can redefine education to fit the needs of the moment—frequently, to solve economic problems. The neglect and in some cases abandonment of bodies of knowledge and subjects (which has occurred to different degrees in different countries and different parts of education systems, as is explored in this book) means that education can be seen as a 'generic service', making it easier to treat it as a mere commodity to be delivered on the market by the most competitive provider. At the same time, people are denied access to bodies of knowledge which could enable them to better understand, critique, and challenge their current circumstances.

The idea that curricula should not be primarily aimed at the acquisition of bodies of knowledge, nor influenced and constrained by the structure of bodies of knowledge; the idea that knowledge can be acquired anywhere, whether in education institutions or the course of everyday life, and more extreme ideas like 'deschooling', produce fantasies about learning unconstrained by institutions, and individuals free to choose from a wide range of learning possibilities. This is very similar to the free market fantasy about education. Outcomes-based qualifications frameworks resonate with both sets of ideas. The progressivist fantasy gives moral support to the free market fantasy, and enables a labelling of opponents as conservatives. What neither sets of fantasies take into account is, firstly, what the necessary conditions are for the acquisition of knowledge, and secondly, how and why institutions emerge to enable knowledge acquisition, and how they can be sustained, particularly in poor countries.

I turn in the final chapter to a consideration of ideas which offer alternatives for thinking about reforming education systems. I do not offer an alternative policy that can achieve all the goals which qualifications frameworks have failed to achieve. Many of these goals are unrealistic, or based on misdiagnoses of problems, and some may be problematic goals. It is also unrealistic to expect one policy mechanism to be a 'magic bullet'. This does not mean that none of the goals of qualifications frameworks can be achieved at all—there may be other ways of making education systems more flexible to learners, for example, and ways need to be found to assist, say, admissions tutors in understanding qualifications from other countries. I explore some possibilities. But any alternative education policies need to start from the right place—with clearer ideas about what distinguishes formal education from other human activities, and what gives it intrinsic value, as well as what its limitations are, and what it cannot achieve. I suggest that thinking about the acquisition of significant bodies of knowledge is a good starting point for this endeavor.

These bodies of knowledge allow us to account for and explain the natural and social world in systematic ways as well as to participate in and reflect on key human experiences such as the literary, visual, or musical. At its best, this is what the traditional curriculum has done. But we also need curricula which, whilst preserving some subject areas of traditional curricula, challenge presumptions and prejudices, and enable us to go beyond the idea of a 'given' curriculum for all time, with subjects and knowledge within subjects based simply on what has always been taught. A focus on the knowledge itself, its intrinsic characteristics and values, as well as on how and by whom it is developed, can assist. Such a focus is a good starting point for thinking more clearly about reforming curricula, educational delivery, the intrinsic value of education, and the role of education in society, as well as in the world of work and in the economy.

NOTE

[1] The Eighteenth Brumaire of Louis Bonaparte. Karl Marx. 1852

A NOTE ON TERMINOLOGY

Many different policy interventions seem to go by the same name. Also, the same terminology is often used for very different policies. This leaves me in the difficult position of deciding what terms to use. In my experience in debating education policy, critics either suggest that I am lumping things together that are different, or they distance their favourite policy from those that I am criticizing by assigning it a different label.

National qualifications frameworks, for example, are different policy interventions in different countries, as will be explored later. There are also considerable differences in understandings of the terms 'learning outcomes', 'competences', and 'skills'in different countries and contexts (see, for example, Bohlinger, 2007; Brockmann, Clarke, & Winch, 2008; for a discussion of different uses across European countries). This partly reflects difficulties in translation between different languages and is partly because terms like outcomes always have to be understood in terms of the national traditions in which they are located. Various authors point out the complexity of the notion of 'competence' (Hyland, 1994). Linda Clarke and Anneke Westerhuis (2011), for example, make it clear that while European countries such as France and Germany use terms with similar meanings to outcomes and competences, they are seldom considered outside of the context of a curriculum. This is substantially different to both the use of the word 'competence' in competence-based training, and the most common use of the term 'learning outcomes', as both are explicitly separated from, not embedded in, curricula. There is also a difference between a notion of competence in relation to nationally agreed and recognized occupations (Netherlands, France, Germany) or competence as job-specific requirements (England) (Brockmann, Clarke, Winch, *et al.*, 2011) as the former tend to be much broader. In the former sense, competence has been embedded and interpreted in vocational education systems for some time. Georg Hanf (2011), for example, argues that the idea of 'kompetenz' was built into the German system from the start. The word 'skill' is sometimes used as a component of both competence and learning outcome, but its own meaning varies substantially, meaning anything from narrowly defined tasks requiring manipulation and hand-eye coordination, to activities with substantial intellectual and social elements (Brockmann, Clarke, Winch, *et al.*, 2011).

Even within the narrower notion of outcomes or competencies developed separately from curricula, some use terms like 'competencies' and 'outcomes' interchangeably, while others argue that 'competencies' are a sub-set of 'outcomes'. Others even distinguish between 'competencies', 'competences', and 'competency'. Brockmann *et al.* (2011) distinguish between competency and competence, but point out that the European Qualifications Framework uses the word 'competence' to refer to both of their meanings, and argue that the way it is used favours the English conception, which is embedded in a notion of a managerial hierarchy, rather than the German notion of an autonomous and responsible worker. Competencies are also sometimes prefixed with the words 'generic' or 'key'. Recently, some literature which uses the idea of 'capabilities' seems to use it to mean much the same as 'competences'.

Not only are the same words used for different things, but different terms are used for what seem to be the same things. Sometimes, policy makers seem to change from one term to another to signal a policy shift or hoped for shift. In many cases, authors or policy makers seem to attempt to use a different term to distance themselves from an approach with which they disagree or which is seen to have failed. For example, in post-apartheid South Africa reformers took up the flag for 'learning outcomes', but were highly critical of 'competencies', seeing them as narrow and behaviourist. The adoption of the term 'outcomes' was intended to signal that the South African approach was broader. But the policy mechanisms produced were for all intents and purposes the same as the training packages that are part of the competency-based training system in Australia. In many countries there has been a continual series of slightly different types of competence or outcome specifications, often with different names. Structures too have continually altering names and mandates, so that, for example, in Bangladesh the National Council for Skills Development and Training has been replaced by the National Skills Development Council. While to those involved differences between terms may be significant, this area of policy is so laden with jargon that it tends to be opaque and tedious to outsiders, contributing perhaps to a lack of critical engagement in this area of policy. This is aggravated by the way in which terms that have a general usage in everyday language, such as 'standards', are recruited with very specific technical definitions and applications. For example, Stewart and Sambrook (1995, p. 97) argue that

> Statements of *competence* which form the basis of NVQs [national vocational qualifications] consist of specifications of occupational standards. The concepts of *competence* and *standards* appear to become synonymous in practice as illustrated by the following quote: 'An element of competence, with its performance criteria and range statement, constitutes a standard' (Mansfield, 1991:14).

'Competence-based training' (sometimes competency-based training) is a phenomenon specific to the reform of vocational education. 'Outcomes' is often contrasted with this, seen as a broader and more general term, not limited to the requirements of workplaces, and expressing the broader goals of education in general. Many people say that competency-based training has nothing to do with outcomes-based education. They are right and wrong—different policies in different countries and at different times always have differences.

Something else that makes terms like 'outcomes-based' and 'learner-centred' difficult to deal with is that the terms both contain value-judgements and implied criticism of any alternative—which is clearly either not at all concerned with outcomes (nonsensical) or disregards learners (unacceptable). Some notion of aims or objectives, and some concern for learners, is inherent to any educational process, but invoking these terms in association with specific policy reforms seems to imply that other policies have no regard for such matters.

There is no generally accepted or standardized use of these terms. Thus, while you may find in one policy document or analysis an attempt to distinguish between these various terms, in another the same term will be used in a different way. This is complicated by the fact that the concept of a competency or outcomes-based education system is an evolving idea, the details (and terminology) of which are constantly changing (Spreen, 2001). Michael Young (2009b) argues that the terms 'learning outcomes' and 'competences' have become almost synonymous in recent policy documents, partly because they are both expressions of the increasingly instrumental approach to education, in which emphasis is placed on the economic benefits of general, as well as vocational, education, and all education is judged in terms of potential benefits for the labour market and economy.

I do not want to develop my own definitions of each of these terms—an exercise which seems pointless as others will use them in different ways. Rather, I am attempting to draw attention to what are underlying and fundamental similarities in the ways in which learning outcomes, competencies, and competences are used in many policy reforms across the world today. Consequently, I will use the terms more-or-less interchangeably, except where referring to specific policy interventions which use one or the other. I argue that there is a broad and common trend—differently expressed in different countries, with different effects on the ground, but nonetheless common. The trend is attempting to describe activities, mainly in the workplace but sometimes also in the citizenry or family, and using these descriptors of activities as the basis of curriculum reform, as well as to serve various other goals of qualification reform. This is a trend which must be taken seriously. Finding specific examples on the ground which don't entirely correspond with all aspects of the trend does not refute the fact that there is a trend.

The word 'qualification' also has different meanings in different countries and sometimes within the same country depending on whether it is used in relation to education systems or to labour markets. A traditional usage of the word 'qualification' relates to a formal means of signifying that someone has completed a prescribed process linked to an education or training programme offered in an educational or training institution. But where qualifications are linked to official statements that an individual has been accepted to practice in a certain area (such as a lawyer, plumber, or teacher), the term 'qualification' means something close to a 'competence' for a given occupational practice. Thus, Phillipe Méhaut (2011), for example, distinguishes between diplomas and qualifications, with the former associated with education systems and the latter with workplace requirements.

In relation to qualifications frameworks as well as outcomes-based qualification reforms, a slightly different use of the word 'qualification' has emerged. Here it is mainly used in reference to (or as a short-hand for) the sets of formal requirements needed for achieving awards. This usage is common in official policy documents relating to qualifications frameworks. In this usage, the 'qualification' is the statement of learning outcomes and associated requirements needed for awards. As outcomes-based qualifications are a key focus of my argument in this book, I will in most instances be using the word in this sense, unless indicated otherwise, or unless context clearly suggests otherwise.

CHAPTER 1

QUALIFICATIONS

Culture, Currency, Commodity

What should be taught, to whom, how, and who should foot the bill? These questions underpin much debate and research in education, and my work is no exception. My particular interests are in the curriculum (what should be taught?); the organization of education (what kinds of institutions should offer what kinds of education, who should pay, and how?); and in the role of education in society (why do we need education?). These are not questions that have easy answers. They raise difficult issues concerning the nature of knowledge, how it is developed and acquired, the nature of society, the possible and likely roles education can play in societies and economies, and so on. They have become increasingly complex as more and more people have completed, or attempt to complete, higher and higher levels of formal education. Tackling them inevitably draws on a range of disciplines—at a minimum these include sociology, philosophy, politics, economics, and, of course, education.

But education policies are often not informed by any of these disciplines, or draw on them very loosely. As Wallis and Dollery (1999, p. 5) cited by Bob Jessup (2012, p. 62) argue,

> Policy paradigms derive from theoretical paradigms but possess much less sophisticated and rigorous evaluations of the intellectual underpinnings of their conceptual frameworks. In essence, policy advisers differentiate policy paradigms from theoretical paradigms by screening out the ambiguities and blurring the fine distinctions characteristic of theoretical paradigms.

As education has taken centre stage in the minds of policy developers, governments, and people concerned with development, and as education has been increasingly touted as the solution to social and economic problems, education policies have become increasingly instrumental: what can people do with the education that they are getting? This is of concern to left and right-wing reformers alike, although the end points that they have in mind for education are different. Policy makers on both sides of the political spectrum often seem to believe that if they start from this question, education systems will be able to respond, producing according to societies' requirements, and alleviating societies' problems. When this fails, education *per se* is blamed, instead of misguided notions of what education is, and what it can do for individuals and societies. In this book I explore a recent example of this type of education reform: outcomes-based qualifications frameworks.

In this chapter, I discuss the international prevalence of the idea that education is the key to economic and social success, and the growing popularity of outcomes-based qualifications frameworks as one of the main policies intended to ensure that education solves economic and labour market problems. Advocates of learning outcomes and qualifications frameworks claim that these policies can reform education systems in various important ways. The claims can be boiled down to three key areas: improving relationships between education systems and labour markets; reforming curricula, pedagogy, and assessment; and assisting governments to improve the quality and quantity of education available. Over 120 countries are currently reported as developing or implementing outcomes-based qualifications frameworks (Keevy, Chakroun, & Deij, 2011). This is an extraordinary development, considering that the first qualifications frameworks were launched at most only 20 years ago, and that there is little empirical evidence that they can achieve their goals.

I explain the context in which these policies have become popular with governments: education has taken on ever-greater prominence, touted as the solution to individual, social, and economic problems. Because of this, more and more has been expected of education systems, leading to reforms that are both utilitarian and unrealistic, as well as to ever increasing criticisms of the (inevitable) failures of education systems. I then explore why qualifications in particular have become the focus of policy reform, and why governments and policy makers have come to assume, without any theoretical grounding or empirical evidence, that qualifications can be used as instruments to influence education systems. This is followed by an examination of the specific claims made about learning outcomes and qualifications frameworks. Finally, I discuss the little existing evidence for the claims made about outcomes-based qualifications frameworks. I argue that the available research evidence suggests not only that qualifications frameworks do not achieve their goals, but also that they have many negative effects on education systems. In the rest of the book I explore the underlying problems with this policy mechanism, and why it nevertheless seems to have been so seductive.

Why start from exploring a policy that I disagree with, instead of developing positive propositions about education and society? For one thing, it is important to explain precisely why and in what ways a policy is flawed, particularly if, as is the case with this one, the policy seems to have captured the imaginations of policy makers internationally. We need to study the policy carefully, both in terms of empirical evidence for and against it, and in terms of its conceptual soundness, considered not in its own terms (this particular policy has an internal logic that seems quite plausible) but in relation to broader bodies of knowledge about society, knowledge, and the economy. Questions about the purpose and role of education in society are not easy to answer, and equally difficult are more practical questions about the organization of education systems. Engaging carefully with the policies that dominate our education systems can assist in thinking about why education frequently doesn't do what is expected of it, what education cannot do, and, conversely, what it can do, and what the conditions of possibility are. My analysis of the problems leads to ideas for alternatives: why thinking about the nature and importance of knowledge is a better starting point for thinking about the curriculum; why education systems should be collectively organized and funded; and why economic and social problems need to be tackled directly, and not through education policy.

'RELEVANT' EDUCATION AS THE SOLUTION TO ECONOMIC AND SOCIETAL PROBLEMS

Let's consider first the expectations that policy makers have of education systems.

"A new grand narrative of the role of education has emerged on a truly global level", argues political scientist Jurgen Enders (2010, p. 209). The essence of this grand narrative is, in the words of Tony Blair, former British Prime Minister, that "education is our best economic policy". For poor and rich countries alike, education is described in policy documents as the route out of poverty for individuals. As Phil Brown, Andy Green, and Hugh Lauder (2001) demonstrate, it is argued increasingly widely that economic competitiveness rests on the skills of the labour force. It seems that education's importance is hard to overstate. For example, the OECD argues:

> Recent research reinforces the view that human capital [by which they mean education] not only plays a critical role in economic performance, but also brings key individual and social benefits such as better health, improved well being, better parenting, and increased social and political engagement. (OECD, 2010, p. 7)

This could sound like a great opportunity for those of us who are concerned with expanding access to education, and many educationalists have enthusiastically embraced this narrative. But it has caused serious problems for education systems, as I will discuss below, after considering the origins and context of the 'new narrative' about education.

The new emphasis on education stems partly from a belief that while nation states have increasingly less control over the outcome of economic competition, education can be used as a weapon for individuals and governments to improve their prosperity (Reich 1997). A.H. Halsey, Hugh Lauder *et al.* (1997) argue that one of the reasons that education is treated as a universal panacea could be that it remains one of the few areas of social policy over which governments believe they can exert a decisive interest, and demonstrate their power to improve the conditions of everyday life. They go on to argue that exaggerated claims about education reflect political ideology—for instance, it is in the interests of the new right to argue that unemployment, poor productivity, and sluggish economic growth are supply-side problems, caused by education not being in tune with the needs of industry, rather than admit that neoliberal economic policies are not delivering even on their own terms (neoliberalism is discussed further in Chapter 3). Another factor is that education is an area in which governments can make claims which sound attainable, and which potentially have appeal to a huge group of voters: parents. This role for education in improving individual and national prosperity came to prominence through the influence of the idea of 'post-Fordism'[1], which found support from many left-wing thinkers after the collapse of the so-called socialist bloc. Where socialism was seen to have failed as an alternative to capitalism, the reorganization, reinvigoration, and democratization of production were seen as the basis for achieving a reformed, more productive, and more egalitarian capitalist society (Kumar 1992). The post-Fordist approach to the economy *seemed* to many to provide a paradigm in which, by increasing the skills levels of a nation, international competitiveness could be achieved, thereby increasing the general prosperity of the nation. This was posited as the only alternative to the harshest forms of neo-liberalism. However, it was also seen as desirable because its more flexible organization of production was linked to the 'democratization' of the workplace (Desaubin 2002).

Related to the idea of 'post-Fordism' is the idea of the 'knowledge economy'. Policy makers refer to this idea to suggest that the workforce and the economy require high levels of education. Since the 1970s, analysts such as Daniel Bell (1973), Peter Drucker (1969) and Alvin Tofler (1980) have argued that societies previously based on industrial manufacturing were being transformed into 'information societies', in which knowledge would become the dominant factor of production. New types of work were emerging, particularly in information management, finance, marketing, and sales, leading many to suggest a fundamental change in the advanced economies (Carlaw, Oxley, Walker, Thorns, & Nuth, 2012). As D. W. Livingstone and David Guile (2012, p. iii) note, today the existence of a 'knowledge-based economy' is "widely taken for granted by governments, mass media, public opinion, and most scholars today".

The promise of the knowledge economy is a 'win-win' scenario: the boom and bust business cycle could be abolished through a new stage of capitalist development that would lead to a fundamental shift in power from the owners and managers of capital to knowledge workers (Lauder & Brown, 2009). According to analysts such as Nan Lin (2001), different social classes could come to share the same interests: "labourers can become capitalists, as they enjoy the surplus of their labour... The confrontation and struggle between classes becomes a cooperative enterprise – 'What's good for the company is good for the worker and vice versa'" (Lin 2001, p. 13).

Education particularly came to prominence in social policy within the ambit of 'third way' politics, which came to dominate the United States and Europe in the mid 1990s when previously left-wing parties started accepting many of the tenets of neoliberalism (Crouch, 2011). Alex Callinicos (2001, p. 48) cites former British Prime Minister Gordon Brown arguing "where the success and failure of an economy depend on access to knowledge more than access to capital, individual liberation arises from the enhancement of the value of labour rather than the abolition of private capital"[2]. Improved education and training was supposed to improve the competitiveness of industries, because, it was believed, "in the 'knowledge economy' competitiveness depends on the skills of the workforce" (Callinicos, 2001, p. 48). At the same time, education was supposed to benefit individuals. Thus, education was seen as a substitute for welfare provision. Anthony Giddens (1998, p. 117) describes this as "investment in human capital wherever possible, rather than the direct provision of economic maintenance".

As many rich states pulled back from industrial policy, and social democracies came under attack, policy makers turned to market mechanisms to play an increasingly greater role in delivering goods and services. Many poor countries also attempted to implement more market-oriented policies, dramatically restricting their already limited ability to deliver services to their populations. In this context, where public spending on social welfare is decreasing, education reform has been increasingly posited as the key factor in reducing social inequality (Lauder, Hughes *et al.* 1999), as well as the single best way of achieving national and individual prosperity (Ashton and Green 1996; Lauder, Brown, Dillabough *et al.* 2006).

The 'third way', argues Sally Tomlinson (2009, p. 5), was an "attempt to marry social democracy with market capitalism, to explain the diminishing of collective public welfare provision, the incursion of private capital and business, and the increasing expectations on individuals to provide for themselves", based on the widely accepted political view that the costs of the welfare state were prohibitive. It makes sense, then, that a discourse of duties, rights, and responsibilities is invoked to ensure that individuals do not expect too much from the state. This supported a shift in policy rhetoric from 'full employment' to 'full employability' (Brown & Lauder, 2006). In the former paradigm, governments see it as part of their role to create jobs and support and develop industries which will create jobs, to ensure that individuals are employed. In the latter, their role is to encourage individuals to make themselves 'employable'. The onus is on the individual to get a job, because, it is believed, it is wrong, or not possible for governments to play a role in ensuring that jobs exist. This is a characteristically neoliberal idea: it is the moral duty of human beings to arrange their lives to maximize their advantage to the labour market.[3] The emphasis on the skills of the workforce and therefore on training has enabled governments to describe unemployment as a temporary phenomenon, resulting from economic change and individuals' (and educational providers') failure to meet the needs of the economy. Unemployment, according to this line of thought, is caused by the lack of 'skills' in the workforce, and not by structural problems with the economy, or by the economic philosophy dominant in the world, neoliberalism. The learner must be in a continual state of "up-skilling and re-skilling" in order to respond to shifts in the world labour market (Spreen 2001, p. 62). The victim, rather than the system, is blamed for unemployment (Foley, 1994). Education is seen as a significant component of a comprehensive approach to workplace restructuring and workplace organization, with a highly skilled, mobile workforce making industry internationally competitive (Foley 1994). Thus, Kennedy (2012, p. 178) describes the expansion of post-compulsory education as "the most prominent policy to contain and manage surplus labour and sustain control over 'free time'".

'Third way politics' have been very influential: the idea that "efficiency as the market defines it and justice as socialists have conceived it" are reconcilable was, at the turn of the millennium, "the most politically influential ideology both in the advanced capitalist countries and in the leading Third World states" (Callinicos, 2001, p. 209). Education is central to these promises about both economic competitiveness and social justice, as it is to the promises of the knowledge economy. These promises have proved illusory.

'Third way' politics did not succeed in achieving the claims made for it about 'win-win' systems. The recent dramatic failures of neoliberalism to achieve economic growth and prosperity has forced some degree of reality check on this type of politics. The idea of the 'knowledge economy' proved similarly weak, based on notions of labour markets, economies and employers, in short, capitalist economies, which are implausible. And in many instances the development of 20th century capitalism has involved substantial elements of 'deskilling'. As Livingstone (2012, p. 108) points out,

> The image of contemporary society inherent in post-industrial/knowledge economy and human capital theories proves illusory. While an aggregate upgrading of the technical skills needed for job performance is gradually occurring, our collective acquisition of work-related knowledge and credentials is far outpacing this incremental shift.

Further, as Lauder and Brown (2009) compellingly demonstrate, the promise of the knowledge economy for high paid jobs in return for investment in education has been manifestly broken, with the majority of 'knowledge workers' forced into a global labour market for work that is high-skilled but low-waged. Of course many also remain in low-skilled low-waged work; as Kennedy (2012, p. 169) points out,

> While some authors wax lyrical about the centrality of the development of skilled and autonomous human capital to the knowledge economy, it is also the case that deskilling and temporary low-skill employment contracts remain a core feature of 'knowledge work.'

Brown, Lauder, and David Ashton (2008, p. 4) point out that while much policy literature focuses on knowledge, innovation, and creative enterprise, it has ignored the shift towards global standardisation of work, along with efforts to 'capture' and digitalise knowledge that had "previously remained locked in the heads of high-skilled workers." They refer to this as 'Digital Taylorism'. Much 'knowledge work', they argue, is being standardized in much the same way that the knowledge of craft workers was captured and translated into the moving assembly line in the early twentieth century:

> Standardisation is well-understood in manufacturing, where the same standard components such as wheels, brake linings, and windscreens can be made in different factories around the world and shipped for final assembly at one location, in the knowledge that all the components meet international quality standards and will fit together. This not only gives companies flexibility but enables them to reduce costs. The same logic is now being applied to service-sector occupations which were previously difficult to standardise because

there were no digital equivalents to mechanical drills, jigs, presses and ships, all of which are required to create global supply chains in manufacturing.

They argue that in the same way that Taylorism transformed the distinction between conception and execution of work, digital Taylorism involves a power struggle within the middle classes, for it depends on reducing the autonomy and discretion of the majority of well-educated technical, managerial, and professional employees. Lauder and Brown's 'digital Taylorism' is echoed in Christopher Newfield's (2010) idea of the 'cognotariat', which captures the systematic stratification within the class or group of 'knowledge workers'.

A substantial body of research interrogates whether education causes or follows economic growth, and largely finds that the 'knowledge economy' vastly overstates the role that education can play in the economy (for example, Amsden, 2010; Brown & Ashton, 1987; Brown et al., 2001; Brown & Lauder, 1992, 2006; Brown, 1999; Lauder & Brown, 2009; Lauder, 1997). Development literature emphasizes the importance of economic policy—fiscal, monetary, employment, trade— as well as industrial policy and land reform, and not of education, which cannot solve the structural problems of economies (Amsden, 2010; Chang, 2003, 2007).

However, despite these broken promises, education policy has been substantially dominated by the 'new narrative' of education as the solution to economic problems, with many negative consequences for education systems.

One such consequence for education systems is that education is blamed for social and economic problems, and this is linked to the first problem, the idea that education must be relevant to the needs of the economy. Norton Grub and Marvin Lazerson (2004) talk about the 'education gospel' in the United States: the idea that education is both the reason for and the solution to the key problems facing society. Education is positioned as the key to solving social problems—in order to 'socialize' people, to help them to find constructive ways of solving their problems, to enable them to become 'employable' or self-employed. But it is also seen as the cause of these problems—for example, societal problems and 'unemployability' are put down to weaknesses in the current education system. Various problems in the world of work—growing unemployment, particularly amongst young people, industrial stagnation, or lack of economic growth—are ascribed to a lack of skills in the workforce or potential workforce. Since the 1970s, increasing levels of unemployment have been blamed on the supposed lack of relevance of the education and training received. Thus, as Grubb and Lazerson (2006, p. 295) explain,

> in many countries, an amazingly similar rhetoric has developed, one that first stresses the failures of schools and universities and then proceeds to reform them with more economic and utilitarian goals.

This has led to a tendency towards narrow, utilitarian approaches to education— what Grub and Lazerson (2006, p. 301) call 'the dark side' to the new arguments

7

for the usefulness of education and the need to expand it. If education is to be the solution to economic problems, it is thought that education must be 'relevant' to the perceived needs of the economy, not driven by what are believed to be the self-regarding interests of the academy or educationalists. This has led to a stressing of vocational education as well as the vocationalizing of general education. Vocationalizing the curriculum has been a major concern both at the level of rhetoric and in a plethora of education reforms since the mid-1970s. Generic preparation for employment is increasingly viewed as "a basic and essential condition of all school education" (Sedunary, 1996, p. 369). J.D. Marshall (1997) argues that ideas about the vocational purposes of education and business values are so embedded in education that 'vocationalism' has little or no meaning, for there is no alternative to it in the educational realm of discourse. Linked to this is the belief that education should be driven by employers because they best understand the specific skills required by the economy, and the role of the state should be to encourage individual enterprise as well as incentives for people to invest in their own 'human capital', i.e. education.

The idea of 'relevance' is one which has long dogged educational reform. In the following chapter I explore in more detail how reformers from various political perspectives have criticized the 'traditional' curriculum as 'decorative', 'cultural capital' of the elite, and of no practical value in the world. Tongue in cheek, Stephan Collini (2012) calls the debate one between proponents of 'useful' and 'useless' education. This debate has intensified in the light of changing economic conditions prevailing in the late 20th century. It has also intensified as more and more people have achieved higher and higher levels of education, and as education has been used more and more in labour markets. When belief in a meritocracy based on educational achievement is dominant, some researchers have responded by questioning the validity of this notion of meritocracy, but many others have turned to reforming education systems, with one particular aim being to assist children from poor socio-economic circumstances to perform better in education, in the belief that this will assist them in the labour market. This practical and laudable work has often brought into question traditional curricula, which were developed for elite education systems, and have often, as is explored in the following chapter, emphasized the notion of relevance to learners.

The paradox of education as both the solution to societal and economic problems and the cause of them is, perhaps, inevitable given the implausible roles ascribed to education. The desire to change education systems in such a way that they stop causing, and start solving social and economic problems, lies behind much contemporary education reform. *Qualification* policy in particular is being used to drive educational reform[4].

QUALIFICATIONS, CURRICULUM, ECONOMY

Why have governments come to believe that qualifications can be a useful lever to reform education systems?

A qualification is traditionally seen as a token of sustained study for a designated period in a designated area. In the past, it *qualified* an individual to do something in the labour force. Because qualifications are used when people move between education and the workplace, they are seen as a mechanism for translating something obtained in one area to something desired in another. They have come to be seen as an indicator of the skills people have gained through education which make them more productive, and hence as an indicator of an individual's economic value in the labour market. This is, perhaps, the common sense notion of the role of qualifications in the labour market, and human capital theorists have tended to assume that this is how education always functions in relation to work. But while this is sometimes the case, there are many different ways in which qualifications play a role in the jobs that people get, and the salaries that they earn.

For example, instead of being used as indicators of productive skills, qualifications can function in labour markets as vehicles for social closure. Here qualifications are a mechanism for legitimating inclusion and exclusion, for example, in regulated access to an occupation or profession, and qualifications create labour market shelters for those who possess them (Freidson, 2001).

A different way in which qualifications function in labour markets is as positional goods—your qualification buys you a place in the queue. Here, employers use qualifications as a screening device, and will hire at the highest qualification level they can, regardless of the relationship between the specifics of the job in question and the qualification in question. For many job vacancies there are surpluses of qualified workers, so employers look for ever higher levels of qualifications, to obtain information about individuals *relative to each other* rather than as indicators of the attainment of skills necessary for the job in question (Collins, 1979; Shields, 1996). In other words, the value of a qualification may be dependent on how many other people have it, and not on its intrinsic worth. This phenomenon is referred to as 'credentialism'.

The presence of educational credentials dominates increasingly professionalized and formally organized societies, and this role for qualifications has taken on increasing significance over the course of the twentieth century. In the latter half of the century, more and more people started to obtain qualifications (Collins, 1979). In describing this phenomenon, Ronald Dore (1976) coined the phrase 'diploma disease', suggesting that credentialism had a distorting effect on education systems. Credentialism is also referred to as 'qualification inflation', because the social and economic value of qualifications diminishes while the level of skills and knowledge in the programmes they represent remains the same. This, Dore argued, leads to a vicious circle of more and more people trying to obtain qualifications, which in turn further lowers the value of qualifications. Randall Collins (1979) argued in the late 1970s that this was sustaining a false sense of meritocracy, and had serious negative consequences for people as they felt compelled to obtain higher and higher levels of qualifications, losing money in fees as well as in income whilst studying to obtain knowledge and skills that they didn't need and may not have wanted.

Qualification inflation or credentialism is a major contributor to what are perceived as education/labour market 'mismatches', because, while the common sense idea is that qualifications should be indicators of 'productive skills', the actual content of learning programmes is seen as having an ever-diminishing relationship with the skills needed for specific jobs. This is part of what policy makers want to address. Angela Little (1997), in a review of Dore's arguments twenty years later, concludes that education systems have become more preoccupied with qualifications and qualification reform as a result of qualification inflation: more qualifications are on offer and more money is spent by public authorities on administering qualification systems, and by individuals in gaining qualifications (Little, 2000).

Qualifications have also become a mechanism for trade in international markets for education (Holmes, 2003). Governments that want to encourage markets in education need common 'currencies', or at least 'exchange rates' which are reasonably consistent, and which are understood. Keith Holmes (2003) and Young (2005) point out that in relation to international trade in qualifications as well as international movement of people, poor countries and small countries are under pressure to get their qualifications recognized internationally.

All of this perhaps provides some indication of why governments around the world seem to have become preoccupied with reforming qualifications. Enter learning outcomes: a policy mechanism which is claimed not just to reform qualification systems, but to use qualifications to reform education systems.

WHAT CAN OUTCOMES-BASED QUALIFICATIONS FRAMEWORKS DO FOR YOU?

In most countries around the world someone familiar with their national education system could draw a sketch on a single piece of paper which demonstrated the main national qualifications available, and how they related to each other. Occasionally, the term 'national qualifications framework' is invoked to label such a grid.

Outcomes-based qualifications frameworks are meant to go considerably beyond this. There are many claims made about what they can achieve, and it is difficult to make sense of the documentation surrounding them. Documents are frequently normative, written as if they pertain to actually existing education systems and policies, when in fact they describe what policy makers hope will be the case. They are also prescriptive. Both the prescriptive and normative aspects of these documents may be largely due an assumption that learning outcomes have a 'common-sense plausibility'. However, closer examination shows that they are not common sense at all, but are based on extraordinary assumptions.

The claims[5] made about outcomes-based qualifications frameworks can be reduced to three main (related) areas:

- If governments and policy makers can change the way qualifications and credentials are used in labour markets, they can improve the functioning of economies, increasing general prosperity and opportunities for individuals. Learning outcomes provide a mechanism to achieve such a change.

- By specifying the desired outcomes of an education programme, instead of specifying the content to be learned during such a programme, the curricula, pedagogy, and assessment will change in ways that make education more socially and economically useful.
- Qualifications frameworks can change the way education is managed, delivered, or regulated by the state, in order to increase the supply, flexibility, and quality of education provision. Learning outcomes provide a useful mechanism for this type of reform, as they specify required outputs, which can be used to introduce market or quasi-market mechanisms in governance and finance, as well as providing regulatory agencies with benchmarks against which to evaluate provision, and facilitating more inclusion of stakeholders in education systems.

Learning outcomes are the central mechanism through which qualifications frameworks are presumed to precipitate these changes. They are also, as I demonstrate throughout this book, the source of many of the problems that are experienced when countries try to implement qualifications frameworks. As Nigel Norris (1991, p. 339) argues, "The trouble with competence is that it now has a currency way beyond its operational or conceptual reach." This currency has grown, and not shrunk, in the years since Norris made this observation. Below, I provide a brief overview of how, according to advocates, learning outcomes are supposed to play these roles.

It must be noted that the use of 'learning outcomes' here is very specific, and is not the same as a more colloquial use of the word which focuses on actual learner achievements; here, learning outcomes mean descriptions of what learners should have attained in order to be awarded a particular qualification (see *A Note on Terminology* preceding this chapter). All qualifications invoke some sense of 'outcomes'. A qualification is a statement about an outcome of learning. The 'outcomes' of education systems—such as, how many people have qualified to become engineers in a particular year in a particular country, or what the graduation or throughput rate of a particular institution is, or what levels of mathematical ability are obtained by school students—are obviously of concern to governments and citizens. But in outcomes-based qualifications frameworks the term 'outcomes' is used in a very specific way: providing an exact and transparent (clearly understandable to anyone) description of competences. These outcomes are also supposed to provide a benchmark against which assessment can be conducted, learning programmes can be developed, and educational quality can be evaluated.

Let's consider the first set of expectations about how outcomes-based qualifications can improve relationships between education and labour markets. The idea is that qualifications which have clearly specified outcomes will enable employers as well as other educational institutions to know exactly what it is that the qualified learner is competent to do. One problem ostensibly being tackled here is the education/labour market 'mismatch' discussed above, whereby traditional qualifications are seen to provide inadequate information to employers, who are then not able to know whether or not they should employ someone. I

11

have suggested above that the so-called 'mismatch' has its roots elsewhere, and in Chapter 5 I explore this in more depth.

Advocates also suggest that traditional qualifications provide inadequate information to learners, who are not, therefore, able to make clear choices about whether or not to invest in education and training and, if they do, which programmes to invest in, as well as to governments, which do not know which programmes to fund. It is indisputable that qualifications do not always play these roles, although the extent to which qualifications could ever make labour markets function perfectly smoothly is very disputable. The assumption behind outcomes-based qualifications frameworks is that a clear specification of exactly what competences or learning outcomes a particular qualification signifies will fix this problem. What is not considered is what it actually means to try to specify outcomes in this manner, whether it is possible, and what the consequences of trying to do it are for education systems. Further, the underlying issues in economies and labour markets which may be the real source of unemployment problems are also downplayed.

Another ostensible problem that outcomes-based qualifications frameworks try to solve is lack of mobility for learners, through education systems, between education and work, and across different countries:

> The changing nature of work creates demands for more flexible, multi-skilled workers who are mobile across the economy and internationally. For efficiency, and fairness, this requires that a qualification or skill, however or wherever acquired, should have common meaning among employers selecting workers throughout the country. For individuals it implies they should be able to have their qualifications and skills recognised for entry into further studies or relevant forms of employment. (APEC Human Resources Development Working Group, 2009, p. 5)

Like much policy discourse in this area, the document cited above states a wish that 'a qualification or skill, however or wherever acquired, should have a common meaning'. Of course this is to some extent applicable to some qualifications and some institutions, but the larger the geographical area in question, and the greater the number of types of institutions offering learning programmes and types of qualifications on offer, the less likely it is that qualifications will have a common meaning. The document above, like many others in this area, seems to reflect the idea that simply stating that something *should* be the case makes it possible that it *will* be the case, without a consideration of why qualifications and 'skills' do not currently have common meanings, what it would mean for them to have such meanings, and from where qualifications and skills derive their meanings. Outcomes are supposed to assist learner mobility, because, it is claimed or believed, they can give both education institutions and employers a clear sense of what learners have achieved.

Countries (as well as education institutions, and different areas of economies and disciplinary areas) have their own traditions and systems. "The new learning outcomes based levels", argues the European Centre for the Development of

Vocational Training, Cedefop, (2009, p. 5) "can be seen as introducing a neutral reference point for diverse qualifications and qualifications providers". Countries hope that learning outcomes will improve their ability to compare their qualifications with those in other countries, as well as to provide clearer information to employers at home and abroad about what qualifying learners are in fact competent to do:

> Universal approaches to reference points, based on learning outcomes, make cross-border judgements as to the level, nature and equivalence of qualifications easier and more accurate. (Adam, 2008, p. 13).

Jörg Markowitsch and Karin Luomi-Messerer (2008) suggest:

> The focus on learning outcomes, irrespective of learning paths, opens up possibilities for recognising non-formal and informal learning and, finally, the EQF [European Qualifications Framework] supports the transfer of qualifications between countries, and hence mobility of learners and workers.

In other words, learning outcomes are seen as a useful tool to mediate between different systems of provision, different types of institutions, different disciplines, and so on. What this actually means, and how it would work in practice, is not discussed; what is also not discussed is what the real causes of mobility problems in labour markets are.

Now consider the second set of claims made about learning outcomes—that they can reform curricula, pedagogy, and assessment. The logic here is that the specification of outcomes will ensure that curricula are developed appropriately and to the right standard, because outcomes can be determined outside of educational institutions, and crucially, can involve industry in setting standards. This last aspect—industry involvement in developing learning outcomes or competences—is also supposed to address the education/labour market 'mismatch'. The ostensible problem, usually unstated but implied, although sometimes explicitly stated in policy documents, is that education programmes are 'irrelevant' to the needs of the labour market because educationalists are ignorant of these needs. The assumptions are that employers know what they want and can state it in terms of 'competences' or 'outcomes' that will have common meanings understood by all, and that once these outcomes have been developed by employers, it will be a simple matter for education institutions to develop programmes that lead to these outcomes. Because of this, Wheelahan (2010, p. 126) argues, "competency-based training models of curriculum are now the basis of vocational education and training (VET) qualifications in many countries because governments believe that they meet the needs of industry and ensure industry 'control' over VET".

But the role of learning outcomes in the reform of curricula, pedagogy, and assessment is supposed to go further than this. Learning outcomes, Cedefop (2008, p. 9), argues,

> ... form part of an innovative approach to teaching and learning, which some have identified as part of a new learning paradigm. Learning outcomes are the

focus, and provide a key role in organising systemic aims, curricula, pedagogy, assessment and quality assurance. Increasing use of learning outcomes is expected to have profound implications for making systems more learner-centred, organising institutions, curricula and for the roles and training of teachers and trainers.

What are these profound implications? The Commonwealth of Learning and the South African Qualifications Authority (2008, p. 44) argue that qualifications frameworks based on learning outcomes represent 'new notions of knowledge', and a 'new hierarchy' in which "education providers are no longer the leaders and standards-setters, and content (or inputs) is no longer the starting point". What these 'new notions of knowledge' actually are is never really explained, but they are described as more learner-centred than 'traditional' systems or ideas about knowledge.

Like many ideas in educational reform, the notion of learning outcomes is proclaimed as a new 'paradigm', often invoking Thomas Kuhn's notion of a paradigm (in ways that Kuhn would not be comfortable with). For example,

> A paradigm shift is a change from one way of thinking to another. It is a transformation in thinking that is driven by change agents. In the context of learning outcomes a case can be made that they are an essential part of a Bologna paradigm change driven by the imperatives of the need to respond to globalisation. They are at the heart of an educational revolution that has been slow to gestate but is beginning to have a profound impact. (Adam, 2008, p. 6)

Steven Adam (2008) argues that due to the 'Bologna' process, whereby European countries have been attempting to align their higher education systems through learning outcomes,

> Institutions are slowly moving away from a system of teacher-driven provision, and towards a student centred concept of higher education. Thus the reforms are laying the foundations for a system adapted to respond to a growing variety of student needs. Institutions and their staff are still at the early stages of realising the potential of reforms for these purposes. Understanding and integrating the use of a **learning outcomes** based approach remains a key medium-term challenge. When achieved, it will enable students to become the engaged subjects of their own learning process. [emphasis in original]

Adam goes on to argue that the "humble learning outcome has moved from being a peripheral tool to a central device to achieve radical educational reform of European higher education". The use of 'radical' here, as well as the notion of a 'new paradigm', are invoked because the changes implied involve reforming education in a range of different ways—addressing curricula, pedagogy, assessment, provision of education, accountability of educational institutions, and the use of qualifications in society and in labour markets.

I do not, in this discussion, consider whether or not the changes that Adam *says* are being achieved have in fact *been* achieved, and whether it would be a good thing if they were, except to note that many people who teach in higher education in Europe may be surprised to read it. For now my focus is on the nature of the claim being made about outcomes-based qualifications. The essence of the claim is that it is possible and desirable to specify the outcomes of education programmes to education providers, and that this will change the way education systems operate.

'Learner centredness' is an idea frequently associated with learning outcomes. Advocates suggest that outcomes-based qualifications enable learner-centred curricula and pedagogy because they will force education institutions to teach to 'outcomes' that learners want to acquire. The idea of learner centredness is extended to the organization of education. National qualifications frameworks present ladders of qualifications described in terms of learning outcomes, suggesting that individuals are free to climb up them over the course of their lifetime, and free to choose and select the learning that is relevant to them. Once again this seems to be policy as wish-fullfillment: creating a framework that says that it is possible for people to 'move up' the education system seems to make it possible. When the background of the idea of the 'knowledge economy' discussed above is added to the mix, and the ideology that individuals who invest in education can become 'knowledge workers', and will be rewarded financially as well as with power, greater autonomy, and scope for creativity in work, it all seems very desirable. With these grand pictures of qualifications ladders within and across education and training systems and countries, the messy details of why, in fact, individuals do not move up education systems, what the real social and educational barriers are, and so on, are swept aside. Qualifications frameworks are also seen as ways of supporting learners to move between and within the different 'tracks' of education systems (such as between general and vocational education), which in many instances are designed with little possibility for student transfer (Hodgson, Spours, Isaacs, & Grainger, 2013).

The discussion above has touched on the third area in which outcomes and qualifications frameworks are supposed to be a reform tool: they are seen as mechanisms to increase the supply, flexibility, and quality of education provision, and solve what are seen as rigidities in the management and delivery of education. Let's now consider this area in a bit more detail. Education systems are described as 'supply driven'. This term is used to describe the traditional role educational institutions play in determining what education is offered and how. In many countries, particularly in school education and sometimes vocational education, this is associated with centralization of educational provision—in other words, the state, and not individual institutions, takes these decisions. The term 'supply driven' also invokes a sense of professionals in educational institutions acting in their own narrow self-interest. This, and the other 'rigidities' in education institutions are linked by advocates of outcomes-based qualifications frameworks to putative rigidities of the subject-based curricula and teacher-centred pedagogies. The alternative idea is that by using learning outcomes as the standard against which provision and assessment takes place, institutions can be forced to be more accountable for what they are providing, as well as being forced to compete with other educational institutions. In other words, learning outcomes provide a mechanism whereby governments can shift from being primarily providers to being primarily regulators, or, as will be discussed in more detail in later chapters, such outcomes can be a mechanism for introducing quasi-markets into education systems.

In traditional systems of issuing certificates, diplomas, degrees, and so on, qualifications are linked to the completion of specific learning programmes. Behind the growing emphasis on learning outcomes and qualifications is a belief that this traditional approach gives education institutions an unfair monopoly on the issuing of qualifications. Learning outcomes, it is claimed, provide a vehicle for recognizing experiential learning by providing a benchmark against which it can be compared with knowledge taught inside education programmes (Jessup, 1991). This belief contains an implicit notion of knowledge, and what the conditions for its acquisition are, which I will for now just note, and will return to in Chapter 6. Policy makers argue that skills and knowledge obtained on-the-job or through informal learning are not recognized by educational institutions, and assume that they are frequently and substantially the same as learning obtained through formal education. It is assumed that this leads to serious wastages of skills within economies, as well as exacerbation of inequality as the skilled but unqualified fall behind the qualified. The same logic is used to claim that learning outcomes increase access to education by making entrance requirements more fair and transparent, because the outcomes provide an objective benchmark against which individuals can be evaluated.

As can be seen from the above discussion, the three sets of claims in favour of outcomes-based qualifications (improving education/labour market relationships; reforming curricula, pedagogy, and assessment; reforming how the quality of education is evaluated and how education is delivered) are related. The idea is that liberalized systems of education provision, or education provision which places more emphasis on employer requirements, will be responsive to the market needs of both direct consumers (students) and indirect consumers (employers), and will therefore produce the kinds of graduates that the labour market requires, as well as meeting the needs of individuals. Further, using learning outcomes as the starting point for curriculum design can break what is perceived as the monopoly or dominance of educators in curriculum design, and open up space for employers to contribute, thus again ensuring that education programmes are more relevant, and at the same time, enabling different providers to compete against each other in provision of the specified learning outcomes. Learning outcomes are also intended to improve the relationship between education, the economy and the labour market, as well as ensuring individual satisfaction.

There are other issues interwoven into these three sets of issues in different ways. For example, in many countries it is predominantly disadvantaged learners who are enrolled in vocational education programmes, and there is concern about the low status of vocational qualifications. There are concerns that this low status discourages learners from enrolling in vocational programmes, which policy makers believe are more useful than general education programmes. They hope that qualifications frameworks will raise the status of vocational qualifications—by showing that they are at the same 'level' on a framework as other qualifications, and thus should be seen as equal by society. Thus, qualifications frameworks are seen as a tool to ensure that more people will obtain education which is 'relevant', and which produces 'useful skills', and therefore develop the economy. At the same time, the fact that outcomes or competencies are specified for all qualifications is seen as a way of ensuring that *all* education is more relevant to the economy and to the needs of individuals. It is also seen as a way of ensuring 'world-class standards' against which students must perform.

There are, no doubt, many problems with education systems, in terms of who can access them, what people get out of them, what they have to sacrifice in order to access them, and so on. Qualifications frameworks are claimed to solve many of these problems. Looking at the speed at which this policy has spread around the world, it seems as if at least some of these claims are believed by many policy makers.

AN EXPLOSION OF QUALIFICATIONS FRAMEWORKS AND LEARNING OUTCOMES

Antonio Novoa (2002) draws on Pierre Bourdieu (2000) in positing the spread of 'banalities' around the world, which become universally accepted as truth, and are then transformed into 'magic concepts' which claim to provide solutions to a wide range of problems. Learning outcomes seem to be a 'magic concept' sweeping the globe at the moment, together with lifelong learning, qualifications frameworks, and recognition of prior learning. Policy makers in many countries, with vast differences in their education systems, wealth, levels of industrialization, demographic trends, and so on, are involved in developing qualifications frameworks, and attempting to use outcomes to change their education systems.

In the late 1980s and the 1990s a handful of countries were introducing outcomes-based national qualifications frameworks, and implementing outcomes-based curriculum reforms. By now, as mentioned above, over 120 countries are reported to be developing a national qualifications framework. Policy makers in many countries, with vast differences in their education systems, wealth, levels of industrialization, demographic trends, and so on, are involved in developing qualifications frameworks, and attempting to use learning outcomes to change their education systems.

As I discuss in more detail in Chapter 3, the qualifications framework phenomenon started in the reform of vocational education in the United Kingdom in the 1980s. A Scottish reform in the 1980s which introduced outcomes-based, portable, 'institutionally versatile', modules for vocational education is sometimes seen as its origin (Raffe, 2009b). In the rest of the United Kingdom, a competence-based framework of vocational qualifications, known as National Vocational Qualifications, was developed in the late 1980s.

This approach to educational reform spread to Australia and New Zealand, both of which were engaged in major reforms of their economies and education systems during this period. Qualifications policy became a major tool in educational reform in both countries. Australia, using the English model as a base, developed a competence-based training system for its vocational education in the 1990s, which was institutionalized through 'training packages' in 1997. In 1990, the New Zealand Qualifications Framework was created. This framework was not restricted to vocational education, and embraced the entire education and training system.

For a decade or so, most development was seen in countries in the developing world, drawing heavily on the models developed in the United Kingdom. These were mainly countries directly influenced by the United Kingdom, such as former colonies, or Asian and Pacific states with strong relationships with Australia. In 1995, South Africa, like New Zealand, created a National Qualifications Framework for its entire education and training system. In the 1990s, various countries started developing frameworks of qualifications for vocational or workplace-based education and training—including Chile, Malaysia, and Mexico. The English National Vocational Qualifications were used as a model for these reforms. Competence-based training became a major feature of vocational education in Latin America and the Caribbean in the 1990s and early 2000s (Vargas Zuñiga, 2005). Qualifications frameworks *per se* are more recent in Latin America, with Argentina, Brazil, Chile, Colombia, Mexico, and Suriname being reportedly involved in developing frameworks, and in Central America the one country with British colonial heritage, Belize, is developing a qualifications framework. In the Caribbean Community, a single set of Caribbean Vocational Qualifications was created, with a regional coordinating mechanism established in 2003. This framework has been specifically focused on the adoption of competency-based education and training, and includes the five-level framework of occupational standards which had already been developed in the region; a process of standards development; and a specific process of training delivery and assessment for certification (Keevy *et al.*, 2011). Many Caribbean islands[6] are involved in qualifications frameworks according to Keevy *et al.* (2011).

In Africa, besides South Africa which has already been mentioned, Namibia, Mauritius, Botswana, and the Maldives were involved in developing qualifications frameworks from the late 1990s and early 2000s. By 2002, under considerable influence from South Africa (Chisholm, 2007), a number of countries in southern Africa were developing qualifications frameworks, mainly with a focus on vocational education. By 2003, besides the frameworks in the countries mentioned above, Malawi, Mozambique, Zambia, and Zimbabwe had established an authority or department to further develop and implement a framework, and preliminary work towards developing a qualifications framework had taken place in many other African countries[7].

In Asia and the Pacific, there was similar growth, also mainly in vocational education. From 2002, many islands started developing qualifications frameworks[8]. In 2007 the Malaysian Qualifications Framework was adopted, and Pakistan started developing a qualifications framework. In East Asia, Hong Kong, Malaysia, Singapore, Thailand, and The Philippines are reported to have national qualifications frameworks established, and Brunei Darussalam and the Republic of Korea are reported to be developing frameworks (APEC Human Resources Development Working Group, 2009). In South and Central Asia and the Middle East there are moves towards developing qualifications frameworks in many countries[9] (Keevy et al., 2011).

Some European countries started developing frameworks in the late 1990s and early 2000s. Ireland, France, Malta and the United Kingdom are the only countries where there were fully developed qualifications frameworks, but almost all European Union countries, as well as Iceland, Liechtenstein and Norway, which are all European Economic Area members, have signaled that they will introduce or are introducing comprehensive, overarching qualifications frameworks covering all parts of their education, training and qualifications systems (Cedefop, 2010).

In 1999, the Bologna Declaration was signed, through which 29 (now over 40) European countries agreed to start aligning their higher education systems, using learning outcomes and levels, both of which are intrinsic to qualifications frameworks. This declaration was a big step towards a supranational education framework in higher education and arguably started the move towards qualifications frameworks as a Europe-wide phenomenon. There is also a long history in Europe of trying to align vocational education, which was brought to a head with rising youth unemployment since the 1970s (Brockmann, Clarke, Winch, et al., 2011). In 2008, the idea of qualifications frameworks received a huge burst of energy in Europe with the adoption of the European Qualifications Framework for Lifelong Learning.

Besides the European Qualifications Framework, other regional frameworks are being designed or implemented. The Southern African Development Community (SADC) has been talking about a regional framework since 2001, and a concept document was released in 2005. The focus is on vocational education and training as well as promoting the development of qualifications frameworks in individual countries (Keevy et al., 2011). According to Chisholm (2007), the process has been substantially influenced by the South African Qualifications Framework as well as the 'expertise' and 'advice' of South African consultants. She cites David Atchoarena and André Delluc (2002, p. 341) who argue: 'For SADC, the development of compatible national qualifications frameworks represents a strategic instrument to increase the competitiveness of the sub-region and contribute to further economic and labour market integration' (Chisholm, 2007, p. 301).

The need for a qualifications framework is also being considered for nations within the Asia Pacific Economic Cooperation (APEC 2009). The Association of Southeast Asian Nations[10] is in the preliminary stages of developing a regional framework, using the European Qualifications Framework as a reference (Keevy et al., 2011). The Pacific Islands countries[11] also intend to develop a qualifications framework, and have started with a unified register of qualifications, the Pacific

Regional Qualifications Register, as well as the development of an inventory of technical and vocational education and training programmes (Lythe, 2008).

In 2007, the Commonwealth of Learning facilitated the development of a Transnational Qualifications Framework for 29 small (population-wise) states[12] which are members of the Commonwealth, regardless of their geographical location. It is defined as a 'translation instrument', and includes higher education and post-secondary technical and vocational qualifications (Commonwealth of Learning and SAQA, 2008). Various members of the regional qualifications frameworks listed above are also members of this framework.

Many of these frameworks were predated by conventions or declarations developed through UNESCO (for example, the Lisbon convention and Bologna process in Europe and the Arusha declaration in Africa), which aimed to ensure that countries recognized qualifications and part qualifications within different regions[13].

The major and notable exception to this international trend is the United States. There are no proposals for federal or state frameworks. However, many of the underlying trends are still the same: there has been a rapid increase in industry credentialing programs, and emphasis on 'external certification of skills' as opposed to the traditional college and university credentialing system. This is specifically for 'continuing education', which is offered through a diverse range of providers. David Bills (2004, p. 198) notes, quoting Lewis *et al.* (2000, p. 3), "what was once an eclectic assortment of individually accessed, non-credit educational courses is quickly being knit into comprehensive degree- and certificate-granting programmes".

It is not just governments who are involved in outcomes-based qualifications frameworks. Learning outcomes and national qualifications frameworks, together with associated policies such as lifelong learning, recognition of prior or experiential learning, and competency-based reform of vocational education systems, as well as the idea of learner centreness, dominate the policy agenda of international agencies[14]. As Young (2010, p. 2) argues: "Not only does every country seems to want a National Qualification Framework, but virtually all the leading international agencies are involved in persuading any countries that show reluctance, that there is no other alternative if they want to be 'modern' and improve their economic competitiveness."

Powerful international organizations including the World Bank, the OECD, and many donor and development agencies, are increasingly advising poor and middle income countries to develop qualifications frameworks (for example, World Bank, 2002). The International Labour Organization (ILO) has in the past recommended the adoption of national qualifications frameworks (Departments of Education and Labour, 2003; Jane Stewart, 2005), and has suggested the promotion of national, regional, and international qualifications frameworks (ILO, 2004). Donor funding to poor countries has increasingly been channeled into this kind of education reform. The South African Qualifications Framework, for example, has been largely funded by the European Union, as well as partly by the Canadian government, and the

Dutch government's funding arm has recently funded the processes of exploring the regional qualifications framework in the SADC area (SAQA, 2003). The European Commission is funding qualifications frameworks in many countries, including Somalia, Bangladesh, and India, and the European Training Foundation is assisting countries to develop qualifications frameworks.

EVIDENCE OR IDEOLOGY-BASED POLICY?

Despite their sudden and rapid rise to prominence in education policy internationally, there has been very little research on qualifications frameworks. This may in part be a by-product of their opacity and tendency to generate jargon which makes them difficult and tedious to engage with. It may also be because, in the eyes of most critical researchers and analysts, the exaggerated claims about what they can achieve are so implausible that they are simply not worth the effort.

Much of the international documentation in support of qualifications frameworks tends to be self-referential, mainly consisting of claims about what frameworks can do or are doing as policy reforms. For example:

> National qualifications frameworks (NQFs) have, during the last five years, turned into key instruments for the restructuring and reform of education, training and qualifications systems in Europe. While very few countries had considered this approach prior to 2005, the situation today is very different. (Cedefop, 2009, p. 1)

> Qualifications Frameworks have become important structures in deepening access, inclusion, and achievement in education. (Donn 2003, p. v)

> The [Mauritius national qualifications] framework was developed to ensure greater articulation between education, training, and the world of work and that training responds to standards set by industry. At the same time, it aims to encourage lifelong learning through recognition of prior learning and flexible delivery of training. (http://www.logos-net.net/ilo/195_base/en/init/mau_2.htm accessed 9th September 2006)

None of these claims are linked to empirical evidence or clear examples of where frameworks have in fact led to the kinds of goals stated. For example, the reasons provided for a framework for the Southern African region by a SADC technical committee document are that it will benefit the development of frameworks in member countries (a circular argument) and will lead to "standardized terminology to ensure effective comparability of qualifications and credits across borders in the SADC region" (Technical Committee on Certification and Accreditation 2005, p. 9). The document goes on to spell out the advantages that a framework will have for states, education systems, students, society, employers, stakeholders, and the global community. The document does not explain how a qualifications framework is likely to lead to these aims; it simply claims that it will.

The small amount of research which is available suggests there are serious problems with this type of policy reform. In 2009, I conducted an international comparative study for the ILO. Leading a team of researchers around the world, I compared qualifications frameworks in 16 countries,[15] as well as surveying available research into qualifications frameworks around the world (Allais, 2010b). The focus was on how qualifications frameworks had been or were being implemented, and what impact they had had to date. The countries we investigated[16] were selected to ensure a spread across geographic regions, favouring countries where implementation of the qualifications framework was advanced or at least underway, as many countries are in very preliminary stages. In most countries, (exceptions being Australia, New Zealand, Malaysia, South Africa and Scotland) qualifications frameworks were focused on the reform of vocational education. The countries were a diverse mixture: in geographical size, they varied from the largest country on earth to a very small island; in population size, from the most densely populated country on earth to countries with tiny populations. They included very rich and very poor countries, countries with high and low levels of social equality, and countries on both ends of the spectrum of the United Nations human development index. We found that, despite the diversity of the countries studied, the goals of policy makers for qualifications frameworks were very similar. Equally similar was the litany of woes about education and training systems that qualifications frameworks were being introduced to solve: the 'mismatch' between education and the workplace, the 'irrelevance' of education and training to the alleged needs of employers, the lack of 'transparency' of qualifications, the lack of 'accountability' of education institutions, the lack of official recognition for learning acquired out of formal education systems, and the low status of vocational education.

What was stark in the findings was the paucity of evidence supporting the claim that qualifications frameworks have contributed to solving these problems. We found no publicly available research which presented clear evidence in favour of outcomes-based qualifications frameworks, despite the flurry of countries developing qualifications frameworks. In some instances, lack of positive evidence was because qualifications frameworks were a recent intervention, and so it may have been simply too early to tell. It could also be the case that there have been successes, but that they are not recorded, researched, and publicized, or that my researchers simply failed to find them. Nonetheless, the absence of clearly available evidence of successes, particularly for the older frameworks, is an important finding for a policy that has been so widely accepted internationally, and that is growing at such a rapid rate: representatives of qualifications authorities, government agencies, and industry bodies interviewed did not have concrete evidence, evaluations, or research that showed clear achievements, and publically available information from these organizations also did not contain such evidence. The framework which emerged as the least *unsuccessful* was the Scottish Credit and Qualifications Framework. This framework, which had the fewest ambitions with regard to the typical goals of frameworks I have discussed, is discussed further in Chapter 8.

The research found little evidence that qualifications frameworks have substantially improved communication between education systems and labour markets—a key goal in all the countries. The strongest evidence found was in Scotland, where there was some indication that the framework was being used by a national career guidance service. This is hardly a startling achievement, and is a long way from solving the so-called education/labour market mismatch. None of the case studies found evidence demonstrating that employers found qualifications easier to use than they had prior to the introduction of a framework, nor were other data found to demonstrate that competence and outcomes-based qualifications had improved the match between education and training systems and the labour market.

With regard to articulation amongst educational providers, there is some evidence of successes, but also evidence that in some countries, qualifications frameworks have *reduced* learner mobility across different sectors of the education system (Blom, Parker, & Keevy, 2007; Wheelahan, 2009). There is also some evidence of increased numbers of certificates being awarded that recognize existing skills, knowledge, and abilities of workers and potential workers. But in all cases this was on a small scale, and our researchers could not find evidence that it had benefited workers in any way other than improving their self-esteem.

Further, while we didn't find evidence of successes, we did find considerable evidence that implementing qualifications frameworks had caused problems in many countries.

In a number of the countries with longer experience of qualifications frameworks, a common problem was that many new qualifications had been designed and registered on the frameworks but not used. South Africa had the greatest number of unused qualifications—by 2007, 787 new qualifications had been developed, but only 180 of them had ever been awarded to learners. Of the well over 10,000 'unit standards' (outcomes-based part qualifications) that had been developed, just over 2000 had been awarded. The remaining unit standards were just documents in cyberspace which took considerable resources to produce. This is not unique to South Africa. In Mauritius *none* of the new, outcomes-based qualifications that were developed through the qualifications framework for the vocational education system had been used, eight years after the introduction of the framework. In Botswana, a mere ten courses had been developed against unit standards, a very small fraction of total provision of vocational education, and even government colleges did not use the newly designed unit standards. In Mexico, 630 'labour competence technical standards' had been registered by 2008. 530 of them had not been awarded to any learners. The situation with regard to the English National Vocational Qualifications was similar. Australia and New Zealand also had many qualifications with low take-up, and some which are completely unused. In all these countries, the new qualifications were designed by all relevant stakeholders, particularly representatives of industry—which policy makers claim ensures that they will be relevant to employers' needs. Further, in all these countries, the problem of overspecification was found—long, detailed qualification documents were produced in the name of increased transparency, which became impossible to work with, and highly opaque.

There is, then, on the face of it, a fascinating conundrum: this policy mechanism is growing very fast, and yet has very little evidence in its favour. What is particularly interesting is the role that international agencies are playing in pushing this agenda. Strong claims continue to be made about the benefits of outcomes-based qualifications frameworks, and yet supporters and implementers have not yet produced evidence to back up these claims. How can this state of affairs be explained, and what does it tell us? Policy borrowing as well as the influence of donor and development agencies have been significant factors in the spread of qualifications frameworks, as is discussed in Chapters 2 and 3. But this does not explain why it is that this specific set of policies have become the policy *du jour*.

I start my story by considering the educational ideas which have been drawn on in order to justify qualifications frameworks, and show that many of the ideas which are claimed as part of a 'new learning paradigm' in contemporary policy documents have, in fact, a long history in educational debates and reform.

ENDNOTES

[1] The notion of 'post-Fordism', although fraught with difficulty and highly contested within economic and social theory, is important to introduce here because of the extent to which it has proved popular with governments and education policy formulators. Post-Fordism is sometimes seen as a description of how economies are changing, and sometimes a prescription about how they should or could change. It emphasizes a move away from mass production (Fordism) to niche oriented, flexible production. Advocates argue that through this kind of reorganization, nations will all find their comparative advantage in the global market place, and thus prosperity will follow for all. The idea is both premised on and advocates for a 'skilled' and 'flexible' workforce, and is often linked to discussions about the 'knowledge economy', which are discussed further below.

[2] Gordon Brown, "My Vision of a Fairer Britain for Everyone" Times, 3 June 2000, cited in Callinicos (2001, p. 48).

[3] Brown (2006) suggests that the idea of 'employability' signifies a shift in the meaning of life, whereby people are economically enslaved by 'opportunities' for employment.

[4] Another dominant trend in education policy is national and international standardized achievement tests. Critics argue this is leading to a narrowing of curriculum content, an increasing prescriptiveness of curricula, and narrow notions of what is 'worthwhile knowledge'. For example, Emery Hyslop-Margison and Alan Sears write that "[t]hese 'policy as numbers' moves have affected pedagogies, thinning them out and reducing curriculum content to that which is valorized in tests and examinations" (Hyslop-Margison & Sears, 2006, p. 96). The prevalence of international achievement tests is often linked to neoliberalism, and what is described as 'performativity' or an audit culture, as well as to marketization: "National and international league tables and rankings for schools and universities have grown enormously in popularity and have become a growing market of consumer information" (Enders, 2010, p. 209). There is a huge wealth of critical literature on this area, and it is, therefore, not explored in this book.

[5] Of course, how outcomes-based frameworks have been implemented in practice differs from country to country, and many do not make claims as strong as these, as is discussed later in this book. However, in general policy documents from countries as well as advocacy documents for learning outcomes-based approaches make these claims.

[6] Antigua & Barbuda, the Bahamas, Barbados, Dominica, Grenada, Guyana, Haiti, Jamaica, Montserrat, Saint Kitts and Nevis, Saint Lucia, Trinidad & Tobago, St. Vincent, and the Grenadines.

7 Angola, the Comoros, the Democratic Republic of Congo, Ethiopia, Egypt, Eritrea, the Gambia, Ghana, Lesotho, Madagascar, Malawi, Morocco, Mozambique, the Seychelles, Sierra Leone, Somalia, Swaziland, Tanzania, Tunisia, Uganda, Zambia, and Zimbabwe, according to Keevy *et al.* (2011), SAQA (2003), and personal communications with agencies involved in qualifications design. Kenya, Nigeria, and Rwanda were said to be investigating implementing frameworks.

8 Fiji, Kiribati, the Philipines, Samoa, Vanuatu, Maldives, Tonga, Tuvalu, Papua New Guinea, and Vanuatu started developing frameworks.

9 Afghanistan, Bangladesh, Burma, India, Pakistan, Maldives, Nepal, Sri Lanka in South Asia, Armenia, Azerbaijan, Kazakhstan, Kyrgyzstan, Mongolia, and Tajikistan in Central Asia, and Bahrain, Cyprus, Georgia, Oman, Jordan, Kuwait, Lebanon, Turkey, and the United Arab Emirates in the Middle East.

10 Including Brunei Darussalam, Cambodia, Indonesia, Lao People's Democratic Republic, Malaysia, Myanmar, Philippines, Singapore, Thailand, and Viet Nam.

11 Supported by Cook Islands, Federated States of Micronesia, Fiji, Kiribati, Marshall Islands, Nauru, Niue, Palau, Papua New Guinea, Samoa, Solomon Islands, Tokelau, Tonga, Tuvalu, and Vanuatu.

12 This includes Antigua & Barbuda, Barbados, Belize, Botswana, Cyprus, Dominica, Grenada, Guyana, Jamaica, Lesotho, Maldives, Malta, Mauritius, Namibia, Papua New Guinea, Samoa, Seychelles, Sierra Leone, St. Kitts & Nevis, St. Lucia, St. Vincent and the Grenadines, Swaziland, The Bahamas, The Comoros (non-Commonwealth), The Gambia, Tonga, Trinidad & Tobago, Tuvalu, and Vanuatu.

13 The lists in the preceding 6 footnotes seem repetitive as many countries are involved in both national and regional frameworks, and some are involved in more than one transnational framework.

14 See for example (APEC Human Resources Development Working Group, 2009; Bjornavold & Coles, 2007; Cedefop, 2008, 2010; Coles, 2006, 2007; Commonwealth of Learning and SAQA, 2008; Lythe, 2008; OECD, 2007; Sellin, 2007).

15 The full report is published by the ILO, and an overview of the findings has been published in the Journal of Education and Work, along with some of the case studies, as well as in Young and Allais (2013).

16 Australia, Bangladesh, Botswana, Chile, England (the National Vocational Qualifications), Lithuania, Malaysia, Mauritius, Mexico, New Zealand, Russia, Scotland, South Africa, Sri Lanka, Tunisia, and Turkey.

CHAPTER 2

PLUS LA MEME CHOSE

The Early History of Learning Outcomes and Learner Centredness

The novelties of one generation are only the resuscitated fashions of the generation before last. George Bernard Shaw, *Three Plays for Puritans*, Preface (1900)

Current attempts to ensure that education delivers according to the needs of the economy, as well as current critiques of subject-based curricula, are less new than they appear. Ideas about 'relevance', objectives, and learning outcomes, as well as the idea that subject-based curricula are obsolete, both of which have re-gained prominence in contemporary education policy, particularly through outcomes-based qualifications frameworks, have been influential periodically in the history of educational reform. And both sets of ideas have been supported by both left and right-wing educational reformers and policy makers.

For over a century, criticism of 'traditional' academic education and subject-based curricula has come from business leaders who wanted economy and efficiency in schools, and work-ready, relevantly skilled, and compliant workers. Politicians and industrialists (and people who claim to speak for industry) have argued that the traditional subject-based curriculum has caused economic decline. The subject-based curriculum has been associated with the ideas of an out-of-touch aristocratic elite, labeled by business leaders as out of touch with the needs of industry, contributing to industrial decline, not training people to be 'enterprise-minded', and not giving them useful skills.

Raymond Callahan's detailed study of North American educational reform at the turn of the twentieth century demonstrates that reform in the early 1900s was focused on making education more 'relevant' and 'practically useful':

While the most specific outcomes of this pressure were the establishment of vocational schools and vocational courses in the existing secondary schools and the decline of classical studies, the utilitarian movement pervaded the entire school system from the elementary schools through the universities. A less tangible but more important corollary of the practical movement was a strong current of anti-intellectualism which, when it was given expression, generally appeared in such phrases as 'mere scholastic education' or 'mere book learning'. (Callahan, 1962, p. 8)

27

Callahan describes popular journals and magazines in early twentieth century North America which featured prominent educationalists arguing that education should not be concerned with "culture". A "gentleman's education" was seen as being of no used in the business world and, it was suggested, also not "desired by the mob". Such education was seen as inappropriately "preparing our children for a life of scholasticism" (Callahan, 1962, p. 50). This was linked to a campaign for running educational institutions as businesses. Callahan argues that the main procedure for educational reform between 1900 and 1925 consisted of making unfavourable comparisons between schools and business enterprises, applying business-industrial criteria (economy and efficiency) to education, and suggesting that business and industrial practices be adopted by educators. An interesting theme which Callahan picks up on, and which was to be a source of similar concern across the Atlantic for many years, was a comparison with Germany, and an argument that Germany's industrial superiority was due to its greater emphasis on vocational education; this led to attempts to vocationalize the school curriculum.

Ironically, as Doll (1993, in Flinders & Thornton, 2004, p. 253) points out, the late nineteenth and early twentieth century curriculum was at least in some ways highly focused on the workplace: arithmetic, not mathematics, was taught to young learners, with an emphasis on "store clerk functionalism, keeping the sales slips and ledgers accurate and neat. Problem solving was introduced as early as the second grade, but it was heavily, if not exclusively, associated with buying in an urban store". Ivor Goodson (1994, p. 49) laments the loss of 'the science of common things' from the 1840s, which he suggests was empowering for ordinary people. He argues that subsequently, "[k]nowledge increasingly became decontextualized and disembodied as the 'disciplines' developed closer and closer ties with the state and with university scholars", by implication becoming disempowering to ordinary people.

Many progressive educationalists have shared Goodson's concerns. Like the industrial reformers mentioned above, progressive educationalists have associated the subject-based curriculum with elites. They have argued that the school curriculum should be more aligned with the needs of society, and the interests and needs of individuals. Many, but not all of the educational reformers who have pushed for 'child-centred' or 'learner-centred' reforms have seen them as part of a broader left-wing struggle for an education system which can play a part in creating a more democratic and more egalitarian society.

Thus, from very different political perspectives, subject-based curricula and the idea of the acquisition of bodies of knowledge as a key purpose of education and the focus of curriculum development have been the target of much criticism. One early alternative for conceptualizing and designing the curriculum has been associated with terms such as objectives, outcomes, or competencies. Objectives or outcomes-based approaches start with tasks or activities in the everyday world, and specifically the world of work. Analyzing such tasks or activities, and then attempting to design a curriculum which prepares learners for them, it is seen as a way of overcoming the problems of 'traditional education', and ensuring the relevance of education.

The second approach, which is very different although also concerned with the need for education to be relevant to individuals, is child- or learner-centred reform. As I discuss below, this is sometimes presented with an emphasis on pedagogy only, but frequently slips into an approach to the curriculum. Reformers in this (very broad) tradition have suggested that the knowledge acquired at school must be more continuous with the knowledge of the everyday world of the learner as well as the knowledge of the working and social world into which they will progress.

In both approaches, the starting point for thinking about education, and designing curricula, is the projected or immediate utility of knowledge in the life of the learner. For some, the interests and life experiences of individual learners must drive the curriculum, while for others the workplace becomes the curriculum authority. These two approaches have frequently been at odds with each other politically, the former emphasizing humanism, autonomy and democracy, and the latter economic efficiency, the needs of employers, and the market. But in both cases, existing bodies of knowledge are not the *starting point* for designing a curriculum. This does not mean that either educational outcomes or child-centred education are *inherently* incompatible with the idea of subjects. Invariably subjects do still feature in various ways in many approaches which are labeled 'child-' or 'learner-centred', as well as in some objectives/outcomes-based approaches, as will be discussed below.

Both objectives/outcomes-based approaches and child- or learner-centred approaches have spawned many different lines of thought about educational reform. Neither can be associated with one simple reform agenda. They have sometimes been at odds with each other, and sometimes seen as sharing similar concerns. However, criticism of traditional subject-centred education has been a dominant feature of much educational thinking that has gone under both these labels.

Before considering the specific histories of qualifications frameworks (Chapters 3, 4, and 8), as well as the conceptual issues that they raise, it is worth taking a brief look back in time, to consider the predecessors of the current ideas about outcomes and learner-centredness. The cursory accounts below, both of outcomes/ objectives-based approaches, and of child-/learner-centred approaches, are roughly chronological. This is not meant to imply a clear progression or move from one thinker or movement to another, but simply to show some of the ways in which similar ideas have emerged in the history of educational reform. I start with learning outcomes, and afterwards consider learner-centredness.

LOOKING BACK ON LEARNING OUTCOMES

Current policy documents describe learning outcomes as a new idea, even a 'new learning paradigm'. But actually this idea has rather a long history. Previous versions of it have surfaced particularly when reformers have wanted to improve relationships between education and labour markets, or increase the 'relevance' of education to work. Developing statements of objectives, competences, or learning outcomes is one way in which reformers have attempted to make education relevant, accessible, and useful to the individuals acquiring it, to their employers, and to society at large. The premise seems to be that if we can just figure out *exactly* what it is that we want learners to *be able to do* by the end of education, we can design education systems that enable them to learn it.

Many researchers trace outcomes-based education to teacher education in the United States in the 1980s, where there was a focus on developing and measuring teacher 'competence', largely as a result of political pressures as school education came under public criticism (Spreen, 2001; Stewart & Sambrook, 1995). But, as Terry Hyland (1994) points out, this idea had already gained prominence in the United States in the early twentieth century, under the influence of Frederick Taylor and the 'efficiency' cult. Taylor conducted time and motion studies in order to increase the productivity of workers in manufacturing. His most famous study was on the processing of pig iron. This led to a flurry of publications on 'Scientific Management' between 1910 and 1916 (Callahan, 1962; Wainwright, 1994). Various reformers and curriculum writers developed this into the notion of the 'Scientific Curriculum'. For example, W.W. Charters, an influential north American educationalist propounded the idea of 'activity analysis': the notion that curriculum construction should begin by listing the major objectives of schooling, creating details of the lists of activities associated with work in which the student planned to engage, and then preparing study units on the basis of these objectives and descriptions of activities (Ravitch, 2001).

Franklin Bobbit (1876–1956), who claimed to write the first book on 'the curriculum', is an exemplary representative of this approach. I will consider his ideas in some depth because of their startling similarity to recent educational reforms. Bobbit was an enthusiastic follower of Taylor's Scientific Management, and wanted to use it to improve schools. He argued that schools needed clearly specified objectives, based on analysis of tasks and roles in the 'real' world. His strongest criticism of the contemporary curriculum was a lack of clearly articulated objectives. The essence of the theory of the 'Scientific Curriculum' was that one should "go out into the world of affairs and discover the particulars of which these affairs consist" (Bobbit, 1918, p. 11). The task of the curriculum developer was to "discover the total range of habits, skills, abilities, forms of thought, valuations, ambitions, etc, that the members of any particular social class need for the effective performance of their vocational labours, as well as for their civic activities, health activities, recreations, language, parental, religious, and general social activities".

Bobbit (1918, p. 11) argued that the curriculum was "that *series of things which children and youth must do and experience* by way of developing abilities to do the things well that make up the affairs of adult life". As opposed to nineteenth century education, focused, wrongly in Bobbit's view, on 'facts', the new education that he advocated would "train thought and judgement in connection with actual life-situations, a task distinctly different from the cloistral activities of the past. It is also to develop the good-will, the spirit of service, the social valuations, sympathies, and attitudes of mind necessary for effective group-action where specialization has created endless interdependency" (Bobbit, 1918, p. 10). He emphasized the continuity between education and experience:

> ... as education is coming more and more to be seen as a thing of experiences, and as the work- and play-experiences of the general community life are being more and more utilized, the line of demarcation between directed and undirected training experience is rapidly disappearing. Education must be concerned with both, even though it does not direct both. (Bobbit, 1918, p. 11)

Bobbit suggested that just as steel plants had precise specifications for their products, which were not determined by the mill but by those who had ordered the rails, education must have standards specified by the community, and not by educators. "A school system can no more find standards of performance within itself than a steel plant can find the proper height or weight per yard for steel rails from the activities within the plant," he argued, and went on:

> ... the commercial world can best say what it needs in the case of its stenographers and accountants. A machine shop can best say what is needed in the workers that come to it. The plumbing trade contains the men who are best able to state the needs of those entering upon plumbing; and so on through the entire list. (Bobbit 1913b, cited in Callahan, 1962, pp. 83-84)

Teachers' expertise, according to Bobbit, lay in achieving the standard which had been specified by the experts:

> After society has given to the school its ultimate standard in any particular case, it then is certainly the business of the educational and psychological experts to determine the time of the beginning, the intensity of the work, and the standards to be attained in each of the successive stages. (Bobbit 1913, cited in Callahan, 1962, p. 84)

The analysis of tasks and roles would lead to a list of desired skills, which could then be broken down into constituent elements, and specified as the objectives of the curriculum. Based as it is on the ideas of Scientific Management, which used manufacturing as a template, this 'Scientific Curriculum' may be the origin of the tendency to use notions such as 'inputs', 'outputs' and 'efficiency' in educational discussions.

Bobbit's work was largely focused on *behavioural* objectives. He parts company with contemporary learning outcomes discourse in his attitude towards learners. Whereas the contemporary discourse puts emphasis on 'learner centredness', he saw "the interest of children as irrelevant to the educational process". Instead, "curriculum work was a practical task whose only need for theoretical justification had been 'discovered' analyzing the behavior of successful adults" (cited in Flinders & Thornton, 2004, p. 3). In this, he was at odds with his better-known contemporary, John Dewey (1859 – 1952), who stressed the importance of 'child-centred theory', and whose ideas I will return to below. Bobbit was also at odds with many of the educational thinkers and reformers who re-used, re-worked and developed his ideas, who increasingly took on the notion of learner centredness. For, as discussed in the previous chapter, recent documentation about learning outcomes and qualifications frameworks places emphasis on both the notion of learning outcomes *and* the idea of learner-centredness, the modern version of child-centredness. The two ideas are seen as intertwined, and policy makers, advocates and researchers increasingly describe learner-centredness and learning outcomes as part of the same package of policies.[1]

Elliot Eisner (1967), a critic of objectives-based approaches to the curriculum, argues that the 'Scientific Curriculum' movement of the early twentieth century collapsed under its own weight in the 1930s, because of the large number of objectives and very complex curriculum which emerged. Bobbit's approach led to long and unwieldy lists of learning objectives, something that remains a dominant feature of outcomes-based qualifications today. Herbert Kliebard, an authority on the history of the curriculum in the United States, quotes just a small selection of Bobbit's objectives, to give a flavour of the types of objectives that were developed: "the ability to keep one's emotional serenity, in the face of circumstances however trying", "an attitude and desire of obedience to the immutable and eternal laws which appear to exist in the nature of things", "ability to read and interpret facts expressed by commonly used types of graphs, diagrams, and statistical tables", "ability to care properly for the feet", "keeping razor in order" and "ability to tell interesting stories interestingly" (Kliebard, 1975, p. 40).

In the late 1940s and 50s, outcomes and objectives re-emerged. Specialists reintroduced the importance of specific educational objectives, often with links to, or invoking support from, the 'Scientific Curriculum' movement (Eisner, 1967). Ralph Tyler (1949), for example, although advocating broader objectives than Bobbit's, had a similar notion of curriculum making as linear: content must be selected on the basis that it achieves specified objectives. The means must only be determined once the end has been decided upon. Tyler argued that subject specialists should be consulted in curriculum design, but the focus should be on what the subject can contribute to the education of young laypeople; for example, how science can contribute to personal health, meet needs for responsible participation in socially significant activities, or encourage reflective thinking. Tyler emphasized studying young people and contemporary life outside the school in order to design the curriculum (Tyler, 1949). Tyler's doctoral thesis was supervised by W.W. Charters, champion of 'activity analysis', whose particular focus was on describing the competencies of teachers in order to better train them (Norris, 1991, p. 338).

The ideas of Benjamin Bloom (Bloom, Engelhart, Furst, Hill, & Krathwohl, 1956), particularly his notion of a taxonomy of learning domains, were very influential from the 1950s, and continue to be part of mainstream educational thinking, still widely taught to trainee-teachers in many countries. Bloom, and others working in his tradition such as Anderson and Krathwohl (2001) who have developed a 'Revised Bloom's Taxonomy', have a very different idea of the curriculum to those of Bobbit and the Scientific Curriculum movement. Bloom's original Taxonomy of Learning

Domains describes different kinds of cognitive processes. These are not specified competencies to be mastered and then moved on from, but rather, ongoing aims of educational processes. There may, however, be some continuities between these different schools of thought. The original taxonomy is dedicated to Ralph Tyler, and many later advocates of outcomes-based education link their ideas to Bloom. What the taxonomy developed and made mainstream is the notion of cognitive 'skills' disembedded from specific subject matters. Bloom's taxonomy also contains the idea that cognitive 'skills' can be organized on a hierarchy, from the lowest level of simple recall or recognition of facts, through increasingly more complex and abstract mental levels, to the highest order, classified as evaluation. This notion of a generic hierarchy in the absence of the context of a specific subject or knowledge area re-surfaces in contemporary outcomes and qualifications frameworks policies.

Behavioural objectives acquired particular popularity in the United States in the 1950s, and were associated with the idea of 'mastery learning', as advocated, for example, by William Glasser, a psychiatrist outside of mainstream psychiatry in the United States who wrote an influential book, *Schools Without Failure* (Glasser, 1969). Glasser criticized traditional schooling for using norm referenced assessments in which students were ranked against each other according to achievements on assessment tasks, arguing that this just focused on selecting the 'fastest horses in the racecourse'. The idea of setting objectives which all students should be able to master in their own time was seen as more progressive, enabling all students to succeed in education, instead of setting some up for failure. In mastery learning the specification of objectives is tied to a notion of learner-centredness. While it is not necessarily opposed to a subject-based curriculum, Glasser raised other themes familiar from much contemporary education policy, including criticisms that schools do not prepare students for life, and criticism of memorization and focus on 'facts'. Schools, he argued, "usually do not teach a relevant curriculum; when they do, they fail to teach the child how he can relate this to his life outside of school" (Glasser, 1969, p. 50).

Another relative of the outcomes and objectives focus in educational reform is the criterion-referencing movement. Advocated by Glasser and others such as William James Popham, this movement gained force from the early 1960s, arguing for the clear specification of criteria against which learners would be assessed (Wolf, 1995). Popham (1972) also argued for more specific behavioural objectives. Drawing on Bloom's taxonomy, he argued that educational objectives need to be disaggregated according to the types of behaviours they are designed to promote.

Criterion-referencing has been a major influence in mainstream educational thinking, with a far broader reach than outcomes-based curriculum reforms and qualifications frameworks. It could be argued that this notion has been, to a large extent, mainstreamed in educational thinking today. For example, the notion of "supposedly clear and free-standing descriptors of what pupils at different 'levels' should attain" (Wolf, 1995, p. 3) is a key part of the National Curriculum of the United Kingdom. It is often also linked to ideas about learner-centredness and mastery learning, and invoked in opposition to norm-referencing[2]. While it is not necessarily opposed to subjects, as criteria can be set within subject areas, it has also emerged in relation to the outcomes-based qualifications movement, as Alison Wolf describes in her book about the competence-based reform movement in the United Kingdom and the National Vocational Qualifications which emerged, and to which I will return in the following chapter.

The ideas of Bobbit, Tyler, and Glasser show that outcomes approaches have a long lineage. However, as mentioned above, most accounts link their current popularity to their use in teacher education during the 1970s in the United States. Here the focus was on the competencies that teachers were expected to have, echoing the work of W.W. Charters. It is to this movement that the current spread of outcomes and competencies is usually linked:

> CBET [competence-based education and training] can be traced to education of primary and vocational teachers in the US, starting in the 1970s. Performance-based modules were developed, starting in Ohio. By 1977 some 23 states had implemented performance-based vocational education, and in the late 1980s the concept shaped many programmes of vocational education and training. (Deissinger & Hellwig, 2005, p. 8)

I have shown above that this movement has clear roots in the earlier ideas of outcomes and objectives, and traces its genesis from Bloom and Glasser.

The same lineages can be seen in another figure who influenced the more recent outcomes-based curriculum reforms, particularly in the schooling sector: William Spady, sometimes referred to as "the Father of outcomes-based education". He is described by Spreen (2001, p. 86) as "[p]robably the most significant actor in the OBE [outcomes-based education] arena". Spreen traces Spady's intellectual lineage from Tyler as well as Bloom. Like Bobbit, a central feature of Spady's notion of education is that its prime purpose is to prepare learners for 'life roles' after their formal education is complete (Killen, 2007).

Roy Killen, Australian outcomes-based education advocate, argues in an unpublished memo on Spady that

> Spady has never felt bound to conform to traditional ways of viewing education, particularly the organisational and systems aspects of school education. He is very much a "systems thinker" and this is why his ideas about educational reform are so challenging. They are not just ideas about what teachers should do in classrooms. They are ideas about how educational systems should be structured, how schools should be managed, how curricula should be designed and, ultimately, how learning and teaching should be driven by significant outcomes. (Killen, undated, p. 3)

This argument is one made by many contemporary advocates of outcomes-based qualifications frameworks, as will be seen below in this chapter and in later chapters. The specification of learning outcomes is seen as a way of thinking about the curriculum, but also of changing the way education is managed, funded, organized, and evaluated. Spreen links the emergence of learning outcomes in the United States to market-oriented influences, and points out that outcomes-based education incorporated corporate sector concepts into education. This is evidenced by a focus on notions such as 'client satisfaction', 'efficiency' 'measurable productivity' 'accountability', 'standards', and 'quality assurance'. Defining learning outcomes was seen as a key part of institutional strategic planning, in much the same way as quality management literature emphasizes goals. It is striking how naturalized these concepts are in education policy today.

Spady's ideas never became a major tenant of educational reform in the United States. They had a far greater influence on curriculum reform in Australia, New Zealand, and South Africa. Spady provided consultancy services and advocacy visits to these countries, all of which had lengthy experiments in various types of outcomes-based reforms (Spreen, 2001).

Two common threads are worth highlighting across these different thinkers and attempts at educational reform. One has been mentioned at length above: a general tendency to oppose a subject-based curriculum, or reject the idea of subjects as the starting point for curriculum design. This is not necessarily inherent to all the positions mentioned above. However, what is common, despite substantial differences, is that the various outcomes/ objectives/ competencies movements all entail attempts to describe skills, including cognitive 'skills', as disembedded from specific subject matter. In most instances this has led to difficulties, for although some sense of outcome, purpose, and standard is inherent in educational processes, pinning down exactly what this should be has proved difficult, particularly when outcomes are specified outside of specific contexts and subjects or bodies of knowledge. It is perhaps this problem which leads to the second common thread: a desire for dramatic change to education systems. The change desired differs— from empowering individual learners to improving the 'usefulness' of education to employers—but substantial change is believed necessary; the current system is seen as failing. And perhaps a third common thread is that while reformers aim for system-wide change, their mechanism is often the production of detailed and narrow technical specifications. Wolf's observation about reforms in England and Wales applies equally to outcomes-based approaches as a whole:

> [a] curious aspect of competence-based reform, at least in England and Wales, is that, although the reformers' ambitions are very wide, their focus has been very narrow. They would like to see major changes in the whole institutional context of vocational education and training but they have themselves treated the approach as an essentially technical affair. (Wolf, 1995, p. 131)

This 'technicalism' has in many instances been argued to have led to the downfall of outcomes-based approaches. Early and more recent criticisms of objectives and outcomes pointed out that they tend to trivialize education. This, Lawrence Stenhouse argues, (1975, 2002), is the consequence of an over-emphasis on endpoints and a neglect of processes. Others (e.g. Scott, 2008) have examined how outcomes-based approaches have led to an atomized model of knowledge. I will pick up some of these critiques and debates in Chapter 6, after discussing more recent developments using outcomes and competencies. But first I turn to a brief and necessarily selective consideration of the history and major tenants of child/learner-centredness, as this is another key component of recent educational reforms.

LOOKING BACK ON LEARNER-CENTREDNESS

Many advocates of child-centred or learner-centred education are opposed to a narrow instrumental notion of education and oppose the notion of outcomes because they value the importance of process, and do not like the idea of fixed end points. Others are critical of the behaviourism that has been part of many outcomes-based approaches. But many reformers and thinkers who have adopted the terms 'child-centred' or 'learner-centred' have argued that allowing learners to determine what they want to learn, as well as how and when, helps to ensure not only that they do learn, but that they learn something useful to *them*. Following from this has been hostility, in the ideas of *some* advocates of learner-centredness, to the idea of subjects as the basis of the curriculum. In emphasizing the notion of relevance, the idea of learner centredness has at times developed common ground with the idea of learning outcomes. This is particularly visible in contemporary policy documents advocating for outcomes-based qualifications frameworks, but can also be traced back through the history of the idea of learner-centred education.

Educational reformers attacking the subject-based curriculum under the rallying cry, 'we teach children, not subjects' have a long intellectual lineage. Although usually associated with the works of John Dewey in the early 20th century, some track it as far back as John Amos Comenius in the 17th century, and others to Jean-Jacques Rousseau, Johann Heinrich Pestalozzi, and Herbert Spencer in the 18th and 19th centuries. Rousseau (1712-1778) is probably the best-known early figure in this history, frequently cited by later educational reformers. John Darling (1994), British expert and advocate for child-centred education, argues that he may not be the starting point of child-centred educational thinking, but he is the most brilliant early exponent, and that the remainder of child-centered or progressive educational theory can be seen as a series of footnotes to him. Rousseau argued that we should observe the mind's pattern of development, and discover ourselves through education. Education should not be about learning an approved body of knowledge, but rather, discovering our individual nature and focusing our attention on creating the conditions for its fullest growth (Egan, 2008).

Rousseau wrote about a hypothetical boy, Emile, who would learn only from unmediated experience: from the real world, not in a classroom. As Barrow (1978) points out, his experience is not completely *unmediated,* because Emile would not be allowed to experiment with anything really dangerous. Further, in the sense that Emile's experience would be completely artificial, removed from society, it would be entirely *mediated*. What Rousseau principally implies is that Emile would have no academic teaching and no moralizing or rules. The former is qualified, for, while there is to be no direct *instruction*, there is a tutor who could take advantage of situations in order to advance learning; thus Barrow (1978, p. 20) suggests that rather than having no teaching *per se*, "the tutor must not be detected by Emile in the act of teaching". For the first twelve years of his life he will not be actively introduced to books or reading. After this, he may start to gain some knowledge, starting with that most practical and relevant: for example, he will learn geography starting with the town he lives in, and science by the problems that confront him. Rousseau placed a strong value on practical learning—Emile should learn a trade. In the final stage of his education, from age 15 to 20, Emile would live with other people for the first time. At this time he would be introduced to 'facts' and books, including history and poetry, which, Rousseau argued, he would appreciate, as they would be new and interesting (Darling, 1994). Rousseau also wrote, more briefly, about the education of 'Sophie', who was to be brought up to be Emile's wife, her main role being to delight Emile.

Many of Rousseau's ideas are still popular today. His notion of child-centredness was based on the idea that education must be individualized. He also distinguished between "learning for the sake of learning, and the desire to find out about things that affect oneself and one's wellbeing" (Darling, 1994, p. 8), which is related to current ideas of useful or relevant knowledge. Other ideas that still have considerable currency are: the danger that education is preparing learners for a world that no longer exists; the primacy of sense experience, learning through experience, and learning by doing; 'learning how to learn', which is seen as more important than learning any particular skill or content; an insistence on useful or relevant knowledge; and suspicion of art and abstract study with a complementary emphasis on the dignity and value of learning a trade (Barrow, 1978, p. 183).

A lesser-known figure following Rousseau, and sometimes cited as a key early thinker about child-centredness, was Johann Heinrich Pestalozzi. Darling (1994) argues that there is a clear intellectual lineage of child-centred thought, and that Pestalozzi, like other child-centred reformers, knew the work of his predecessors, and developed or revised it, and suggests that Pestalozzi called his son Jean-Jacques as a testimony to his 'intoxication' with Rousseau (Darling, 1994, p. 17). Pestalozzi, who lived in Switzerland in the late 18th and early 19th century, also emphasized that instead of dealing with words, children should learn through activity and through interaction with objects, and should be free to pursue their own interests and draw their own conclusions (Darling 1994, p. 18). Like later child-centred reformers, Pestalozzi strongly emphasized the laws of nature, spontaneity, and self-activity. Children should not be given ready-made answers but should arrive at answers themselves; their own powers of seeing, judging and reasoning should be cultivated, their self-activity encouraged (Silber, 1965, p. 140), although Pestalozzi actually had very specific and prescriptive ideas about curriculum and pedagogy, which he saw as derived from nature (Pestalozzi, 1894).

Herbert Spencer (1820 – 1903) came to prominence later in the nineteenth century. He was an English philosopher who expounded similar ideas, although he did not link them to Rousseau, perhaps because of the latter's left-wing politics, with which he disagreed (Egan, 2002). Spencer claimed superiority to earlier philosophers of educational reform because, he argued, his ideas were based on science. He argued strongly for the now commonly accepted notion that education should be about educating 'the whole person'. He also believed that children's understanding could expand only from things of which they had direct experience, and that education should start with the concrete. He emphasized that the process of self-development should be encouraged, and children should be told as little as possible. He argued that traditional subjects were ornamental affectations of the elite. His publications were widely read by those involved in building the new state schools in the United States in the late nineteenth century: by the end of the 1860s, his book, consisting of four essays initially published separately, had been republished in 15 editions by seven publishers. During the 1870s it was reprinted in New York nine times by one publisher, D. Appleton, alone, and in the 1880s there were fifteen printings, all but two of them in the United States (Egan, 2002). He was offered honours in the United States, England, Italy, Denmark, Belgium, Greece, Austria, and Russia. However, as Egan (2002) points out, despite this popularity, Spencer is rarely mentioned in educational texts today, and many of the ideas that he argued for are attributed to John Dewey, who held very similar ideas about education[3].

John Dewey, mentioned above, was an educational reformer whose ideas dominated much educational thinking in the twentieth century and beyond. He is probably the most well-known voice of educational reform in the English speaking world, associated, amongst other things, with having "helped to legitimate child-centred educational theory" (Darling, 1994, p. 25). He is also linked with what is referred to as 'progressivism'[4] in education, which is often used as a synonym for child/learner-centred education. The Progressive Education Association in the United States codified many of Dewey's ideas to guide teachers, including examples such as, "Teachers will inspire a desire for knowledge, and will serve as guides in the investigations undertaken rather than task-masters"; and "Interest shall be the motive for all work" (Novack, 1975, p. 229). According to Darling (1994, p. 3), the progressive view "is that education should be designed to reflect the nature of the child". Dewey argued that education needed to shift its 'centre of gravity' so that it was centred around children. In terms that are very similar to the ways in which the current 'new educational paradigm' is discussed, he suggested:

> Now the change which is coming into our education is the shifting centre of gravity. It is a change, a revolution, not unlike that introduced by Copernicus when the astronomical center shifted from the earth to the sun. In this case the child becomes the sun about which the appliances of education revolve; he is the center about which they are organized. (Dewey, 1956, p. 34).

Like his predecessors and followers, Dewey positioned his ideas as new, and emphasized the out-datedness of the contemporary system: "... our present education is ... an education dominated almost entirely by the mediaeval conception of learning" (Dewey, 1956, p. 26). He emphasized "its passivity of attitude, its mechanical massing of children, its uniformity of curriculum and method" (Dewey, 1956, p. 34). Dewey argued that the knowledge presented in the curriculum must be driven by and related to the child's interests:

> An end which is the child's own carries him on to possess the means of its accomplishment. But when material is directly supplied in the form of a lesson to be learned as a lesson, the connecting links of need and aim are conspicuous for their absence. (Dewey, 1956, p. 25).

Dewey's idea, much in line with the contemporary popularity of the idea of teacher as 'facilitator', was that "...the teacher becomes a co-planner of work, whose expertise is based less on academic knowledge—though a broad general knowledge will be necessary—than on an understanding of children and groups" (Darling, 1994, p. 27). The children would carry out the educational process, guided and aided by the teacher.

Another idea explored by Dewey which remains popular today is 'learning to learn', which was linked to a preoccupation (equally prevalent today) with what was seen as a rapidly changing world. As mentioned above, this was also a concern of Rousseau. Like today's reformers, 'learning to learn' was juxtaposed with learning 'a fixed stock of information'. Like reformers who preceded and followed him, Dewey emphasized that 'changes' in society required 'changes' in education. In particular, he discussed the growth of science-based inventions that

> have utilized the forces of nature on a vast and inexpensive scale; the growth of a world-wide market as the object of production, of vast manufacturing centers to supply this market, of cheap and rapid means of communication and distribution between all its parts ... One can hardly believe there has been a revolution in all history so rapid, so extensive, so complete. ... That this revolution should not affect education in some other than a formal and superficial fashion is inconceivable. (Dewey, 1956, p. 9)

In the works of Dewey and many others the idea of 'learner-centredness' is often linked with ideas about student motivation—the assumption being that students will be more motivated if they can see the purpose of what they are learning, or if the starting point is their immediate interests. This has been influenced by the idea that children learn naturally, easily, and pleasurably if left to their own devices, and the idea, derived from psychological research into cognitive development, that learning involves the 're-construction' of knowledge by learners. It is believed that shaping education around learners' interests and inclinations will enable them to be active constructors of their own knowledge, instead of passive recipients (or memorizers) of inert knowledge. So, for example, Gay (2003) discusses teachers who draw on learners' life experiences to teach "higher-order math knowledge" to African-American middle school students in the United States:

> To teach algebra, they emphasize the experiences and familiar environments of urban and rural low-income students, many of whom are at high risk for academic failure. A key feature of their approach is making students conscious of how algebraic principles and formulas operate in their daily lives and getting students to understand how to explain these connections in nonalgebraic language before converting this knowledge into technical notations and calculations of algebra. Students previously considered by some teachers as incapable of learning algebra are performing at high levels—better, in fact, than many of their advantaged peers. (In Flinders & Thornton, 2004, p. 320)

The example above shows that the idea of *learner-centredness* is not inherently incompatible with the idea of subjects or a knowledge-based curriculum. Some advocates of learner-centredness see it as a primarily pedagogical notion: that the knowledge which is in the curriculum must be presented in ways that resonate with children's interests and existing knowledge. Thus, for some, disciplines or subjects should be the core of the *curriculum*, but *pedagogy* should be child-centred, to ensure that learning has meaning for the child. "Learning should be child-centred in that the learner comes to possess what he knows" argues Entwistle (1970, p. 203), who also suggests that ideas of child-centred education are focused on ensuring that schools are happy places.

But there is a frequent slip from arguments about learner-centred pedagogy to a notion of learner-centred curricula. The idea of the 'motivating curriculum'—that the curriculum will motivate learners to succeed in education if it is relevant to their interests and experiences—can contain a conflation of pedagogy and the curriculum. Some advocates of learner-centredness have gone so far as to denounce the idea of learner-centered pedagogy as a 'sugar coating', that simply appeals to learners' interests in order to in continue to teach predetermined subjects. Dewey argued: "When education is based in theory and practice upon experience, it goes without saying that the organized subject-matter of the adult and the subject specialist cannot provide the starting point" (Dewey (1993, p. 83) cited in Wheelahan, 2010, p. 114). Diane Ravitch (2001) discusses advocates of this line of argument who suggest that teachers must not just *start* with learners' interests in order to make the subject matter more interesting to them, but must *genuinely* work with what learners are interested in. This would mean, for example, that the pedagogical strategy of locating the teaching of mathematics in the everyday experiences of learners to help them make sense of mathematical concepts is not sufficient. Instead, as William H. Kirkpatrick, an early exponent of 'the project method' in the United States, argues, the teaching of mathematics should only involve mathematical ideas derived from, logical to, or embedded in the learners' everyday experiences. Kirkpatrick, a mathematician by training, published an influential article in 1918, and later a textbook, in which he argued that projects in school must genuinely interest the learner and be chosen by them, in order to motivate them, promote democracy, and teach character and creativity. Others go further still, and argue against the teaching of 'mathematics' as a subject, and of subjects in general. Ravitch (2001), critic of child-centred education and progressivism, argues that while in some of his writings Dewey defended subjects as the basis of the curriculum, he did not oppose, and often endorsed, the writings of contemporaries which were more explicitly opposed to a subject-based curriculum.

Dewey was, of course, a highly prolific philosopher whose views shifted over time, and so cannot always be pinned down. The extent to which his notion of child-centredness is opposed to subjects is the focus of much debate. Like some present-day advocates of learner-centredness, (for example, Hyslop-Margison & Sears, 2006), he also argued against a neglect of knowledge in education, and suggested that children's interests should be seen as leverage to teach them more, not as accomplishments in their own right (Dewey, 1956).

Nonetheless, throughout the history of learning outcomes and learner-centredness, argument emerge to the effect that the boundaries between subjects are arbitrary, the structure of bodies of knowledge is unimportant and structured bodies of knowledge are not particularly important, nor should they be the starting point in curriculum design. Boundaries between subjects as well as between school knowledge and everyday knowledge are seen as similarly arbitrary and as counteracting effective learning. In Chapter 6, I will provide some epistemological arguments against this position, but for now I will merely mention the view of Egan (2002), who argues that the 'motivating curriculum' is often not motivating at all. He points out that children are frequently bored by curricula that are derived from their 'everyday' experiences, and are often more interested in dinosaurs and distant heroes than social studies focused on 'my community'.

What ideas of learning outcomes and the ideas of learner (and child) centredness as they have manifested at various points in the last century have in common is hostility, to varying degrees, to the subject-based curriculum. Both outcomes-based and learner-centred approaches have questioned the idea that subjects handed down by tradition should be the basis of education (Thornton & Flinders).

In the 1960s and 70s, the 'freeschoolers' took up the call against subjects, suggesting fundamental changes to schools. A.S. Neill, Neil Postman and Charles Weingartner were the prominent voices. Like Rousseau, they were suspicious of 'book learning', and, like most of the progressivist or child-centred reformers discussed in this chapter, emphasized 'natural' learning instead. They all argued for a learner-centred starting point for education, and generally argued against the 'traditional' curriculum and against subject division in the curriculum. In discussing the idea of starting from the 'interests' of the child, A.S. Neill extended the use of the word 'interest' to one similar to that advocated in policy documents today:

not just what fascinates a child, but what they perceive as being to their advantage (Barrow, 1978). The idea of the constantly changing world emerges again. Postman and Weingarter, for example, wrote in 1971 that "change—constant, accelerating, ubiquitous—is the most striking characteristic of the world we live in" (Postman & Weingartner, 1971, p. 13).

The ideas of radical literacy educator Paulo Freire (e.g. Freire, 1974), and the struggles of liberation movements against colonial education systems, are sometimes used to oppose subject-based curricula, although Freire did not advocate an anti-subject approach. Freire's emancipatory pedagogy emphasized that education should help learners to connect their personal problems to broader structural issues in society, arguing against what he described as 'banking' education, where facts are seen as things to be deposited into empty learners. Instead he advocated an approach which was based on dialogue. These ideas are often *invoked* as arguments against a subject-based curriculum. However, teaching people subjects does not necessarily mean treating them as blank slates, and, many of Freire's ideas were not about formal schooling, but about conscientization; he was concerned with the role of literacy in political activism, and the ways in which it could be used to develop self-awareness and insight into the world. Freire's approach is sometimes invoked to justify an anti-subject stance in the sense of working with issues of immediate concern to learners; this is something which may well be appropriate in activist groups. But, as I will argue in Chapter 6, it is less appropriate in formal schooling. I cannot here do justice to the nuance of Freire's ideas, nor evaluate their strengths and weaknesses. The point for now is to note that he was a key left-wing figure who is often presented as being against subject-based curricula.

The concept of 'deschooling' is another idea that has emerged again and again in the history of educational reform. Many reformers in the 1960s and 70s referred back to earlier theorists, arguing, for instance, that the logic of Rousseau's ideas implied that the school system itself was the problem. The 'deschoolers', who included Ivan Illich, Paul Goodman and Everett Reimer, argued for the abolition of educational institutions (Barrow, 1978). Although Illich later distanced himself from the term 'deschooling', what is common to these three thinkers is profound hostility to institutions, including, or perhaps particularly, educational institutions. Reimer, quoted in Illich (1970, p. 105), argues that "learning occurs only with great difficulty in the role of the classroom student"; it occurs "naturally at work and at play, but must be artificially stimulated when separated from them". Like earlier reformers, and like today's policy makers, they emphasized the changing world as a key motivating factor in radically changing education. Goodman was not completely against schools, but was strongly against teachers and professional training for teachers, and argued, like Rousseau, that there should be no prescribed curriculum until the age of 12. After 12, he argued for an extended apprenticeship system, in which an individual could be apprenticed in anything that interested them[5]. The 'deschoolers' were concerned with efficiency, and saw schools as wasting children's time. Like many of today's enthusiastic reformers, they were excited about the possibilities of technology replacing schools, and, like Pestalozzi before them, were critical of teachers. As Entwistle (1970, p. 167) writes:

> Enthusiasm for the mechanization of schooling often conceals a mistrust of the average teacher which is nowadays rarely expressed as candidly as it was by Pestalozzi, himself a central figure in the child-centred tradition.

The passage below gives some indication of Pestalozzi's mistrust:

> I would take school instruction out of the hands of the old order of decrepit, stammering, journeymen-teachers as well as from the new weak ones, who are generally no better for popular instruction, and entrust it to the undivided powers of Nature herself, to the light that God kindles and ever keeps alive in the hearts of fathers and mothers, to the interest of parents who desire that their children should grow up in favour with God and man. (Pestalozzi, 1894, p. 97)

Thus, the ideas which dominate qualification reform today have a rich and long ancestry, despite their presentation by policy makers as 'new learning paradigms'. In fact, this tendency to present their ideas as new, forward-looking, and progressive innovations is another commonality across time and space between outcomes-based approaches and learner-centred approaches (Egan, 2002; Muller, 2001). Many of them have been associated with new developments in technology, which are seen as changing knowledge, the role of teachers, and the ways in which learners can access knowledge.

Presenting 'newness' as a virtue is common in education. Those concerned with social justice tend to position newness in juxtaposition to ideas that are seen as conservative or elitist simply by virtue of being old. Left-wing educational reformers have usually wanted to achieve 'radical' change, in the sense of dramatic and substantial change, and so favour ideas which seem to be new and forward-looking. Reformers associated with market-oriented approaches or economic efficiency link 'old' or 'traditional' approaches to education with backwardness, inefficiency, and irrelevance to industry. Callahan (1962), for example, writes that this type of charge was made by industry-oriented reformers in the United States in the early twentieth century. Educational reformers today likewise argue that the 'archaic' content and pedagogy of traditional education are out of touch with emergent social realities, including the impact of the mass media and the 'knowledge explosion' (Sedunary, 1996). David Harvey (2005) argues that the fetishization of newness as well as of technology is a product of capitalism, because new technologies often lead to profit increases and new market shares. As the ideas dominating qualification reform show, it doesn't even matter whether the ideas are really new, only that they are presented as such.

THE PENDULUM OF IDEAS

Conservatism in education has been associated with an invocation of tradition, and the arguments that the traditional curriculum embodies traditional wisdom, values, and authority, and that the culture represented in 'traditional' subjects transforms and enriches individuals (Moore, 2009, p. 4). Matthew Arnold's notion of education as the 'best that has been thought and said' is usually invoked[6]. The traditional division of the disciplines and disciplinary knowledge "are endowed with timeless and universal features. The role of the curriculum is to transmit timeless truths through contemplative processes, and to inculcate appropriate deference to traditional bodies of knowledge, and instill respect for authority and traditional values" (Wheelahan, 2010, p. 107). Pring (1976, p. 144) expresses it thus:

> Conservative restorationists argue that the curriculum should be anchored in the past and they emphasise canons of influential texts, formal and didactic modes of pedagogy, the inculcation of values rooted in stability and hierarchy, strong insulations between disciplinary and everyday knowledge, strong forms of classification between different aspects of knowledge, and indeed in some cases a belief that curriculum knowledge is either intrinsically justified or transcendental.

This is why the traditional curriculum is associated with conservative social and political agendas, and has led many to argue that the notion of 'an educated person' is circular: "What is often meant in calling people educated is that they have learned the kind of stuff that has traditionally been taught in educational institutions" (Darling, 1994, p. 63).

As discussed above, various arguments against this have been laid out through the course of educational reform movements. Reformers from the nineteenth-century onwards have observed that the "richness and abundance of understanding that should have come to all students from literacy through an education in the classics had too often descended into dry pedantry" (Egan, 2008, p. 21). Many have argued that the traditional curriculum is alienating, and leads to failure and students dropping out of education. And the idea of 'tradition' dictating subjects has a serious practical problem: it does not provide criteria with which to make decisions about which knowledge should be chosen for specific individuals or groups, either in terms of broad subject areas or in terms of selection of knowledge within subject areas.

And yet, learner centred approaches to the curriculum do not have a great track record in achieving the claims made for them—neither the more modest claims of ensuring student success at school, nor the more radical claims of ensuring that schools disrupt rather than reproduce the *status quo*. Egan (2002) points out that while learner alienation, drop-out and failure are usually discussed in relation to an assumed subject-centred approach, in fact learner-centred curricula are in many instances the orthodoxy in schools, have been *attempted* in different forms for over the past 100 years, and have not solved these problems.

One reason given to explain this state of affairs is that learner-centred approaches have not been 'properly' or 'thoroughly' implemented, or have become distorted and diluted in their implementation. Paul Goodman, a 'deschooler', argues that progressive ideas are distorted through their institutionalization (Goodman 1964). Some supporters of progressivism (for example, Hyslop-Margison & Sears, 2006), argue that while aspects of progressivist or learner-centred reforms in Canada and the United States may have been adopted to some extent, or in official rhetoric, they were never fully implemented, and where they were implemented, conservative backlashes have mainly reversed them. Some researchers suggest that, while they have had some successes, particularly at specific times in history, vested elite interests have unleashed backlashes which have ensured that the subject-based curriculum prevails. Darling (1994), for example, describes progressivism as the established orthodoxy in the 1960s in primary education in the United Kingdom, a situation he attributes to the intellectual freedom of the 60s, but describes a 'backlash' against it in later decades. Scott (2008) agrees that in the 1970s and 80s curriculum theorists put more focus on knowledge, in particular transcendental knowledge, and Tomlinson (2009, pp. 26–27) links this with a return to education "as an allocator of occupations, a defender of traditional academic values, teaching respect for authority, discipline, morality and 'Englishness' and preparing a workforce for the new conditions of flexible, insecure labour markets". Darling (1994) describes this shift as culminating in John Major's announcement to the Conservative Party Conference in 1991: "The progressive theorists have had their say, and they have had their day".

However, nearly all commentators agree that *some* reforms and ideas introduced under the banner of child-centred or progressivist reforms have been positive. These include, for example, acceptance that failure to learn the curriculum might be "due to faults other than the child's recalcitrance" (Entwistle, 1970, p. 24), and that schools should not be dreary places. Tomlinson similarly (2009) suggests that the reforms actually instituted through the child-centred movement in the United Kingdom were much more modest than their critics suggested, and were generally necessary, with positive effects. There is also some agreement that child-centred or progressivist reforms have been influential, regardless of whether this is seen as positive or negative. Darling (1994), arguing in favour of progressivism, and Egan (2002) and Ravitch (2001), arguing against it, all agree that many aspects of it, or of the child-centred tradition, have become common-place and accepted wisdom, particularly in primary schools. Darling (1994, p. 32) points out that Dewey's influence was massive in the United States and United Kingdom, as well as in Russia and China, countries which he visited and toured, and in many other countries which learnt of his ideas. Entwistle (1970) also claims that child-centredness is a foundation of much educational thought. Egan (2002) and Ravitch (2001) both argue that progressivism has become conventional wisdom in North American education; Egan argues that even where progressivism is not the default in terms of practices in schools, it is the default in terms of the concepts and vocabulary that dominate educational research and teaching.

But they and other critics suggest that there are problems with progressivism which are intrinsic to it. Young and Muller (2010, p. 19), for example, argue that when boundaries between knowledge areas are not made explicit (as they are in a subject-based curriculum) learners who stumble are less able to see what causes them to stumble. Drawing on the extensive work of Bernstein (for example,

Berstein 1977; 2000), they demonstrate that the difference between 'progressive' and 'traditional' curricula is not the presence or absence of rules, but rather their *visibility* or *invisibility;* in other words, the degree to which they are made explicit to the learners, as well as the degree to which learners are prepared by their home background to perceive and understand what is expected of them. They argue that progressive curricula are likely to *entrench* social inequalities (Muller, 2001; Taylor, 2000; Young & Muller, 2010). Even if learner centredness is only considered from the point of view of pedagogy, and not as the basis for curriculum construction, in other words, where learner centredness means using learners' everyday experiences and interests in order to draw them into prescribed subjects, some argue that over-emphasizing context can sometimes make it more difficult for learners to acquire systematically organized knowledge in educational institutions. Bernard Charlot (2009, p. 92), for example, argues:

> José leaves home with thirty euros and loses ten euros: how many euros will he get back home with? The pupil solves this problem without difficulty because the meanings "lose" and "subtract" converge. Now, José leaves home with thirty euros, earns money and comes back home with fifty euros: how much did he earn? To solve the problem the pupils have to do a subtraction, which they do not find logical, given that José earned money. One can give lots of examples in which the reference to the every-day world creates a difficulty for the pupil.

The effects, positive or negative, of learner-centred reforms and learning outcomes and objectives are difficult to evaluate empirically. One obstacle to such evaluation is the enormous number of uncontrollable variables which will always be present in research in schools. But more importantly, the different perspectives involve different notions of what education can and should achieve, and hence different criteria for educational success. For example, while some researchers (for example, Donnelly, 2005) argue for teacher-centred classrooms and prescribed syllabuses on the grounds that this leads to improvement in international and national achievement tests, critics argue against international and national achievement tests on the grounds that they lead to teacher-centred classrooms and prescribed syllabuses (for example, Rizvi & Lingard, 2010; Zajda & Zajda, 2005).

The continued rediscovery of educational ideas may be located in the different manifestations of both subject and learner-centred curricula, and the fact that different uses and interpretations of outcomes, objectives and competences have also taken different forms across different levels and sectors of education systems. The extent to which a curriculum is centrally prescribed, and how prescriptive it is, also tends to confuse matters[7]. There are inevitably substantial differences between the education policies of various countries, between policy rhetoric and the reality of education institutions and education systems within countries, and between policies implemented at different times in the same country. In some instances the same education systems have some policy mechanisms which support 'subject centred' approaches and others which tend towards 'learner centred' approaches. 'Subject-centred' approaches have tended to hold stronger ground in senior secondary schools and universities, and 'child-' or 'learner-centred' approaches have been more prominent in adult education, primary education, and nursery schools, as well as in vocational education, especially in competence-based training. Elite education, particularly exclusive private secondary and tertiary institutions, has generally taken a more traditional subject based approach[8].

What is contested is not just the merits of the arguments for and against these approaches, but the extent to which curricula and education systems are influenced by them today. On the one side, researchers and policy analysts argue that narrow subject-based curricula are increasingly entrenched internationally (Scott, 2008). Goodson (1994) talks about the 'impregnable fortress' of the subject-based curriculum, drawing the term from Kliebard, who concludes his study of the history of the American curriculum with the observation that "by and large, dethroning school subjects turned out to be a much more formidable task than the proponents of such change ever imagined" (Kliebard, 2004, p. 218). David Scott (2008) suggests that contemporary curricula are governed entirely by disciplines, and that any debates within governments about the correctness of this have been put aside:

> governments around the world, although not exclusively so, have sought to reinforce strong boundaries between disciplinary and everyday knowledge in developing the contents of their curricula, and have reinforced strong insulations between learners, between learners and teachers, between knowledge domains and between institutions which focus on teaching and learning. (Scott, 2008, p. 146).

He argues that the ideas which predominate in contemporary curriculum thinking are: that traditional knowledge areas and the strong boundaries between them need to be preserved; that each of these knowledge areas can be expressed in terms of lower and higher level domains, and the former have to be taught before the latter and sequenced correctly; that certain groups of children are better able to access the curriculum than others, and therefore a differentiated curriculum is required; and that the teacher's role is to impart this body of knowledge in the most efficient and effective way possible. Other contemporary critics bemoan how 'conservative' schools and the subject-based curriculum are (for example, Murgatroyd, 2010). Like advocates for earlier child-centred reforms, Murgatroyd (2010, p. 260) attributes the problems with contemporary education to a focus on 'content' at the expense of 'learning how to learn' or 'skills and competencies', and makes much of the 'speed of discovery' of knowledge, which, he argues, means that "much of what is taught in schools is, by definition, outdated".

But still other researchers call for knowledge to be 'brought back into the curriculum' (Young, 2008), and suggest that knowledge is undermined or marginalized in contemporary curricula (Muller, 2000; Rata, 2012; Young, 2007). Young and Muller (2010) argue that this results in tracked or streamed systems, which preserve classical education for the elite, and provide vocational or practical alternatives for the rest. Ravitch (2001), fiercely critical of progressivism in the United States, and until recently associated with conservative political agendas, suggests that progressivism has dominated educational thinking in the United States since the 1890s. She laments the loss of subjects in North American education, arguing that it has led to poor students being denied access to meaningful education.

It could be hoped that the different schools of thought would have moderating effects on each other. Entwistle discusses the notion of a counter-cyclical theory of education: when the needs of children dominate, theorists assert the claims of the disciplines, and vice versa: "Out of this, it is hoped, would emerge a satisfactory synthesis, a stabilizing of educational practice at a point mid-way between the extremes to which the pendulum swings" (Entwistle, 1970, p. 211). On the contrary, he argues that the problem with the swinging pendulum is that it leads to the worst sides of both approaches. Instead of producing some kind of happy medium, educational theory is perceived as in perpetual conflict: "There can be no gain, least of all for children .... For the middle ground is not a neutral territory where reasonable men come together to fashion a treaty of peace; it is a no-man's-land where virtually nothing of rational educational theory survives at all" (Entwistle, 1970, pp. 211–121). Similarly, Egan (2008, p. 26) describes the history of education in the twentieth century as "a bizarre war between those who were 'subject-centered' and those who were 'child-centered', between traditionalists and progressivists". The war has manifested itself, he suggests, in swings from the one to the other, as well as uneasy, (and, according to him, ultimately unworkable), compromises between the two. And, in Egan's view, it is precisely the *failures* of *both* approaches that lead to this periodic and unsatisfactory swinging between the two.

Much educational literature assumes that learner-centred policies are intrinsically left-wing, and subject-centred policies intrinsically right-wing. Darling (1994), for example, suggests that attempts to halt the advance of the child-centred movement are the product of social conservatism. The clash between child- and subject-centred education, he suggests, is not a clash of intellectual ideas, but of ideologies. Referring to the opposition to child-centred education of R.S. Peters, Paul Hirst, and Robert Dearden, he argues that these "[p]hilosophers of education are therefore not spectators at the revolution, but counter-revolutionaries" (Darling, 1994, p. 86).[9] However, as can be seen in the very brief discussion above, the inherently conservative nature of the subject-centred curriculum is disputed. Indeed, Marxist Antonio Gramsci saw traditional education as empowering and necessary, as I discuss in further detail in Chapter 6. And many contemporary researchers (e.g. Young, 2008) argue for a left-wing approach to a subject-based curriculum, on the grounds that the knowledge which the elite are taught in school is useful or powerful, and hence should be taught to everyone: Young argues that it is the *power* of this knowledge that makes education a social justice issue. In other words, while most critical writers on education agree that it is inevitably political,[10] it is much less clear that particular ideas about education and the curriculum, as well as about epistemology, are inherent to particular political agendas. Thus while it is difficult to separate ideas about what should be taught, to whom, by whom, and at whose cost, from broader political questions, the relationship between different approaches to the curriculum and particular political ideologies are not straightforward. This issue will be explored most thoroughly in Chapter 7. In order to lay the basis for this discussion, I will now pick up the story of learning outcomes and objectives, as well as learner centredness, as they emerged in qualification reform in the 1980s and 90s. The following chapter examines outcomes-based qualifications in vocational education reforms in the United Kingdom and Australia, and an outcomes-based National Qualifications Framework in New Zealand which was intended to reform the entire education and training system.

ENDNOTES

[1] Dewey also supervised the doctoral thesis of W.W. Charters, leader of the 'Scientific Curriculum' movement, so there may have already been relationships between these two schools of thought (Ravitch, 2001).

[2] Criterion-referencing and norm-referencing are often positioned as two alternative ways of conducting assessment. Advocates of criterion-referencing tend to suggest that norm-referencing is an unfair system of assessment. The very term 'criterion-referenced assessment' implies that there are ways of assessing that invoke no criteria at all. This does not make sense. All assessment is based on criteria, whether implicit or explicit. Norm-referencing is about what happens to the results of assessment; how they are used for ranking students within schools or for selection into professions. Although there is no necessity for this, in policy documents norm-referencing is usually associated with written examinations, and presented as a package with other 'bads' like memorization and 'passive learning'.

[3] Egan attributes this to Spencer's unpalatable political ideas, such as social Darwinism and racism, as well as his opposition to public education, particularly for the 'lower classes', despite the fact that the educational ideas which he advocated were in many substantial ways the same as those of earlier and later 'progressive' reformers.

[4] The term 'progressivism' is highly contested both by those who align themselves to it and those who are critical of it. Some suggest progressivism is so diverse that it can't be pinned down (for example, Kliebard, 2004), while others (for example, Ravitch, 2001) suggest that the different strands, diverse as they are, have certain core things in common—particularly, she argues, hostility to subjects as the basis of curricula.

[5] Even those sympathetic with the deschooling 'school of thought', such as Ian Lister (1974), have pointed out that in most instances apprenticeships are just as likely, if not more likely, to be as exploitative and oppressive to learners as schools.

[6] Although Arnold and his idea are usually associated with a conservative political agenda, a close consideration of his works reveals that they are not open to easy labeling. His argument was that culture "seeks to do away with classes; to make the best that has been thought and known in the world current everywhere; to make all men live in an atmosphere of sweetness and light, where they may use ideas, as it uses them itself, freely—nourished, and not bound by them" (Arnold, 1993, p. 79).

[7] A centrally prescribed curriculum often seems, in critical educational writing from the United Kingdom and United States, to be assumed to be bad. Hyslop-Margison and Sears, for example, argue for a subject-based curriculum, but argue that it should not be centrally prescribed: "Policies such as centralized curricula development enforced by rigid testing and teacher accountability are designed more to constrain teachers than they are to define and measure student achievement" (Hyslop-Margison & Sears, 2006, pp. 16–17). It is possible, however, to be highly prescriptive without having a subject-based curriculum. The South African outcomes-based curriculum prescribed

learning outcomes to a very fine level of detail, without any subjects or indeed any content at all being prescribed. Ravitch (2010) discusses extreme examples of prescriptiveness around pedagogy in literacy and maths programmes in North American schools, as well as the negative effects of 'skills-based' accountability tests which are de-linked from a curriculum because there is no prescribed curriculum, and suggests that a prescribed curriculum may liberate teachers from this.

[8] Young (2008) suggests this may be a key factor in perpetuating the idea that traditional education systems produce inequality, because it creates a perceived link between elites and the subject-based knowledge learned in elite schools, which is then seen as elite knowledge, or knowledge that operates in the interests of elites.

[9] Although less critical of their intentions, he suggests that an 'unintended' consequence of their ideas was to give ammunition to conservatives in a 'back to basics' agenda.

[10] There are exceptions, a recent one being Frank Furedi (2009), who argues for the depoliticization of education.

SOMETHING NEW, SOMETHING OLD

*The Rise of Neoliberalism and the First Institutionalization of
Outcomes-Based Qualifications*

We have seen that over the course of the twentieth century many educational reformers supported the idea of learning outcomes or objectives, as well as the idea of learner centredness, and that in many instances these ideas were positioned as an alternative to subject-based curricula. In the 1980s these ideas once again came to the fore in the reform of vocational education in the United Kingdom and Australia. This was in the context of the rise of neoliberalism as an emerging and soon to be dominant political and economic force throughout the world. In this chapter I start with a short discussion of neoliberalism and its implications for education. I then discuss outcomes-based qualifications in vocational education in the United Kingdom and Australia, and in a national qualifications framework in New Zealand. We see a reemergence of the same ideas about knowledge considered in the previous chapter: that subjects as defined by teachers or disciplinary experts in universities are not the best starting point for curriculum design, because they are outdated and irrelevant, and cause a 'mismatch' between education and labour markets. Learning outcomes are introduced in the belief that they can ensure that curricula are more responsive to the needs of employers and learners. In the context of the growing influence of neoliberalism, critiques of teachers and education institutions as elitist or irrelevant are used in a push for the marketization of education provision. Here we see the other two major roles claimed for outcomes-based qualifications emerging clearly: that they can improve the relationships between educational institutions and labour markets; and that they can improve how education is delivered, by making it more competitive and therefore more responsive to market needs.

NEOLIBERALISM

Over the past 40 years, regulatory changes across the global capitalist system have prioritized market-based and market-oriented approaches, striving to intensify commodification in all areas of social life (Brenner, Peck, & Theodore, 2010). This tendency is usually referred to as neoliberalism. In the 1930s and 1940s, free market economists such as Frederich Hayek, harking back to the classical liberal project of 'self-regulating' markets in late nineteenth and early twentieth century British imperialism, developed the doctrine of neoliberalism to criticize the emerging

Keynesian system (Brenner *et al.,* 2010): in the Western world, between World War II and the 1970s, various forms of government 'demand management' of the economy became dominant, as did state provision of welfare to its citizens (Crouch, 2011). Despite significant differences between countries, in common was "an acceptance that the state should focus on full employment, economic growth, and the welfare of its citizens, and that state power should be freely deployed, alongside of or, if necessary, intervening in or even substituting for market processes to achieve these ends" (Harvey, 2005, p. 10). This was a reaction to what were seen as the failures of minimal state intervention in liberal capitalist economies, and the serious problems with the two other alternatives which had emerged in the 1930s—fascism and Soviet-style communism.

The decades between World War 2 and the late 1970s saw increasing prosperity in many developed and developing countries around the world (Crouch, 2011; Harvey, 2005; Palma, 2003). In many cases this was accompanied by declining social inequality, and increased collective responsibility for social needs (Crouch, 2011). Both increased levels of prosperity and increased social equality were achieved through the power of the nation state, through different combinations of welfare policies, state spending on infrastructure, and state driven industrialization, driven at least in part by well-organized cores of the working class (Chang, 2002; Crouch, 2011). By the late 1970s, however, in many Western countries unemployment and inflation were rising, the working classes were weakening, and the system which had delivered strong economic growth and raised prosperity levels in the Western world was in crisis.

In the 1970s the first "real-time experiments in neoliberalization were elaborated" (Brenner *et al.,* 2010, p. 336). This included experiments in Chile after Pinochet's coup in 1973, carried out with the assistance of the United States government and military, as well as a group of neoliberal economists known as 'the Chicago boys' because of their attachment to the ideas of University of Chicago-based neoliberal economist Milton Freidman (Harvey, 2005). It also included "post-IMF bailout Britain, Reagan's deindustrializing USA, and various crisis-stricken cities and regions across the older capitalist world attempting to attract 'footloose' transnational capital investment through various forms of regulatory arbitrage" (Brenner *et al.,* 2010, p. 337). The election of Margaret Thatcher in 1979, Ronald Reagan in 1980, and Deng Xiaoping's first steps towards liberalizing the Chinese economy in 1978, signalled a turning point in world history (Harvey, 2005). During the 1980s, "a repertoire of neoliberal policy templates began to circulate transnationally and to acquire the status of all-purpose, 'silver bullet' solutions to diverse regulatory problems and crisis tendencies" (Brenner *et al.,* 2010, p. 337). Neil Brenner *et al.* (2010, p. 338) describe the process by which neoliberalism became dominant as follows:

> [t]hrough a series of trial-and-error maneuvers, manipulations, negotiations, and struggles, many of the core neoliberalizing regulatory experiments of the

1970s—such as privatization, financialization, liberalization, workfare, and urban entrepreneurialism—subsequently acquired something approaching 'prototypical' status, and became key reference points for subsequent projects of neoliberalization.

From the 1980s onwards, there was a turn towards neoliberal thinking in almost all states around the world, sometimes initiated by governments themselves and sometimes in response to coercive pressures on governments, such as through the structural adjustment programmes advocated by the World Bank and International Monetary Fund, which were used as conditions for financial assistance to poor countries. Poor countries were made to privatize many of what were previously state provided services and welfare, as well as enforce 'user fees' for even very basic services, such as basic health care and education. They were also pressurized into opening their economies to international markets by removing exchange controls and tariffs. By the 1990s, neoliberalism had become the "dominant, if not hegemonic, process of regulatory restructuring across the world economy" (Brenner *et al.*, 2010, p. 331). Many parties in the developed world that had previously defined themselves as centre left or social democratic started accepting much of neoliberalism, starting with Clinton's 'New Democrats', spreading to 'New Labour' in the United Kingdom, and affecting centre left parties in much of the Western world.

Neoliberal advocates argue that the market is the best possible way of distributing goods and services internationally, and that the market should, if possible, be intensified and expanded to all aspects of human life (Fine 2002a). They believe that competition allocates physical, natural, human, and financial resources with the greatest possible efficiency. Ben Fine (2002a) characterizes this type of thinking as 'free market virtualism', because it sees the world through the image of the free market, and attempts to remake it as such. As Simon Clarke (2005, p. 58) puts it, "the neoliberal model does not purport so much to describe the world as it is, but the world as it should be".

Many analysts point out that neoliberalism is utopian, and the tenets of its political philosophy have been selectively implemented; for example, governments advocating for the benefits of free trade have not advocated for removing immigration controls to create free labour markets (Chang, 2010). Munck (2005, p. 60) draws a distinction between "neoliberalism as a system of thought and actually existing neoliberalism". Harvey makes a similar distinction. He concludes that while the political philosophy argues that "human well-being can best be advanced by liberating individual entrepreneurial freedoms and skills within an institutional framework characterized by strong private property rights, free markets, and free trade" (Harvey, 2005, p. 2), in practice neoliberalism is

a class project that coalesced in the crisis of the 1970s. Masked by a lot of rhetoric about individual freedom, liberty, personal responsibility and the virtues of privatization, the free market and free trade, it legitimised draconian policies designed to restore and consolidate capitalist class power. This project has been successful, judging by the incredible centralisation of wealth and power observable in all those countries that took the neoliberal road.

Advocates for neoliberalism argue that states should be as limited as possible, and should 'get out of the way' as much as possible, allowing the free market to deliver goods and services. Governments, according to neoliberalism, transgress the rationality of the market and work against efficiency and liberty (Munck 2005), they are defined as inefficient and rent-seeking, and, as a result, are considered to reduce general well-being (Palley 2005). It is claimed that markets, on the other hand, if allowed to operate without restraint, would "optimally serve all economic needs, efficiently utilise all economic resources and automatically generate full employment for all persons who truly wish to work" (Shaikh 2005, p. 41). One of the implications of neo-liberalism is that the public sector must be drastically downsized, because it does not and cannot obey the basic law of competing for profits or for market share. In reality most governments in wealthy countries have continued to use macro-economic intervention such as controlling interest rates, and have maintained social welfare to varying degrees (Lapavitsas 2005). But "actually existing neoliberalism does not really believe in a straightforward 'roll back' of the state" (Munck, 2005, p. 62). Most analysts agree that the issue is not whether there should be a state, but what the state should do. As Colin Crouch (2011, pp. 170–171) points out:

> Neoliberals rarely call for a roll-back of those state activities that hearken back to an earlier pre-democratic age when governments served the interests of elites only: the extension of official honours and symbolic privileges to the rich and powerful; the establishment of an elaborate apparatus of law, prisons and police forces to protect private property and guarantee its rights; the awarding of lucrative public contracts.

Generally neoliberalism is seen as reducing the role of the state with regard to development and social welfare (Dumenil and Levy 2005). The state is meant to do not much more than sell itself as an investment location. Restrictions on foreign investment should be reduced, as, it is believed, economic development can only happen through privatization, export-led growth, and integration into the global economy (Hahnel 2000). As a result, privatization has been one of the major economic transformations of the past thirty years. Neoliberalism has also been linked to the mobilization of "speculative financial instruments to open up new arenas for capitalist profit-making" (Brenner *et al.,* 2010, p. 330). This includes a desire to intensify and expand the market *within* the state—with the ultimate aim of enabling as many human interactions as possible to be market transactions conducted in competition with others.

According to Thomas Palley (2005), the two key aspects of neoliberalism are its theory of income determination and its theory of employment determination.

Advocates of neoliberalism, he argues, assert that the market ensures that labour is paid what it is worth, thereby removing the need for social protection and trade unions. They also assert that price adjustment automatically tends towards full employment. A key feature of neo-liberalism is thus an emphasis on 'getting the prices right', i.e. pushing for cost-recovery or 'user-fees' for public services, and providing as few subsidies as possible for those who can't afford these services.

Neoliberalism is sometimes referred to as the 'Washington Consensus', as the influential organizations promoting it—the International Monetary Fund, the World Bank, and the United States Treasury—are based in Washington DC. Fine (1999; 2000; 2001) distinguishes between two variants of neoliberalism: the 'Washington consensus', and the 'post-Washington consensus'. The latter is sometimes positioned as a challenge to neoliberalism. The post-Washington consensus is associated with 'Third Way' politics (Palley 2005). Whereas the Washington consensus treats all economic and social phenomena as if they were a perfectly functioning market, even where the market is absent in practice—for example, all exchanges in the household or the firm are considered equivalent to market exchanges—the post-Washington consensus sees the world as an imperfectly functioning market. The notion of imperfect information that prevents markets from clearing is an important part of this analysis, influenced by the work of the former Chief Economist at the World Bank, Joseph Stiglitz (Fine 2001; Palley 2005). The post-Washington consensus is still premised on the assumption of rational and egoistic individuals buying and selling goods and services in a market, but they are assumed to possess different amounts of information. The better informed individual is at an advantage, which means that free-market trading is not efficient (Lapavitsas 2005). Thus, Lapavitsas (2005, p. 30) describes a new "interventionism" emerging, "seeking to regulate markets, but without challenging the notion that they comprise the optimal organising mechanism for capitalist economies".

Because of its emphasis on the role of the state, the post-Washington consensus has a broader appeal across the political spectrum. Fine (2001) suggests that because the shift from the Washington consensus to the post-Washington consensus retained a role for the state, neoliberal economics managed to win support from left-wing thinkers. The new interventionism argues that state actions are legitimate if they improve information flows, create or mend institutions, or promote social customs that allow markets to perform better (Lapavitsas 2005). By improving information flows, governments support individuals to make better choices in the market. And if markets fail to provide essential services such as health and education, the state contracts for these services and has the private sector provide them rather than trying to provide them itself (Palley 2005).

The post-Washington consensus is not a challenge to neoliberalism (Fine 2001; 2002b; 2002a; Lapavitsas 2005; Palley 2005). The basic philosophy remains the same: that the market is the best way of distributing goods and services, and should be extended to as many aspects of human existence as possible. The difference is that while the Washington consensus advocated for states to be as small as possible—the leaner the state, and the less it interferes, the more the market will deliver—the post-Washington consensus advocates for the state to play an active role in expanding markets to aspects of human existence which were previously seen as non-market. Thus the primary role of the state has become the use of regulation to support and create markets. Christopher Hood (1995), Christopher Pollit (1998) and David Phillips (1998) have analyzed how states have come to see their role as primarily a regulatory one, believing that efficiency is created through the market, and through increased competition. States thus implement policies aimed at intensifying the amount of competition (and therefore the number of transactions) that occur in a sector (Palley 2005). Neoliberal public sector reform has focused on forcing state institutions to either compete in a market or operate 'as if' they were in a market. The role of the state becomes that of regulating contracts, and assessing the adequacy of its contractors against performance statements. Reforms attempt to lessen or remove differences between the public and the private sector and shift the emphasis from process accountability towards accountability in terms of results (Hood, 1995; Pollit, 1998). This trend in public sector reform, which emerged initially in English-speaking liberal market economies, and was pushed into many developing countries, has focused on increasing contractualization in the state by privatizing state entities, and breaking state entities into smaller units and forcing these smaller units to compete through contracts (Hood, 1995; Phillips, 1998; Pollit, 1998). For example, instead of a large state entity supplying a particular service (transport, water, education), it is seen as preferable for an ever-increasing number of small contractors to provide small components of this service, as this means increased competition and so, according to the advocates of marketization, increased efficiency.[1] The creation of quasi-markets in education and health has particularly been pushed by reformers. This type of reform is often referred to as New Public Management.

New Public Management and other similarly oriented reforms have been associated with the introduction of economic standards for the evaluation of governance. Wolf, 2010). The focus is on quantifiable outputs and performance targets, rather than input controls, bureaucratic procedures, and rules. Trends in public sector reform accordingly advocate a greater degree of monitoring of certain kinds of behaviour and performance, through a range of new 'accountability' mechanisms, such as performance indicators, performance appraisals, and other forms of control (Phillips 1998). New Public Management encourages private ownership, contracting out, performance-linked remuneration, concern for corporate image, cost-cutting, and monetary incentives rather than incentives such as ethos, ethics, and status (Phillips 1998). "The ideological triumph of neoliberalism", Crouch (2011, p. 166) argues, "has led to too much reliance being placed on the bundles of quasi-market and corporate forces that constitute the economy. No problems are seen in these dominating polity, the world of values and the rest of society".

Karl Polanyi (1944, p. 146) argued, in relation to nineteenth century liberalism, that "[t]he road to the free market was opened and kept open by an enormous increase in continuous, centrally organized and controlled interventionism". The same is the case with neoliberalism. Various analysts have pointed out that while governments have attempted to increase the variety of actors involved in delivering services, and decrease the role of the state in this delivery, this has meant *increasing* the regulatory role of the state, which obviously does not correlate with the neoliberal orthodoxy of a 'small' state (Hudson, 2010). Thus, while in theory advocates of neoliberalism promote the idea of a state that does as little as possible, in reality it has led to a state that is no smaller than the state it replaced. But whereas the state it replaced provided services to its citizens, the neoliberal state creates pro-market mechanisms within which necessary services are meant to arise, making the state provision of services redundant. Neoliberalism has transformed the state, rather than rolling it back (Munck, 2005). As Colas (2005, p. 70) argues, neoliberal globalization is a political project that "privileges the private, economic power of markets over the public, political authority of states, but does so, paradoxically, through the state-led, multilateral *re-regulation* of markets". Crouch (2011) shows that, because this expanded role of the state is presented as a response to market failure, it is often (wrongly) presented as critical of markets and so the fulfillment of left-wing ideas which held that markets were not the answer. This apparent appeal to the left made it a key idea of 'Third Way' politics, advocated most famously by New Labour in the United Kingdom. But in fact, it cedes ground dramatically to the right, by accepting that markets should be the starting point, and that individual preferences should be the basis for all societal decisions.

All of this has had many implications for education. In the context of what Crouch (2011) calls privatized Keynesianism, where individuals go into debt to secure general economic prosperity, education policy is being used as part of the story about individuals taking responsibility for their own welfare (including going into debt to obtain educational qualifications), and making sure that they are employable. Hein Marais (2011, pp. 137–138), citing Gillian Hart (2006), argues that neoliberalism

> represents a new modality of government predicated on interventions to create the organizational and subjective conditions for entrepreneurship—not only in terms of extending the 'enterprise model' to schools, hospitals, housing estates, and so forth, but also in inciting individuals to become entrepreneurs themselves [....] This process of 'responsibilization' often goes hand-in-hand with new or intensified invocations of 'community' as a sector 'whose vectors and forces can be mobilized, enrolled, deployed in novel programmes and techniques which encourage and harness active practices of self-management and identity construction, of personal ethics and collective allegiances.'

The winding back of the welfare state in the Western world since the 1980s, and the drive to market liberalization in poor countries—which has in most instances increased impoverishment—has led to education and training being seen as personal insurance against risk, in the sense that education leads to a job, which leads to a wage, which allows the individual to buy the welfare services previously provided

57

by the state, and so as a replacement for welfare provision by the state (Wheelahan, 2010). This has led governments to seek reforms that 'vocationalize' education, or to attempt to make it more 'relevant' to what are *perceived* or *claimed* to be the needs of employers. Thus neoliberalism has curriculum implications: business interests are meant to drive the curriculum. This is often accompanied by a plethora of superficially attractive terms such as 'upskilling', 'lifelong learning' and 'transferable skills' which have obvious economic connotations but do not have a clear meaning in practice (Phillips 1998).

Neoliberalism has also dramatically affected how education is delivered. Increasing criticisms of the state in general have been linked to arguments that state provision is the cause of irrelevant and low quality education. This has led to a growing emphasis on privatization, pressure on governments to use market-based policies even where the state is still involved in the delivery of education, and, following from this, pressure to introduce or increase payments by learners. Outcomes-based qualifications in vocational education reform in the United Kingdom, and competence-based training in Australia, were some of the earliest attempts to encompass neoliberal ideas about public sector reform into a single education policy. Young (2003, p. 232) suggests that qualifications frameworks represent an "almost paradigm case of government intervention in a neo-liberal economy", as they are attempts both to gain greater central control and to give greater 'choice' to individuals.

THE UNITED KINGDOM AND AUSTRALIA

The National Vocational Qualifications (NVQs) developed in England, Northern Ireland, and Wales in the 1980s were "the first national attempt to base vocational qualifications on the idea of competences" (Young, 2009b, p. 6). The policies which were being developed in Scotland at the same time were somewhat different, and I will return to them in Chapter 8.

A major impetus for the introduction of the National Vocational Qualifications was the idea that the existing vocational education system needed to be dramatically changed in order to contribute to solving Britain's relative economic decline (Hyland, 1994). As discussed by many educational researchers in the United Kingdom (Dale *et al.,* 1990; Moore & Ozga, 1991; Wolf, 2002; Young, 2008), the notion that the curriculum was out of touch with the needs of industry, and did not contribute to an 'enterprise' minded population, was a dominant theme in British education reform, and was particularly prevalent in the 1980s. At the same time, some reformers from left-wing political perspectives also supported the competence/ outcomes approach. Educational reformers who wanted to open up access for non-traditional learners, and who felt that education institutions were overly academic and self-interested, saw focus on outcomes as a useful mechanism for doing so (Wolf, 1995; Young, 2009b). Reformers hoped that the 'new standards' would provide a rigorous and more 'relevant' alternative to the 'knowledge-based' approach associated with written examinations (Young, 2009b). As the discussion below, and in the following chapter, shows, the popularity of outcomes-based qualifications frameworks with reformers from opposite sides of the political spectrum is a trend that has continued throughout their history.

In 1981, a *New Training Initiative* introduced 'standards of a new kind' (Wolf, 1995; Young, 2009b). Gilbert Jessup (1991, p. 11), influential advocate of learning outcomes, described the new approach as a "radical departure from most existing practice". What was new, according to Jessup, was that the new standards made the *outcomes* of education explicit, instead of focusing on the 'inputs' to the learning process. On this familiar claim to 'newness', Norris (1991, p. 338) commented: "We have been here before and others have been here before us." Terry Hyland (1994, p. 2) pointed out:

> The parallels between the social-efficiency philosophy and the more recent vocationalizing elements surrounding the establishment of the NCVQ [National Council for Vocational Qualifications] in the early 1980s are quite striking. All the essential ingredients of the NVQs are present in the early American model – a conservative ideology, a foundation in behaviourist psychology and a determination to serve the specific needs of industry.

The outcomes-based approach was intended to make a break from two main elements of qualification design prior to the 1980s: the specification of time for an apprenticeship, and the specified syllabus (Young, 2009b). Apprenticeships were seen by the government of the day as leaving too much control to the trade unions (Raggat & Williams, 1999; Wolf, 1995). The specification of the syllabus as the basis for teaching programmes and the assessment of off-the-job learning was seen as giving too much control to teachers, colleges and Awarding Bodies (Young, 2009b). Instead, the new standards would specify the expectations and requirements of employers, in terms of expected work performance, expressed as outcomes Stewart & Sambrook, 1995, p. 98). Other perceived problems which this policy attempted to solve were "lower than desired levels of post-compulsory participation; lower than desired levels of achievement; significant levels of disengagement from learning (i.e. the not in education, employment or training [NEET]) group" (Keep, 2005, p. 534). Ewart Keep suggests that the assumption underlying the reform was that these problems could be solved through "reform of the curriculum and associated systems of assessment".

There was increasing criticism of the existing system of vocational qualifications, which had developed at a time when many jobs required few skills and little knowledge (Young, 2009b). A review of vocational qualifications reported in 1986. The review was partly a response to the fact that the government wanted a basis for accrediting the learning of young people who had participated in the recently launched Youth Training Scheme. In late 1987 in England, Northern Ireland, and Wales, a National Council for Vocational Qualifications was created, to develop "a new system of qualifications that will deliver the skills needed by industry" (Phillips

1998, p. 64). Key to this new system was the idea of reforming vocational education through outcomes-based qualifications.

The Council was launched in 1987 "with much fanfare as a 'revolution' in education and training across the whole of the UK" (Young, 2003, p. 223). Its main task was coordinating the development of National Vocational Qualifications. Many occupational sectors had little training available or qualifications which could be obtained, few existing qualifications had any links with each other, and many vocational qualifications were not available at lower levels. To capture its complexity, the qualification system was described as a 'jungle', and this term has subsequently been invoked in many countries which are attempting to develop qualifications frameworks.

The initial idea was to replace all existing vocational qualifications. What emerged was a new set of outcomes-based qualifications, replacing some existing qualifications. 'Standards of competence' were developed in England, Northern Ireland, and Wales, in 200 occupational sectors. Each was associated with a national vocational qualification (Wolf, 1995). The qualifications were made up of a number of units, which attempted to spell out exactly what the student had to do, and to what standard, through specifications of learning outcomes and performance/assessment criteria (Phillips 1998).

A key aspect of these 'standards' or 'outcomes' was the idea of 'functional analysis', which, though different in the detail, harkened back to Bobbit's idea, discussed in Chapter 2, that we should start from activities in the real world when thinking about the curriculum. The idea was that the starting point in designing a qualification should be an analysis of occupational functions, conducted by employers (Stewart & Sambrook, 1995). Industry-led bodies would develop 'statements of competent workplace performance' from sets of individual 'elements of competence' and their associated 'performance criteria'. These 'elements of competence' (later known as 'occupational standards') were then grouped together into 'units of competence'. Each national vocational qualification was made up of a number of related 'units of competence' (Young, 2009b). The first National Vocational Qualifications were awarded in 1988.

In 1991, Jessup published his influential book, *Outcomes: NVQs and the Emerging Model of Education and Training*. He explained how the outcomes or standards could be organized in a 'framework', which would "provide the reference grid within which different forms of learning provision can be related" (Jessup, 1991, p. 12). The standards or outcomes were then 'packaged' in the form of credit or qualifications. A hierarchy of five levels of 'competence' was created (Hyland, 1994). Here, then, emerges the idea of organizing qualifications into a framework—a grid derived from an attempt to create a logical hierarchical arrangement of outcomes or competencies. The appeal of this apparently simple idea has endured, although implementing it in reality has proved very complex.

Young (2009b) argues that what was new in this outcomes-based reform was the idea that qualifications could drive educational reform. A key driving force behind this was the government's belief in 'market' solutions. Education and training providers were seen as 'monopolizing' provision, and unions' role in apprenticeships was similarly seen as hindering a 'free market' in education. Education institutions were seen as tending to focus more on the interests of their staff and what they could—or wanted to—teach than on their role as providers of a public service that was responsive to employer and learner needs. This was referred to with the term 'provider capture'. Dale *et al.* (1990, p. 157) argue that "the concerted attack on education, throughout the mid- and late 1970s, for its apparent failure to maintain standards and move towards greater relevance to adult and working life, had quickly given way to an attack on the educational establishment itself, as defenders of an outdated system."

Very similar ideas can be seen in reforms of vocational education taking place in Australia. Australia is often considered the prototype of competence-based training,[2] but its reforms were based on the English model. Guthrie (2009, p. 6), in a comprehensive review of the Australian competence-based training system, describes it thus:

> The model was strongly based on the functional competency approach in use in the United Kingdom (UK), and based around a system of national vocational qualifications. It was workplace focused and performance oriented, like its UK counterpart. Australia therefore drew heavily on the UK experience and literature, and many of the issues raised about CBT [competence-based training] and its implementation had parallels. Like its counterpart, the Australian conception has tended to downplay the importance of underpinning knowledge and a holistic view of the 'craft concept' compared with, say, the German and Austrian models of competence.

A major reorganization of vocational education and training was intended to improve economic performance and international competitiveness (Phillips 1998; Spreen 2001). Vocational education and training was seen as having a "significant role in enabling" the "improvement of Australia's productivity and international competitiveness" (Guthrie, 2009, p. 5). A key moment in the history of Australian (and thus international) competence-based training was the introduction of 'training packages' in 1997 (Deissinger & Hellwig, 2005). Training packages, described as the "architecture of CBET [competence-based education and training]", are the nationally endorsed standards and qualifications, which contain competence standards in a specified format, and are thus seen as defining skills and knowledge required in workplaces within specific occupational fields (Deissinger & Hellwig, 2005, p. 32). The training packages were intended as the basis for course development, and as a mechanism to enable articulation and portability within vocational education and training (Crawford, 2003). Another aspect of the reform was to establish a recognition system which allowed qualified assessors to assess endorsed units of competency outside of any formal learning programme, thereby "giving equal status to formal, informal, and non-formal learning" (Byron 2003, p. 66). Assessment against competence standards would be "evidence based", although, predictably, in practice most learning remained institution based (Byron 2003, p. 67).

While much of the literature focuses on the curriculum-related aspects of the system, equally central to it was the idea of reducing "the monopoly of the public training providers" and introducing "a more open training market, to develop a more demand- and industry-led VET [vocational education and training] system" (Byron, 2003, p. 66). Like the English National Vocational Qualifications, the competence-based training reforms in Australia were explicitly focused on creating markets, forcing public providers to compete with each other and private providers, and shifting to a regulatory role for government (Wheelahan, 2010). The competence standards were crucial for this: they were introduced to function as a regulatory mechanism against which all providers, public and private, should operate (Wheelahan, 2009).

This was located in a broader socio-economic context of a neoliberal social pact introduced by the Labour government in 1987. Trade unions had participated in this process with the production of a publication, *Australia Reconstructed*, which emphasized improving Australia's economic performance and competitiveness through a more highly skilled workforce. The impetus for change was primarily economic, based on an analysis that Australia had experienced serious economic problems as a "primary producer and exporter of largely unprocessed materials" (Skilbeck, Connell, Lowe *et al.* 1994, p. 86, cited in Phillips 1998, p. 78). Exposing established providers to competition was a major aim of the reforms, through processes to support the registration of private providers. The assumption was that this would both drive up quality and force providers to be more responsive to industry needs.

As in the United Kingdom, there was a strong social justice drive behind some of the advocates of competence-based training. The idea of 'new vocationalism' was invoked, and Sedunary (1996, p. 371) argued, for example, that new vocationalism "embraces and gives new direction and legitimacy to many of the core principles and practices of the progressive tradition". She suggested that:

> ... the new vocationalism shares with the earlier radical education movement an antagonism to the esoteric nature of the academic curriculum and revives radical education's rejection of the social distinctions produced by it. In its dissatisfaction with general education, the new vocationalism contends that the academic curriculum does not, in its present form anyway, adequately prepare young people for the changing requirements of the workplace, particularly new work practices and the nature of new technology.

Outcomes-based education also became a driving force for the reform of school curricula in many states, as well as a focus on what were described as 'key competencies'. Both outcomes-based curriculum reforms in the school system and the competence-based training system for vocational education were positioned as necessary to produce the knowledge, skills, attitudes, and values needed to operate competently in a "globally-based, technologically advanced economy" (Spreen, 2001). American thinking, especially the ideas of William Spady[3], who was discussed in the previous chapter, were influential, particularly in the school reforms, as were the English National Vocational Qualifications in the vocational sector.

Common Threads

Deissinger and Hellwig (2005, p. 43) argue that the National Vocational Qualifications "quite ideally represent the central premises of CBET", and, as I have discussed above, the Australian reforms directly drew on the English National Vocational Qualifications. Let us, then, reconsider some essential features of this model in the two countries. In both countries, governments were trying to reform vocational education to improve economic performance. A focus on competence or learning outcomes was supposed to ensure that vocational education achieved "knowledge and skill and the application of that knowledge and skill to the standard of performance expected in the workplace (Deissinger & Hellwig, 2005, p. 8). This led to models of curriculum development[4] which started with analyzing tasks, jobs, competences, and tools associated with certain types of workplaces, or defining the central tasks of an occupation (Deissinger & Hellwig, 2005). How education was delivered and accessed by learners was as much a focus of the policy interventions as curriculum reform. There was a key emphasis on ideas such as flexible delivery, self-paced learning, learner choice, and so on (e.g. Guthrie, 2009). Learning outcomes and learner centredness were explicitly brought together in both countries: learning outcomes were presented as the vehicle to empower learners and put choices in their hands.

Deissinger and Hellwig (2005, p. 8) argue that in competence-based training the individual is "rated higher than teachers, government or other stakeholders". Learning outcomes were seen as a way of ensuring choice for learners, competition amongst providers, and of giving a regulatory role to government. Giving the central role to the learner was directly linked to attempts at creating a market in educational provision; learner-centredness was explicitly linked to marketization and 'choice'. Jessup's book, for example, starts with a chapter entitled 'Learning and Individuals', in which a 'learner-centred' system is advocated, with the 'individual learner' defined as the 'client' of education: "Individuals differ in the way they prefer to learn and the time and opportunity they have available. In a customer-oriented system, in which the learner is the customer, this should determine what is provided" (Jessup, 1991, p. 4). Thus, Wheelahan (2010, p. 127) argues that while competence-based training "is tied to a putatively progressive policy which promises to empower the most disempowered", it in fact only gives learners the autonomy of the consumer. I return to explore this issue in more depth in Chapter 7.

Jessup placed considerable emphasis on how much individuals learn outside of educational institutions, how inefficient traditional education and training institutions are, and on maximizing choice for individuals. All of this resonated with educational reformers and their ideas of recognizing learning outside of formal education institutions, and challenging the traditional authority of educational institutions. Also, inefficiency could be removed, Jessup suggested, if the focus was on the assessment of the outcomes learners had achieved:

> Qualifications reformers picked up on this idea. ... the shift to an outcomes-led system of Education and Training *thus means a qualification-led or assessment-led system*... As candidates do not have to undergo any particular programme of learning, the *award of an NVQ is based solely on the outcome of assessment.* (Jessup, 1991, emphasis in original)

There is another way in which outcomes-based qualifications have been related to the marketization of education—through the ways in which they have been positioned to support neoliberal public sector reform. These include the drive towards a state which primarily contracted for services, as opposed to providing services, and the attempt to create markets in sectors that had previously been seen as best provided by the state.

It is no coincidence that early qualifications frameworks emerged in countries preoccupied with New Public Management as a way of reforming their civil services, as the logic is essentially the same (Allais, 2007a; Phillips, 1998; Strathdee, 2011). Young (2003b) argues that qualifications frameworks have generally emerged in countries with weaker traditions of central government involvement in education and training, and which most readily embraced neo-liberalism, with the exception of the United States and Canada. He argues that the first countries which attempted to introduce national qualifications frameworks had had histories of education and training systems characterized by "inequalities, deep divisions", and "low rates of participation in post-compulsory education and training" (Young 2003b, p. 6).

As discussed above, the outcomes-based New Vocational Qualifications in the United Kingdom and the competence-based reform of vocational education in Australia both explicitly attempted to marketize vocational education. Education was argued to be a sector in which 'provider monopolies' must be broken in order for markets to be able to 'provide'. Following this line of thought, educational institutions should not have a monopoly on providing education and training—the role of governments must be to allow the entrance of other 'service providers' into the market, to increase competition, which, under neo-liberalism, is believed to lead inherently to better quality. Teachers and lecturers are seen as an obstacle to market-based efficiencies, and scenarios are sought which make education less dependent on teachers[5] (Levidow 2005).

The shift to a regulatory and contracting role for the state in the provision of education, in which there is no need to distinguish between the private, state, semi-private, or corporatized entities which deliver services to the public because they all have to measure up in the same way, requires targets against which learning can be assessed. One of the driving ideas behind the early outcomes-based qualification reforms was that qualifications consisting of statements of learning outcomes appear to offer the competence criteria against which education can be delivered, assessed, and evaluated, and against which cost recovery can be implemented, thus opening up markets in education. The key mechanism through which they operate is the creation of explicit, formal, and measurable performance statements, in the form of learning outcomes or statements of competence, against which all education must be measured. These learning outcomes are captured within qualifications and part qualifications (smaller components of qualifications which learners can acquire separately but which can be accumulated towards the award of a full qualification), which then are supposed to become the tool for driving the education system.

Learning outcomes were to be used to ensure that any provider could compete; the learning outcome would be the mechanism for contracting and evaluating their service. Educational institutions, as separate cost centres, were to deliver 'competences' in students, according to the specified 'standards'. The citizen was to be a consumer of a market good, whether they were buying from a private provider or from a state provider, or even obtaining subsidized provision from the state. Thus, the focus in educational reform was on setting the learning outcomes to be specified in the qualifications. The rest would follow from the learning outcomes. The role of the state was to lead and drive a process of setting learning outcomes, and not necessarily to build or develop educational institutions.

In this model, separate educational 'competences' are seen as 'goods' or 'services' that can be delivered through the market. Stipulation of educational outcomes is supposed to be able to disaggregate the provision of education, so that providers can deliver just the required outcomes, and consumers can purchase only the outcomes that they want, without having to sit through long educational programmes which are perceived as irrelevant. Instead of education being 'dominated' by the concerns of educators and the academy, education can be opened up to a wider range of 'service providers', who can all provide programmes that lead to the outcomes or competences in question. The primary role of the state is to regulate this market, through contracted or government-owned agents. Instead of the state being a collective body which delivers goods and services which are seen as outside of the market, the state tries to increase the ways in which the market can 'deliver services' to society, using regulation to *create* the market, to turn something into a market deliverable 'good' or 'service'. This fits with the broader neoliberal idea that educational providers must behave as though they are business corporations, even when they are state institutions.

The outcomes-based qualification model sees colleges and other educational institutions becoming entrepreneurial, offering qualifications desired by businesses, and marketing themselves to learners. This model is often linked to funding models whereby funding is directed to training providers through employers commissioning training for their staff, or when colleges choose to offer industry-designed competence-based qualifications. The college is the seller, the learning programmes are the products, and the consumers—whether in the form of learners and their parents, or employers—are supposed to dictate their requirements for the product. Advocates believe that competition improves quality. But, particularly when the 'commodity' being purchased is as complex as education is, and where there is no direct way of testing its benefits or evaluating its quality, the likely effect is a pressure on institutions to keep prices as low as possible, keep quality as low as possible, and focus on short-term desires of 'consumers'. This may well be at odds with more long-term ideas about what learners should learn.

As discussed above, various analysts in the political sciences have looked at how privatization and New Public Management, two key features of the new 'governance' notion, require additional regulatory mechanisms from governments, as well as new regulatory agencies to manage and support markets (Hudson, 2010; Jakobi, Martens, & Wolf, 2010). In education, this has meant the establishment of statutory or quasi-governmental organizations which establish requirements or practices that the providers of education and training need to meet if they are to be allowed to offer their services; in other words, quality assurance agencies. The need to regulate the new market in education providers delivering under qualifications frameworks is one reason why 'quality assurance' is often linked to qualifications frameworks, and, *vice versa*, frameworks are often introduced specifically to facilitate the establishment, or hoped for better functioning, of a quality assurance system. Quality assurance agencies define the nature of the performance expected of the providers, and the systems which they expect providers to develop to demonstrate their capacity to deliver approved courses and qualifications. Policy makers argue that this type of arrangement will improve accountability, transparency, efficiency, and quality. Defining standards of performance is seen to contribute to the 'raising of standards' (Phillips 2003). This notion can be traced right back to the efficiency movement described in the previous chapter, and Bobbit's ideas about setting standards outside of educational institutions, in order for them to 'produce' the 'goods' to specification. Dale *et al.* (1990, p. 72) describe this sort of approach as follows:

> ... a role for the State not unlike that of the 'head office' of a national commercial or industrial concern, i.e. the checking of standards and quality control. The interest of the State in testing and assessment now becomes more concerned with the external measurement of the effectiveness of institutions in maintaining standards. The question of how students are hierarchically differentiated for their placement in the workforce is no longer an issue for the State; it is to be resolved at the interface between education and employment. Neither is pedagogy a central source of worry; that is the responsibility of the teaching profession. The concern of the State is to ensure that educational institutions are held accountable to market forces via 'measurable' criteria, i.e. performance indicators.

Because of the emphasis on 'accountability', this approach is often seen as compatible with and indeed supportive of democratic reform. It is argued that it enables electorates to hold governments more accountable for the delivery and regulation of services. In countries that have enthusiastically adopted this approach, various new forms of 'accountability' and performance indicators are also used to ensure greater competition amongst educational institutions. This leads to a model dominated by 'arms-length' state institutions "…whose aim is to facilitate employer needs, when employers are often reluctant to articulate these, not least because their needs are, in many cases, extremely limited" (Winch, 2011, p. 85, drawing on Keep, 2001). This type of intervention can become centralized and top-heavy. As pointed out earlier, the regulatory state is not a small state.

A review of Callahan's (1962) account of the 'efficiency' movement in early 20th century educational reform reveals many parallels between today's qualifications frameworks and the earlier reforms, including the idea that the community or industry (stakeholders/users) should specify learning outcomes, the way in which educationalists agreed or capitulated, the impossible conditions that schools were operating under *before* they had the added strains of the 'efficiency police', and the extra money which was 'found' to pay for 'surveys' of 'efficiency experts' where the aim was to reduce expenditure on actual education. Callahan (1962, p. iii) also argues: "So long as schoolmen have a knife poised at their financial jugular vein each year, professional autonomy is impossible". This type of financial relationship between education institutions and government funding of education is largely accepted in today's climate of marketization, and in fact is explicitly introduced to make institutions more 'responsive'. Ironically, in many instances, particularly, as will be seen in Chapter 4, in poor countries, and specifically in vocational education systems, such a relation makes responsiveness impossible, as lecturers have no time to dedicate to research, curriculum design, and so on, because they are constantly chasing the next enrolment cohort. If the consumer reigns supreme in educational provision, the professional autonomy of educators is automatically reduced—and in all but the most elite private education systems, which have the luxury of a long-term perspective and the resources to spend on high salaries and good conditions of employment for well-trained professionals, this leads to sacrificing educational quality.

Other related market-oriented educational policies have also emerged over the same period as neoliberalism became increasingly influential, all of which purport to facilitate greater 'consumer choice', such as charter schools and voucher systems whereby governments allocate funds to individuals and let them select which institution to attend or enrol their children in, as well as site-based modes of school management and greater emphasis on competition between pupils, teachers, and schools.

Achievements in Australia and the United Kingdom

How successful and influential were these reforms? Despite its grand aims, the National Vocational Qualifications framework in the United Kingdom "became the subject of increasingly sharp criticism … and has staggered to a position of ever increasing marginality" (Young, 2003, p. 223). The critiques have been many and devastating (for example, Hyland, 1994, 1998; Norris, 1991; Raggat, 1994; Wolf, 1995, 2002). Wolf (2002) describes how the qualifications created through this framework were seen as undesirable not only by parents and youth, but also by employers, the very constituency they were primarily aimed at. She also provides empirical evidence and theoretical arguments to show that the specification of outcomes and assessment criteria, as well as assessment on the basis of assessment criteria, proved unsustainable (Wolf, 1995). Young (1996, p. 28) argues that "[a]ll the experience of NVQs in England and other outcomes-based systems indicates that attempts to increase the precision of outcomes can only lead to them becoming trivialized". This is reminiscent of Bobbit's objectives discussed in the previous chapter, which turned into long detailed lists of behavioural specifications which were often trivial; why this should be the case, and further manifestations of it, are discussed in Chapter 6. Hyland (1994, p. 10) provides additional evidence of lack of employer support, and quotes a major report which described National Vocational Qualifications as "a disaster of epic proportions". The vast majority of qualifications were awarded at low levels, in areas in which there were no perceived additional needs in the labour market. Supporters argued that people who had previously not been able to access education were now doing so. Detractors do not deny this, but point out that they were being given access to low-level qualifications with few labour market benefits.

Young (2009b) points out that while the assumption by the government of the United Kingdom when launching National Vocational Qualifications was that colleges should be giving more attention to employer needs, in practice, employers were not as interested in defining qualification outcomes as the government had hoped, and qualifications became 'captured' by 'assessors' and consultants. He speculates that another possible problem was that the National Vocational Qualifications were associated with the certification of those on youth training schemes for unqualified school leavers who in a previous period would have gained unskilled manual jobs (Young, 2005). They thus became associated with low-level qualifications with limited currency on the labour market. Young (2009b), Wolf (2002), and Hyland (1994) all argue that National Vocational Qualifications contributed to lowering the status of vocational education and polarizing education and training. Successive attempts have been made to reform National Vocational Qualifications in response both to the criticisms of researchers and the complaints of employers. They are still used in the United Kingdom, although the original National Vocational Qualification model has been changed many times.

Competence-based training in Australia has been more successful than the National Vocational Qualifications were in the United Kingdom, in the sense that it has remained central to vocational education policy. There has, however, been substantial criticism and debate about it in Australia (Guthrie, 2009; Wheelahan, 2010). For example, a high level review of training packages suggested that outcomes are poorly differentiated, and that the same groupings of units of competence could lead to "multiple qualification outcomes for vastly different content and training effort" (Schofield & McDonald, 2004, p. 10). A recent OECD review has also been critical of training packages (Hoeckel, Field, Justesen, & Kim, 2008), citing problems including the length and complexity of documentation associated with the training packages, as well as a lack of national assessments. Even the National Council for Vocational Education Research (1999, pp. 2–3) argue that:

> CBT [Competency-based training] seems particularly effective for imparting procedural knowledge and routine problem-solving skills, making it well-suited for technical skill acquisition. It is not as well suited to the development of conceptual and experiential knowledge.

> CBT may have been less successful in developing flexibility, adaptability and capacities to innovate, all features seen as necessary for a workforce that will be competitive in a fast-changing, global marketplace.

There are many training packages which are not used at all, and many others with very low enrollments. Despite the fact that the system is explicitly 'industry-led', and the structures which design training packages are dominated by industry representatives, there continue to be criticisms of the lack of a 'fit' between qualifications and the labour market needs, and criticisms that training packages are not in touch with the 'needs of industry' (Hoeckel et al., 2008; Wheelahan, 2009). Wheelahan (2009) also describes considerable hostility from college teachers to training packages, as well as confusion about the relationships between teaching, learning, and assessment. Sedunary (1996, p. 370) suggests, with regard to both competence-based training reforms in vocational education and the key competencies agenda in schooling, that "conservative critics" have offered a "defence of the integrity of the traditional subjects and the social and vocational benefits of a liberal education", while "progressive critics" have also found fault, identifying:

> those elements that represent a resurgence of older, often discredited practices (like behaviourism and assessment-led education), to argue that such reform of the post-compulsory years may exacerbate existing social inequalities, to question the claims of generic usage of current notions of competence in future workplaces, and to point out the clear links between the Key Competencies movement and broader New Right and economic rationalist approaches to social management dominant since the 1980s.

Despite these debates and discussions, commitment to competence-based training has remained strong and substantial, particularly from structures set up to provide industry inputs and from government policy makers.

AN OUTCOMES-BASED QUALIFICATIONS FRAMEWORK IN NEW ZEALAND

New Zealand was the first country to take something similar to the two models discussed above, the United Kingdom National Vocational Qualifications model and the Australian competence-based training model, and apply it to the whole education system. The qualifications framework which was developed exemplifies many of the trends described above. These include, firstly, an attempt to use an outcomes-based qualifications framework to marketize the delivery of education. This was part of broader New Public Management-style public sector reforms emphasizing: a reduced role for the state; increased consumer choice, competition, and accountability; and improving efficiency and promoting enterprise through public sector finance management aimed at greater provider accountability and higher levels of user fees. Secondly, outcomes were intended to improve the relevance of education, and thereby increase the ability of individuals to get jobs, and improve the economy. Thirdly, the specific use of outcomes-based qualifications as a policy mechanism to drive these goals was the product of policy borrowing, substantially derived from the two models described above. The New Zealand framework has also been a key model from which many countries have borrowed. It is therefore discussed in some detail below.

Political and Economic Drivers

New Zealand was experiencing relatively high unemployment, particularly for young people between 15 and 19 years, for whom it reached 17 per cent, in the late 1970s and early 1980s (Strathdee, 2009). Rob Strathdee argues that the economic problems of this period, as well as significant economic restructuring and moves to a less regulated economy in the 1980s and '90s, were important factors in the implementation of the national qualifications framework in New Zealand. David Phillips (1998) describes how the Labour Party in New Zealand won an election in 1984 and took over a country heavily in debt, and with significant social welfare in place. It proceeded to institute a series of changes which have generally been characterized as neoliberal. These included drastic attempts to reduce state expenditure, slashing the workforce of the public sector, privatizing key state-owned enterprises such as the railways and the post office, and introducing user fees for health and education. Legislation was introduced to increase efficiency and accountability, the main mechanisms of which were unbundling government departments into smaller units with greater autonomy, and performance-related contracts for top civil servants. The existing Department of Education was broken into ten separate units, each of which worked under a regulatory framework set by the Ministry of Education. One of these new agencies was the New Zealand Qualifications Authority (NZQA), which came into existence in 1990, the date at which the proportion of the cost of post-compulsory education borne by students started to increase (Van Rooyen, 2003). The series of reports, investigations, and discussions leading up to the establishment of the NZQA emphasized: a desire to break down the 'monopoly control' that the Department of Education had over all aspects of education; a vision for a series of independent organizations with discrete functions taking over various roles from the Department of Education; and a belief in the necessity of separating policy making from operational work as a way of functioning in a more business-like manner (Phillips 1998). Van Rooyen (2003) also argues that reform in New Zealand focused on moving education from centralized provision and organization to, on the one hand, greater regulation, and on the other hand, increased autonomy for providers.

Various reports criticizing the state of the economy had raised questions about the skills levels of the labour force, as well as pointing to the need to reform various aspects of the curriculum, assessment, and qualification policies and practices in order to develop 'human capital'. The main issues were: an emphasis on economically relevant content (interpreted as skills as opposed to knowledge); defining standards of performance or competence; replacing academic examinations with competence-based assessment methods; an emphasis on quality assurance (registration and accreditation of providers); and the notion of a comprehensive framework of qualifications (Phillips 1998). James Marshall (1997) argues that since the 1984 Labour government, the dominant educational ideology in New Zealand has been that schools should prepare people for work, with an emphasis on vocationally oriented education, and a neoliberal view of self-serving individuals pursuing economic rewards in the world of work, rather than an emphasis on the intrinsic value of education.

Policy papers leading to the New Zealand qualifications framework emphasized that if New Zealand was going to be economically competitive, it would need a highly skilled, flexible workforce, and a more efficient and responsive vocational education and training system. The increasing pace of economic and technological change required a "culture of lifelong learning" (Department of Labour and Ministry of Education 1996, cited in Van Rooyen 2003, p. 49). A 1988 report addressing post-compulsory education and training recommended a single qualification structure which would specify national standards in all areas, evaluate courses against the standards, and endorse claims that learners were competent against the standards. It also emphasized the notion of enabling a variety of routes to allow learners to obtain the same standards. In other words, the emphasis was explicitly on standards, and not on institutional organization. A series of reports, committees, and working groups moved swiftly towards the establishment of a national body that would "promote and maintain quality standards based on student-centred, competency-based learning and assessment" (Van Rooyen 2003, p. 49). A major review of the school curriculum in 1986 recommended the introduction of achievement-based assessment, and legislation in 1990 created the New Zealand Qualifications Authority. Documentation leading up to the creation of the New Zealand Qualifications Authority drew heavily on the United Kingdom National Vocational Qualifications model, and emphasized the notion of competence, as well as the certification of on- and off-the-job training. During this period, there was also extensive engagement with key officials in the Scottish Vocational Education Council (Phillips 1998).

The qualifications framework was an attempt to use outcomes-based qualifications to introduce more efficiency and greater marketization into the provision of education and training at all levels and in all learning areas (Strathdee, 2009). Reform of

71

post-compulsory education was intended to improve the range of choices available to students, so that an increasing number had the chance to gain qualifications. Increasing flexibility between 'tracks' (vocational education, schooling, and higher education) was considered to be key to increasing choice, and the qualifications framework was seen as a tool to achieve this (Phillips, 1998). A unitary framework was thought to be a way of breaking down what were perceived to be the "false boundaries" between two important "styles of learning" (vocational and academic), and the idea of a single framework had a "seductive simplicity" and a "strong equity flavour" (Phillips 1998, p. 244).

The focus on outcomes and unit standards appeared to enable the development of 'useful' qualifications (Phillips 1998). Phillips also argues that the mechanisms for control introduced through unit standards and outcomes supported the neoliberal framework of market competition, in which, firstly, anyone in theory could be a provider of qualifications as long as they met certain outcomes as specified through the outcomes-based qualifications framework, and secondly, *homo economicus*, the "rational, self-interested seeker of qualifications" could chose to obtain them from any provider (p. 246). Van Rooyen (2003, p. 61) notes that one of the results of qualification reform has been a rapid growth in the number of private training providers.

Phillips stresses two factors that led to the adoption of the qualifications framework: the creation of a set of competing devolved state agencies—including the New Zealand Qualifications Authority; and policy engagement with the Scottish Vocational Education Council and the National Council for Vocational Qualifications in the United Kingdom. The borrowed idea of a unitary framework allowed the Qualifications Authority to keep ahead of its potential competitors in the government with a strong foundation with which to forge a new organization and provided it with a mechanism for exerting power or control over other state agencies. In other words, the fact that there were competing government agencies, and the fact that this particular agency, the Qualifications Authority, was able to keep ahead by borrowing an appealing sounding policy from the United Kingdom and Scotland, and the fact that the policy in question emphasized economic growth, relevant education, and so on, led to the adoption of the New Zealand Qualifications Authority's qualifications framework.

Achievements in New Zealand

Initially there was strong support from the government, with a focus on the importance of skills to the economy and on the national qualifications framework as a key mechanism for increasing skills and for providing a clear expression of what had to be learnt. Qualifications were to be based on 'unit standards' with a standard format. The framework would be a national catalogue of these units of learning, written in terms of outcomes, and bearing credits towards named qualifications. There was an intention to develop qualifications and standards in sectors of employment which had not had any previously (Van Rooyen 2003). And a record of learning was to be kept centrally for all learners.

It was intended that the unit-standards based framework would be fully operational by 1997, at which time all existing qualifications would be phased out (Strathdee and Hughes 2001). After an initial period of frantic writing of standards, both for vocational and school qualifications, implementation began, and the Qualifications Authority started to hit resistance. While it had significant support from industry, and support from some polytechnics and schools, there was opposition from other schools and almost total opposition from universities (Phillips 1998). Strathdee (2009) argues that in some areas of vocational education the new outcomes-based qualifications took hold, with progress in developing unit standards and new qualifications, but in many other areas they failed to win the hearts and minds of users. But the New Zealand national qualifications framework suffered a similar fate to the National Vocational Qualifications, facing near collapse after five years (Phillips, 1998; Strathdee, 2011; Young, 2005).

Much of the criticism was similar to that leveled at the National Vocational Qualifications, in particular criticisms of the endless spiral of specification which the outcomes-based qualifications descended into (discussed in depth in Chapter 6). In 1994, the New Zealand Vice-Chancellors' Committee withdrew the university sector from the qualifications framework (Strathdee, 2009). The Qualifications Authority could not convince the universities to adopt the unit standard model and the then government would not force them to. A white paper in 1999 signaled that the framework would be reconceptualized and 'broadened' in various ways (Strathdee and Hughes 2001). This included allowing for whole qualifications. By 2001, the unit standards model for schools was abandoned. The New Zealand framework was incorporated within a broader New Zealand Register of Quality Assured Qualifications, which brought together other non outcomes-based qualifications along with qualifications already registered on the framework (Phillips 2003). The Register is the structure that brings together all approved qualifications available in New Zealand. With the adoption of the Register, institutions do not have to carry out assessment against outcomes or unit standards in the way that was first envisioned (Strathdee, 2009). In light of this, one of the first executives of the New Zealand Qualifications Authority argued that the idea of a national qualifications framework is a waste of time, and is unlikely to lead to any of its stated goals (Blackmur 2003).

MOVING OUT

Young (2009b) contends that National Vocational Qualifications remain, over 20 years after their introduction, "the most widely known, widely copied and most heavily criticized model for a vocational qualifications framework in the world". Hyland (1998, p. 370) discusses an international conference held in London in November 1997, at which the British Council "was openly and unashamedly seeking

73

to sell the NVQ system to countries from all over the world." Quoting the then Education and Employment Secretary, David Blunkett, who described the National Vocational Qualifications as "one of Britain's best kept secrets", Hyland argues that the 'best kept secret' about National Vocational Qualifications "at least until relatively recently—has been the fact that they have failed, comprehensively and spectacularly, to achieve any of the objectives set for them." Gerhard Bosch and Jean Charest (2010, p. 14) are equally blunt when they argue that: "The case of the British National Vocational Qualifications (NVQs) framework demonstrates that it is possible—surprisingly—to export schemes that do not work in the country of origin".

These three policy models—the English National Vocational Qualifications, the Australian competence-based training, and the New Zealand national qualifications framework—all provided substance for the models of qualifications frameworks and competence-based reforms to vocational education that have been adopted in many countries. This has particularly been the case in the developing world, often with assistance and advice from international organizations and consultants (Loose, 2008). As is clear from the discussion above, while many countries have looked to the models developed in Australia and New Zealand in developing their own reforms, those two countries both drew on the English model.

The English, Australian, and New Zealand models are not the only ways to design a qualifications framework, or indeed to reform vocational education. For example, the national qualifications framework in Australia—the framework that incorporates all qualifications across higher education, schools, and vocational education—did not use the competence-based model, despite its strong use in the vocational education sector. The Australian national qualifications framework was introduced in 1995 in an attempt to create clearer relationships between schooling, vocational education, and higher education. It was a rather loose policy, as it had to accommodate federal power with regards to schooling, a large and influential private schooling system, a highly autonomous and powerful higher education sector which has close links with schooling, and the national and competence-based vocational education and training system that I have described above (Keating, 2003; Wheelahan, 2009). It was been described as a relatively 'weak' qualifications framework, because it did not have regulatory functions over the three sectors; what it essentially did was to provide some kind of map of the main qualifications on offer in the country, and show possible relationships between them. However, the original framework was the subject of a series of reviews, and it has been changed in an attempt to bring greater national coherence across the three sectors, and to facilitate student transfers between education sectors (Wheelahan, 2009). The Scottish qualifications framework, widely regarded as one of the most successful frameworks internationally, is also a much looser model, which did not aim to create new qualifications or reform educational delivery, but rather to bring together existing qualifications, and improve relationships between the different educational sectors which awarded qualifications. I briefly consider these other models in Chapter 8.

However, as I show in the following chapter, poor countries which have adopted qualifications frameworks have tended to develop policies which look like the English National Vocational Qualifications, the Australian competence-based qualifications, and the original New Zealand national qualifications framework. It is therefore these models that are of chief concern for now. It is true that Scottish policy makers played a role in the creation of the New Zealand qualifications framework, as discussed above, but the actual framework in the latter country was designed very differently to that in Scotland. Similarly, as I will discuss in the following chapter, many poor countries have sought advice from Scottish experts, but they have produced qualifications frameworks which look rather more like the outcomes/ competence-based systems described above.

To briefly re-cap: all three countries experimented in using outcomes/ competence-based qualifications to reform their education systems, for vocational education in both the United Kingdom (except Scotland) and Australia, and for the whole education system in New Zealand. The qualifications framework in New Zealand, and the English National Vocational Qualifications survive, albeit in substantially altered forms, but neither of these reforms can be seen to have been particularly successful, even on their own terms. The relatively more successful competence-based training system in Australia is also the subject of serious criticism. All have seen a series of organizational and institutional changes. The outcomes and competence-based reforms in the United Kingdom, Australia, and New Zealand were as much reforms to the state as they were educational reforms, and they were located in broader public sector reforms which were focused on marketization and privatization. The outcomes-based qualifications frameworks—whereby educational institutions were offered increased autonomy in exchange for meeting targets, set through outcomes/ competence-based qualifications—were the educational component of this broader political trajectory.

In all three countries discussed, the links between qualifications frameworks and a broader neoliberal programme were explicit. The increased emphasis on qualifications by British governments since the mid-1980s was closely linked to marketization policies forcing educational institutions to compete for students (and therefore funds). Similarly, in Australia and New Zealand, the explicit aim was to create a market in the delivery of vocational education through 'industry-led' competence-based qualifications that were independent of educational providers. The achievement of this is regarded by some as evidence of success in Australia and New Zealand.

Despite their differences, what the frameworks discussed above had in common is that they were implemented in relatively wealthy and developed countries, with well-established education institutions. In the next chapter, I will explore what happened when this model was transported to poorer countries.

ENDNOTES

1 Of course there is still a cost to the taxpayer—the increase of competition and transactions means an increase of contracts and assessments, as well as regulation. It also creates considerable possibilities for corruption.

2 While all vocational education works to a greater or lesser degree with the idea of competence, competence-based training is something specific.

3 However, Spady himself disassociated himself from much of what was done in his name, as he did later in Australia and South Africa (Spreen, 2001).

4 The approach which starts with the bits that make up a job, and gradually builds on these, is referred to as DACUM, which stands for Developing A Curriculum. Functional analysis, on the other hand, is the term given to the approach which starts with defining the central task of an occupation, and then deriving complex functions from it (Deissinger & Hellwig, 2005). In both cases, though, the essence is starting from thinking about and analyzing work, and designing a curriculum backwards from this.

5 The rise of computer-based distance learning and various other applications of technology in education such as televised lessons are also in some instances linked to attempts to remove teachers from education, or to minimize the need for them.

CHAPTER 4

SOMETHING BORROWED, SOMETHING SOLD

Outcomes, Competences, and Qualifications Frameworks
Spread to the Developing World

In the 1990s and early 2000s, it was to poor and middle income countries that most work on qualifications frameworks (and competence-based training) spread. What happened is the focus of this chapter. The patterns that emerge in these countries seem to be, in the main, similar to those already seen. However, the problems caused by this type of reform are more serious.

Some of early uses of the ideas of learning outcomes and learner centredness were discussed in Chapter 2. Chapter 3 considered how these ideas re-emerged in qualifications in the United Kingdom, Australia, and New Zealand. Outcomes-based qualifications were used to drive marketization of provision and reform the role of the state in educational delivery; change curricula, thereby improving their relevance to individuals and employers; and improve how education related to labour markets by providing better information to employers about the abilities of the holder of a qualification. We also saw how these policies had support not only from the right of the political spectrum, but also from the left, firstly, in the context of the centre-left shifting substantially to the right through 'Third Way' politics, and secondly, through drawing on left-wing educational traditions that were critical of subjects as the basis for the curriculum, and of educational institutions as elitist or conservative reproducers of class inequalities.

Drawing on the English National Vocational Qualifications directly or indirectly, qualifications frameworks emerged next in South Africa, Botswana, and Mauritius, competence-based frameworks for vocational education were developed in the Caribbean and some Asian countries, and labour competence frameworks were developed in some Latin American countries. All generally followed the model of getting stakeholders, particularly representatives of employers, to develop outcomes- or competence-based qualifications (Allais, 2010b). There are also some examples of qualifications frameworks which were not narrowly modelled on the English National Vocational Qualifications.

There is very little research on qualifications frameworks in all of these countries. The framework on which there has been the most research is that developed in South Africa. The South African case is useful because it is an extreme instance of a qualifications framework, and thus highlights, in almost ideal-typical fashion, the nature and limits of the outcomes-based qualifications framework form. (However, it could also be argued that it was a *reductio ad absurdam* of policy which could be sensible if adopted in a more moderate way; I will return to this possibility in Chapter 8). In most countries, from the advocacy and descriptive documents which are available, it is hard to establish the extent to which frameworks have actually been implemented, never mind how effective they are. In most cases qualifications frameworks are relatively recent policy interventions, and it is not always clear what they will look like, and how they will operate in practice. Nonetheless, there are some indications of trajectories, particularly in the countries with more years of experience.

Across the globe, developing countries are adopting outcomes- and competence-based approaches to vocational education. I argue in this chapter that one of the reasons outcomes-based qualifications frameworks and quality assurance systems have great appeal in developing countries is because education systems, and particularly vocational education, are weak, and the state has no viable policy to ensure employment for all citizens. A policy focused on regulation of provision, rather than trying to build and improve providing institutions, and which claims to make people 'employable' without government intervening to create employment, seems like it would be appealing to policy makers. In all the cases I have studied, developing countries have attempted to follow the model of creating a framework of qualifications, using employers (and other stakeholders) to define 'competences' or 'learning outcomes' that are the basis of the qualifications, and setting up state (and in some cases private) regulatory bodies to regulate both private and public providers against the stipulated outcomes. The specification of outcomes is supposed to improve the quality and relevance of education, as well as to improve the ability of government to regulate education, which is often linked to a desire to open up markets, and ensure that new providers can emerge, as well as provide a means of holding existing providers to account without the state having to play a central role in delivering education.

But this approach, with the emphasis on a regulatory state 'quality assuring' different providers, has not increased the quantity or quality of provision, and in some cases (such as South Africa) may have decreased it. In most instances, the main achievement has been to develop paper qualifications that in fact are never used, despite the involvement of industry and other stakeholders in their development. This is a tragedy not only due to the pointless expenditure of resources in a context in which governments have very limited finances for a number of competing priorities, but because many more serious priorities—such as developing and supporting educational institutions—are neglected because the policy *appears* to be taking care of them. This chapter will provide some evidence of these trends, with a particular focus on South Africa, but also drawing on experiences from a selection of poor and middle-income countries. The analysis draws largely from the study I led for the International Labour Organization discussed in Chapter 1 (Allais, 2010b); the detailed case studies for the individual countries, which were all conducted by different researchers, are available online.[1]

SOUTH AFRICA

A qualifications framework was developed in South Africa in the mid-1990s. It was strongly supported across the political spectrum because of a broad consensus on a need for dramatic change, heralded by the liberation movement, and in response both to apartheid education and to problems with the economy as South Africa tried to reenter the global economy. Perhaps because of the political support, as well as the high ambition for what it was to achieve, the South African national qualifications framework was designed as a rather extreme model of an outcomes-based qualifications framework. In South Africa, outcomes-based qualifications were intended for all sectors of the education and training system, at all levels, and, according to the original policy, were meant to replace all existing qualifications. Given that it was introduced as a key policy to entirely change the system of education inherited from apartheid, it was seen as the most ambitious framework in the world. The stakes were much higher. Its failure would matter much more.

It is also one of the most advanced frameworks in the world in terms of the number of years it has been implemented, and is one of the few qualifications frameworks in the world that has been subjected to considerable scrutiny by researchers. What is evident is that the attempt to turn an outcomes-led qualifications framework into a real policy vehicle in which learning outcomes were stipulated separately from educational contexts led to a model that spiralled out of control, becoming completely unwieldy and unusable as a basis for educational reform. The outcomes-led framework model led to a system which was not only very complex and cumbersome, but also a very poor basis for educational reform. What's more, the education system in South Africa survived this reform only where the reasonably strong education institutions *ignored* the outcomes-led qualifications framework model. In the sectors where educational provision has been historically very weak in South Africa—such as vocational and adult education—the existence of outcome statements has not led to increased provision or improvements in quality, and there is considerable evidence that it has made provision more difficult. The failures of the South African qualifications framework are important beyond South Africa, because, despite these failures, the outcomes-led model is being pushed in poor countries as a major mechanism for educational reform. Angola is probably one of the starkest examples. Ravaged for twenty years by civil war, desperately needing new educational institutions, it is attempting to create a national qualifications framework with guidance from the South African Qualifications Authority.

High Hopes for Learning Outcomes

The idea of a qualifications framework emerged in South Africa in the early 1990s, shortly prior to the transition to democracy. The South African national qualifications framework was officially introduced in 1995. It was seen as a major policy intervention to contribute to overcoming the educational, social, and economic problems caused by apartheid. Like the Australian competence-based training and like the National Vocational Qualifications and competence-based models in the United Kingdom, it was supported by both progressive educators anxious to democratize education provision and policy makers anxious to marketize the education system.

The need to dramatically improve the education system in South Africa was (and still is) much greater than in Australia, New Zealand, and the United Kingdom. The educational, social, and economic problems in South Africa were much deeper than they were in these other countries. The idea of an education policy which increased relevance and competence, ensured that education contributed to eradicating economic problems and social inequalities, enabled democratization, and increased levels of provision, whilst also being a mechanism for ensuring quality provision, had appeal across the political spectrum.

Apartheid has been described as "the most notorious form of racial domination that the postwar world has known" (Thompson, 1990, p. 189). It was a political system which disenfranchised the black majority, and restricted most of the population to intentionally inferior 'bantu education'. Black people had very limited possibilities for participation in the economy. Education and training policy reinforced social and economic inequality by destroying and restricting access to education and training, by providing poor quality education and training to most black people, and by controlling the content of syllabuses for all population groups to reflect the interests of the apartheid state. The workforce was deeply divided, with higher skilled and higher paying jobs frequently reserved for white people, and 'unskilled' low paying, insecure jobs or unemployment as the primary options for black people.

The extreme inequality of the South African education system under apartheid, as well as the extreme social and economic inequality, the inefficiencies of the economy inherited from apartheid, and the rapid liberalization of the economy after re-entry into the global economy, meant that the qualifications framework took on extraordinary significance in South Africa (Allais, 2007c; Mukora, 2006). A policy which appeared to bring unity, to create a single *national* system, and which claimed to integrate mental and manual training, theory and practice, academic and everyday knowledge, and academic and vocational education, achieved widespread support. The idea of a qualifications framework resonated with groups and organizations across the political spectrum, and obtained a high degree of support from educationalists in many different communities. It also seemed to articulate the concerns of a diverse range of contemporary thinking on education and training policy, as expressed in a report commissioned by the Ministers of Education and Labour:

> It was characteristic of South Africa's transition to democracy that people of different political persuasions, bodies working within the formal schooling, training and higher education sectors, public servants and organised business and labour were able to find a strategic patch of common ground … The National Qualifications Framework was established as an emblem and an instrument of the single national high-quality education and training system

that democratic South Africa aspired to create. (Departments of Education and Labour, 2002, p. 5)

Outcomes-based qualifications were seen as a solution not only to the educational problems, but also to the economic problems of apartheid. In a structure called the National Training Board, in the late 1980s and early 1990s, industry representatives involved in discussions with unions and the apartheid state saw the qualifications framework and the idea of outcomes- or competence-based qualifications as a way of addressing the low levels of skills in the workforce and labour market (Allais, 2003; Badroodien & McGrath, 2005; Cooper, 1998; Ensor, 2003). A national qualifications framework that overarched all education and training promised to be a mechanism that would ensure that learning was 'relevant' and of high quality, produce learners who were competent in the workplace, provide access to those previously excluded, recognize the learning that had been achieved informally, ensure that all qualifications were of equal status, and ensure that assessment was transparent and fair. It was hoped that organizing all qualifications and parts of qualifications on a hierarchy of levels would force society to value types of learning programmes which had historically been of low status, which would increase efficiency and encourage more learners to enroll in vocational programmes (HSRC, 1995).

The democratically elected government oversaw a rapid liberalization of the economy (Desaubin, 2002; Marais, 2011). Public sector reform was complex, but there was a strong emphasis on New Public Management-style reforms, introducing performance contracts for public servants and public entities, disaggregating government functions into different cost centres, and privatizing or corporatizing aspects of the state. It was believed that these types of reforms would introduce efficiency and effectiveness. As in the examples in the previous chapter, outcomes-based qualifications seemed to provide a basis for the measurement of private provision as well as the regulation and control of public provision, through providing explicit, formal, and measurable standards against which all education would be measured. This gave weight to the idea that outcomes-based qualifications would become the tools for driving the education system.

The framework was strongly supported by people and organizations who were part of the liberation movement, and who saw it as an emancipatory policy. This was particularly notable within the trade union movement, as it formed part of discussions between trade unions, business representatives, and government about industrial training. Union representatives saw the framework as a way of improving the poor education provided to black people, the difficulties faced by black people in accessing education, and the racist job reservation system which denied jobs to competent black people and sometimes used their lack of formal qualifications as a justification (Bird, 1992). The idea that skills and knowledge learnt through non-formal programmes and informal processes[2] should be certified was important to the unions, who hoped that certification of non-formal learning programmes, as well as of prior learning or informal learning, would formally recognize these forms of knowledge as 'equivalent' to what was learnt in formal educational institutions. They further hoped that this certification would provide redress and facilitate equity in employment. Outcomes seemed to provide a way of validating the knowledge of people who had been deprived of formal education, a way for them to describe their knowledge outside of a deficit model in which their knowledge was seen only in relation to the formal knowledge that they lacked.[3] Because outcomes would be developed separately from specific institutions or specific learning programmes, it was thought that they could be the benchmarks against which all learning was measured—whether the learning had happened in the classroom, the workplace, or simply in the course of life.

In the early 1990s, the policies that the unions developed were fed into the policy development processes within educational organizations that were part of the liberation movement—teacher unions, student organizations, non-governmental organizations, and so on. Although there was obviously much debate within the democratic movement, a national qualifications framework was ultimately adopted by the policy structures of the African National Congress, the then leader of the liberation movement, and soon-to-be dominant party in the new government.

However, despite support from the unionists, and with the exception of adult educationists within the democratic movement, the idea of an outcomes-based curriculum had not emerged from the *educationalists* within the democratic movement, and it had not been a part of the thinking about the curriculum. Curriculum policy was very under-developed in the African National Congress and amongst its allies. Many argue that educationalists were taken by surprise when the idea of learning outcomes emerged (Jansen, 2001).[4] Some were critical, associating outcomes with behaviourism. Others saw commonalities with progressive educational traditions.

There had been intense struggles against apartheid education, under the slogan 'people's education for people's power'. The question of what to teach—what the curriculum should look like—was particularly problematic in South Africa, where education during apartheid had been so clearly used as part of a brutal social engineering project. The ideology of Christian National Education[5] was firmly located in a strongly authoritarian tradition, and the curriculum had been designed to instil a sense of final authority, downplaying the importance of interpretation and debate. Content-based curricula and even the idea of a syllabus came to be seen as authoritarian, and associated with using education for ideological control. People knew, for example, that history as they learnt it in school could not be correct, because in history textbooks they learnt about 'peaceful separate co-existence' and about how all the different 'national groups' in South Africa and the 'independent' countries surrounding it (the so-called Bantustans, which were the small areas of land within South Africa into which different ethnic groups were divided) were happily pursuing their own development within the confines of their own cultural ideas and preferences.

What was clear to the liberation movement was that something more than just arguing for increased access to education was needed. Education must be 'transformed'. The idea of learning outcomes as the vehicle for this transformation gained support amongst educational reformers in South Africa. Outcomes appeared to enable a policy whereby the knowledge of elite groups in educational institutions would not be able to take precedence over the knowledge of the socially disadvantaged. The qualifications framework was designed to remove the power of defining knowledge and skills from formal institutions, and to do away with educational institutions as the source of authority on qualifications. They would no longer define the benchmarks of what was worth knowing, nor be the only arbiters of what learners had achieved. Everyone would have a say in the outcomes of the educational process, instead of only the experts in a particular field. In particular, industry would be able to play a much larger role in defining standards, thus ensuring that education programmes were relevant to the needs of industry, and that industry invested in training[6]. Outcomes were also thought to enable academic freedom, because they would allow academics and teachers to "interpret the meaning of specified learning outcomes in their classrooms in contextually sensitive ways" (Higher Education Quality Council 2003, p. 18).

The notion of competence-based qualifications had already been introduced in the reform of vocational education in the apartheid state in the early 1990s (Gamble, 2004). Jeffy Mukora (2006) suggests that the curriculum reforms developed shortly before the end of apartheid had some similarities with the outcomes-based approach. Perhaps the late apartheid state wanted to appear to be implementing curriculum reforms that were modern and in line with international trends. Or perhaps, seeing the end of their control over the syllabus in sight, educationalists in the apartheid state were sympathetic to an approach which said that no form of knowledge should take precedence over another, because such an approach would make it possible that even after the transition, enclaves of Afrikaans schools would be able to continue teaching what they had in the past. Outcomes-based education, and outcomes-based qualifications seemed to fit in with the spirit of negotiation, reconciliation, and tolerance which characterized the South African transition, because difficult debates about which content to include in the curriculum—which version of history was 'right' for example—could be avoided. Instead, only learning outcomes would be specified nationally. Each teacher would be free to select the appropriate content which would 'lead' to the outcomes (SAQA, 2000c). This not only avoided difficult debates but seemed to provide an alternative to the highly-authoritarian and prescriptive apartheid curriculum: providing an alternative to the idea of 'truth' seemed more radical than providing different 'truths' in the curriculum.

Outcomes were seen as a mechanism for improving quality, because they would specify standards for all educational provision, and all educational institutions would have to meet the standards. Outcomes-based qualifications would indicate to institutions the standard expected of them, and regulatory bodies would be able to check up on what institutions were offering against the prescribed outcomes (SAQA, 2000d). Increased supply of education would lead, it was believed, to competition, which would, it was assumed, improve quality. It was also believed that outcomes-based qualifications would lead to new provision and new institutions (SAQA, 2000d, 2000e). Because any 'provider' would be able to offer learning programmes against the outcome statements, it seemed as if access to education could be increased, and other 'providers' that were not tainted by their role under apartheid, as many educational institutions were felt to be, would also be able to offer educational programmes. And because all providers would be offering programmes leading to the same outcomes, the qualifications framework would "remove the obsession with institutional learning as the measure of a person's worth, because national qualifications will be blind as to where the learning takes place" (HSRC 1995, p. 15).

Further, the model was supposed to facilitate a disaggregation of provision. Instead of learners attending one educational institution to follow one set learning programme, they could go to different providers for smaller parts of a programme. These small parts would all be designed against learning outcomes, which could be put together again into a qualification. Similarly, the idea was for learning programmes to be designed against single unit standards (single competence statements), allowing learners to acquire competences as and when they needed to or were able to. It was hoped that this would empower learners. Outcomes were also seen as the basis for stimulating entrepreneurial provision of new programmes, as, once learning outcomes had been registered on the qualifications framework, any provider would be able to design a learning programme against them. This is the same idea as that discussed above in relation to the National Vocational Qualifications in the United Kingdom: the idea that they would break the 'provider capture' of the 'educational market' (Hursh 2005).

Finally, learning outcomes would be used to remove barriers to education: institutions would have to be clear which outcomes learners needed to have met in order to attain access, and individuals would have a chance to be tested against these outcomes. This would prevent what were widely perceived to be unfair and elitist admission criteria. Outcomes appeared to enable qualifications to be recognized between institutions, because it would be clear what it was that the learner had achieved—what their 'competences' were. Because the competences that someone had achieved would be transparently specified and available for general scrutiny, it would be straightforward to decide which competences were applicable in other courses or programmes that a learner wanted to undertake, meaning that there would be minimal duplication (SAQA, 2000e).

In Chapter 1, I discussed three areas of educational reform that qualifications frameworks are supposed to reform: how qualifications and credentials are used in labour markets; curricula, pedagogy, and assessment; and how education is managed and delivered by the state. All three of these can be seen in South Africa. A national qualifications framework seemed to be a key mechanism to improve how education related to the labour market, and contributed to the economy, by making it more relevant to industry (curriculum reform through learning outcomes), and by increasing quantity, quality, and accountability of provision (learning outcomes as targets for regulatory agencies). It was supposed to improve efficiency of provision, in the interests of the economy and of individuals, by removing unfair barriers, and by ensuring that competences already achieved were recognized through a benchmark provided outside of educational institutions. It was supposed to reform the authoritarian and ideologically-laden apartheid curriculum, but at the same time, by not stipulating content, to contribute to the idea of national unity. It also created unity in a fragmented system by bringing everything within a single national framework. As was seen in Chapter 3 in the United Kingdom, Australia, and New Zealand, in South Africa the idea of outcomes-based qualifications appealed to people with very different political sympathies.

By the early 1990s, then, the idea of outcomes-based education and a national qualifications framework had become central to the education policy of the African National Congress, and, accordingly, was a keystone in the policy reforms introduced by the newly elected government. When the South African Qualifications Authority Act (Republic of South Africa Act No. 58 of 1995) was introduced in 1995, this approach had the backing of all major groupings in South Africa. It was seen as symbolic of the transition to democracy, and the appropriate education policy to unite the divided nation.

Policy Borrowing

We saw in the previous chapter that the policies developed in Australia and New Zealand were both substantially influenced by the earlier English policies. This trend continued in South Africa. While the concerns and aspirations of those involved were specific to South Africa, the substance of the policy ideas was borrowed from the competence-based training system in Australia, the qualifications frameworks in New Zealand, and the English National Vocational Qualifications. Detailed policy proposals drawing on all three countries were developed by representatives of unions and industry in the early design stages (Badroodien & McGrath, 2005; Lugg, 2007).

The English National Vocational Qualifications were not frequently invoked in the design of the South African qualifications framework. One influential policy maker refers directly to them (Vorwerk, 2004), but others sought explicitly to distance themselves from this model, and develop what they believed to be a 'broader' notion of outcomes (French, 2009). The negative associations of the English model may in part have caused the South Africa policy makers to abandon the word 'competence', and adopt instead 'learning outcomes'. South African policy documents argued explicitly that the latter term was broader and less behaviourist. It could also be that policy makers were looking for policy coherence, as the notion of outcomes had already become prevalent in curriculum reform of the school system, mainly through the ideas of William Spady discussed in Chapter 2. South Africa did not officially adopt 'functional analysis'—as described in the previous chapter, the idea that the starting point in designing a qualification should be an analysis of occupational functions, conducted by employers. Unlike in the United Kingdom, the South African qualifications framework was comprehensive, aiming to cover all education at all levels, so it would have been impossible for all learning outcomes to be derived from the workplace; many of the unit standards and qualifications developed did not have a direct relationship with specific industries. Nonetheless, the outcomes-based approach, where it did not directly relate to a specific area of work, still started from 'activities in the real world', as opposed to knowledge areas or subjects—much along the lines of the invocation of Bobbit's 'activity analysis' discussed in Chapter 2. What's more, although functional analysis was not adopted, a very similar approach to functional analysis was used in the detailed requirements and specifications for qualifications and unit standards that were created, as well as in the manuals and guidelines for their development (SAQA2000a, 2000b, 2000c, 2000d, 2000e), with the resultant qualifications looking substantively the same as the English National Vocational Qualifications and the Australian training packages.

It is interesting to note the curious balancing act in the policy community of, on the one hand, using international experts, and referring to models in other countries as a way of legitimating their ideas, and, on the other hand, stressing the homegrownness of the policies developed (Spreen 2001). Spreen (2001, p. 186) argues that once outcomes-based education had been indigenized, its international origins "vanished from official documentation". This is evident in various official histories. For example, writing on the history of the qualifications framework in one of its reports, the South African Qualifications Authority argues:

> The [South African] NQF is a distinctly South African phenomenon that has been developed in a unique political and historical context. The concepts and organizing principles were drawn from similar developments in Scotland, England, New Zealand, and Australia in the mid to late 1980s. Nevertheless, it is important to emphasize the essentially South African nature of the NQF and its roots in opposition to apartheid. (SAQA 2004f, p. 22)

New Structures, New Qualifications

The idea of the qualifications framework in South Africa was to replace *all* existing qualifications in the country with a set of new qualifications and part qualifications (called unit standards) designed by new, stakeholder-based structures, and expressed in the form of learning outcomes. This, it was hoped, would ensure that new learning programmes and curricula would be developed. No existing educational provision would remain untouched—all educational institutions would be obliged to redesign their programmes on the basis of these specified outcomes, or to develop new programmes to meet the requirements of specified outcomes, and new providers would be able to emerge to offer new programmes against the specified learning outcomes. All would be held accountable by newly created quality assurance bodies. The apartheid education system would, in this way, be completely transformed.

A South African Qualifications Authority (SAQA) was created through an Act of Parliament in 1995, as an independent statutory body under the joint oversight of the Ministries of Education and Labour. A single comprehensive framework of eight levels and 12 fields was developed. This grid was supposed to include all learning that took place in South Africa, at all levels, in all areas. The key design feature was learning outcomes, developed separately from educational institutions and educational programmes, against which learning would be delivered, assessed, quality assured, and certified.

The South African Qualifications Authority created both permanent and *ad hoc* structures to develop the outcomes-based qualifications and unit standards which would populate the eight levels[7] and 12 fields[8] of the national qualifications framework. These included 12 permanent national standards bodies and a large number of standards generating bodies, created on an *ad hoc* basis. The national standards bodies were stakeholder-based bodies, which were given responsibility for overseeing the development of qualifications and unit standards in each of the fields of the qualifications framework.

The standards generating bodies, comprised of representatives of experts and interest groups (SAQA 2000c, d), were supposed to develop the outcomes-based qualifications and unit standards for all education and training in South Africa (SAQA, 2000a, 2000b). These would then populate the levels and fields of the qualifications framework. Gradually, it was hoped, all previous qualifications would disappear. Only the new qualifications and unit standards would remain. None of them would have a direct relationship to an educational provider—they would all be national qualifications.

New qualifications and unit standards soon started rolling off the mill, apparently in every conceivable area: from National Certificates in *Macadamia production and de-husking, Cigarette Filter Rod Production,* and *Resolving of Crime,* to Further Education and Training Certificates in *Victim Empowerment Coordination* and *Real Estate.*

All of these qualifications were outcomes-based, and most were comprised of unit standards, which had titles ranging from the extremely specific—*Manage venomous animals, Assist a frail care patient to relieve him/herself using a bedpan, Prepare, cook and assemble hot filled baked potatoes,* or *Pack customer purchases at point of sale*—to the curiously broad—*Show, explain, discuss and analyse the relationship between society and natural environment, Demonstrate an understanding of climate and weather in the context of renewable energy, Apply biblical models of transformation to perceived needs of the community, Explain and apply the principles of conceptual thinking,* and *Describe ideologies in community contexts.*

According to the original model of the qualifications framework, educational providers would be accredited by quality assurance bodies to offer programmes leading to specific qualifications. The quality assurance bodies would check up on how well they were doing this, and on whether or not they were assessing learners appropriately against the learning outcomes (SAQA 2000e). A set of quality assurance bodies was created. Two were created under the Minister of Education: one for all education below tertiary education, and one for Higher Education. These bodies were created through acts of Parliament. Another 25 were created for different sectors of the economy, as parts of bodies called Sectoral Education and Training Authorities (SETAs), which were under the authority of the Minister of Labour. These bodies were set up through a 'skills levy', whereby employers were levied one per cent of their payroll (Republic of South Africa, 1998). The employers could get most of it paid back by proving to their relevant SETA that they were conducting training. Ten per cent of the levy funded the running costs of the SETAs. These bodies had to apply for accreditation from the South African Qualifications Authority in order to be recognized as quality assurance authorities.

Outcomes-Based Education for the School System

At the same time as the South African Qualifications Authority was developing the qualifications framework along the lines described above, the Department of Education started developing an outcomes-based curriculum for the primary and junior secondary education system, known as Curriculum 2005. This was to be the major curriculum reform of the democratic South Africa, intended to be phased first into the primary and junior secondary system, and later into the senior secondary system. This is similar to the situation in Australia and New Zealand, where an outcomes-based curriculum for the school system was introduced alongside the competence-based training system for vocational education (Australia), or as part of the qualifications framework (New Zealand).

Curriculum 2005 will not be discussed or evaluated in detail here. Briefly, the Department of Education tried to do away with disciplinary areas or subjects, through the specification of learning outcomes, and by putting a strong focus on learner-centredness (Harley and Wedekind 2004). Sixty-six specific outcomes were specified, which were supposed to contain "the specific knowledge, understanding, skills, values and attitudes which should be demonstrated by learners in the context of each learning area", and each outcome, like the unit standards and whole qualifications of the qualifications framework, was associated with assessment criteria that identified "the kind of evidence that must be gathered in order to be able to report that learners have met a specific outcome" (Spreen 2001, p. 112). In other words, this curriculum separated the idea of learning outcomes from the idea of content or knowledge (Curriculum 2005 Review Committee, 2000; Muller, 2000; Taylor, 2000).

Initially, there was a clear relationship between the emerging national qualifications framework and the outcomes-based curriculum for the school system (Lugg, 2007). However, the Department of Education developed its curriculum separately from the structures and processes of the South African qualifications framework. It drew heavily on the ideas of American education reformer William Spady whom, as Spreen

(2001) points out, the unions had also encountered in outcomes-based education in Australia. Many analysts have emphasized the differences between the outcomes-based curriculum developed by the Department of Education and the qualifications framework. Muller (2004), for example, describes the school curriculum as drawing on a progressivist thread that, he argues, had long existed in certain circles in South Africa. Because of its emphasis on continuous assessment and against examinations, and because of its long progressivist heritage, he argues that it was at odds with the qualifications framework, which he characterizes as systemically-driven, with a centralized framework and a 'one-size-fits-all' epistemology. Curriculum 2005, on the other hand, was teacher and learner driven, with highly particularized and individualized assessment procedures. But reformers within adult education and some within vocational education who could be characterized as progressivists saw the qualifications framework as similarly individualized. Both the qualifications framework and Curriculum 2005 were based on the idea of centrally prescribed 'outcomes', with individual teachers and trainers designing their own courses around the needs of their specific learners, using decentralized assessment instead of examinations. The two policies shared the same premises, as well as sharing much of the same terminology and jargon. However, although the Department of Education bought into the idea of outcomes-based education, it went on its own in terms of actual implementation of the outcomes-based curriculum for the schools, creating the impression that it was doing something fundamentally different. The Department continued exploring the policies of other countries, specifically engaging with policy makers from New Zealand, Canada, Scotland, England and the Netherlands, and in 1996 was involved in a set of study tours to look at competence-based education, invited and paid for by the Australian government (Spreen 2001). William Spady was a particularly significant influence (Spreen 2001). Visiting South Africa in 1998, he spoke at two conferences, and worked with the departmental officials who pushed the development of outcomes-based education in the Department.

The outcomes-based school curriculum led to a crisis in schools very quickly after its implementation, as many teachers simply had no idea what to teach, and the technical complexity of the curriculum was overwhelming for teachers (Allais, 2010a; Curriculum 2005 Review Committee, 2000; Jansen, 2002; Taylor, 2000). A review was commissioned by the Minister of Education, which reported by 2000 (RSA Department of Education 2000). Major changes were made to the curriculum, without, however, officially abandoning the idea of outcomes-based education.

Failures of the NQF in South Africa

Very few concrete claims are made, even by the South African Qualifications Authority, about what the qualifications framework has achieved. The main achievements which are claimed are the development of qualifications and the 'shifting of consciousness'. With regard to the former, most of the qualifications that were developed have not been used. And most people who obtain qualifications in South Africa obtain qualifications that were developed and designed outside of the elaborate representative structures established to develop outcomes-based qualifications and unit standards. These structures have in the main been disbanded. Thus there is little that has concretely been achieved. With regard to the latter, a report published by South African Qualifications Authority (French, 2009) claims that the qualifications framework has shifted thinking about educational quality, curriculum design, and assessment, and a relatively recent presentation by the Authority's former Chief Executive argues that the existence of the qualifications framework has "increased awareness" about quality assurance in higher education (Isaacs, 2009). Even if these claims were testable and found to be true, it is far from clear that the 'shifts' that they purport to have achieved are desirable.

Despite its well-meaning goals, as well as its wide support across the political spectrum, the implementation of the South African qualifications framework was fraught with problems. Critics described it as "complex and esoteric" (Breier 1998, p. 74), and "large, unwieldy, expensive, complex and somewhat unstable", as well as "out of line with the *modus operandi* of the formal education sector" (Ensor 2003, p. 334). Many people and organizations felt alienated by the terminology and structures that were set up around the qualifications framework, as they were unfamiliar to them, and did not fit with the traditional concerns of educational institutions (RSA Departments of Education and Labour 2002). Lugg (2007) documents the increasing unease of trade unionists, who were unable to participate meaningfully, partly due to the huge number of structures that had been created, and partly because of the alienating jargon that had increasingly been adopted. An employee of the South African Qualifications Authority, Nadina Coetzee, describes the implementation of the qualifications framework as characterized by "intense debate, tension and even resistance" (SAQA 2004a, p. 79).

In 2000, only three years after implementation had really started, there was an announcement of an official review. A lengthy (seven year) period of policy reviews ensued. Before it had even started, there were disagreements about the terms of reference for the review between the Ministry of Labour and the Ministry of Education (Lugg, 2007). When the review was completed, the two departments were unable to agree with each other on the review recommendations (French, 2009; Lugg, 2007). The review team suggested that both in terms of their analysis of the problems and in terms of their ideas about what should be done about them, the Departments of Education and Labour were "mirror-images" of each other (RSA Departments of Education and Labour 2002, p. 33).

During the review period (2000 to 2008), with no resolution and no policy pronouncements coming from its sponsoring departments, the South African Qualifications Authority continued to develop the qualifications framework largely according to its original design. Standard generating bodies continued to generate standards, quality assurance bodies to accredit providers, the Authority to register qualifications and unit standards, and so on. As Merlyn Mehl put it, writing in the *SAQA Bulletin*,

> ...[u]nit standards, qualifications, qualification-sets and qualifications frameworks are more and more rapidly coming off the production line. (Mehl, 2004, p. 42)

By March 2005, 696 unit standards-based qualifications and 8,208 unit standards had been registered on the qualifications framework. The vast majority of the new qualifications and unit standards that were developed were never used—by 2007, only 180 of the then 787 newly developed qualifications had ever been awarded to learners. In other words, many hundreds of qualifications which were developed had not been taught, assessed against, or awarded.[9] By 2007, 130 qualifications were allowed to lapse after their official term ended, signalling that no one was interested in offering them, and 2,013 unit standards similarly elapsed, although some were replaced.

At the same time as these new qualifications were being developed, educational institutions were asked to submit their existing qualifications to the South African Qualifications Authority, for 'interim registration' on the framework (SAQA, 1997). These qualifications were referred to as 'legacy' qualifications; the intention was that they would be phased out as soon as new qualifications had been designed. A transitional period of five years (from 1 January 1998 to 31 December 2002) was announced, after which they would fall away. A dual reality soon emerged. On the one side was the national qualifications framework, with its unit standards, ideas about individualized assessment conducted by registered assessors, and particular ideas about quality assurance. On the other side was the formal education and training system, which never complied with the new models introduced through the qualifications framework.

For example, the individualized approach to assessment which was central to the design of the qualifications framework was not adopted by the formal education system. Young (2005) argues that outcomes-based qualifications frameworks are really assessment frameworks—because they aim to stipulate the competences or outcomes that learners should have achieved, by whichever route. The idea was that instead of national examinations, which, it was argued, tested limited skills, and did not cater for individual strengths and weaknesses, individuals would all be assessed against the learning outcomes, and found competent or not yet competent. Standards would be maintained through the outcomes:

> Reliability is ensured in that specified standards, outcomes and competences and their accompanying criteria are the basis upon which assessment is planned and administered. These are a constant, regardless of who is assessing and who is being assessed. Laying down these specifications makes it incumbent upon the assessor to use them as a guide in planning, developing and administering

assessment. Because they are specific, known and clearly understood by all who are affected, they act as an in-built mechanism against assessor inconsistency, deviation or error. (Mokhobo-Nomvete, 1999)

Further, anyone who wanted to conduct assessment would have to be registered as an assessor. An assessment unit standard, with various learning outcomes, was developed. Quality assurance bodies were supposed to 'register' assessors who were found competent against this standard. The South African Qualifications Authority gave a four-year grace period for this to happen, ending in May 2004 (SAQA, 2001b). In some areas, particularly amongst providers of vocational or workplace-based training who had to deal with the new sectoral quality assurance bodies, there was a rush to get registered as an assessor, and correspondingly, a flurry of income-generation for institutions offering 'assessor training' against the standard. But despite the Authority's official proclamation that registration against this standard would be a requirement for all assessors, the Department of Education did not require educators under its auspices (i.e. teachers in state schools, and lecturers in public colleges and universities) to be registered as assessors. People working in schools and universities did not rush down this route, and very few were registered as assessors. School and college certificates continued to be assessed through a national examinations system.

Sometimes there was formal compliance with the qualifications framework. For example, higher education institutions would develop their qualifications and curricula as per their usual practice, and then have them 'translated' into learning outcomes in order to formally submit them to the South African Qualifications Authority. The Department of Education operated largely without reference to the qualifications framework. It developed a new senior secondary qualification for the school system, with an accompanying new curriculum, using its own systems and structures.

During this period in which the framework was under official review, the period of 'interim registration' of the 'legacy' qualifications was extended, until June 2006. The South African Qualifications Authority started referring to 'provider' qualifications instead of 'interim' qualifications, suggesting a shift in the way these qualifications were thought of, and perhaps an acceptance that they might start to be a permanent feature of the qualifications frameworks. The National Standards Bodies were disbanded. So while the intention was for the framework to replace all existing qualifications, it soon started incorporating them instead. And these previously existing qualifications were the ones which, in the main, were awarded to learners. The formal education and training system contained the vast majority of learners studying and qualifications being awarded in South Africa. Thus, the national qualifications framework, at least according to its design, was largely ignored by the systems issuing the vast majority of qualifications.

From the point of view of formal institutions, it seems that the qualifications framework was a house of cards. However, it was not entirely ignored. It increasingly came to dominate organisations providing workplace-based training, short courses for communities, on-going professional development, as well as any kind of community development work that involved education and training. The sectoral quality assurance authorities increasingly required all providers wishing to be accredited with them to offer unit-standard based courses. Complex quality assurance procedures were set up that were highly onerous for providers and gave limited information about the actual quality of provision (Marock, 2011). Given that these bodies had large amounts of money at their disposal—they were set up through a payroll levy which providers were desperate to access—many converted their offerings to comply with the unit standards and unit standards based qualifications. The National Skills Fund, a fund set up to channel 20% of the payroll levy into training programmes for unemployed people and training focused on community development, also required applications to be based on unit standards-based qualifications or unit standards.

With hindsight, the different behaviour of formal and informal institutions was probably inevitable. Formal education institutions, for better or for worse, tend to be conservative bodies. The formal system in South Africa was no exception. Although uneven—with some strong and many very dysfunctional institutions—there were institutionalized ways of doing things that continued to operate. But the world of training, informal education, community development, and so on, did not have the same institutionalized ways of operating, and, further, was in general much more fragile. It did not have the same ability to continue with business as usual. The non-governmental sector in South Africa suffered enormously when funding dried up after the end of apartheid, and donors started to channel their money directly to the state. This fragile sector, desperate for funds, tried in whatever ways it could to comply with the official requirements of the education and training system which were, ironically, ignored by the actual education and training system.

A Revised Framework

The lengthy policy review was finally terminated in 2008. The qualifications framework was split into three separate but linked frameworks—one for higher education, one for schools and vocational education and training, and one for trades and occupational education. The first two of the sub-frameworks were to be under the Minister of Education, and the third under the Minister of Labour. The outcomes-based model was partially abandoned. The unit standards and unit standards-based qualifications remain on the framework, but most have still never been used.

The first of the two sub-frameworks represent the formal education and training system—the learning programmes offered and qualifications issued in universities, colleges, schools, and adult learning centres. As discussed above, in practice they had abandoned the original model of the qualifications framework years before. The frameworks that emerged, then, were much more in keeping with the practices and systems of the formal system—they functioned more to describe the system than to shape it, although some changes to types of qualifications were introduced, and there is still much debate about relationships between qualifications at the time of writing. Both sub-frameworks comprised a small number of 'qualification types', such as Bachelor's Degree. By 2011, the higher education framework contained 9, and the general and further education and training framework contained 12, as compared with the thousands of qualifications registered on the original framework. In 2009, the Minister of Basic Education introduced changes to the school curriculum, and finally declared that outcomes-based education is officially dead in South Africa.

The third framework is less developed at the time of writing. Some initial policy documents stipulated a combination of different types of reconceptualized unit standards. The initial approach was to develop qualifications and awards based on an Organising Framework for Occupations, which contained a 5-level classification system for organising occupations into clusters and identifying common features at successively higher levels of generalization. The claim was that by starting from a framework of occupations, and by ensuring that qualifications were designed by 'occupational practitioners', learners would qualify in an occupation, as opposed to in a knowledge domain, which would ensure that they would get a job. This framework, then, seems closest to at least some of the original claims made about the national qualifications framework. In the training or vocational education world, outcomes-based education seems to be very much alive, as in many instances providers are still required to use unit standards-based qualifications (Allais, 2012b), although a Green Paper released by the Department of Higher Education and Training says explicitly that this should no longer be seen as a requirement (DHET, 2012). The same document signals further possible changes to the qualifications framework.

In Chapter 1, I introduced a distinction between frameworks that primarily describe existing systems, and frameworks that are intended to replace existing qualifications and so introduce substantial changes to education systems. The South African framework was clearly of the latter type in its original design, with major claims or hopes about what it could achieve. The revised framework abandons the original design, and by implication, although not official policy proclamation, abandons the claims or hopes about what it can achieve. This is particularly worth noting because the differences between the old and new framework are not immediately apparent to an outside observer. A framework of sorts still exists, and strong claims continue to be made about the role of outcomes-based qualifications frameworks.

Despite the serious problems and manifest lack of success of the South African qualifications framework, it has played an important role internationally. Linda Chisholm (2007) explores the role of financial and technical 'assistance', as well as of conferences and consultants, in spreading outcomes-based education and the national qualifications framework to southern and eastern Africa, and the ways in which "particular coalitions in South Africa have tried hard to export their own brand of the NQF and OBE." Referring to a 'discourse coalition' brought together by the South African Qualifications Authority "in the wake of the review of the

NQF which had proposed a significant diminution of its authority", Chisholm describes how "the donor, Danish International Development Agency (DANIDA), a team from qualifications framework structures and NGOs in South Africa, and consultants, trainers and others working in the field of qualifications and industry training from Australia, New Zealand, the United Kingdom, Mexico and representatives from 9 SADC countries" contributed to the popularization of this approach internationally, even as serious doubt about it was growing in South Africa (Chisholm, 2007, p. 203).

SIMILAR TRAJECTORIES IN OTHER POOR AND
MIDDLE INCOME COUNTRIES

The limited evidence available from other developing countries suggests many similar problems.

Unused Qualifications

The most startling common research finding is that qualifications frameworks have led to the creation of new qualifications which do not get used. In other words, qualifications based on learning outcomes, developed in processes which attempted to be participatory, and involved industry or relevant stakeholders, led to the development of new qualifications which then sat on qualifications frameworks, with no corresponding provision of education programmes. This is not unique to poorer countries. As discussed in the previous chapter, it is the case even in the relatively successful Australian competence-based training system. In most of the small number of countries internationally that have actually attempted to implement a framework, qualifications have been developed and not used. But it is most dramatically visible in countries where education levels are low, and provision is weak or haphazard. Besides the South African case, the starkest examples of this are Botswana, Mauritius, and Mexico.

In Botswana, a qualifications framework was created specifically for vocational education: the Botswana National Vocational Qualifications Framework. The Botswana Training Authority, an institution created in 1998, was mandated to develop a framework, and, after a four year planning and staff development programme that started in 2000, began to implement the framework in August 2004. As in South Africa, qualifications consisted of parts—known as unit standards—which could be separately awarded, and which were defined through learning outcomes or competences. Like in the United Kingdom and all the countries which have followed this model, the intention was that employers would be involved in creating these unit standards, in order to ensure that training would be relevant to the labour market. In line with the notion of 'functional analysis', workplace operations were to be the context for setting outcomes statements, which would be broken down into specific outcomes and performance criteria for the purposes of assessment. Task teams were constituted, initially located in 15 key economic sectors. Stakeholders were trained in designing unit standards. The unit standards produced look similar to their counterparts in other countries. Similar rules and structures were established.

The results? The development of unit standards was slow. Even slower, however, was the uptake of the unit standards once they had been developed. In 2008, 124 training providers were registered by the Botswana Training Authority, offering a total of 643 approved programmes. In a country with a small population, this probably accounted for a sizable percentage of educational providers. However, most of these providers did not offer courses based on the newly developed standards. Only ten of them used the unit standards registered on the qualifications framework. In other words, out of the 643 programmes offered across the 124 institutions under the qualifications framework, only ten programmes complied with the unit standards specifications.

Although the belief was that industry involvement in standards-setting would lead to relevant training programmes, the Botswana Confederation of Commerce and Industry did not adopt the unit-standards based qualifications. At the time of our research, government-run vocational colleges were also not using them. There were no official records of how many learners had actually been awarded unit standards, but based on the numbers of courses offered, they would be extremely low. Most of the unit standards have never been used.

The most used unit standards were 'generic' ones, such as using computers and learning about HIV/AIDS, which have no direct workplace link. Although no formal evaluation or tracer studies had been conducted, individuals interviewed felt that where courses had been conducted and unit standards awarded, they have not led to jobs or further study, the former because of a lack of available jobs, and the latter because there is no articulation between the vocational qualifications framework and the rest of the education system. However, in two instances, employer organizations which participated in the development of curricula and the formulation of unit standards felt that the qualification acquired by employees was relevant to the workplace.

In Mauritius, legislation was passed in 2001 that created the Mauritius Qualifications Authority and a qualifications framework. This framework was a bit like that in Australia, where a fairly loose comprehensive framework encompasses a much tighter framework for vocational education. For higher education, the focus was on making sense of the 'jungle of qualifications', rationalizing the number of qualifications, and attempting to make them easier to understand. In vocational education, where the now familiar outcomes-/ competence-based model was introduced, the aim of the qualifications was to introduce substantial reform to both the curriculum and the delivery of education and training. The Mauritian Qualifications Authority was in charge of the qualifications framework, but it had far more jurisdiction over vocational education and training than over other areas. In vocational education, it was made responsible for the generation of new qualifications and unit standards. As in South Africa, Australia, the United Kingdom, and New Zealand, the model was essentially competence-based training, with the intention of giving industry a central role in defining its required competences. Industry Training Advisory Committees were created. It was anticipated that the qualifications developed would replace the existing qualifications as well as create qualifications and unit standards in areas that had previously not had formal qualifications. According to the qualifications authority, 66 qualifications were generated, although public information is only available on about 20 of these qualifications and 476 unit standards. In 2009, at the time of our research, *none of these qualifications had been used by educational institutions or employers*, and there was no designated awarding body for them. The main state provider, the Industrial and Vocational Training Board, as well as many private providers, continued to offer the National Training Certificate that predated the qualifications framework. This qualification has a specified curriculum, and is assessed and certified through the Mauritian Examinations Syndicate or relevant international bodies.

In Mexico, a labour competence framework was initially envisaged as a framework for qualifications in vocational education and training, as well as in workplace-based training, but ended up focused on the latter, where it was used mainly for the assessment of prior learning. Providers of vocational education did not accept or use the standards. The competence standards developed described mainly low levels of competence in the workplace, and many competence standards were developed that were never used.

A five level framework was developed, with the levels derived from an analysis of the complexity of labour involved, the degree of autonomy of performance, and the different activities included in the qualification (Klapp, 2003). Lead bodies, including representatives of employers and workers as well as sector experts, used the English National Vocational Qualification 'functional analysis' approach to produce competence standards. Awarding bodies were accredited to verify the quality of the assessment centres in which candidates were to be assessed against standards. From 1996 to 2003, 601 competence standards were registered. A very small number of these were ever issued to learners. From 1998 to 2003, 256,282 certificates were issued against these qualifications. One qualification generated 29.7 per cent of the certificates, and 80.7 per cent of the issued certificates corresponded to only 26 qualifications. Those qualifications which were used were linked to specific government-driven programmes. Although the overall project included a focus on educational institutions, in most instances the standards developed did not relate to their courses, so they developed their own standards. Pilot projects were commenced in seven priority industries, and Tourism and Electricity reported some gains in terms of learners achieving certificates.

One reason for this is the inherent clumsiness of outcomes-based qualifications, as well as contradictions between them and the way in which educational institutions usually develop curricula, which will be discussed in Chapter 6. Another is the shift to a regulatory state *à la* New Public Management, in contexts where state provision was already poor; in other words, reliance on the emergence of a market of providers, in the context of weak educational institutions. This is explored below.

The Regulatory State and Weak Institutions

Neoliberalism in the developing world, implemented through structural adjustment programmes and other types of loans with heavy conditionalities which have prevented the building of welfare states, has entrenched the privatization of limited state provided services and welfare, as well as deregulation of the economy. Simon McGrath (2010) describes a 'toolkit' of reform for vocational education in developing countries which is very much within the paradigm of New Public Management. This 'toolkit' starts from the premise that improving individual's 'employability' is a better way to bring the poor into the social and economic mainstream than is the redistribution of wealth. It includes systemic reform focused on: giving more power to employers in the shaping of policy directions, often through qualifications frameworks; quality assurance systems; outcomes-based and 'institutionally-neutral' funding (such as voucher type systems); and managed autonomy for public providers. In recent years, aid money for vocational education in developing countries has increased, as has technical assistance from a variety of international organizations. The World Bank, long-time critic of vocational education, has started advocating building vocational education systems. With this has come a shift from traditional notions of building technical skills, to a focus on skills as the basis for entrepreneurship. 'Aid' money has been channelled into reforms that fit within this toolkit.

In our study, the rationales given for the introduction of qualifications frameworks mainly included this type of logic (Allais, 2010b). In Botswana, South Africa, and Sri Lanka (as well as in more developed countries such as Russia and Turkey, although these are not the focus of the current chapter), outcomes-based qualifications were explicitly described by policy makers as necessary to shift what was seen as a 'provider culture' or a 'provider captured' system, to a 'user-led' or 'learner-centred', competition-based or marketized system. In Mauritius, the Industrial and Vocational Training Board, the main provider of vocational education in that country, was responsible for the registration of private vocational education providers prior to the introduction of the qualifications framework. One of the rationales of the qualifications framework was to introduce a new institution, the Mauritian Qualifications Authority, to take over the function of registration of providers, in order to separate provision from quality assurance, and to have a body which could hold *all* providers accountable, including the state provider. In Bangladesh, a framework for vocational education was supposed to bring coherence to a large and complex set of providers, including many government ministries, private institutions and non-governmental institutions. But at the time of our study, the documents associated with the qualifications framework had very little to say about these institutions—how they would be funded and supported, where provision will come from, and so on. The idea seemed to be that designing new qualifications which contained competence statements or learning outcomes as the benchmark for all provision, whether offered in formal education and training, workplace training, or on-the-job training in the formal and informal economy, would in itself regulate and therefore enable provision.

In some of the countries, this type of approach was explicitly based on commitments to neoliberal market policies and principles. In many others this was not explicit. What was common to many of the countries in our study was an emphasis on treating state and private institutions in the same way through contractualization and the introduction of accountability measures, in the belief that this would increase efficiency and effectiveness.

Most critical commentary on quality assurance agrees that it has a strong focus on marketization (for example, Vidovich & Slee, 2001). But most of this commentary is in the developed world. Marketization is applied to education systems that *exist*, and that are reasonably strong. Using market-based or New Public Management type models where delivery systems do not exist, or are very small and/or very weak, is an entirely different matter.

Some years ago, Young (2005, p. 14) pointed out that

[t]he sub-Saharan countries … are attempting to introduce an NQF with relatively low levels of institutional provision. They presumably hope that an NQF will either act as a substitute for the lack of institutional provision by encouraging the accreditation of informal learning, or that it will act as a catalyst to motivate new provision, especially from the private sector. The danger is that qualifications will proliferate where there is no provision leading to them. An expensive activity without obvious wider benefits.

The limited body of critical research into qualifications frameworks that has been carried out since then, describes the failures of this type of reform in developing countries almost exactly along the lines of Young's prediction. As Gert Loose (2008) argues, one of the biggest problems with the promotion of competence-based training in developing countries is that what these countries actually need is the creation of an effective training system—the development of institutions, programmes, and curricula. These are just the things that outcomes-based qualifications frameworks and competence-based training do not address: competence-based training, Loose argues, has provided "*the definition of competencies and the methodology for assessing them*; but it *failed* to provide the "T" in CBET, a learning process as the basis for the creation of *training* itself" (Loose, 2008, p. 76, emphasis in original). So, for example, policy makers that I interviewed in Bangladesh argued that including a specification of 'pre-vocational' qualifications on the Technical and Vocational National Qualifications Framework would lead to increased access, as many people would not have the basic education needed to access vocational qualifications. However, there were no policy mechanisms under consideration other than specifying these qualifications. The assumption was that once qualifications had been specified, provision would start: institutions would take them up and start offering them, thereby increasing access to education and training. But there was no plan for which institutions would offer them, no notion of developing a curriculum or learning programme, no clear notion of who would teach them. This epitomizes Loose's point above: this model fails to provide the 'T', the training itself; it simply assumes that it will happen.

I was approached recently by an international non-governmental organization that had won a European Commission grant to develop a national vocational qualifications framework for Somalia. The assumption behind the project was that once clear standards had been set, educational providers would be able to emerge, and offer programmes against these standards, and that their provision could be evaluated against them. This is an extreme example: a country which for many years has not even had a functional government, far less any kind of systematic education provision provision, is given development aid on the premise that specified standards will be developed which will somehow lead to or enable provision. But the extremity of this particular situation is not that far removed from many other countries—from Angola to Afghanistan—that are implementing outcomes-based qualifications frameworks with assistance from development agencies and colleagues in qualifications authorities of other countries. And in South Africa, with a relatively extensive school and higher education system, but where provision was still extremely weak—in adult education, vocational and occupational education, and so on—the specification of outcomes-based qualifications resulted in little more than a large set of outcomes-based qualifications, never used by anyone. The irony is that reliance on the market to expand provision may make it less likely that education is responsive to the needs of the economy or society.

The focus on outcomes/ standards/ competences, as well as quality assurance and accreditation, shifts attention away from learning processes, and the need to build and support educational institutions to ensure that learning happens. Quality assurance systems do not *build* quality, they build procedures that *claim* to *measure* quality. Sadly, they can end up being used as a substitute for building quality. Poorer countries, and countries with weak institutions, may find themselves facing a whole new set of problems if they rely too much on such mechanisms. This issue may be most stark in technical and vocational education, where a considerable infrastructure of workshops and other facilities is required in order to ensure quality. Models which narrowly link funding to learner enrolments and outcomes-based qualifications may not encourage institutions to take a long-term perspective, and are unlikely to provide the necessary incentives for building and developing institutions. Qualifications frameworks and competence-based reforms are often introduced with the professed aim of promoting the 'autonomy' and 'empowerment' of vocational institutions. However, 'autonomy' without increased capacity, without increased financial support, and with a series of new 'accountability' requirements, may turn out to be rather less empowering for institutions than is claimed, and governments are unlikely to get the desired results. This is why, as Claudio de Moura Castro (2000, p. 263) writes, "all industrial countries—with absolutely no exceptions—operate large public training systems financed from regular budgets". De Moura

Castro (2000) also points out that governments which are not strong enough to repair institutions often have enough power to destroy them. This, sadly, may be the net effect of neoliberal public sector reform and the focus on contractualization in the delivery of education.

Further, setting up a viable accreditation system is a costly endeavour, and is based on the assumption that bureaucracies which are putatively incompetent at delivering good training are likely to be good or at least better at contracting it out and managing quality, or, that new institutions created for this purpose will be able to do so with no track record or institutional history. Conducting meaningful evaluation of educational quality is costly and time-consuming, and demands high levels of professional capacity amongst staff. This type of approach can lead to more emphasis on building quality assurance institutions and accreditation systems than on building educational institutions.

A model of decentralized, institution-based assessment has most potential to be effective when it is based on very strong institutions. Where institutions have substantially divergent standards, the outcome statements—notwithstanding all their detailed specifications—are not sufficient to 'hold the standard', to ensure that all teaching and/or assessment is at the same or a similar level. Thus, far more quality assurance is required—checking up on the institution, each assessment, and so on. The weaker the institutions, the more expensive this type of model is. Clearly, no country wants to spend more on quality assurance than it spends on provision. While registration and accreditation processes are important, they prove costly, time consuming, and ultimately ineffective, in the absence of more traditional quality measures such as prescribed curricula and centrally-set assessments[10].

In the context of vocational education systems which are underfunded, countries which want to improve educational quality need to make serious choices between focusing on improving the capacity of education institutions or on increasing quality assurance. Managing contracts and evaluating the performance of contracted institutions, whether public or private, demands enormous regulatory capacity from the state, and possibly leads to many additional expenses for the various players in the education and training system. South Africa, for example, now has a huge and complex set of regulatory institutions and processes that oversees a tiny, diverse, but mainly extremely weak system of vocational and occupational education (Allais, 2012b).

Our research, although conducted while qualifications frameworks were in fairly preliminary stages in many of the countries, suggests that there may be problems in many of the countries in the study; while there have been new developments in all the countries, there is little research available. In Botswana, the training authority which was supposed to accredit providers found this work difficult to carry out, particularly when donor funds that had initially supported it dried up. Subsequent to our research, a comprehensive National Qualifications Framework for Botswana has been developed, and legislation passed to create a new authority, as well as a human resource development council; however, implementation has not yet begun.

101

In Mauritius, while the qualifications authority officially took over the function of registering providers of vocational education and training, the Industrial and Vocational Training Board, the state provider of vocational education, continued to play a role in quality assurance for private providers that offered the National Training Certificate, the qualification that predated the new outcomes-based qualifications framework. In Mexico, because the criteria to become an assessing or awarding centre were so stringent, there were few assessment agencies, and these bodies charged high prices for assessment. In South Africa the plethora of quality assurance institutions initially introduced has been substantially changed after there was very little evidence of improved quality, and even some evidence that it had made it impossible for non-profit and community-based organizations to offer education programmes.

Reiterations of Policies and Complex Institutions

Another commonality across many countries is the reiteration of different versions of standards, outcomes, and so on, as well as of structures. 'Embedded' knowledge is renamed 'underpinning' knowledge, range statements (which attempt to define the context in which the learning outcomes or competences will be evaluated) are developed, and changed; the format of assessment criteria is changed.

The Mexican labour competences, for example, were reiterated in many different ways, as each proved to be differently interpreted by key stakeholders. The labour competence framework was developed through two complex multi-faceted projects. Both of these projects were concerned with vocational, technical, and workplace training, as well as broader human resource development. The first project, which began in 1994 through the Secretariat of Labour and Social Provision and the Secretariat of Public Education, was funded through a World Bank loan. This project established the National Council for Standardization and Certification of Labour Competence, CONOCER (which means 'to know' in Spanish). CONOCER is a government agency with broad stakeholder and inter-departmental representation. One of its key aims is the creation of a labour competence framework. The plan was for CONOCER to establish an integrated unitary framework of 12 competence areas and five levels, and to develop the labour competence technical standards with which to populate this framework. It was also meant to develop an assessment and certification system and a regulatory framework for awarding bodies.

There was a whole host of complex problems with the initial project, leading to long periods of impasse. These ranged from problems with the implementation of the framework, to problems with its administration and financing. In 2005, a new project began, funded by the Inter-American Development Bank. CONOCER was reorganized, with an emphasis on stakeholder participation, developing better relations with educational institutions, and working with employers. A new format was developed for competence standards, and new standards were developed. However, despite a stronger sectoral organization, with 10 strategic sectors identified, many of the sectors had poor industry participation. From 2006 to 2009, CONOCER issued 121,598 certificates using 128 of the competence standards, out of over 601 existing standards. Around 20 per cent of these certificates were based on the older standards from the first project. Both projects of which the labour competence framework was a component have seen many different formulations of the competence standards, as well as other technical modifications. For example, the framework originally had 12 horizontal divisions, but this was later reduced to 11, and then later again increased to 20. Despite the changes, the problem of unused qualifications persisted.

In 2008, the Mexican government relaunched CONOCER *again*, with what they implied was a new approach of focussing on working closely with enterprises and producing demand-oriented standards. But while there may have been many substantial differences, the two previous projects had also both claimed to be working with industry and to be producing standards that industry wanted. This is a recurring pattern in the development and implementation of competence-based training models: in many of our case studies, countries implemented models which were described as industry-led and competence-based, and then re-launched them with new names and new structures, with the main claim that the newer version was industry-led and competence-based.

As mentioned in the note on terminology, in Bangladesh, the National Council for Skills Development and Training was introduced to replace the National Skills Development Council. This body would oversee and monitor all activities related to the National Technical and Vocational Qualifications Framework. Supposedly the new council had greater representation from relevant Ministries and other stakeholder groups, in the hope that this would give it a higher profile. However, the previous structure was also ostensibly stakeholder-based, and also had industry representation.

Many countries introduce qualifications frameworks, outcomes- or competence-based approaches, and describe them as new policy models, despite having attempted similar approaches before. In almost every country in our study, competence- or outcomes-based education and training was used in the reform of vocational education systems to replace *previous versions of competence-based models*. Almost every country had various iterations of competence-based models. A new model would be introduced as the solution to the problems that the old model tried to solve, and the same reasons would be given for why it would succeed: industry-developed outcomes would ensure that learners had the appropriate competences; competences would allow an appropriately modular approach, and so would create more flexibility for learners; and so on. In almost every case, the previous system of vocational education was already modular, and based on competences which were developed in the name of industry. In each case, there is no record of an examination of *why* the original model failed. It seems to have been assumed that either the standards were formulated in the wrong way, or that industry was not involved enough, so that solving these two things would ensure that this new version would succeed.

Chile is an interesting example of this phenomenon. For many years, competence-based training has been the focus of most reforms of vocational and workplace-based training in that country. Various attempts have been made to specify competences, and many reforms involving competences have replaced other reforms which had already involved competences. International organizations have been influential, including the World Bank, which played a major role in financing and supporting various reforms, the Inter-American Development Bank, the German development agency the GTZ (Gesellschaft Technische Zusammenarbeit), and the Organization for Economic Cooperation and Development (OECD). The competence framework was only one of many attempts to implement the idea that seems to be so compelling to policy makers, and which Bobbit had argued for nearly a century earlier, as discussed in Chapter 2: if industry specifies the competences it requires for competent workers, providers will be able to produce them.

In Sri Lanka as well, a new competence-based training model was introduced to replace an old competence-based training model. One difference between the old and the new systems, according to Gajaweera (2010), was the scope of the system—the previous National Skills Standards and Trade Testing system was largely focused on the construction sector and was limited to four grades, the highest of which was the Tradesmen category. This competence-based training system was modelled on the English National Vocational Qualifications, through a World Bank project with British Council assistance. Policy makers wanted, firstly, to extend the system, and secondly, to make competence standards more relevant to industry, as a problem identified with the previous system was that industry was not involved in the development of standards. According to our research, although official documents championed the role of industry, and although the 'difference' between the new system and the old was meant to be active involvement from industry in setting the new competence standards, so far industry has not been very involved. This is a pattern the world over—involving industry in the setting of competence statements does not create a strong relationship between vocational education and work, nor does it seem to provide a good basis for developing strong vocational education, an issue that will be discussed in more depth in the following chapter.

Vocational Education Focus

Outcomes-based qualifications frameworks seem mainly to affect vocational education and training. In the poorer countries included in our study, those classified as middle and low income, qualifications frameworks have mainly been focused on vocational education. This is the most marginalized and low status sector of education systems, particularly in Anglophone countries. And in some cases, this type of reform has taken place only in the most marginalized section of the vocational education system—for low-level workplace-based training, or even, in some instances, not for training at all, but simply to recognize the competences workers already demonstrate in the workplace. In most instances, it is implemented in response to what is diagnosed as a problem with the irrelevance of education and training to the needs of the labour market. Even where the framework was ostensibly comprehensive, such as, for example, in Malaysia, Mauritius, and South Africa, the outcomes-based approach seems to have had the greatest impact in the vocational sector. In South Africa, as discussed above, the rest of the education and training system largely ignored the qualifications framework, and in Mauritius, it was only in the vocational sector where the qualifications framework was introduced as part of developing new outcomes-based qualifications. In Malaysia, while the framework as a whole was more focused on higher education, there was a competence-based framework of qualifications for low-level workplace-based qualifications. In this sector, mainly low levels of qualifications were awarded, and they provided limited opportunity to move up the education and training system. In Chile and Mexico, the frameworks were initially envisaged as frameworks for qualifications in vocational education and training as well as in workplace-based training, but in both they were only really used in the latter, and there they were used mainly for the assessment of prior learning. Providers of vocational education did not accept or use the standards. In both countries, the competence standards developed described mainly low levels of competence in the workplace.

None of this was very different from the early-starter rich countries which began the trend for qualifications frameworks. Although New Zealand attempted a comprehensive unit standards-based model, in the United Kingdom (except for Scotland), as well as in Australia, the competence-/ outcomes-based qualification model was targeted at vocational education[11]. It makes sense for vocational education to be the focus of these models, firstly, because it fits well with the claims made about outcomes-based qualifications' ability to improve education/ labour market relationships, and secondly, because vocational education programmes have always contained some notion of being 'competent' to do a particular job. It is also the case that in many countries vocational education does not have strong and organized voices speaking on its behalf, perhaps making it easier for policy makers to fiddle with it.

Frameworks in most countries are positioned as contributing to solving problems of increased unemployment, skills shortages, and perceived failures in the education and training system. It seems a strange irony that it is the weakest parts of most educational systems that are being called on to solve the problems of the economy through a reform which places no emphasis on supporting provision, perhaps suggesting the largely rhetorical nature of such reform initiatives.

Recognition of Prior Learning

One of the strongest and most consistently made claims about qualifications frameworks, as well as outcomes- and competence-based qualifications, is that they provide a basis for recognizing, validating, and certifying learning that has happened outside of the formal education system. This is variously known as recognition of prior learning, accreditation of prior experiential learning, and by other similar terms. It is thought to be helpful for individuals, because, it is hoped, having certificates will assist them to enter education programmes, get jobs, or get a promotion.

Some of the theoretical and conceptual issues raised by recognition of prior learning will be discussed in Chapters 6 and 7. For now, I merely want to point out that there is little evidence that learning outcomes and qualifications frameworks help people to gain qualifications on the basis of prior learning, and even less evidence that the qualifications thus obtained lead to further learning, jobs, or promotion. In South Africa, for example, the Qualification Authority's research in 2005 found that the South African qualifications framework had had "...minimal positive impact or a mix of positive and negative impact" with regard to portability of full qualifications (SAQA 2005, p. 45), and that the framework had also not facilitated credit accumulation and transfer (SAQA 2006). A more recent report produced for the OECD found that recognition of prior learning was not widely implemented, and had taken place only in small pockets of the education system (Blom, Parker, and Keevy 2007). One of the few examples of 'success' was found in our case study on Chile, which suggested that awards recognizing existing competences had improved workers' self-esteem. However, there was no evidence that they had led to workers gaining promotion or getting better jobs. They had simply received certificates which did nothing more than prove that they could do what they were already doing. In no county was there any clear evidence that workers who were given certificates benefited from them in terms of promotion, salary, or job security.

A particularly poignant story comes from Botswana, where the Botswana Training Authority developed unit standards for traditional dancers in the Kalahari. This project was funded by the government, and encountered many problems, such as the fact that the unit standards were in English, which none of the traditional dancers could speak. At great expense, the unit standard was translated into Setswana, and experts assessed dancers against the learning outcomes. Dancers were awarded certificates in a ceremonial and celebratory event. However, although policy makers were convinced that providing individuals with certificates for their existing skills would help them, these traditional dancers discovered that the certificates did nothing other than certify that they could do something that they were already doing. After the initial excitement had died down, some of the dancers approached the authorities to ask what they could do with their certificates. They were told that they could practice as traditional dancers—which is what they were doing before. There were no increased educational or work opportunities for them on the basis of this certificate. As Christopher Winch (2011, p. 96) puts it, "the award of a qualification for an existing workplace ability does not create a new skill but merely assigns a name to the skill an individual already possesses".

While the recognition of prior learning has particular appeal to policy makers and governments in developing countries, as it seems to hold out an alluring possibility of increasing qualification levels relatively cheaply, it is unlikely to be successful on a large scale. One reason for this is the prevalence of informal labour markets:

while skills and knowledge may be useful in informal labour markets, it is less likely that *qualifications* will be required than in more organized and regulated labour markets. Another reason recognition of prior learning is not a policy solution for poor countries is generally low educational levels. While workers may have acquired practical skills at work, lack of formal education will often remain a barrier to progress in workplaces where, say, literacy is necessary. Poor education is the real problem to be solved, and putting resources into awarding qualifications and certificates of dubious labour market value may well divert resources away from building education systems and ensuring access to them. Furthermore, this trend towards certification often ignores other barriers to education and training: over-emphasizing qualification barriers, it under-emphasizes the extent to which user-fees, the inability to take time off work, as well as other financial factors, prevent individuals from accessing education.

Differences

There are some divergences from the patterns discussed above. The Malaysian framework, for example, seems to be more successful than many others, with some degree of functionality and use that is missing in the cases discussed above. The national framework in Malaysia is made up of three sub-frameworks: the National Occupational Skills Standards; a framework for vocational and technical qualifications awarded in the state polytechs and community colleges; and a framework for higher education qualifications. As is the case in Australia, there are weak linkages between the three frameworks, and limited opportunity to move up the education and training system with them. While the qualifications in each of the three sub-frameworks are placed on a common set of 'levels', the relationships between them are relatively weak. Each of the three frameworks has different processes for developing qualifications, there are different assessment and certification systems, and the institutions which provide them are quality assured through different agencies.

One major difference between this framework and most of the others described is that it relates directly to providing institutions: there are clear sets of providers that offer the qualifications on each of the sub-frameworks. Universities provide the higher education qualifications; colleges, polytechnics, and community colleges provide the vocational and technical qualifications; skills centres provide the skills standards. While Malaysia did experience similar problems to the countries described above in the lower level competence-based qualifications—the skills standards—the fact that training for these certificates happened through skills centres which were funded and administered by the Ministry of Human Resource Development meant that at least training did happen. Keating (2010), drawing on Raffe (2003), suggests that one factor behind this relatively successful framework is that it works with the institutional logic of the country—it works with the providing institutions, instead of trying to change them through qualification policy.

Another difference between this framework and those in the other developing or middle income countries is that, like the Scottish framework, the Malaysian framework has been dominated by higher education. In 1996, in a drive to regulate a very active private higher education sector, the Malaysian government established a National Accreditation Board for higher education. It had responsibility for regulating the standards of private higher education institutions—colleges and universities—which had increased in number following the liberalization of markets and increased public investment. The Malaysian Qualifications Framework was subsequently set up in 2007 with the aim, amongst others, of extending this quality assurance system to the public providers. The stated intention of the government was to establish an overall framework that incorporated qualifications across all three sectors, but so far, the three frameworks have been mainly developed in parallel with each other, without developing relationships between them.

In Sri Lanka, a potential difference, and possible strength, of the new system under development is the much more centralized approach to curriculum development. This diverges from the general thrust of competence-based training models, where learning outcomes are centrally developed, but curricula are developed by each provider. There seems to be some emphasis on building education institutions—for example, a University of Vocational Technology has been established, and has had its first intake of students. This institution is intended to provide higher education to students who have carried out vocational education and training, as they are unable to enter the conventional universities. So far most provision of vocational education is through state institutions: 90 per cent of provision is through Vocational Training Centres under the Ministry of Vocational and Technical Training, and these centres have been the focus of the implementation of the vocational qualifications framework. This is another difference with other countries implementing frameworks, and its effects would be worth monitoring.

The emerging system in Sri Lanka seems, therefore, to be some kind of hybrid of a traditional state-based provision system, and a competence-based training/ qualifications framework model. It is hard to untangle the two, or to see which is dominant in practice. However, private and non-governmental sector vocational training centres have also been registered and accredited to provide courses within the framework, and so where the system may fit with the general pattern of qualifications frameworks described above is in this treatment of all providers, state and private, as competitors, to be evaluated against their performance in training learners against the competence-standards. The vast majority of education and training providers are government institutions, and government is concerned that its institutions should be accountable. Policy documents state that the national vocational qualifications framework will play an important role in managing resource allocation to these institutions. This could be a centralized system with a state monitoring its delivery institutions, but it could also be a move towards the regulated market and quasi-market which qualifications frameworks or competence-based training systems have been used to implement in many countries.

Policy Borrowing and 'Technical Assistance'

Policy borrowing—the role of international agencies, as well as the dominance of the English National Vocational Qualifications model and the Australian competence-based training system (itself modeled on the English model)—is a striking feature of this story. To give just a few examples, the framework in Mauritius was influenced by frameworks in Scotland, New Zealand, and South Africa. The framework in Botswana was developed with assistance and advice from 'experts' from the United Kingdom, South Africa, and New Zealand. Mexico and Chile both drew explicitly and heavily on the English National Vocational Qualifications model. In Bangladesh, while processes had been established to involve a range of stakeholders, in practice much work so far has been dominated by ILO experts through a technical assistance project being implemented by the ILO with the Ministry of Education, in coordination with the Ministry of Labour and the Ministry of Overseas Workers, and in partnership with the European Union.

As discussed in the previous chapter, Hyland (1994) prophetically pointed out that the British government would spread the model of the National Vocational Qualifications. The story of learning outcomes, qualifications frameworks, and competence-based training is a complex one, and there are various ways in which it can be read. As Ball (2007) discusses, a tension in all policy analysis is the need to attend to local particularities of policymaking and enactment, while being aware of general patterns and apparent commonalities. The national stories described above are based on varying amounts of research and yet, even where there is limited research, it is clear that although each country displays local particularities, they also all share some general patterns and commonalities, making Hyland's argument seem very plausible: the national stories of qualifications frameworks could be collected into one volume, entitled, perhaps, 'How NVQs Conquered the World.'

CONCLUSION

Based on my detailed analysis of the South African national qualifications framework (Allais, 2007c), and also drawing on research in other developing countries (Allais, 2010b), I suggest that outcomes-led frameworks in poorer countries are likely to be worse than a waste of money and time. Outcomes-led qualifications frameworks cannot realize the extensive claims made about them. Learning outcomes developed by employers or 'stakeholders' separately from educational contexts cannot provide a basis against which learning programmes can be designed, delivered, assessed, and evaluated. Neither can outcomes-led qualifications frameworks be the stimulus or the regulatory mechanism for provision. However, by being claimed as mechanisms to drive educational reform, they divert attention and resources away from increasing the quality and quantity of education provided. Because outcomes-led frameworks in poorer countries are positioned and described as mechanisms for overhauling education systems, increasing provision and improving quality, they appear to remove the need for the state to support and build institutions. They are likely to drive energy and resources away from institutions and into the fruitless project of defining disembedded outcomes. They force institutions into unhealthy and unnecessary competitive relationships, and undermine the very nature of the work of educational institutions, by making them work to objectives that are external and artificial to them. They provide an inappropriate basis for the state to attempt the complicated business of regulating and monitoring educational provision.

At the same time, such frameworks are frequently used as a basis for privatizing educational provision, or for creating a contractualized basis for it, even where there is state provision, introducing quasi-markets, with very detrimental effects, particularly in poor countries where there are small numbers of strong educational institutions. The problems with this approach are more visible in poorer countries because there are fewer strong institutions—education providers as well as other state institutions—which can make policies appear to be working, regardless of those policies' inherent strengths or weaknesses. Thus, in poorer countries, the policies are on display in their essence, and what becomes clear is that the emperor has no clothes.

The tragedy of qualifications frameworks in poorer countries may also have lessons for wealthy countries. When qualifications frameworks are introduced to *describe* existing systems of provision, existing education programmes, and existing qualifications, they may have a reasonable chance of successfully achieving limited goals. But most of the claims made to justify the introduction of qualifications frameworks are far stronger than this. It may be the case that the strength of educational provision in rich countries *hides* the failures of this model to live up to its claims. In other words, what the lessons of poorer countries show is what these policies do in their own right, what the real logic of them is, and the serious theoretical and practical problems with them.

Outcomes-led qualifications frameworks give the impression that a problem is being solved when it is not. They thus represent a significant waste of time and money, both in terms of policy development, and in terms of the enormous bureaucratic burdens they impose on underfunded and overworked educational institutions. It is more useful for poorer countries, or countries with weaker education and training systems, to concentrate on building or supporting institutions that can provide education and training. Similarly, poorer or weaker states should be cautious when assuming that adopting regulatory models which rely on contracts and accountability mechanisms will solve the problems that they have had in delivering education and training. Where provision does not exist in the first place, or where it is weak or uneven, and where an outcomes-led qualifications framework is introduced to drive educational reform, the *best* such a framework can do is reflect the (weak or non-existent) provision that is already there in the system. But it can have a worse effect, which is to damage the already weak educational provision.

Why this model continues to be pushed, despite lack of evidence of its success, extensive criticism of it in the United Kingdom, and growing criticism in Australia, is considered in the following three chapters, which also provide analysis of the conceptual problems with this model. I start, in the following chapter, with a focus on the chimera of employer-specified competences, and why they have not succeeded in improving education/labour market relationships. I argue that outcomes-based qualifications frameworks and competence-based training reforms are more likely to be a symptom of weak relationships between education and labour markets than a solution to them.

ENDNOTES

[1]   Bangladesh: Mia (2010); Botswana: Tau and Modesto (2010); Chile: Cabrera (2010); Malaysia: Keating (2010); Mauritius: Marock (2010); Mexico: De Anda (2010); Sri Lanka: Gajaweera (2010); they are all available on the ILO website, www.ilo.org.

[2]   Here I am distinguishing between non-formal education, meaning non-certified education, but organized with some degree of institutionalization; and informal education, referring to what an individual learns in life, outside of all organized educational experiences.

[3]   Activists, for example, who often did not have much formal education training, had often been engaged in high levels of strategic planning, analysis, and organizing in the struggle against apartheid.

[4]   Mary Metcalfe, provincial minister of education for the Gauteng province in 1994, and influential member of the National Education Coordinating Committee, for example, confirmed in a discussion with me that the idea of learning outcomes had not been present in ANC education policy circles prior to its introduction by the Department of Education (Personal communication, 3 February 2006).

[5]   For more information and analysis on Christian National Education, see, for example, Hofmeyer (1982), Hyslop (1993), Kallaway (1984), Lowry (1995).

[6]   The union most active in this process, the National Union of Metalworkers, had become very influenced by the idea of post-Fordism, and consequently was very concerned about raising skills levels of the workforce; it was also very influenced by Australian advocates of competence-based training (see Allais, 2007c, for an elaboration).

[7]   From basic education equivalent to the first 9 years of schooling at level one, and Masters and above at level 8.

[8]   The division into the 12 fields was explicitly not supposed to represent 'fields of learning' derived from or based on disciplinary areas (SAQA, 1997, p. 7), but rather was seen as a pragmatic division, necessary to facilitate the creation of structures for the 'standard setting' process. The twelve fields were: Agriculture and Nature Conservation; Culture and Arts; Business, Commerce and Management Studies; Communication Studies and Language; Education, Training and Development; Manufacturing, Engineering and Technology; Human and Social Studies; Law, Military Science and Security; Health Science and Social Services; Physical, Mathematical, Computer and Life Sciences; Services; Physical Planning and Construction.

[9]   In 2007, 172 unit-standards based qualifications and 2,211 unit standards had awards made against them to a total of 37,841 and 562,174 learners respectively (many of these will be to the same learners. The figures reflect the total number of awards, not the number of awards per learner). Data was supplied by the National Learner Records Database of the South African Qualifications Authority.

[10] Outside of university systems, where assessments are usually not centrally set.

[11] This trend may have changed in more recent qualifications frameworks in richer countries, as higher education has been included in many since the adoption of the European Qualifications Framework.

CURE OR SYMPTOM?

Why Outcomes-Based Qualifications Frameworks Don't
Improve Education/Labour Market Relationships

Developments in vocational training cannot be understood solely by examining the inner dynamics of education and training systems. They do not acquire their societal significance and their value for companies and trainees until they are embedded in the labour market. In particular, differences in industrial relations, welfare states, income distribution and product markets are the main reasons for the persistently high level of diversity in vocational training systems. (Bosch & Charest, 2010, p. 22)

The previous two chapters considered neoliberal public sector reform whereby states have tried to shift from providing public goods to regulating markets and/or creating quasi-markets. One of the intended roles of outcomes-based qualifications frameworks is to provide the basis for quality assurance of provision. The learning outcomes are intended to operate as mechanisms for regulating and contracting provision of education. Stephen Ball (2007) points out that decoupling education from direct state control and tying it more closely to economic interests are two complexly related contemporary policy agendas. Qualifications frameworks represent attempts to do both. The previous chapters have considered the former, and this chapter considers the putative role of qualifications frameworks in improving relationships between education systems and labour markets. I suggest that outcomes-based qualifications frameworks are a *symptom* of weak relationships rather than a viable mechanism to improve relationships.

Qualifications are seen as the nexus between education systems and labour markets. Policy makers believe that improving how they function will improve both the efficiency of labour markets and the functioning of education systems. The perception that improvements in education will improve labour markets is unsurprising given that many policy makers see education systems as little more than markets for human capital acquisition. I argue in this chapter that this approach to policy reform ignores the ways in which notions of skill as well as skill formation systems are deeply embedded in different ways of organizing economies and societies. Specifically, I argue that the way labour markets are structured, as well as the nature of social and industrial policy in a country, are far more likely determinants of the nature of vocational education, and the strength of education/ labour market relationships, than qualification frameworks.

BRINGING EDUCATION CLOSER TO LABOUR MARKETS
THROUGH EMPLOYER-SPECIFIED COMPETENCES

Many countries have introduced qualifications frameworks and/or competence-based training to reform vocational education, and sometimes other parts of the education system as well, in the hope that such reforms will lead to education programmes being more relevant to labour market needs. The idea is that industry representatives or employers would specify competences or learning outcomes, which education providers could then use to design their curricula. This, in policy jargon, is usually defined as giving more emphasis to *users* rather than *providers* of education in the process of defining what is included in a qualification. This is why, in many instances, it is claimed that qualifications frameworks based on outcomes or competences are *industry-led* policies.

Competence-based training systems and labour competence-standards are based on the same idea: that employers specify what they require, and then educational institutions design programmes that enable people to acquire the required outcomes. The hope is that if industry representatives are involved in specifying the qualifications, then educational providers will develop learning programmes which develop the required competences, and learners will get jobs after qualifying. An interviewee from one of the qualifications authorities in our study captured this sentiment as follows: "the process means that industry has developed the qualification. If the training provider offers it, they know that these people will get a job because it was done by industry people". Outcomes or competence statements are also supposed to provide a 'language' through which education systems can communicate with labour markets.

As will be elaborated in Chapter 7, inadequate information, or unequal access to information about what the bearers of qualifications know and can do, is believed to be a reason for failure in labour markets. Qualifications frameworks, particularly based on outcomes-based qualifications, are seen as a way of improving the information available to all parties in the market. In our research, in many of the interviews with people in countries which have introduced national qualifications frameworks, the term 'jungle of qualifications' was invoked to describe the system that the qualifications framework was supposed to replace. The perception was that there were so many qualifications on offer, that people could not make sense of them. Learners didn't have enough information about which to enrol for, and employers didn't know whom to hire. By improving the availability of information, qualifications frameworks were seen as a way to clear up this 'jungle', and so were considered key to improving the education 'market'. The outcomes specified in qualifications are intended to provide information to learners—seen as 'investors in skills'—about which jobs specific training programmes will lead to, and to industry—seen as the buyers of labour—about what skills potential employees have. This, it is hoped, will improve the functioning of labour markets, as employers can, it is hoped, employ people with greater confidence. Education markets should also improve, as individuals will be clearer on what skills and abilities they will be acquiring through an education programme.

THREE 'LOGICS' OF LABOUR MARKET ORGANIZATION

Eliot Freidson (2001) distinguishes between three ideal types or logics of labour market organization: those which are 'free'; those which are organized bureaucratically; and occupational labour markets. All three are *markets* in which labour is bought and sold, but they operate in substantively different ways. Each 'logic' or type has different implications for "how tasks are organized and divided among workers, and for the organization of labour markets" (Freidson, 2001, p. 83). He argues that the differences between the three have major implications for the possibilities of developing successful training programmes.

A free labour market would be one in which the consumers of labour were completely sovereign, with no controls or restrictions on them. By virtue of having the money to pay for a service, and in the absence of any other constraint, they would decide what goods and services to demand, whose labour to employ, and what they were willing to pay. Production would follow consumer demand, and workers would compete equally for jobs. Such conditions are very rarely achieved in real life, although different labour markets may have some aspects of them; most economists, Freidson (2001, p. 65) suggests, agree that "the conditions for a perfectly free labor market are virtually impossible to find in all but minor and marginal segments of modern economies". A free labour market requires "an island in which there is no immigration or emigration and neither workers' organizations nor employers' associations, while all workers are equally skilled and efficient, employers are indifferent to the personal characteristics of those they hire, and workers have complete knowledge of the pay rates prevailing for different work, choosing work solely on the basis of what it pays" (Freidson, 2001, p. 64). Freidson suggests that in the marginal segments of modern economies there are something like free labour markets, as for most workers there is no stable specialization, and little public or official recognition of their work as distinct occupations. In this context, it makes no sense for individuals to attain high levels of education. As Freidson (2001, p. 87) points out, a free labour market works against skills development because demand is so fluid that it is "difficult to imagine many workers investing in training for specialized skills before entering the market". This is because precarious or casualized work makes it risky to do a training course in the skills currently required, as they may not be required next month or next year. This is why Guy Standing (2011, p. 40) asks, "Why invest in an occupational skill if I have no control over how I can use and develop it?"

No substantial education and training programme can be designed and delivered to learners in a short space of time. However, employers are interested in the development of discrete skills for the immediate job at hand. They require an education system that responds quickly to changing demand for specific skills in the workplace. It is thus very difficult for institutions to develop programmes which both prepare learners for the workplace and also provide them with a broader education. In labour markets with casualized or constantly changing jobs, vocational education programmes can either be somewhat removed from the immediate needs of the labour market, leading to the accusation that they don't meet the needs of the labour market, or they can be comprised of ever-changing short courses in narrow skills.

By contrast, a bureaucratically controlled division of labour is one in which a directing authority and their support staff decide what work shall be done, and how it shall be divided into different jobs. This could take the form of either centrally planned markets, in which the division of labour is planned, and wages are specified for recognized categories of workers, or of internal labour markets within large firms or state bureaucracies, in which workers hold particular jobs, and gradually gain rises in salary and promotions or transfers internally. In labour markets that operate according to this logic, allocations of work and decisions about job structures are made by specialists in personnel management, who are responsible to the authorities in charge, rather than to the workers who do the work, or the consumers of this work or its products. Training is necessary to take on these jobs, and this training is often very specific to the internal requirements of the given firm or state bureaucracy.

The third logic is an occupationally controlled division of labour. Here, members of distinct occupations have exclusive right to perform the tasks associated with them, with some overlap or ambiguity with related occupations. Consumers and managers who want to contract for the tasks connected with those specializations are obliged to use *bona fide* members of the occupation; they are neither free to employ any willing worker, nor to train workers for the purpose. It is the occupations themselves which determine what qualifications are required to perform particular tasks, and which control the criteria for the licensing or credentialling procedures that are enforced by the state (Freidson, 2001, p. 56). Empirical examples of this type of labour market are craft guilds and professions. In this third type of labour market, not only is training likely to be strong, it is essential. It is the acquisition of bodies of knowledge and skill that enable the creation of these 'labour market shelters' for given occupations or professions. Within the professions, the acquisition of bodies of theoretical knowledge, and the relationship with universities that teach, develop, refine, systematize, and expand the body of knowledge over which each profession claims jurisdiction, gives workers more power over their work.

Professions are generally regulated even in very liberal economies, although many have seen a considerable onslaught against this in the name of the free market. Friedson describes how governments have argued against occupational regulation, and have in some instances substantially weakened professions in the name of the 'free market', and of 'breaking monopolies'. Standing (2011, p. 39) concurs, arguing:

> In the globalization era, governments quietly dismantled the institutions of 'self-regulation' of professions and crafts, and in their place erected elaborate

systems of state regulation. These removed the capacity of occupational bodies to set their own standards, to control entry to their occupation, to establish and reproduce their ethics and ways of doing things, to set rates of pay and entitlements, to establish ways of disciplining and sanctioning members, to set procedures for promotion and for other forms of career advancement, and much else.

Dismantled is probably an overstatement, particularly for the classic self-regulating professions. Nonetheless, there is always political contestation about who has the right to restrict and regulate labour markets. Where it is an option, people attempt to free themselves from 'free labour markets' by obtaining a qualification in a more protected and socially recognized occupation—an occupation where there is some kind of labour market shelter. One way of doing this is attaining the knowledge and skills of a protected occupation or profession. Higher levels of general education are also generally seen as leading to the possibility of a white collar or so-called 'knowledge-based, knowledge-economy' job.

LABOUR MARKETS, TRAINING, AND QUALIFICATION REFORM

It is striking that the particular notion of 'industry-led' outcomes- or competence-based vocational education described above emerged in Anglophone liberal market economies in which there were *very weak relationships between education and training systems and labour markets*. It is also interesting that they were targeted at the lowest and most fragmented sections of the workforce. Vocational education systems in such countries (such as the United Kingdom, Australia, and New Zealand) have been aimed at providing individuals with options for developing their own 'employability'. This is in contrast to vocational education and training systems focused on education for an occupation, such as the German dual system (Brockmann, 2011, drawing on Rauner, 2007).

In the latter systems, vocational education and training aims to develop vocational competence and identity for a *regulated occupational labour market* which relates occupations to the corresponding tracks of vocational education. An occupation is a formally recognized social category, with regulations in terms of aspects such as qualifications, range of knowledge required, both theoretical and practical, and promotion. The employment relationship is a long-term one. This makes it possible for it to be founded on broad abilities, such as an understanding of the entire work process and of the wider industry, and on an integration of manual and intellectual tasks, in order to be able to plan, execute, and evaluate, and not just carry out narrowly specified tasks. The nature of this labour market makes strong vocational education both necessary and possible. Vocational education "is provided through comprehensive programmes that are part of the national education system and thus constitutes the continuation of 'education' (commonly based on a curriculum, with a broad content) rather than 'training' as more narrowly focused on the labour market and the job" (Clarke, 2011, p. 108). Clarke further argues that in this system, vocational education aims to develop vocational competence and identity, and is

...designed to develop the ability to act autonomously and competently within an occupational field. Qualifications are obtained through the successful completion of courses developed through negotiation with the social partners, integrating theoretical knowledge and workplace learning.

Of course the word 'occupation' itself is used in different ways across different contexts. Winch (2011) distinguishes between a restricted sense, usually used in Anglophone contexts, in which an occupation is considered to concern occupational standards and a series of skills—in other words, a set of related tasks bundled together—and the broader German notion of *Beruf*. As explained by Georg Hanf (2011), the concept of a *Beruf* structures the German labour market, mainly at the level of intermediate qualifications and the vocational education system. To pursue a *Beruf*, an individual needs a systematic combination of formal knowledge, skills, and experience-based competence, and their deployment is not linked to a specific workplace. *Berufe* are strongly linked to the collective bargaining system as well as to the welfare system. They are also part of a broader concept of 'cultivated and qualified' labour, and linked to the idea of dignity as opposed to humiliation in work (Hanf, 2011, p. 55). This organizes and reduces competition in the labour market, and protects those who have a *Beruf;* it provides, in Friedson's term, a 'labour market shelter'.

In liberal English speaking countries, which saw the first emergence of outcomes-based qualifications frameworks and competence-based reforms, education is regulated through a 'market of qualifications' (Brockmann, Clarke, & Winch, 2011). Individuals can choose from this market, and compose their own qualification profiles according to what they think will improve their position in the labour market:

a 'market of qualifications' enables individuals to enhance their employability through continuing vocational education or certification of sets of competencies acquired either through work experience or modularized courses." (Brockmann, 2011, pp. 120–121)

This type of arrangement is premised on the notion of a free labour market. But even in the most liberal economies, labour markets are probably the least 'free' and most regulated of markets, starting with the immigration policies of any given country, which are a major determinant of relationships in the labour market.

Qualifications frameworks and the idea of employer-specified competences or learning outcomes emerged in places with a weak relationship between education, particularly vocational education, and the labour market. The outcomes or competence statements are supposed to improve this relationship. As Rauner (2007, p. 118) explains:

When competence development is disconnected from occupationally organized work and the related vocational qualification processes, the relationship between vocational identity, commitment and competence development becomes loose and fragile. In which case, modularized systems of certification function as regulatory frameworks for the recognition and accumulation of skills that are largely independent from each other and disconnected from genuine work contexts.

Of course there are labour market shelters in these economies, particularly at higher levels, so in many instances individuals aim at ever-higher levels of general education. This leads to qualification inflation, as employers use qualifications as a screening device, and potential workers are obliged to strive for higher and higher levels of qualifications to improve their place in the queue, and to have a chance in the increasing competition for good jobs. This leads to many people acquiring qualifications which they don't need for the substance of the work that they will be doing, which in turn leads to increasing criticism of education, both in terms of content and form. The perception that education does not prepare people for work becomes ever-more entrenched.

This context makes it difficult for providers to develop strong vocational education programmes. Vocational education is seen as a last resort for several reasons: many jobs do not require any substantial qualifications; where qualifications are required in order to get jobs, the connections between vocational education and work are so weak that graduates often do not get the jobs they are ostensibly trained to do; and when they do get jobs, they are often low-waged and short-term. All of these factors create a negative cycle of neglect of vocational institutions and curricula. Individuals with low levels of education are generally perceived by employers as inefficient workers, and are left trapped in low-level, 'unskilled' work.

SOCIAL POLICY, TRAINING, AND QUALIFICATIONS REFORM

The two models of skill—the first aimed at developing general employability and the second aimed at long-term training for regulated occupations—map onto the two main types of capitalist systems described by the 'varieties of capitalism' literature: coordinated market economies and liberal market economies (Hall & Soskice, 2001). In this literature, which takes its name from Peter Hall and David Soskice's book *Varieties of Capitalism: The Institutional Foundations of Comparative Advantage*, coordinated market economies (for example, Germany, France, and Scandinavian countries) are described as resting on multiple mechanisms of institutional coordination, including tight coupling between the financial and industrial wings of big business, collective wage determination, and strong and well-funded systems of general and vocational education, supported by the state. Liberal market economies (such as the United States, the United Kingdom, Australia, and Canada) operate more closely to the textbook model of the unfettered 'free market'.

The former set of economies have liberalized since this body of literature emerged, which might mean that the differences between the two types are diminishing with implications in the long-term for training systems in the former coordinated market economies. This may to some extent explain the increasing interest in competence statements, learning outcomes, and qualifications in Europe, an issue which I will return to in Chapter 8. For now I simply want to make the point that the descriptive purchase of the varieties of capitalism literature has diminished in today's world due to increasing similarities between the two main models of capitalist economies. The varieties of capitalism literature is also critiqued for downplaying power relations, particularly in relation to the role of trade unions in building the welfare state. Furthermore, the models it describes are all models of advanced capitalist economies. Nothing in the analysis helps to work out how best to build the general and vocational skills systems of developing and middle-income countries. Nonetheless, the findings regarding complementarities between different systems of the labour market, social policy, and training policy remain salient, for this literature usefully highlights the *relationships* that different systems of education and training have with distinct modes of capitalist production and social protection. It shows that the relationships are not coincidental, but are *intrinsic* to the way the different systems are structured.

Torben Iverson and John Stephens (2008) argue that there are strong links between specific and general skills at the bottom of the distribution of educational achievement and employment protection, unemployment replacement rates, and active labour market policies. This is because high levels of social protection in the coordinated market economies encourage individuals to acquire specific skills: unemployment protection and other active labour market policies support individuals who lose their jobs, making it easier for them to look for a job that uses their skills, as opposed to being forced to take the first job that comes along. This supports a vocational education system that enables firms to specialize in international niche markets—often with quasi-monopolistic competition and high mark-ups. Where there is strong vocational education provision, workers at the lower end of the achievement distribution have strong incentives to work hard in high school to get into the best vocational schools or get the best apprenticeships. This raises the skills of at those at the low end of the educational achievement distribution, and supports a more compressed wage structure.

Within the Scandinavian coordinated market economies, a historical domination by centre-left coalitions has led to high levels of wealth redistribution. This has enabled heavy investment in public education, including high quality public day care and preschools, and industry-specific and occupation-specific vocational training, which have led to high levels of *both* general skills *and* industry-specific skills. Flexibility in the labour market is supported by extensive spending on retraining. The result of this *combination of policies* is compressed skill distribution: workers at the lower end of this distribution have specific skills that the equivalent workers in liberal market economies do not have; they also have better general skills, due to good general education, making it easier for them to acquire additional technical skills. The high level of specific skills supports high value-added production in international niche markets, and the high level of general skills supports service industries. Provision of public day care provides jobs, allows parents to enter the workforce or increase their working hours, provides early childhood education, which is particularly important for children of less educated parents, and facilitates higher fertility rates, which in turn enable more stability in the long-term funding of the welfare state. In other words, *social equality* fosters the development of high levels of both general and specific skills, especially at the bottom end of the skill distribution, which in turn reinforces social equality. General skills at this level are strongly related to day care spending, as well as to strong vocational education. Iverson and Stephens also argue that in general 'information age literacy', including reasonably high levels of general literacy as well as information technology ability, is "extremely strongly and negatively related to the degree of inequality", which is why levels of achievement in this area are high in the Scandinavian countries (Iverson & Stephens, 2008, p. 621).

In other coordinated market economies where there are alliances across class lines, such as in those dominated by strong Christian Democratic parties, demands for redistribution are fewer. Support for heavy public spending on preschool and primary education is lower than in the Scandinavian countries, and spending on overall education, higher education, and day care is closer to that in liberal regimes. Nonetheless, general skills at the bottom are significantly higher than in liberal regimes. Most continental European countries have well-functioning vocational training institutions, which offer opportunities for reasonable levels of general education. They also have strong collective bargaining systems, which have facilitated well-paying stable jobs. High social insurance and job protection, as well as strong vocational training, have facilitated acquisition of firm-specific and industry-specific skills.

In contrast with both types of coordinated market economies described above, liberal market economies have much lower redistribution of wealth to public schooling and social welfare. The middle and upper-middle classes self-insure by attaining high levels of general education, often through private institutions. Students who expect to go to higher education have strong incentives to work hard. Because vocational education is weak, learners in the bottom third of the achievement distribution have few incentives to do well in school, and few opportunities to acquire skills. Skills at the bottom end are therefore low, and workers end up in poorly paying jobs with little prospect of advancement. Manufacturing uses mainly low and general skills. Wages for labourers are based on outputs, generally at variable rates (Clarke, 2011). Intellectual functions—planning, coordinating, evaluating, controlling—are sharply separated from execution. It is difficult for unions to gain bargaining leverage, as workers are easily replaced. This means incentives to join unions are low, which weakens unions, which in turn makes the regulation and protection of occupations less likely. Training is aimed more at specific short-term jobs, or even tasks, than at broad 'occupations'. In short, in liberal market economies, *the structure of the economy and the labour market leads to weak vocational education.*

It is in this labour market and social policy context that the idea took hold that if employers specified competences and learning outcomes, education would produce the required results. The starting point was an analysis of a 'mismatch' between skills 'supply' and 'demand'. This was seen as largely the fault of the education system. However, relationships between education systems and labour markets are complex, and many examples can be found of where 'mismatches' are not caused by the poor functioning of education. To cite just two, Chang (2010) points out that bright Koreans are increasingly becoming doctors, rather than engineers or scientists, not because there is no need for the latter two professions in industry, but because the government has reduced already low social security nets, and many companies retrench or otherwise get rid of older people. Because this is not a threat for doctors, medicine is seen as a more secure profession. Here, the social welfare system, not education institutions, is a crucial factor in skewing the supply of qualified professionals. In another example, Wildschut and Mgqolozana (2009) point out that there is a shortage of nurses in South Africa, despite more than adequate numbers being trained, because nurses are recruited to work overseas; similarly, Breier (2009) shows that from one-fifth to one-third of South African doctors are working abroad. These are merely two examples of a whole host of complicated reasons why education systems may not 'produce' according to 'demand'.

As described in Chapter 3, the idea of employer-specified competences was first systematically implemented in England, Northern Ireland, and Wales in the 1980s, through a framework of National Vocational Qualifications. Seen as an alternative to 'knowledge-based' curricula, these qualifications introduced the idea of learning outcomes derived from an analysis of work functions. The outcomes were specified according to the requirements of employers, and hence were described as 'industry-led'. This attempt to link vocational education to the workplace through employer-specified competence statements would be better seen as an attempt to regulate the 'market of qualifications' in order to compensate for the lack of well-defined and protected occupational roles in the labour market, particularly at lower levels. As Dale *et al.* (1990, p. 70) explain, the *assumption* is:

> ... an ideal labour market in an ideal free market economy would function such that the wage nexus determined the long term supply and demand for labour, so the education system would be responsible for generating the supply of labour to an economy which generated demand for it. Like in a commodity market, educational credentials must indicate the potential 'value' of individual labourers to employers. At the same time the output of the education system should mirror the divisions of labour (which would be differentiated horizontally and hierarchically in the most technically efficient and profitable ways) and the subjects taught should serve the needs of the economy.

This assumption lies behind much of the interest in qualifications frameworks and qualifications reform, as policy makers attempt to improve how qualifications supply information in labour markets, hoping that this in turn will have an effect on the organization and content of education systems. This reform of vocational qualifications in the United Kingdom in the 1980s was designed to legitimate constantly shifting, job-type specifications, by making them easier to accredit (Winch, 2011), and accordingly there was a strong emphasis on the development of separate 'units of competence'. This, perhaps, explains why Clarke and Westerhuis (2011, p. 146) argue: "In its almost exclusive focus on skills, the English meaning of competence ... is almost incomprehensible in most countries". The English notion of competence is seen as narrow and 'task-based', as opposed to a broader, more holistic notion in continental European countries (Bohlinger, 2007; Hanf, 2011; Méhaut, 2011). Brockman, Clarke, and Winch (2008, p. 106) write: "On the continent, in contrast, LOs [learning outcomes] are interpreted as broad outcomes or competences, implicitly linked to curricula in the context of a broad occupational field."

The narrower notion of competence lies behind competence-based training reforms as well as outcomes-based qualifications frameworks. Reforming qualifications systems is easier than regulating labour markets or developing strong social policy, which provides some insight into the why outcomes-based qualifications frameworks and competence-based training appeal to policy makers. None of the developing countries in our study have the factors found in coordinated market economies that support strong vocational education systems: strong social welfare, well-developed and well-regulated industries, and active labour market policies. They do not have the labour market regulation and social policy which are necessary in order for vocational education systems to develop strong linkages with regulated occupations. Instead, informal ('free') markets dominate, often supported by structural adjustment programmes or the equivalent, as well as 'technical assistance' and conditional loans and grants which have pushed neoliberal policy models. It is thus not surprising that vocational education policy models in developing countries are derived largely from those in liberal market economies. Education reform, as described in the previous two chapters, is focused on forcing education providers to behave like corporate, profit-driven entities, competing in markets or quasi-markets. As described in this chapter, education reform is supposed to improve the functioning of labour markets by supplying the required skills, with outcomes-based qualifications both indicating to providers what skills to provide, and to employers what skills learners have acquired. The policy does not engage with the substantial reasons for the weaknesses of vocational education, or with the poor relationships between vocational education and labour markets, because these are much harder things to fix.

For example, as discussed in the previous chapter, frameworks of labour competences influenced by the British National Vocational Qualifications were developed in some Latin American countries in the 1990s, in the context of major economic shifts and political reforms aimed at reducing the role of the state and liberalizing economies (Palma, 2003). De Moura Castro discusses the strong national training institutions that were established in these countries mainly through payroll levies. He argues that they had "financial stability, comfortable budgets and a long-run perspective" (de Moura Castro 2000, p. 252), that they were successful and prestigious, in some instances far more so than the schooling system in their countries, and that they trained several generations of highly-skilled workers. However, these workers worked in industries nurtured by import substitution policies. These industries later collapsed when economic crises led to import substitution being abandoned. The weakness of the industrial sector was *not* caused by lack of skills. The education institutions had met the needs of industry while industry flourished, and while there were stable jobs within industry. But when skilled workers suddenly had no industry to work in, because of broader economic conditions as well as the responses of their governments to these conditions, education and training came under the spotlight. The idea of competences and competence-based training was seen to offer a way of improving the relevance of training, particularly in the informal sector, and in a context in which the previous systems no longer seemed to be working. As one of the advocates of this approach argues:

> work in the current situation requires subjects who actively construct their labour career, and who have the capacity to identify and value their resources and capacities with an attitude of seeking help and the will to overcome their limitations, and this makes them managers of their own employment opportunities. (Vargas Zuñiga, 2005, p. 89)

My analysis above also goes some way towards explaining why there is so little empirical evidence that the 'industry-led' competence/ outcomes-based model has created strong relationships between education systems and the world of work: besides creating a model for educational delivery which is unsustainable, it does not address the root of the problem in labour market and social policy. As Keep (2005, p. 546) argues, "policy interventions that simply attempt to enhance the quality of labour supply through addressing the individual 'deficiencies' of young people are unlikely to succeed and that policy interventions to *decasualize* the labour market are needed" (my emphasis). Winch (2011) argues that the notion of 'skill' partly derives from the fragmentation of the labour process, which is why countries with broader occupational categories tend to use it less: "When reference to workplace ability is almost exclusively centred around skill, it becomes difficult to allow for the concept of occupational integration, as skill is a fragmenting rather than an integrating concept" (Winch, 2011, p. 92). Drawing on Braverman, Winch points out that, whilst 'skill' is suited to conceptualizing the segmentation of the labour process into particular episodes of work or tasks, at its limits, this fragmentation removes any aspect of personal ability, or, ironically, skill, from an operation. This is the dilemma of casualized and precarious work, and it is the dilemma of the 'market of qualifications' approach. Brockmann *et al.* (2011, p. 19) argue further:

> ... the English output-related qualification system, such as the NVQ, rests on the certification of narrowly defined skills and reinforces the fragmented nature of the labour process, resulting in weak occupational identities and an obsession with managerial control.

There are a few other reasons for the problems experienced with this type of model, which I will mention briefly below.

OTHER PROBLEMS WITH EMPLOYER-SPECIFIED COMPETENCES

A common practical problem with the employer-specified competences model was the involvement of industry. All the countries in our study were developing qualifications frameworks and competence-frameworks in the hope of improving relationships between education and training systems and labour markets, and all were premised on industry participation, but, at the time of our research, and with the exception of Australia, this participation was very limited in all countries. Despite policy makers claiming that these were 'industry-led' systems, industry often appeared reluctant to lead. Where industry did participate, it was often not at the desired level. For example, human resource personnel instead of technical experts were sent to the meetings to develop standards, and in many instances, the process of developing the standards was in fact subcontracted out to consultants, undermining the whole concept of employer-specified competences. For example, in Lithuania, where workplace-based assessment has been officially conducted by the Chamber of Industry, the vocational education and training schools argued that much of the work was delegated to them, leaving the Chamber to the task of organizing and coordinating. The vocational education and training schools argued that the Chamber could not design the actual assessments, due lack of expertise and knowledge in the specific fields. This is borne out by other studies internationally. Keep (2005, p. 543) captures the problem well in relation to English policy: "Unfortunately, the government's obsessive love affair with qualifications is not a passion necessarily shared by employers to anything like the same extent."

Where industry is involved in designing qualifications or specifying competence statements, in many instances the qualifications are not valued in the way authorities hope or intend. Even employers frequently seem not to value the qualifications which emanate from 'industry-led' qualifications processes. In many of the countries in our study, students, parents, employers, and governments value university qualifications above all, and therefore, by extension, value school qualifications which can potentially lead to university. This is usually not the case with qualifications which emanate from competence-based or learning outcomes-based qualifications.

One reason that vocational qualifications which are employer designed are not valued is because employers are likely to focus on their immediate short-term needs. King (2012) points out that in India, for example, while there is a policy emphasis on 'demand-driven training', "the present system is already very demand driven, but driven by a massive demand for using cheap, unskilled labour, and training on the job". Basing a system primarily on what employers *say* they need can trap a country in the production strategies of the moment, which may be based on low-wage, low-skill work. In other words, a so-called 'demand-led' system will be focused on employers' short-term labour market needs, rather than the long-term educational needs of young people or even, perhaps, the long-term needs of the economy. Employers build on the 'skills of yesterday'. Ironically, this leads to lack of labour market currency for many occupational qualifications:

> If a qualification seeks only to mimic a traditional, restricted and shrinking area of labour market activity, then it will inevitably have low labour market currency and become quickly out of tune with changes in the labour market. It is the educational element, in particular the integration of the theoretical knowledge component with practice, which gives a qualification its longer-term value and which can in turn facilitate rather than impede the development of the labour process. (Clarke & Westerhuis, 2011, p. 143)

This, together with the analysis in the beginning of this chapter, may explain why even the 'industry-led' Australian competence-based training system has "weak links between vocational education and training and employment" (Cooney and Long 2010, p. 29).

Further, while they may have some notion of what their immediate needs are, employers may not always be able to articulate what it is that they require, and frequently have unrealistic expectations about what education institutions can achieve. Certainly in most instances they are not able to predict what skills and knowledge will be required in the future[1]. And, as Freidson (2001, p. 130) points out, "at any moment during a period of high change and innovation, old, declining sectors will be better represented by sector-level organizations than new, dynamic ones." Employers in any industrial or service sector also vary widely, in terms of size, how their service or production is organized, and in their demands for knowledge and skills. There is no one "employer view" of qualifications, even in a specific sector. As Wolf (1995, p. 104) argues: "Serious differences which relate to fundamental views of society and people, as well as to job demarcations and future trends, inhere in the process, and are not something which can be solved in a technical fashion."

Designing and developing qualifications and curricula cannot be based solely on the evidence of current employer needs, for the latter will inevitably be based on today's workplaces, which are likely to change. Thus, in our study, representatives of educational institutions interviewed in Lithuania argued that the problem was not so much lack of input from employers as lack of research into present and future skills needs. Qualification design needs to involve specialists making judgements that take account of a range of factors, including the likely development of industries and services and the current needs of employers, as well as how the qualification provides the basis for learner progression.

Another set of problems, which is discussed in depth in the following chapter, lies in the assumption that once competences have been specified, creating a curriculum is a simple process of 'designing down' from them. This idea of employers specifying competences which educational institutions deliver harks back to the Taylorist ideas introduced into educational reform in the early twentieth century, discussed in

Chapter 2. Some passages from American educational reformer Franklin Bobbit are worth re-quoting here:

> ... the commercial world can best say what it needs in the case of its stenographers and accountants. A machine shop can best say what is needed in the workers that come to it. The plumbing trade contains the men who are best able to state the needs of those entering upon plumbing; and so on through the entire list. (Bobbit, 1913a, cited in Callahan, 1962, 83-84)

> After society has given to the school its ultimate standard in any particular case, it then is certainly the business of the educational and psychological experts to determine the time of the beginning, the intensity of the work, and the standards to be attained in each of the successive stages. (Bobbit 1913, cited in Callahan, 1962, p. 84)

This mechanical notion of education suggests that educational institutions are factories which can simply produce on demand, and so it is a simple matter to change the design specifications and produce a different product. Education and training are much more complicated processes than simply producing 'products' to specification. When employers are asked to express needs, they usually come up with long wish-lists, which in many instances are beyond the capacity of educational institutions to deliver, and which take no consideration of, and usually have little knowledge of, what it actually takes to get people to master the skills and knowledge required in a particular occupation. Invariably, they specify things like 'problem solving', 'taking initiative', 'working in teams'. It is highly debatable whether producing all of these can or should be the responsibility of educational institutions, and, if so, what kinds of educational programmes would be needed to produce them. Employers also often expect educational institutions to produce skills which can only realistically be produced in workplaces.

Once policy separates qualifications from educational institutions, and provides specifications to institutions, the question must arise: how can qualifications mediate between educational institutions and the labour market (Young & Allais, 2009)? Qualifications must have a relationship with educational institutions if they are to mediate between them and labour markets. But if they are neither embedded in institutions nor originate from them, and if they do not refer to the activities of educational institutions—in other words, if the outcomes are not linked to the activities that learners are engaged in during a course of study—then the qualifications will have very little to do with education institutions, and will not be able to mediate between these institutions and labour markets. However explicitly learning outcomes or competences are specified, a qualification can only ever be a proxy; it can never summarize all that the holder knows, all that is required to undertake a task or to be trusted as a 'qualified' member of an occupation. The issue of trust cannot be derived from the specification of outcomes. Trust can reside in the providing institution—specific educational institutions build up a reputation over

127

time, or build strong relationships with employers or professional bodies over time. If a qualification refers to the learning that has taken place in an institution, and that institution has built up credibility and trust in its offerings, the qualification is more likely to mediate between the learning that has taken place in that institution and the knowledge and skills needed in the world of work.

People may also trust qualifications examined by institutions whose assessments have an established reputation over time, or awarding institutions which have a good reputation for a particular qualification. They may trust a regulatory body which accredits providing institutions—but this, as discussed below, is only likely if the numbers of providing institutions are not too great, if quality of provision is high to start with, and if the regulatory body has the capacity to make meaningful judgements about the qualifications or institutions it regulates. When a particular qualification is trusted and is seen as a valuable and reliable qualification, a combination of these factors may exist.

This brings me to a final problem: the problem of transparency. This is discussed in detail in the following chapter. I discuss it separately here insofar as it relates to labour markets, and the claim that learning outcomes improve labour mobility nationally and internationally.

LABOUR MOBILITY AND QUALIFICATIONS FRAMEWORKS: 'TRANSPARENCY' AND INTERPRETATION

There is a strong rhetoric about labour mobility in documentation about qualifications frameworks. The European Qualifications Framework is seen as an important tool in creating a single labour market throughout Europe. And a task team from the Southern African Development Community (SADC) that argues for a regional framework also emphasizes that qualifications need to travel across national borders (Technical Committee on Certification and Accreditation 2005), as do other documents emanating from SADC (see for example Pesanai 2003).

It should be noted that the rhetoric about labour mobility is at least partially misleading, as immigration has become more and more difficult in many respects. Furthermore, it seems likely that qualifications frameworks will be used as a way of controlling immigration. For example, the South African Department of Home Affairs, which processes immigration applications, recently tasked the South African Qualifications Authority with validating the qualifications of people seeking work permits in South Africa. This adds an extra hurdle for people wanting to work in South Africa, but also makes the South African National Qualifications Framework a tool for controlling immigration. It seems plausible that the frenetic development of qualifications frameworks in countries surrounding Europe, with substantial assistance from European advisors, is concerned with controlling the supply of 'desirable' immigrants.

Putting this aside, let's consider the actual mechanism which is supposed to increase mobility: outcomes-based qualifications, and specifically, level descriptors composed of learning outcomes. Level descriptors are key to qualifications frameworks and competency-based standards, and in many countries are described as *the* crucial mechanism that enables qualifications frameworks to achieve their goals. Level descriptors are broadly specified outcomes or competences which are supposed to capture what it means to be competent at a particular level of a qualifications framework; in other words, they are supposed to capture qualities or abilities that should be achieved by all learners who achieve a qualification at a specified level. This, it is hoped, will help the process of comparing qualifications across different fields as well as across countries—so that country A's level 5 qualification can be seen as broadly at the same level as country B's. Inside of countries, it is hoped that they can help with clarifying which qualifications are equivalent to which other qualifications, and, perhaps, can be a mechanism with which to convince skeptics that qualifications which are not currently viewed as equivalent can be recognized as such—for they can demonstrate that they lead to the same broad outcomes or levels of competence. The learning outcomes or competences in the level descriptors are also supposed to help designers of qualifications and learning programmes, by indicating to them what broad outcomes should be achieved through the qualification.

For the uninitiated, an example may assist. Below in Boxes 1 and 2 are the descriptors for level one and level four respectively of the South African Qualifications Framework. Level one in South Africa is supposed to be roughly equivalent to the ninth year of formal schooling, or the end of primary education, and level four to the twelfth year of formal schooling, or the end of senior secondary education.

As can be seen from these examples, level descriptors are supposed to capture outcomes or levels of competency across a range of different categories or areas. In South Africa there are ten categories: scope of knowledge; knowledge literacy; method and procedure; problem solving; ethics and professional practice accessing; processing, and managing information; producing and communicating information; context and systems; management of learning; accountability.

By comparing this example to systems in other countries, a potential problem can immediately be seen. Different countries have chosen substantially different categories, revealing that they are by no means self-evident (as seen in Box 3). This partly explains why the process of arriving at these ten categories in South Africa was long, drawn out, and highly contested. Markowitsch and Luomi-Messerer (2008) reveal similar complexities and difficulties involved in reaching agreement on the level descriptors for the European Qualifications Framework, and the continuing differences in interpretation of the key terms. Their description reveals a string of processes which attempted to reach clarity and develop common interpretations, difficulties in pinning down specific definitions and interpretations of different terms, and various reformulations when differences became apparent.

Once the categories have been agreed on, it is by no means self-evident what each category *means*: what, for example, is 'knowledge literacy' or 'accountability' to the uninitiated observer? Bear in mind that a key claim made about qualifications

---

Box 1: Level One of the South African Qualifications Framework

Scope of knowledge, in respect of which a learner is able to demonstrate a general knowledge of one or more areas or fields of study, in addition to the fundamental areas of study

Knowledge literacy, in respect of which a learner is able to demonstrate an understanding that knowledge in a particular field develops over a period of time through the efforts of a number of people and often through the synthesis of information from a variety of related sources and fields

Method and procedure, in respect of which a learner is able to demonstrate an ability to use key common tools and instruments, and a capacity to apply him/ herself to a well-defined task under direct supervision

Problem solving, in respect of which a learner is able to demonstrate an ability to recognise and solve problems within a familiar, well-defined context

Ethics and professional practice, in respect of which a learner is able to demonstrate an ability to identify and develop own personal values and ethics, and an ability to identify ethics applicable in a specific environment

Accessing, processing and managing information, in respect of which a learner is able to demonstrate an ability to recall, collect and organise given information clearly and accurately, sound listening and speaking (receptive and productive language use), reading and writing skills, and basic numeracy skills including an understanding of symbolic systems

Producing and communicating information, in respect of which a learner is able to demonstrate an ability to report information clearly and accurately in spoken/ signed and written form

Context and systems, in respect of which a learner is able to demonstrate an understanding of the context within which he/she operates

Management of learning, in respect of which a learner is able to demonstrate an ability to sequence and schedule learning tasks, and an ability to access and use a range of learning resources

Accountability, in respect of which a learner is able to demonstrate an ability to work as part of a group.

---

frameworks and level descriptors is that they make qualifications systems more transparent.

It could also be argued that not all qualifications should enable learners to achieve higher competency levels in all ten categories. For example, 'working as part of a group' should not be necessary for all qualifications at any particular level.

There could also be considerable debate about what it would mean to have a higher level of competency. For example, South African learners at level one are required to be able to

---

Box 2: Level Four of the South African Qualifications Framework

Scope of knowledge, in respect of which a learner is able to demonstrate a fundamental knowledge base of the most important areas of one or more fields or disciplines, in addition to the fundamental areas of study and a fundamental understanding of the key terms, rules, concepts, established principles and theories in one or more fields or disciplines

Knowledge literacy, in respect of which a learner is able to demonstrate an understanding that knowledge in one field can be applied to related fields

Method and procedure, in respect of which a learner is able to demonstrate an ability to apply essential methods, procedures and techniques of the field or discipline to a given familiar context, and an ability to motivate a change using relevant evidence

Problem solving, in respect of which a learner is able to demonstrate an ability to use own knowledge to solve common problems within a familiar context, and an ability to adjust an application of a common solution within relevant parameters to meet the needs of small changes in the problem or operating context with an understanding of the consequences of related actions

Ethics and professional practice, in respect of which a learner is able to demonstrate an ability to adhere to organisational ethics and a code of conduct, and an ability to understand societal values and ethics

Accessing, processing and managing information, in respect of which a learner is able to demonstrate a basic ability in gathering relevant information, analysis and evaluation skills, and an ability to apply and carry out actions by interpreting information from text and operational symbols or representations

Producing and communicating information, in respect of which a learner is able to demonstrate an ability to communicate and present information reliably and accurately in written and in oral or signed form

Context and systems, in respect of which a learner is able to demonstrate an understanding of the organisation or operating environment as a system within a wider context

Management of learning, in respect of which a learner is able to demonstrate a capacity to take responsibility for own learning within a supervised environment, and a capacity to evaluate own performance against given criteria

Accountability, in respect of which a learner is able to demonstrate a capacity to take decisions about and responsibility for actions, and a capacity to take the initiative to address any shortcomings found

(Sourced from www.saqa.org.za accessed 20 January 2012)

---

demonstrate an understanding that knowledge in a particular field develops over a period of time through the efforts of a number of people and often through the synthesis of information from a variety of related sources and fields while learners at level four must be able to

demonstrate an understanding that knowledge in one field can be applied to related fields.

Is the former at a 'lower level' than the latter?

Finally, what each *specification* means is open to a huge range of interpretation. For example, to "solve common problems within a familiar context" could mean many different things. It is far from clear that, using this as a criterion, people would easily be able to adjudicate between different qualifications, and make judgements about whether they are at the same level.

Consider some examples in Box 3 below, drawn from our study (Allais, 2010b).

Box 3: Some extracts from different countries' level descriptors

Six types of descriptors in Tunisia
This qualifications framework has six types of descriptors of learning outcomes:
Complexity,
Autonomy,
Responsibility,
Adaptability,
Knowledge,
Know-how, and
Behaviour.

Five 'characteristic generic outcomes' in Scotland
The Scottish level descriptors, which were developed based on pre-existing descriptors for the different sectors, specify 'characteristic generic outcomes' for each level (except level one) under five headings:
Knowledge and understanding;
Practice (applied knowledge and understanding);
Generic cognitive skills;
Communication, ICT and numeracy skills;
Autonomy, accountability and working with others.

Eight 'domains' in Malaysia
Malaysia has eight domains of descriptors:
Knowledge;
Practical skills;
Social skills and responsibilities;
Values, attitudes and professionalism;
Communication, leadership and team skills;

Problem solving and scientific skills;
Information management and lifelong learning skills; and
Managerial and entrepreneurial skills.

Concise and detailed descriptors in Lithuania
In Lithuania, levels are defined not only by competences, but also by types of activities. There are two kinds of level descriptors, concise, and detailed or comprehensive. The former are described providing a brief description of qualification levels for general information purposes, and include characteristics of activities, content and acquisition of qualification, and opportunities for further learning. Detailed descriptors, on the other hand, are for the usage of different experts (designers of vocational education and training curricula, experts involved in the assessment of competences and awarding of qualifications, experts responsible for the recognition of qualifications acquired abroad and so on). In these, levels are described comprehensively with detailed indicative characteristics of the level of qualifications. Descriptors of levels are based on two parameters, each of which contains three criteria. Levels are defined not only by competences but also by types of activities.

Ten 'indicators of professional performance' in Russia
In Russia the ten most important indicators of professional performance were identified to formulate descriptors:
Work with information;
Reflection;
Ability to learn;
Business communication;
Responsibility;
Motivation;
Setting up goals;
Independence;
Ability to teach; and
Breadth of views.

Descriptors were developed according to the following rules:

- a descriptor at each level has to be independent of other descriptors. Only at the place of transfer to a higher level does a descriptor have to correlate with the descriptors of higher and lower levels;
- descriptors have to be defined in the affirmative grammatical form;
- they have to be concrete and clear, words with abstract lexical meaning cannot be used ("good", "narrow", "acceptable" etc.);
- they cannot contain professional jargon, they have to be understandable for non-professionals;
- they have to be formulated in a short form to provide clear understanding of the essence of the given level.

Just consider how many different categories of descriptors there are, and how these differ across countries. We have already seen ten categories in the South African level descriptors. The European Qualifications Framework contains three types of specifications: knowledge, skill, and competence. In Tunisia, there are six types. In Scotland, there are five 'characteristic generic outcomes', which must be elaborated for each level (except level one). Malaysia has eight 'domains' of descriptors. The list goes on and on. Note the very last point in the rules for level descriptor development in Russia: that they must provide a clear understanding of the 'essence' of the given level. Considering the length of the descriptors, the variety of different categories across countries, and the various other problems discussed above, this seems extremely unlikely.

There are implicit hierarchies between qualifications in all formal education systems, with some relationship to hierarchies within knowledge areas or disciplines. There is no doubt that a PhD is higher up any such hierarchy than a bachelors' degree, or a post-school vocational qualification. But beyond these very broad specifications, making judgements about levels of difficulty is not straightforward. In some countries in our study, disciplinary specialization was seen as crucial for a qualification to be seen as 'at a higher level', while others specified a greater need for inter-disciplinary knowledge at higher levels. High levels of responsibility or autonomy need not necessarily require or imply high levels of knowledge, and *vice versa*. Leadership and team skills, or communication skills, may not be required at all for some people working at extremely high levels of knowledge specialization. Or, even if some degree of these skills may be required, it does not follow that each type of skill, competence, and ability must be developed to the same level. For example, a theoretical physicist working at the most advanced levels of her discipline may not need level 10 communication or team working skills, even though some communication ability will be very handy for her.

Markowitsch and Luomi-Messerer (2008) argue that there is simply no coherent theory which enables the development of such descriptors. Méhaut and Winch (2011) discuss the substantial differences across European countries in the understandings of words such as 'knowledge', 'skill', and 'competence'—the three categories which are defined for each of the levels of the European Qualifications Framework. In other words, simply saying that to be placed at a particular level on a framework, a qualification must ensure that a learner has "[k]nowledge of facts, principles, processes and general concepts in a field of work or study", or that a learner has "a range of cognitive and practical skills required to accomplish tasks and to solve problems by applying basic tools, methods, materials and information"[2] does not make allocating qualifications to levels a straightforward decision.

While reaching agreement on what the level descriptors should look like is difficult, it will be more difficult still to ensure that everyone interprets these descriptors in the same way. Analyses of the development of these descriptors (for example, Hart, 2009; Markowitsch & Luomi-Messerer, 2008) shows that there are huge differences in interpretation across them. It is precisely because they are so open to interpretation that learning outcomes and competence-based approaches tend to lead to over-specification. This is why we see examples like that of Lithuania, in which there are both 'concise' and 'detailed' descriptors. As seen in the box above, the Lithuanian descriptors are highly complex, and yet all the complexity is supposed to be generic—it is supposed to be generically applied across fields and knowledge areas.

Where countries have similar looking level descriptors, it is because they have been designed using the European Qualifications Framework as a basis. Turkey, for example, has adopted the European descriptors. In Bangladesh, level descriptors drew on the European Qualifications Framework, but with some changes. They are based on 'knowledge, skill, and responsibility', and are linked to very broad 'classes' of jobs. Another reason for commonalities across countries is that level descriptors are frequently designed by consultants who base them on the level descriptors of another country (Scotland was cited as a common source in our study). This could be a potential resolution to the problem of many different descriptors. The existence of the European Qualifications Framework as a powerful force in the world of qualifications frameworks may lead to level descriptors looking similar. But this still does not escape the other problem identified above: what will they mean? How will people interpret them?

Even if we consider only a hierarchy of *cognitive* processes, making judgements about levels is not a straightforward matter. This was illustrated by two curriculum evaluations which I led as researcher for a government agency in South Africa (Allais, 2006, 2007b). We asked evaluators to use an adapted version of the Revised Bloom's Taxonomy[3] (a hierarchy of different kinds of cognitive processes) to guide their judgements about the standards of specified curricula and examinations. In the former evaluation, we compared South African school and college curricula, and in the latter, we compared senior secondary curricula in Ghana, Kenya, South Africa, and Zambia. A hierarchy of types of cognitive operations was produced, derived from the revised taxonomy, which evaluators were then supposed to apply to their analysis of the curricula documentation. What emerged starkly in our evaluation of this research was that subject experts found it very difficult to make meaning of the hierarchy of cognitive skills; they tended to make judgements based on disciplinary knowledge as well as contextual knowledge of teaching and learning. They were not convinced that there existed clear, uncontested distinctions between the various cognitive processes specified in the tools that we had developed. For example, the science evaluators argued that it is often the *way* in which knowledge is tested which determines whether it counts as factual or conceptual knowledge, not the content alone: to *remember a statement* of Newton's Third Law of Motion is simple recall, but to actually *understand the concept* embodied by this statement is challenging, since it is counter-intuitive. In biology, there was some kind of relationship between cognitive operations, types of knowledge and levels of difficulty, but there were also differing levels of difficulty across cognitive operations and types of knowledge. For example, evaluators argued that most of the easy (level one) questions in the South African examinations were in the category *understand conceptual knowledge*, while in the Zambian papers, the easy questions tended to be *recall factual knowledge.*[4] This in itself is not specific to a learning outcomes-approach, and is something that needs to be considered in any assessment design. The point, however, is that a statement of a learning outcome does not contain intrinsic criteria as to how it should be interpreted. A range of factors needs to be considered, and expert judgements need to be made.

To the extent that evaluators were able to make judgements about the nature and quality of the courses, it was only the specification of *content* that enabled these judgements. Evaluators argued that the content specification was essential but not sufficient, and that a careful analysis of examination papers was required. Evaluators also argued that intended and examined curricula need to be evaluated together; or at least in light of each other, as far as possible. They emphasized that there are often vast differences between the intended curriculum, as represented by the official syllabus documentation, and the enacted curriculum, as represented by the full spectrum of possible classroom practices. But they also pointed out that assessment practices, particularly in 'high stakes' assessment, do have a powerful 'backwash' effect, which means that classroom practice is substantially affected by what learners need to know and be able to do in assessments. This meant that it was essential to consider assessment instruments, in this case, examination question papers, to reach any kind of meaningful judgement about relative standards[5].

Even when considering specified syllabuses together with examination papers, evaluators were only able to make limited judgements, as, for example, evaluators could not always make judgements about the predictability of questions, particularly in other countries. Of course, none of the evaluations enabled any insight into the *enacted* curriculum, or into how examination scripts were actually marked, both of which have substantial impact on educational quality. But evaluators were able to gain some insight into the relative standards of the different courses from the content specification in the curriculum documents, together with the examination question papers. None of this will be particularly surprising to educators who work in school systems or do research on school curricula or examinations. But the ways in which judgements were made: subject experts examining context, content, and assessment tools, could not have been done using only learning outcomes. The inability of evaluators to reach agreement across subject areas about the meaning of different words describing cognitive activities raises questions about the possibilities of creating hierarchies of level descriptors (or learning outcomes separate from knowledge areas) in any kind of meaningful way. It also corroborates the argument made by Brockmann, Clarke, and Winch (2011) that outcomes or standards only make sense in the context of the curriculum of which they are a part.

All of these conceptual problems suggest that level descriptors cannot play the roles that are claimed for them. This may explain why our research found very little evidence that level descriptors are actually being used, to say nothing of evidence about *how* they are being used, or how useful they are in making decisions about the location of qualifications on the framework, or about credit transfer, or at comparing foreign qualifications. The only exception was in Scotland, where researchers described level descriptors as 'assisting professional judgements'.

CONCLUSION

The claims made about the role of learning outcomes and outcomes-based qualifications in labour markets do not stand up to critical scrutiny.

The idea of level descriptors is broader than that of employer-specified competences, and applies to almost all qualifications frameworks, while the idea of employer-specified competences dominates some, but not all. I have demonstrated that a broader notion of outcomes in the form of level descriptors is unlikely to improve worker mobility, for the outcomes cannot operate in the way that they are claimed to—level descriptors do not provide a language to translate one education system into another, because they themselves are understood differently in different countries and even between different practitioners in the same countries. Further, outcomes-based qualifications frameworks do not address more fundamental problems with labour mobility—restrictions placed by national governments on emigration. Prior to this I explained why the idea of employer-specified competences and the outcomes/ competence-based qualification model that follows it emerged primarily in countries with *weak* relationships between vocational education and labour markets, and in more liberalized labour markets with weaker social policy. There is very little evidence that competence-based qualifications have solved the problem of weak relationships between education and labour markets, and I have shown that the reason for this is that they do not address the primary causes of the problem. What they do lead to is low-level qualifications containing narrowly specified skills, which have low-labour market currency—ironic for a policy that claims to improve education/ workplace relationships. This is aggravated by the ways in which outcomes-based qualification reforms can weaken education systems, as discussed in the previous two chapters. There are further educational problems with this approach, which I examine in the following chapter.

ENDNOTES

[1] See Wolf (2002) for a useful elaboration of this problem.
[2] These are two of the descriptors for level three of the European Qualifications Framework, and are cited in Brockman *et al.* (2011, p. 7).
[3] Anderson and Krathwohl (2001)
[4] This and other related research is discussed in more detail in Allais (2012a).
[5] The 'backwash' effect of assessment can, of course, have negative effects on education systems, particularly if the assessments are narrow, or if there is too much assessment, but this is a different issue from the problems with learning outcomes, and is certainly not solved by introducing learning outcomes, as is sometimes argued.

CHAPTER 6

KNOWLEDGE, OUTCOMES, AND THE CURRICULUM

INTRODUCTION

The subject of this chapter is the role that is claimed for outcomes-based qualifications in *curriculum* reform, and the explicit and implicit epistemological stance behind outcomes-based qualification frameworks. There is not just one epistemological position inherent to qualifications frameworks. If frameworks are seen as 'light touch' reforms which formalize how qualifications relate to each other, something like a traditional diagram which demonstrates the relationships between the main qualifications on offer in a particular country, sector, or part of an education system, no specific epistemological position is implied. However, most of the claims made about the role of outcomes-based qualifications in education reforms rest on a notion of knowledge as information that can be divided into little bits that can be selected and combined at will. This ignores the extent to which educational knowledge is necessarily organized in bodies of hierarchical conceptual relationships, the value of such bodies of knowledge, and the necessary conditions for their acquisition. I demonstrate that learning outcomes rely on an idea of transparency that they cannot achieve in practice, and that the outcomes approach leads to narrow over-specified outcome statements, and so does not enable curriculum coherence. Starting from activities or roles, whether in workplaces or otherwise, does not enable reflection on what education can and cannot do, but assumes that education must and can lead to any specified outcome—whichever is deemed important at that moment.

The role of subjects and disciplines in shaping curricula is a long-standing and heated debate in education, as touched on in Chapter 2. I suggest that the problems experienced in the implementation of outcomes-based qualifications frameworks provide an indication of why curriculum design needs to start with the idea of the acquisition of bodies of knowledge. This does not mean, however, that I am calling for a thoughtless return to 'traditional' subjects, without questioning which subjects or disciplines should be taught in which educational programmes, or what knowledge should be selected within subjects and disciplines, a point I address in the following two chapters.

KNOWLEDGE AND LEARNING OUTCOMES

It is increasingly rare to find an educational policy document which does not include reference or allusion to the 'changing role of knowledge' or the 'knowledge society', albeit often at the level of rhetorical gestures. But it is seldom clear what exactly knowledge is in this policy world. While it has taken on a new prominence, knowledge also seems to have undergone a conceptual shrinkage in much contemporary policy documentation. 'Knowledge' is sometimes equated with something which would probably be better described as 'information' or 'fact', and, echoing previous ideas about learning objectives and learner centred education, is frequently argued to be less important than what are described as 'skills' (Livingstone & Guile, 2012). Education policies talk about the speed at which 'knowledge' is changing, and that more important than 'knowledge' is the ability to 'learn how to learn', and to learn things like 'problem solving' (Peters 2001). Policies focused on 'core skills' and 'essential skills' have emerged, which suggest that knowledge is not as important as skills that are transferable across jobs and industries (Grubb and Lazerson 2006). Johan Muller (2008, p. 206) argues that contemporary debates about the 'knowledge society' as well as debates about the nature of the labour market in so-called post-industrial capitalism have brought to the forefront questions about what knowledge is for, and have "re-opened the debate about the relative merits of relevant knowledge on the one hand and knowledge for its own sake on the other". This debate has remained fierce and unresolved across the last century or more of educational reform.

Learning outcomes and qualifications frameworks represent, amongst other things, a particular attempt by policy makers to resolve the problem of what education should teach and how it should teach it, by allowing relevant 'stakeholders' to define the required outcomes of any learning process. These outcomes are then supposed to provide the starting point for curriculum design. The South African Qualifications Authority (2001a, p. 7) argues:

> The OBET [outcomes – based education and training] system differs fundamentally from previous knowledge and inputs-based systems in the sense that the learner, not the content or the curriculum, is at the centre of the learning.

A report jointly authored by the Commonwealth of Learning and the South African Qualifications Authority (Commonwealth of Learning and SAQA, 2008, p. 44) and cited in Chapter 1 suggests that qualifications frameworks represent "new notions of knowledge", and a "new hierarchy" in which "education providers are no longer the leaders and standards-setters, and content (or inputs) is no longer the starting point". They refer to this as a 'design down' approach to curriculum development, in which, as captured in Figure 1 below, the knowledge to be taught is supposed to be selected in order to ensure that learners will acquire the relevant learning outcome.

This figure diagrammatically represents the idea that level descriptors, the broadest level of learning outcomes, are the starting point for curriculum design. As discussed in the previous chapter, level descriptors are broad learning outcomes or competences that all qualifications at a particular level are supposed to lead to. The arrow on the top left, moving to the right from 'Qualifications framework', indicates that it is in the qualifications framework that these broad learning outcomes are set. In most qualifications frameworks, level descriptors are supposed to be agreed on

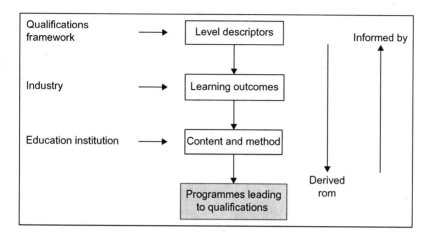

Figure 1. Designing Down (adapted from Commonwealth of Learning and SAQA, 2008, p. 44).

by stakeholders. Industry, or other stakeholders, then designs more specific learning outcomes that are relevant to their specific needs, but which also lead to the broad learning outcomes specified in the level descriptors—as indicated by the sideways arrow from 'Industry' to 'Learning outcomes' in the diagram. This step, advocates argue, enables power over qualifications to shift towards employers and away from educational providers, which is assumed to be desirable. Education institutions then design and select content and teaching methodologies, assembling them into learning programmes that will lead to the specific learning outcomes specified by industry, which in turn will lead to the broader outcomes specified in the level descriptors.

In outcomes-based models, learning outcomes are frequently juxtaposed with 'inputs', which are variously conceived as syllabuses/curriculum, teaching, time, and institutions. In some cases the rhetoric and accompanying policies based on learning outcomes and competences are explicitly opposed to subject-based curricula, while in other cases, subject-based curricula are seen as one amongst many inputs, with the emphasis still on the outcomes or competences that learners have achieved. However, there is a slippage here. Although the emphasis is on *outcomes* as opposed to *inputs*, outcomes which are specified in qualification or curriculum documentation are *not* the outcomes that *have been achieved*, but outcomes which have been *specified as targets or goals* which should be associated with particular qualifications and learning programmes. Learning outcomes are *not* outcomes of learning, but only the *desired* outcomes. In this way, they are the same as aims, syllabuses, curriculum specifications, and so on. They are a means of specifying the intended curriculum, as well as, in theory, a benchmark against which learners' achievements within a curriculum can be measured. They are also supposed to be a benchmark for measuring what learners have achieved in the course of everyday

141

life or work, regardless of whether they have worked their way through a particular educational programme. Unlike the other major international trend in education—the achievement test—which, for all its weaknesses and problems, tries to measure what learners have achieved at various points, the outcomes and qualifications policies specify outcomes which learners *should* achieve, what the outputs *should* be, in order for them to be awarded a particular qualification. In this sense, the learning outcomes are *inputs*, and not outputs. The assumption is that clear statements of learning outcomes will ensure that the appropriate outputs can be achieved.

Learning outcomes differ from traditional mechanisms for specifying an intended curriculum in their attempt to describe desired outcomes separately from bodies of knowledge and skill, distinguishing them from syllabuses which are embedded in and derived from areas of knowledge. A syllabus has aims, whether or not they are articulated explicitly, but these aims are derived from a body of knowledge. A syllabus usually includes information about sequencing—the order in which content should be taught—and can include assessment specifications. A syllabus is designed by specialists within education institutions[1], and is also intended to be interpreted by specialists within education institutions. Learning outcomes can—and indeed, according to much documentation about qualifications frameworks, *should*—be designed by institutions outside of education—whether governments, employers, or other 'stakeholders', and should be understandable to all these stakeholders.

Because learning outcomes have to enable comparisons to be made, not only between different education programmes, but also between learning that has happened outside and inside of education programmes, it is necessary for the learning outcomes to stand above any particular curriculum, education programme, or institution. Similarly, in order for learning outcomes to ensure that stakeholders' interests are met, they must be specified by those stakeholders separately from curricula; the role of the education institution is then to develop curricula that lead to the specified outcomes. This is not a controversial point in advocacy documents for qualifications frameworks; I raise it here because advocacy documents often conflate on the one hand, the idea of teachers setting outcomes within their classroom and within a specified curriculum, with, on the other hand, stakeholders specifying learning outcomes from which curricula are supposed to be developed. For example, a European Union document advocating for learning outcomes uses teachers setting their own outcomes for each lesson as an example of learning outcomes (European Union, 2011). But the claims made about what learning outcomes can do in education reform (improving education/labour market relationships; reforming curricula, pedagogy, and assessment; facilitating recognition of prior learning; reforming how education is delivered; and improving quality) are based on the idea of outcomes specified separately from curricula, which is very different to the process whereby a teacher sets aims for her class within a curriculum. For example, claims that learning outcomes can be used as a mechanism to 'translate' or compare different qualifications to each other, as well as claims that they can be used as benchmarks of attainment for any learning, regardless of whether that learning is linked to a particular learning programme or has been attained by the individual during the course of work or life, assume that the learning outcome is an independent benchmark, that has no intrinsic relation to any particular curriculum or learning programme:

> One of the greatest benefits of an NQF is that it facilitates a *reference* for lifelong learning and for progress in work and social life. (Vargas Zuñiga, 2005, p. 12, my emphasis)

> Progression in learning becomes more than a predetermined path defined and restricted by education and training institutions, but will increasingly be based on an appreciation of the learning outcomes in question, *wherever these have been acquired.* (Cedefop, 2009, p. 5, my emphasis)

The separation of learning outcomes from curricula, learning programmes, and education institutions contains an implicit notion of knowledge, as I explore below.

IMPLIED, 'EMBEDDED', AND 'UNDERPINNING' KNOWLEDGE

The strongest idea of the relationship between outcomes and knowledge in outcomes-based qualifications frameworks and competence-based training can be seen in the policies and systems which talk about 'underpinning' or 'embedded' knowledge. The preference is for no knowledge to be specified in the learning outcomes (or qualification documentation). The belief is that if a particular 'piece' of knowledge is essential to a particular competence or outcome, that piece of knowledge is *implied* when the competence or learning outcome is invoked, and therefore does not need to be specified. Thus, when designing a curriculum, instead of starting from bodies of knowledge, one starts from the competence or outcome, and brings in bits of knowledge as and when they are required. Knowledge must be selected because it leads to the required learning outcome or competence, and not for any other reason, such as its intrinsic value and interest, or because it could provide a foundation for further acquisition of knowledge in a particular area.

This perspective is usually accompanied by arguments that *knowledge* does not need to be assessed; an individual's grasp of any knowledge that they need to know can be *inferred* from competent performance. As Jessup (1991, p. 121), English advocate of an outcomes-based approach to vocational education, argues: "if a person performs competently we need not be concerned with what he or she knows". Similarly, in South Africa, the Qualifications Authority insisted that unit standards (part qualifications) and learning outcomes were not about knowledge:

> If the identified knowledge is that which we need to develop in order to *achieve* identified results or outcomes ... then it *belongs in learning programs,* which are about inputs. We should not say anything about this in unit standards, which are about outcomes. Let us trust teachers, trainers and instructional designers to *do their job*, and identify what must be learnt in order for people to be able to achieve the outcomes! (SAQA, 2000b, p. 27, emphasis in original)

This is common in outcomes-based and competence-based systems. Wolf (1995, p. 26) explains: "A common concern of all competence-based reforms is to counteract what is seen as a 'knowledge bias' within testing procedures". It has also been assumed, she goes on to explain, that "knowledge requirements are legitimate only when clearly required in, and for, performance".

This logic is what informs the idea of 'underpinning knowledge' (the term used, for example, in the English National Vocational Qualifications) or 'essential embedded knowledge (the term used in South Africa). These terms refer to the fact that the specification of some knowledge which 'underlies' the specified competence is allowed, although not preferred. This idea was commonly expressed in South Africa in the notion that content is a "vehicle to achieve the desired learning outcomes" (for example, Malan, 2000, p. 24).

Although the required knowledge should ideally be *implied* within the specific outcomes, it was permissible in South Africa to state the knowledge requirements separately. This is captured in the following extract from a policy document:

> If the standards writers have adopted an integrated approach to standards writing, then the specific outcomes should identify all knowledge to be assessed, and the assessment criteria should identify all knowledge required as proof of competence. If the standards writers have not adopted an integrated approach, embedded knowledge would have to be described at this stage. (SAQA, 2000b, p. 26)

The South African Qualifications Authority goes on to warn: "Caution must be exercised to avoid using this category as a dumping ground for course content. Unit standards are about outcomes, not inputs." In another policy document this organization (SAQA, 1997, p. 10) explains "Background knowledge, cognitive frameworks, assumptions and values essential to the completion of the unit standard are examples of embedded knowledge". The assumption is that the knowledge that 'counts' is the knowledge that is visible in performance. The basic notion of knowledge in the ideas of underpinning and embedded knowledge is that it must have a direct relationship with the learning outcome in order to justify its presence in the curriculum. This confuses knowledge with information. For example, in the South African outcome statement

Apply the arbitration act in dispute resolution (level five, four credits),

the 'essential embedded knowledge' would be knowledge of the act itself. A learner who does not know it, is unable to apply it. Similarly, in South Africa, there are a series of unit standards on banking which mainly focus on knowledge of different pieces of legislation. Each piece of legislation is separately specified as essential embedded knowledge in the respective unit standard.
Christopher Norris (1991, p. 336) points out:

> Competency-based training theorists typically see knowledge as static, as information. They ask what knowledge underpins an activity and more

specifically what does a person need to know in order to do this task or activity effectively. Often knowledge is seen as evidenced in the performance or as supplementary evidence to performance demonstrations that is required to support generalisation. Thus knowledge is largely seen as an issue of assessment. And what lies at the heart of this issue is whether knowledge relevant to an occupation needs to be assessed separately or whether it can be inferred from appropriate and effective action.

This approach to knowledge is reinforced by the idea that outcomes must be measurable. A very common statement by advocates of learning outcomes warns people not to use the word 'understand' because it is not measurable. A google search of the words 'understand is not a measurable learning outcome' turns up millions of webpages from all around the world, in which people are training or advising others in how to specify learning outcomes (I got nearly 18 million hits). They are usually accompanied with advice to use action verbs when writing learning outcomes, and to choose actions which are easy to observe or measure.

KNOWLEDGE AS FLAT

All of this is at odds with any notion of knowledge as hierarchically organized into structured and inter-related concepts, as well as with any notion of bodies of knowledge as intrinsically important. Knowledge is seen as essentially flat, meaning that any 'bit' of it can be selected as required—propositions or fragments of information derived from different conceptual fields can be selected as if they have some meaning on their own.

Not all qualifications frameworks use learning outcomes in quite as extreme a manner, and some advocates of learning outcomes suggest that the specification of learning outcomes can and should include the specification of knowledge, not just 'embedded knowledge, or underpinning knowledge, but knowledge in its own right. So, for example, documents associated with the European Qualifications Framework define learning outcomes as knowledge, skills, and competence (European Commission, 2008). Cedefop (2008, p. 15) states that learning outcomes are "statements of what a learner knows, understands, and is able to do on completion of a learning process". These learning outcomes are juxtaposed with "input factors" such as "the duration, location and particular pedagogical method underpinning a qualification" (Cedefop, 2008, p. 1). But this formal valuing of knowledge is at odds with the notion of learning outcomes as an independent benchmark against which knowledge can be measured and evaluated.

Consider Patrick Werquin's (2012, p. 260) definition of learning outcomes that includes the 'knows, understands, and is able to do' approach mentioned above. He argues:

> Any approach to learning that emphasises learning outcomes is a significant change from the traditional approach that focuses on the content of a course or

a programme rather than on what learners are expected to know and be able to do after the completion of the programme.

Bohlinger (2012, p. 282) argues:

> Implementing qualifications frameworks is hoped to promote a shift from shared practices (what should be learnt? what do teacher and trainers want to teach?) to explicit criteria defining learning outcomes (what are learners able to do? what do they actually know?) and to release qualifications from their traditional links with formal learning and institutionalised educational programmes by validating learning outcomes independently of the context of learning processes.

This is not so different to the 'embedded' knowledge idea described above—because the knowledge is seen as something that is implied in the acquisition of learning outcomes. Similarly, a European Union document argues:

> Increasingly, competence-based approaches and learning outcomes are being introduced as a guiding mechanism to inform general education reforms. The emphasis is on defining key competences and learning outcomes to shape the learner's experience, rather than giving primacy to the content of the subjects that make up the curriculum. (European Union, 2011, p. 9)

The same European Union document goes on to state that learning outcomes "must have an observable behaviour" and "have to be measurable" (European Union, 2011, p. 17). This document, which claims to include knowledge as one of the components of learning outcomes, suggests that instead of 'understand', other verbs must be used, such as "define, recall, list, describe, explain or discuss" or, for more advanced programmes, "formulate, appraise, evaluate, estimate or construct" (European Union, 2011, p. 22). The document goes on to explain that the "verb will usually be followed by words indicating on what or with what the learner is acting and the nature or context of the performance required as evidence that the learning was achieved". This is because "Words such as 'know' or 'understand' do not help with this demonstration of learning and are therefore usually avoided because it is not clear to the learner the level of understanding or amount of knowledge required." (It is not clear how this is solved by stipulating 'recall', 'describe' 'explain' or 'evaluate', as learners will still not know the amount of knowledge required, the level at which each of these so-called measurable actions should be carried out, or the extent of the evaluation required.)

The assumption behind the idea of independently specified learning outcomes is either that people can acquire the same knowledge both inside and outside of education institutions and courses of study, or that different 'knowledges' can all have the same relationship with a given outcome, and so can all lead to that outcome. The primary role of education is to produce learning outcomes which can also be produced just as well elsewhere. There is nothing specifically valuable about the education process.

Implicit in this idea is a notion of everyday knowledge as the same as bodies of knowledge that traditionally have been acquired through sustained and structured courses of study, whether in education institutions or apprenticeships. The implication is a flat, unstructured, undifferentiated notion of knowledge. Structured bodies of knowledge may exist, but they are arbitrary; knowledge can be acquired in other ways, in different orders, in different contexts. This 'flatness' or undifferentiatedness of knowledge is implicit to many of the arguments made for how outcomes-based qualifications frameworks can assist with the recognition of prior learning. This is why knowledge in outcomes or competence statements tends to become relegated to meaning pieces of information or even task specifications.

There are likely to be many examples of ostensibly outcomes-based courses which do teach bodies of knowledge—but this exists in spite of, not because of, the logic of outcomes. For example, in South Africa at one point in the 1990s all lecturers in universities were forced to produce learning outcomes for their courses. This was, for the main, done in a cosmetic manner to comply with the official policy, after the courses had been designed, and had no effect on the courses themselves.

THE SPIRAL OF SPECIFICATION

The currency which competences and outcomes have in contemporary policy derives from the idea that the *essence* of a learning programme, or the *essence* of what an individual *has learnt*, can be mapped in a configuration of clear and transparent learning outcomes. The underlying assumption is that outcomes can disclose meaning to everyone regardless of their level of training in the relevant area, and thus can enable the essence of a programme to be understood *similarly enough* by different stakeholders (Shalem, Allais, & Steinberg, 2004), including all educational institutions. This common understanding is necessary in order for them to select knowledge and pedagogies which will, in all cases, lead to the achievement of the same learning outcomes.

But this does not happen. The previous chapter considered how broad learning outcomes in level descriptors do not represent shared meanings, and are interpreted differently. Similarly, learning outcomes in qualifications or part of qualifications are never sufficiently transparent that they can represent a clear competence that will mean the same thing to different people. Because they are not transparent, the specifications always require additional specifications, but these specifications themselves are also not clear, and in turn require additional specifications. This spiral of specification makes the outcomes or competence statements longer and therefore less usable and, ironically, *less transparent*, because they are so cumbersome: "Clarification leads to complication which is why lists of outcomes grow like mould and become unwieldy" (Knight, 2001, p. 373). Young (1996, p. 28) argues that "[a]ll the experience of NVQs in England and other outcomes-based systems indicates that attempts to increase the precision of outcomes can only lead to them becoming trivialized". Wolf (1995) provides a detailed empirical and conceptual critique showing flaws in the assumption that a specification of outcomes can reveal quality standards. She explains how, in relation to the National Vocational Qualifications in England, while the emphasis of this kind of competence-based system has been on the clarity which it promised to assessors and learners, the creation of competence statements had led to "an ever more complex and complicated 'methodology'". She shows that the desire to reach an agreement on the meaning of learning outcomes and assessment criteria leads to a level of reduction that is educationally unsound:

> The more serious and rigorous the attempts to specify the domain being assessed, the narrower and narrower the domain itself becomes, without, in fact, becoming fully transparent. The attempt to map out free-standing content and standards leads, again and again, to a never-ending spiral of specification. (Wolf, 1995, p. 55)

Like Wolf, Norris (1991, p. 334) suggests that this is a problem inherent to competence-based training:

> Like its forerunner, behavioural objectives, the language of competence invites a spurious precision and elaboration in the definition of good or effective practice. The specification of competence is assessment led in that it is usually associated with a statement which defines performance criteria and expected levels of performance. ... A key principle in the assessment of competence is that assessment criteria should be transparent for all to see .... Such models can be highly reductive, providing atomised lists of tasks and functions, or they can be highly generalised, offering descriptions of motivational dispositions or cognitive abilities such as problem-solving. In the case of the former the sum of the parts rarely if ever represents the totality of good practice; paradoxically the role is under-determined by the specification. In the case of the latter it is difficult if not impossible to provide an operational account of a disposition or ability that does not rest solely on situational judgement. A more significant feature of models of competence is that in their tidiness and precision, far from preserving the essential features of expertise, they distort and understate the very things they are trying to represent.

Hall and Woodhouse (1999, p. 208) provide similar arguments based on experiences in New Zealand:

> [t]he effort and cost needed in making clear an educational standard in writing quickly reaches a point where the law of diminishing returns takes over— additional effort is not matched by educational benefits.

The complicated structures and processes which emerge when countries attempt to implement outcomes-based qualifications frameworks or competence-based frameworks are a *consequence* both of the lack of transparency of outcome statements, and the assumption that learning outcomes should be transparent. They are not the consequence of incompetent bureaucrats or policy makers; they are the product of a logic which is internal to the notion of specifying outcomes outside of educational contexts. The combination of the *need for* and *lack of* transparency leads to increasing elaboration of the 'standards', as well as the development of increasingly narrow standards.

Course aims can be stated broadly, because they are the aims of *something*, and do not have to 'stand on their own', and be interpreted by any 'stakeholder'. They are interpreted by experts in the field in question, and, to a limited extent, by students; of course students will not have a full grasp of what is entailed in something that they do not yet know or understand, but course aims provide them with some sense of where they are going. Similarly, learning outcomes, if they are the outcomes of a specific course, learning programme, or syllabus, can be stated broadly. It is the move of separating learning outcomes from specific courses, learning programmes, and educational institutions that leads, inevitably, to over-specification.

One of the practical problems of the outcomes-based approach is that the process of designing the learning outcomes frequently leads to arcane and complex disputes over terminology that become increasingly opaque to people not involved in the processes—which then contradicts the aim of increased transparency and improved supply of information. As discussed in Chapter 4, in many countries there is constant fiddling with the specifications and formats of the learning outcomes or competence standards, in an attempt to make them more intelligible (Allais, 2010b). Our research in Mexico, for example, found that once it became clear that a particular set of specifications had not reached their aims, then a new set of specifications would be implemented, only for them to fail and be replaced again. In this instance and in many other cases, policy-makers interpreted the problem as being due to inadequately specified standards, or incompetent standards developers. Frequently, this inadequacy was attributed to a lack of participation from industry in the standards setting process and a subsequent failure to ensure that vocational education and other labour-market oriented education and training met the needs of employers – something which, as elaborated in the previous chapter, was one of the main claims of many outcomes-based systems. This might explain not only why particular competence based models are fiddled with, but why, in some cases, one competence based training system is completely replaced by another. In each instance, the previous format of standards is seen as inadequate, and so the systems and structures for developing them are changed in the hope that they can be made more representative.

The complexity of the outcomes or competence documentation could be a contributing factor to lack of industry participation. In our research, some representatives from industry described the approach as one imposed on them by education institutions. This is ironic, as education institutions were found, in most countries, to be the most unwilling partners in the process, and to be generally unhappy with the outcomes and competence-based approach, describing it as something imposed by industry.

Finally, this elaborate system, unworkable because of the documentation generated by the layers of specification, ends up in the place it was trying to get away from: reliance on the judgement of specialists. In other words, if you are trying to measure the performance of specialists in a particular area, it always comes down to specialists in that area making the judgement. This raises the question of why the whole system was necessary in the first place. Outcomes are an unnecessary addition to the judgement of the specialist because despite being so long and cumbersome, they do not capture specialist knowledge.

In order to illustrate the relationship between learning outcomes and knowledge, let's consider some examples. My research demonstrates how the extremes of the spiral of specification in South Africa made the qualifications framework unworkable[2]. The outcomes tended to become narrower and narrower, as developers tried to make them more specific, and less likely to be 'misinterpreted'. This resulted in lengthy documents specifying very narrow and low level tasks, such as packing groceries or washing hands. What makes the South African study particularly interesting was that learning outcomes were not confined to vocational or occupational areas, as will be seen below from the small sample of unit standards extracted from the more than 15 000 which have been registered on the South African qualifications framework. As discussed in Chapter 4 the vast majority of these qualifications were never used, and the main qualifications used in South Africa now are those developed through education institutions, against a set of qualification types that are much broader than the original outcomes-based qualifications.

THE SPIRAL OF SPECIFICATION IN PRACTICE: THE SOUTH AFRICAN CASE

The building blocks of most of the outcomes-based qualifications in South Africa were called unit standards. The first place in which outcomes were specified was in the titles of these unit standards. Titles were supposed to be "a coherent and meaningful outcome (milestone/end point) of learning or training that is formally recognized" (SAQA, 2001a). The title was supposed to represent the outcome or learning achievement that was registered on the qualifications framework and against which learners would obtain credit; the title *was* the learning outcome. A title needed to provide a "concise yet comprehensive and pointed indication of the contents of the unit standard"; and had to contain a maximum of 100 characters, including spaces and punctuation (SAQA, 2000b, p. 5).

Outcomes were developed for high and low level qualifications, and for broad and narrow competences. Some examples are listed below:

Control traffic

Demonstrate knowledge and understanding of the characteristics of Burial Societies in South Africa*

Attend to and handle a domestic violence incident*

Access, process, adapt and use data from a wide range of texts

Apply Maritime Geography

Develop and implement the creative process

Manage one's own development

Match personal lifestyles with Biblical values

Identify and describe learning processes

Interact with people in textile processes

Apply knowledge of anatomy, physiology and medical terminology relevant to phlebotomy

Sweep floors

These examples are typical of outcomes in the South African framework. There are over 15 000 of them which can be viewed at www.saqa.org.za. While some of learning outcomes relate to disciplinary areas, and others more directly attempt to capture workplace competences, none of the learning outcomes in the South African framework have a clear meaning to anyone who reads the title outside of a context. Upon learning that an individual had obtained credit against any of the standards listed above, for example, a member of society, an employer, or a state representative would not really be any the wiser. If an employer was presented with applications for a job, and was told that the applicants could 'Match personal lifestyles with Biblical values' or 'Interact with people in textile processes' they would be none the wiser about what the applicant knew and could do.

For instance, does the learning standard 'Match personal lifestyles with Biblical values' demonstrate an ability to smite one's enemies? The developers of this unit, standard might well argue that what is being described here is the ability to analyze one's own lifestyle, analyze Biblical values, and analyze the extent to which there is a relationship between the two. But this doesn't account for different interpretations of what Biblical values are, or even what a 'personal lifestyle' is, or how the one could be matched with the other. Even if you throw out wild interpretations and take it seriously, this is not a clear and recognizable competence. It could describe anything from a highly complex to a very superficial process: it could mean that a learner has entered into a profound and philosophical venture involving applications of sociology, psychology, and theology to every facet of their existence, or it could mean simply that they have been told that Christianity is charitable and then given money to charity.

The title of the unit standard, which is supposed to clearly represent the learning outcomes to be attained, does not represent some fixed 'competence' that will be recognized in general, outside of a specific context. The title of every unit standard has, to varying degrees, the same problem: they do not mean much on their own. Of

151

course, the appropriate titles could mean something very specific to the designer of a learning programme, for instance, within a specific religious training programme, or a teacher training programme, or a conservation programme. This meaning, however, would be confined to people within that programme. Once the learning outcome was uprooted from that context, it would lose this meaning. But this uprooting is precisely central to the claims made about learning outcomes.

To solve the lack of clarity, various layers of additional specification were added, which were supposed to clarify what is being specified in the title. In South Africa these included "specific outcomes", a "purpose statement", and "assessment criteria" (SAQA, 2001a, p. 22). Furthermore, each unit standard was situated within a field and a subfield[3], and allocated a level and amount of credit.

Let's consider specific outcomes first. Each competence captured in a unit standard title was supposed to be broken down into *specific learning outcomes* which "together reflect and capture the purpose of the unit standard in ways that are *measurable* and verifiable" (SAQA, 2000b, p. 9, my emphasis). Specific outcomes were "smaller, more manageable outcomes" (SAQA, 2001a, p. 22). The specific outcomes, however, had to represent the essence of the title outcome: "[t]he specific outcomes of each unit logically make up the title without going beyond the title or falling short of the title" (SAQA, 2001a, p. 22). Like many outcomes- or competence-based systems, the South African Qualifications Authority emphasized the grammatical structure of the specific outcomes: "Verb + noun + modifying phrase(s)" (SAQA, 2001a, p. 23). For example, the unit standard "Facilitate the optimal functioning of the client with a psychiatric disorder" included:

Differentiate between psychiatric disorders and intellectual disability

Describe the meaning, possible causes and effects of psychiatric disorders

Assist the client and family in coping with activities of daily living

Transfer work related social skills to the client

Explain rights and responsibilities relating to psychiatric disorders

After reading the specific outcomes, we do have a better sense of what the designers meant when they said that a competent learner would be able to 'facilitate the optimal functioning of the client with a psychiatric disorder'. But it is still by no means clear what the specific outcomes mean: How much exactly would the qualifying learner have to know about the 'meaning, possible causes and effects of psychiatric disorders'? What form does the assistance to the client and family in coping with activities of daily living take? How much assistance must be given? Which daily activities must be assisted? What are 'work related social skills' and what does it entail to transfer them to the client? What are rights and responsibilities relating to psychiatric disorders?

The purpose statement further elaborated the competence captured in the unit standard title. The South African Qualifications Authority (2000b) clarifies that the purpose statement, together with the 'specific outcomes', showed what the standard was intended to achieve for individuals, for the field or subfield, and for social and economic transformation. The Authority describes the *purpose statement* in the following way: "The purpose statement succinctly captures what the learner will **know** and **be able to do** on the achievement of the unit standard" (SAQA, 2000b, p. 8, emphasis as in original text). As with all the other features of unit standards, the purpose statement followed a specific format: it had to complete the sentence "Persons credited with this unit standard are able to…"

So, for example, although, the learning outcome "Pack customer purchases at point of sales" could be interpreted as not requiring a sense of customer relations, the purpose statement further clarifies that

> Persons credited with this unit standard will be able to pack customer purchases so that damage is minimised and the customer's image of the organisation is enhanced.

The credit allocated to a particular unit standard gave some sense of how much the learner was expected to learn. As in many outcomes- or competence-based systems, the unit standards were not allowed to include time specifications the way a syllabus would, because individuals were supposed to be able to acquire the outcomes at their own pace. But any educational process is time-bound, even if individuals differ, and outcomes-based approaches cannot run away from this. Credit ratings were based on the idea of 'notional learning hours', which were in turn based on a judgement about how long it would take an average learner with the necessary prior knowledge to master the outcome. Thus, credit ratings gave an indication of required breadth and depth. For example, the unit standard about psychiatric disorders mentioned above ("Facilitate the optimal functioning of the client with a psychiatric disorder") was worth sixteen credits, while a full time learning programme for a year was worth roughly 120 credits. This indicated that learning to facilitate optimal functioning of people with psychiatric disorders was expected to take up a fair amount of time, nearly a sixth of a full time programme of study, and therefore was reasonably in depth.

The unit standard "Develop and implement the creative process" was worth 40 credits. The designers of the unit standard were thereby signalling that this was a broad competence, that would take a long time to acquire; about a third of a full time year of study. However,

> Demonstrate a basic understanding of the physiological processes in plant growth and development

was worth only three credits. This gives us a bit more information about how basic the 'basic understanding' was. Without this information, we may have expected the outcome to be something rather more extensive.

The South African Qualifications Authority suggested that only clear learning outcomes enable assessment that is fair, open, reliable and consistent, and that a unit standard becomes a clear learning outcome if it is supplemented by a purpose statement, specific outcomes, and assessment criteria (SAQA, 2000b). Thus, for each specific outcome, there were *assessment criteria*, which were statements that "describe the standard to which learners must perform the actions, roles, knowledge, understanding, skills, values and attitudes stated in the outcomes. They were supposed to be entail a *clear and transparent* expression of requirements against which successful (or unsuccessful) performance is assessed" (SAQA, 2001a, p. 21, emphasis is mine). The Authority also described assessment criteria as the "associated standard of performance used by the assessor to determine whether the outcome has been met" (SAQA, 2001a, p. 22). They also "must be *sufficiently transparent* to ensure ease of understanding across a range of learning providers, learning services and learners" (SAQA, (2000b, p. 10) (emphasis mine). The format of an assessment criterion was specified in this way: "We will know that you are competent (insert specific outcome) if or when...(insert assessment criterion)" (SAQA, 2000b, p. 9). One of the aims of these criteria was to "minimise the subjective judging required" (Hallendorff, Richardson, & Wood, 1999, p. 82). The Authority (SAQA, 2001a, p. 21) argued that "if different standards are applied across the system, the credibility and integrity of the whole system is placed in jeopardy". Assessment criteria were the mechanism to ensure that this did not happen.

The South African Qualifications Authority (2000b, p. 23) provides the following advice to writers of unit standards, with regards to assessment criteria:

The important question to consider at this stage, is:

What critical evidence do we need as proof of competence?

Be careful to avoid breaking the specific outcome into a set of tasks or steps or things to be learnt. A useful trigger is to ask: "if I walked into the room and a competent person was doing/had done this (insert specific outcome here), what would I expect to see in terms of his/her *performance* and in terms of any *product produced*?" (bold is original emphasis, italics are my emphasis)

One of the specific outcomes for the standard "Demonstrate an understanding of agriculture as a challenging and applied system" is "Analyse the geographical distribution of agriculture and its socio-economic impact." The five assessment criteria for this specific outcome are:

The links between agricultural and other economic activities are explained.

Maps to show the type and distribution of agricultural production are labelled, interpreted, summarised and presented.

Information which summarises and demonstrates the significance of agriculture in society is collected and presented.

Link between society and agriculture is established and clarified.

Link between economy and agriculture is established and clarified.

But much is still open to question: What is 'the link' between society and agriculture? What kinds of agricultural production are included? What would be an adequate summary of agricultural production? What would be an adequate explanation of the links between agricultural and other economic activities?

Young (1996, pp. 31–32) argues that "it is never possible to be 100% certain that a piece of evidence fits a learning outcome and that all assessors would reach the same conclusion". The fifteen assessment criteria for hand washing are a clear demonstration of this problem. In an attempt to ensure that there was no ambiguity, or different interpretation of hand washing across the system, fifteen assessment criteria were specified, as shown in Box 4 below.

Box 4: Assessment criteria for specific outcome "Wash hands effectively".
Extract from South African unit standard, 'Maintain personal hygiene, health, and presentation' (level one, four credits)

ASSESSMENT CRITERIA

ASSESSMENT CRITERION 1

1. Applies soap or hand washing detergent.

ASSESSMENT CRITERION 2

2. Explains why soap and water needs to be used for washing hands.

ASSESSMENT CRITERION 3

3. Lathers hands for a minimum of 10 seconds.

ASSESSMENT CRITERION 4

4. Explains why the lather needs to be on the hands for at least 10 seconds.

ASSESSMENT CRITERION 5

5. Washes palms, backs of hands, between fingers and under jewellery.

ASSESSMENT CRITERION 6

6. Explains the areas where most of the dirt and germs can collect on hands.

ASSESSMENT CRITERION 7

7. Rinses and dry hands.

ASSESSMENT CRITERION 8

8. Closes taps after use.

ASSESSMENT CRITERION 9

9. Dries his / her hands thoroughly after washing.

ASSESSMENT CRITERION 10

10. Explains why hands need to be dried.

ASSESSMENT CRITERION 11

11. Explains why hands should not be dried on clothing.

(*Continued*)

CHAPTER 6

Box 4: Continued

ASSESSMENT CRITERION 12

12. Explains why hand washing is important.

ASSESSMENT CRITERION 13

13. Gives 3 examples of when one needs to wash hands.

ASSESSMENT CRITERION 14

14. Explains the proper hand washing techniques.

ASSESSMENT CRITERION 15

15. Gives an example of health problems that can be prevented by hand washing.

Even with the absurdly detailed list of the different things involved in hand washing, it is still not transparent. For instance, it is not clear what constitutes an adequate explanation of why hand washing is important, or what entails an adequate explanation of the 'proper hand washing techniques', and whether or not, for example, this would include techniques to wash hands when soap is not available, with sand or ash. No matter how important hand washing is to everyday hygiene, it is hard to imagine an education system which could benefit from this type of specification. A content specification located in the context of a specific learning programme at a specific level—which might look something like 'Hygiene requirements'—seems far more practical, and could be done far more simply. Teachers, lecturers, and trainers of surgeons, cooks, nurses, and childminders know what the hygiene requirements are, and how they should be taught to learners. Thus a programme syllabus or content guide only needs to make clear that these requirements must be taught. But when the 'competence' of hand washing is taken out of such a context, this endless spiral of specification occurs, without achieving transparency.

These hand-washing specifications related to one sub-outcome of an outcome which was worth only 4 credits. Bear in mind that a qualification in South Africa was supposed to be a minimum of 120 credits, and think about how much detailed documentation this entailed! These narrow, over-specified, detailed, unwieldy, documents were supposed to be the basis for curriculum design, assessment, and quality assurance. The very length and complexity of these documents made them rather unintelligible to anyone other than those involved in standards design, and very difficult to use in practice. This may account for why so many qualifications and competence-standards are developed but not used (as discussed in Chapters 3 and 4). It also makes the notion that learning outcomes will mean something similar enough to people in different contexts impossible to sustain. Policy makers who make claims about what learning outcomes can achieve in the reform of curriculum, as well in regulating the delivery of education, improving education/labour market relationships, improving worker mobility, and so on, seldom add a caveat that in order to make sense of a particular outcome, it will

156

be necessary to consider a whole lot of additional specifications, and that once these specifications are added, each individual learning outcome is accompanied by lengthy documentation.

The downward spiral of specification is frequently accompanied by an upward spiral. For example, in South Africa, regulations were added to the unit standards, to govern who could make judgements against them, and who could judge whether judgements were made correctly against them. Each learner needed to be individually assessed against the learning outcomes specified in the unit standards and qualifications. Assessors were to be checked by moderators, who were to be checked by verifiers. But in order to be an assessor or a moderator or a verifier, an individual had to be found competent against an assessment unit standard, moderated by a moderator who had been found competent against an assessment and a moderation unit standard, and verified by an individual who had been found competent against assessment, moderation, and verification unit standards. This led to a system which was incredibly cumbersome and complicated.

STRUCTURED, ORGANIZED, COMPLEX BODIES OF KNOWLEDGE

While learning, of course, happens everywhere and all the time, education provides access to knowledge which is *not* typically learnt in the course of everyday life. Organized bodies of knowledge enable us to treat the world as an object of study, and not simply as an environment or place of experience; they are systematized because objects must be seen in the relations they maintain with other objects within bodies of thought, and not only by a direct connection with a individual referent, as often happens in the world of experience (Charlot, 2009). Education allows people to spend time in a non-productive (in economic terms) activity, thus enabling reflection on and analysis of aspects of the social and natural world (Masschelein & Simons, 2013). This distance from everyday life makes education and the knowledge acquired through education powerful, as it enables us to stand back and reflect on the world, as opposed to simply experiencing it by virtue of living in it (Young & Muller, 2013; Young, 2008).

The knowledge that is taught in educational institutions is structured and organized in conceptual relationships. Bodies of theory or groups of concepts hang together because they contain internal conceptual relationships. Disciplinary knowledge is the clearest example of structured specialized knowledge. Disciplines are not static, 'given' bodies of knowledge, beyond questioning or changing, they are socially developed and systematically revisable (Collins, 1998; Moore, 2009; Young, 2008). But they do inherently "take the form of a coherent, explicit and systematically principled structure" (Bernstein 2000, p. 157 in Moore 2004, p. 144) which, to a considerable degree, is independent of specific groups in society that work in them or transmit them.

Some bodies of knowledge build cumulatively and progressively on themselves (Bernstein, 1971; Moore, 2009; Young, 2008). For example mathematics, one of the clearest examples of disciplinary knowledge, has a clear hierarchical structure. This means that some concepts need to be acquired before others. Barring the odd extraordinary genius, most of us need to learn it systematically, with sequencing derived at least in part from its inherent structure. Often we have to have been learning it for a fairly long time before much application can be mastered. Of course there is considerable contestation within the discipline about sequencing, teaching how to apply knowledge, and so on. But nonetheless, it is clearly structured; it is not a set of individual 'facts' or segments of information that can be acquired separately from each other in any order, and that are constantly changing with changes in society. Apart from the geniuses mentioned above, generally people who do not learn mathematics in a (good) educational institution, do not learn much mathematics at all. Similarly, playing music requires mastery of simple pieces first, gradually building up to a reflective and more original practice, which requires not only practice, but insight into musical conventions and boundaries, even if only in order to violate them. Some bodies of specialized knowledge are less 'vertical', and the concepts do not build on each other in as clear a manner as they do in mathematics. They do, nonetheless, build on each other to some degree, and relate to each other. While sequencing of knowledge is less rigid in such cases, acquisition of a systematic body of knowledge is no less crucial, as concepts still relate to each other. Max Weber's ideas did not build on Karl Marx's ideas in the way that calculus builds on algebra, but they did build on them, incorporating insights about society and the economy that were not known before Marx developed his theories. Weber also did not 'replace' Marx in the sense that the idea of a heliocentric solar system replaced the idea of a geocentric solar system. Rather, they offer different but interrelated ways of analyzing the social world. In order to fully appreciate what sociology can explain about the social world, we need to understand both contributions, and how they can relate to each other.

Because of the internal structure of bodies of knowledge, the conditions for their acquisition are different from the conditions for the acquisition of the knowledge acquired in everyday life (Moore 2004). Necessarily, bodies of knowledge are often not directly practically useful, or easy to learn. Learners need to be introduced to them in a sustained way, gradually acquiring greater levels of conceptual depth and breadth. Mastery of particular concepts, principles and facts is needed before progress can be made, and this requires uninterrupted, extended, well-planned and structured educational programmes. Bodies of knowledge cannot be disaggregated easily, as learning needs to be sustained, sequenced, and systematic. Furthermore, they cannot be provided easily. It takes time and resources to build institutions able to deliver sequenced and systematic courses. If this knowledge were easy to learn in the course of everyday life, we would not require education institutions; we could simply allow individuals to acquire knowledge in the world. This is the logical conclusion of the argument that the same 'outcome' can be acquired anywhere, as Jan Masschelein and Maarten Simons (2013) point out.

None of this means that the relationship between education programmes and bodies of knowledge is straightforward. Some professional and vocational qualifications, for example, combine and recontextualize different disciplines; school subjects contain selections from disciplines; and, in discipline-based courses at universities, there is often disagreement about what knowledge to introduce when. But, notwithstanding this complexity, I want to focus on two important points about the idea of structured bodies of knowledge. Firstly, as discussed above, there are necessary conditions for the acquisition of specialized knowledge: learners need to be introduced into it in a sustained way, gradually acquiring greater levels of conceptual depth and breadth. This has substantial implications for curriculum design and delivery. Secondly, structured bodies of knowledge are important: they allow us to account for and explain the natural and social world in systematic ways as well as to participate in and reflect on key human experiences such as the literary, visual, or musical. Some disciplines enable abstraction, reflection, prediction, and application across time and local contexts (Bernstein 2000; Muller 2000a). The knowledge acquired through disciplines can enable people to envisage alternative and new possibilities which are not obvious if they are bound only by what they have direct experience of (Young & Muller, 2013). Thus, as Bernstein (2000) argues, abstract theoretical knowledge enables society to conduct a conversation about itself, and to imagine alternative futures. For example, the theories of Karl Marx can help individuals to understand how and why they are exploited at work, and see their frustrations as more than just a personal problem. This knowledge is valuable, and, rather than being narrowly linked to specific tasks, projects, or situations, can be put to infinite 'uses'.

Specialized knowledge is not just 'information', and so disciplines and knowledge areas cannot be captured in outcome statements, and cannot be read off them. Furthermore, often knowledge, whether theoretical or practical, cannot be inferred from competent performance, as has been demonstrated extensively by Wolf's (1993, 1995) empirical and conceptual research. Some argue that although outcomes-based qualifications frameworks are not appropriate for general or higher education, the specification of learning outcomes is appropriate in a vocational context, in which the learner is ultimately required to be competent in the workplace (for example, Ensor, 2003). Young (1996, p. 28) argues:

> It is not by chance that outcomes-based systems have largely been developed in relation to vocational education where performances are more unambiguously specifiable and where it is far easier and more appropriate to be precise about outcomes.

But this approach does not work for vocational education. Gamble (2002, 2004b) demonstrates that, for example, craft knowledge, which is often a component of vocational programmes, has a part-whole relation inherent to its knowledge structures, and that this part-whole relation is evident from the beginning of a teaching programme, and is in fact the purpose of pedagogic transmission. Thus, craft knowledge is undermined by being fragmented into learning outcomes, and a narrow outcomes or competence-based approach can result in workers receiving a narrow and limiting education (Gamble, 2005; Wheelahan, 2008)

Craft knowledge is mainly tacit, in the sense that it is not written or spoken. As learning outcomes must put into words what is entailed in any particular area of competence, craft knowledge is in some ways even less suited to outcomes statements than disciplinary knowledge. Gamble (2004b) demonstrates that partly because the principles of craft knowledge are implicit, they require sustained and systematic study, and are not easily disagreggated. Much of the teaching in traditional craft training programmes, such as apprenticeships, is not verbal, instead involving teaching through drawing, modelling, or physically working with the learner. It might be easier, during the course of everyday life, to pick up discrete skills in carpentry than in mathematics, and it may be easier to be a self-taught carpenter than a self-taught mathematician, but this does not mean that the teaching of carpentry is irrelevant. The more teaching of carpentry there is, the more people will acquire carpentry skills, and the more carpenters there will be. Thus it is still the case that if a country feels the necessity for carpenters, it is better to create learning programmes to train them, than to hope that enough people will stumble upon the relevant skills in the workplace.

Practical knowledge or workplace knowledge that is not a traditional craft *per se* (such as knowledge of managing a restaurant), is also difficult to reduce to transparent task specifications. The higher the level of professional competence in a workplace, the more difficult it is for someone outside of that particular area to be able to make a judgement. As Wally Morrow (2001, p. 105) puts it:

> Practices are sustained or corrupted to a considerable degree by the ways in which participants and significant others interpret, think about, and discuss, them. But those interpretations, thoughts and discussions do not float freely above the 'reality' of the practice, they are part of that reality.

By emphasizing descriptions and explanations, the learning outcomes approach seems to favour verbal knowledge. Yet skills are not easily verbalized. It is ironic, then, that one of the ideas behind outcomes-based qualifications frameworks is to recognize the *skills* that people already have. Because competences are described in words, writers of outcomes and competence statements frequently emphasize the learners' ability to describe, explain, or talk about, rather than *perform*, the activity in question. Consider the South African grocery-packing unit standard. The following three specific outcomes specify the measurable and verifiable learning outcomes contained in the unit standard title 'Pack customer purchases at point of sales':

> Explain factors impacting on the packing of customer purchases.

> The importance of packing customer parcels correctly is explained.

> Pack customer purchases.

Two of the three specific outcomes of the competence of packing groceries involve talking about packing groceries. It is quite conceivable that many individuals who pack groceries and are quite competent at this would not be deemed competent against this unit standard, as they would not be able to explain factors impacting on the packing of customer purchases. Perhaps the most extreme example I have come across is the standard 'Communicate verbally' which has three specific outcomes:

Explain the importance of being able to communicate effectively.

Describe how to communicate with people who only speak foreign/regional languages.

Describe the various ways of communicating in a particular context.

In other words, while the competence is supposed to be about communication, the specific outcomes are not about communicating, but about *explaining* communication.

In many instances, the criteria for judging competence cannot be articulated by a person who is not relevantly skilled, and are often not verbalizable at all. Thus they cannot simply be written up into a standard or qualification. In Gamble's (2002, p. 79) words, "evaluative criteria reside not only with the master, they reside *in* the master as the carrier of a collective knowledge tradition". This also means that specified outcomes and criteria do not enable quality improvement, as those who are inside the practice do not need them, and those who are novices or outside of the practice cannot understand them.

Furthermore, practical knowledge is often embedded in and dependent on the acquisition of disciplinary knowledge. Many vocational programmes contain a component of disciplinary knowledge that is applied within the vocational area, such as mathematics for engineering, or physics for motor mechanics. With the increasing prevalence of technology, many vocational programmes increasingly require higher levels of disciplinary knowledge, although, as Kennedy (2012) and Livingstone (2012) demonstrate, technology also often has the effect of decreasing the knowledge used in work. In addition, particularly at a junior secondary level and at primary level, where vocational programmes exist at this level, vocational programmes generally contain disciplinary knowledge essential to a basic education, such as language and mathematics. So the belief that outcomes are appropriate for vocational education is wrong. And, as it is primarily applied to vocational education, it is likely to weaken it.

The problem is not poor implementation. The South African experience demonstrates how the outcomes-based approach and its requirement for transparency can distort education and training programmes. Although the South African system was arguably an extreme version of the outcomes-based approach, and had its own idiosyncrasies, the problems the country experienced were not the result of the incompetence of South African policy makers but were inherent to the outcomes-based approach and the requirement for—but impossibility of achieving—transparency.

The specification of particular criteria does not disclose what good practice is. Shalem and Slonimsky (1999) explore this by examining criteria specified for assessing the competence of teachers. They show that the interpretation of any particular criterion—for example, that the teacher can 'use the language of instruction appropriately to explain, describe and discuss key concepts in the particular learning area/subject/discipline/phase'—is always open to debate. A teacher who does not have a reasonable sense of the key concepts will not know whether or not she is explaining them appropriately. Similarly, a teacher who does not know how to communicate key concepts to learners in a manner appropriate to their conceptual and linguistic level will not be in a position to start making a judgement about whether or not he is doing so appropriately. Criteria cannot be provided or legislated or disclosed through the specification of learning outcomes, but rely on a prior understanding of the practice.

It is not inconceivable that different people may design curricula from, teach from, and assess to, learning outcomes in a reasonably similar manner. But where this happens, it is because there is a strong community of professionals or experts who already have an internalized sense of the required standards, with enough professional cohesion to keep this interpretation reasonably similar. In other words, the written outcomes specify enough that they can be interpreted within particular communities or professional groups. But the claims made about learning outcomes are precisely that they provide information to people outside of these specialist communities, and it is this that they cannot do. As Morrow (2001, p. 91) explains:

> I cannot in non-aesthetic language describe what it is I am trying to achieve in teaching someone how to read literature or appreciate music, and nor can I in non-mathematical language describe what I am trying to teach in teaching someone mathematics. From outside these practices it is not possible to understand what these practices are, or even what their value might be. By definition the learner is outside of the practice, or at best is a novice in respect to the practice, thus, it is not possible for the learner to understand in advance what it is she will learn when she learns to become a participant in the practice.

In a research project I led for a South African government institution (Allais, King, Bowie, & Marock, 2007), we asked evaluators to compare the standard of different courses which were ostensibly at the same levels. A key finding of this research was that learning outcome specifications did not appear to be an appropriate vehicle to ensure a commensurate standard. The judgements that could be made about the quality of the courses were very limited, due to serious differences in the kinds of documentation that could be acquired for each course. But to the extent that judgements were possible, it was clear that there were substantial differences between courses which were designed *against the same learning outcomes*. While differences could be attributed to weak capacity or unscrupulous behaviour in some education institutions, in many instances it appeared that there were legitimate and dramatic differences in the interpretation of learning outcomes. In language learning, the same learning outcomes could be interpreted at many different levels. An outcome such as 'show an awareness of manipulative devices' could be displayed by primary school children (for example, through nursery rhymes), newly literate adults (for example, through the understanding of simple slogans), and by those using language with a high level of academic proficiency. The learning outcomes on their own were not enough for providers to know what to teach and assess.

Although this was aggravated by a poorly designed outcomes-based approach (for example, we found mathematics unit standards which contained wrong mathematics), the problem was largely a conceptual one: learning outcomes alone could not express consensus, leading to detailed specifications in an attempt to achieve consensus. However, as discussed above, over-specification is counterproductive because it leads to very lengthy documentation and cannot, in any case, create consensus.

Of course learning outcomes can be stipulated at a sufficiently general level that they mean something to most people (for example, 'be a competent plumber or nurse'). However, the fact that broad outcomes like 'be a competent nurse' can be understood by non-specialists does not mean that non-specialists will always be able to judge whether or not a particular person is sufficiently competent to be awarded this outcome.

A 'softer' approach to learning outcomes would be to use outcomes as useful statements of aim that would enable course designers to describe their understanding of their field of knowledge. Instead of starting with outcomes and designing the content down from them, this approach would derive the aims from within the logic and content of the knowledge field or practice. Aims would be articulated *in relation* to specific content rather than be used to *determine* the content; to a large extent the content would determine the aims. Based on the reasoning that the primary point of providing a course is to give learners access to specialized content, the aims would be designed in relation to the specialized demands of that content. This would not discount the potential instrumental goals of using this knowledge to do useful things in daily life or in the workplace, but would make the relationship between content and aims more iterative, and would not imply that specific 'bits' of content led to specific outcomes.

If a learning outcome is seen as something embedded *within* a knowledge area or learning programme, and derived from the knowledge area, it does not need to be transparent to everybody, because people within the knowledge area, whether it is carpentry or eleven dimensional physics, will interpret it. If institutions that teach knowledge and skills determine what the aim of a programme is, the aim will be located within their expertise. Whether the educator in question has designed their own curriculum, as is usually the practice in higher education, or is teaching a curriculum designed by someone else, its particular specifications—for example that a learner can make Victorian cabinets, offer an interpretation of Kant's transcendental idealism or have knowledge of North American fiction—will be immediately intelligible to them. Specialists within those areas will know what needs to be taught and how it needs to be taught in order to achieve those aims, and will be able to judge whether or not learners have achieved them. Of course, these specialists can be relatively competent or incompetent, dedicated or uninterested. Different educators will teach the same things in different ways and to different standards, and will debate amongst themselves as to what, for example, a reasonable interpretation of Kant's transcendental idealism is, but this is not a problem if the outcome does not claim to be transparent to any outside observers.

If outcomes or competences are seen as educational standards, then they only make sense in the context of that curriculum and the knowledge area that it is derived from. This point is explained in detail in Brockmann, Clarke, and Winch's (2011) discussions of how the European Qualifications Framework will be used in practice to 'translate' across qualification systems. They suggest that a far more detailed mapping, which considers factors such as the length of training programmes and the content of curricula, will have to be brought to bear when comparing qualifications. They also point out that while all four of the European countries in their study (England, France, Germany and the Netherlands) use the idea of learning outcomes or competences, in the three continental European countries, learning outcomes or competences are not abstracted from curricula.

In developing a qualifications framework, the alternative to outcomes is to determine levels primarily with reference to existing qualifications, and the accepted relationships among them. Of course, this is a circular solution, and does not provide a mechanism for resolving disputes. On the other hand, in practice, this approach is often used even in those frameworks which are officially described as outcomes-based. Although they may make it formally possible to challenge implicit and generally accepted judgements, level descriptors and outcomes often do not replace these judgements. Decisions in the end revert to balancing professional judgements against stakeholders' (especially employers') interests.

The lack of transparency demonstrated in the previous chapter as well as in the section above titled the spiral of specification, renders invalid all other claims made for learning outcomes and outcomes-based qualifications frameworks. If the outcomes are seen as part of, or related to, the knowledge that gives education programmes their meaning, if, that is, they are embedded in what they are the outcome of, then they cannot 'cross boundaries', or create transparency for the non-expert, the employer, the manager of a state regulator body, the 'foreigner'. This contradicts the claim that learning outcomes can cross national boundaries. The learning outcome would have to do two things: firstly, capture some essence which can be recognized by different people (employers, admissions tutors, and so on) in different countries; secondly, allow for different routes towards achieving that essence. They would have somehow to capture a 'sameness', or disclose an *essence* which is or could be achieved through a variety of different curricula and learning experiences and even in learning experiences beyond formally taught learning programmes. In other words, the learning outcome must be sufficiently transparent that it can be mapped back onto a whole set of potentially different curricula, selections of knowledge, and learning activities—in different states, different parts of education and training systems, and different education programmes, as well as in life (especially work) experiences.

The argument that outcomes-based qualifications frameworks are an integral component of quality assurance systems is also often based on the assumption of transparency. The idea is that national regulatory bodies would be able to measure programmes against the outcomes, and employers and educational institutions, whether at home or in other countries, would then have a good sense of what it was that the bearer of a qualification was competent to do. Because judgements would be made against clear, agreed, and understood criteria, outside bodies would easily be able to see the *essence* of what needed to be taught, and so could evaluate the quality of provision—whether it was provided formally or informally. This is dependent on outcomes being transparent.

Learning outcomes are also claimed to be a way of 'crossing boundaries' between different *types* of knowledge, as well as enabling all learning to be recognized, as qualifications could be separated from specific institutions and specific (or even any) learning programmes. Thus it is hoped that they could empower everyday knowledge relative to the perceived power of school knowledge. It is this particular claim which reveals the confused notion of knowledge that underpins the advocacy of learning outcomes. Outcomes are situated as the mechanism to capture the 'sameness' of different learning experiences, but in the process of ignoring the specifics of the different experiences, they create an official undervaluing of the important specifics of both everyday and school knowledge. The implication is that it is this sameness—captured in the outcome—that makes the knowledge or experience valuable. And this notion—that it is the outcome which knowledge leads to that makes the knowledge valuable—is the logical conclusion of the idea—found in the works of Bobbit discussed in Chapter 2, and continued through the 'functional analysis' approach developed in the United Kingdom discussed in Chapter 3— that the starting point for curriculum design, and for the selection of knowledge, is activities in the 'real world'.

LEARNING OUTCOMES AND CURRICULUM COHERENCE

Although the idea of learning outcomes implicitly rejects the idea of differentiated, structured bodies of knowledge as the starting point for curriculum design, its advocates do not accept that they have forfeited curriculum coherence, but argue that they have provided an alternative notion of curriculum coherence. For instance, Jessup (1991, p. 4) argues: "Coherence is ultimately a matter for the individual learner. It is only the learner who can make sense of the diverse inputs he or she receives and relate them to his or her perception of the world." In other words, coherence is created when a learner compiles a set of learning outcomes that makes sense for her. Of course each individual's learning path is different, and their experiences and knowledge of other areas will shape how they acquire knowledge, and the nature of the understanding they acquire. But this does not mean that knowledge itself is entirely an open question, simply a flat set of bits of information to be combined in any way at all, blended into some learner-specific whole. The internal coherence and the substance of a learning programme are produced, in the main, by the logic of the knowledge that informs them. As demonstrated above, if the starting point is learning outcomes instead of the knowledge areas in question, then the content knowledge will be marginalized, even when, as in many policy documents advocating learning outcomes, there is a formal assurance to value it.

Thinking about the knowledge area in question is key to the process of designing a coherent curriculum, because, as discussed above, knowledge areas have internal conceptual relationships. Curriculum design should instead be informed by the key procedures, and the concepts that together inform the logic of a field of knowledge and, at higher levels, the practices it adopts for the socialization of practitioners—how knowledge is developed, how research is done, and so on (Shalem, Allais *et al.* 2004). Winch (2012) argues that systematic knowledge is organised both in terms of the classification of its various conceptual elements and the relationships between them, but also in terms of the procedures required to gain and to validate knowledge. Curriculum design, he argues, concerns

> introducing novices into the conceptual field that distinguishes the subject. This conceptual field can itself be seen in hierarchical terms with central organising and methodological concepts at its core and derivative concepts at the periphery. It follows that one cannot be introduced in a serious way into a subject unless one starts to acquire at least some grasp of these central concepts.

There is always much debate and disagreement about the sequencing of curricula, as well as the relative importance of different concepts, and in many instances such debate is not easy to resolve. Developing simple pathways through knowledge areas is not easy, and specialized knowledge is not easy to acquire. But it is nonetheless from the intrinsic logic of knowledge areas that curricula derive their coherence. This is why syllabus documents which specify what knowledge should be taught as well as advise about sequencing and pacing are more useful than outcome statements.

Brockmann, Clarke, and Winch (2008) argue that educational standards and learning outcomes are conceptually at odds with each other. With specific reference to the European Qualifications Framework, they point out that the learning outcomes approach tries to achieve two incompatible goals: providing a notion of progression, whilst also demonstrating competence at a particular level irrespective of competence at any other level. In other words, whilst the learning outcome approach suggests that if one is found competent at a particular level, it must be the case that one would be competent at all levels below the level in question, the official claim is that learning outcomes provide a means of assessing if someone is competent at a particular level, *irrespective of their achievements at any other level*. Qualifications frameworks acknowledge hierarchies of ability and of 'competence'—they are presented as ladders of ever-higher levels of competence—but, unlike knowledge areas such as disciplines or subjects, the hierarchy that qualifications frameworks present is not based on a hierarchy of knowledge itself. In fact, level descriptors go to immense trouble not to draw on such hierarchies, making the explicit claim that learners do not need to work through the hierarchy of knowledge at each level, but can enter at any level. They instead attempt to create hierarchies in terms of other things such as the degree of independence of work. There is a tension, Winch[4] argues, between (1) the idea that learning outcomes are a complete specification of ability/knowledge at a given level, and (2) the idea that learning outcomes exist in a cognitive hierarchy. If (2) is true, then (1) cannot be true, and vice versa. If (2) is true, then the learning outcome does not specify all presupposed knowledge and ability, and if (1) is true then the cognitive hierarchy cannot be taken seriously. For cognitive hierarchies cannot be understood without thinking about fields of knowledge and ability and the relationships within them, both conceptual and practical. Given that these are absent from learning outcomes, then these cannot do the job that they are supposed to do of establishing a meaningful hierarchy.

Brockmann Clarke, and Winch suggest that the contradiction described above leads to an attempt "to produce something that is either of little value or that is bound to throw up paradoxes that undermine its credibility" (Brockmann *et al.,* 2008, p. 100). And, they argue, this is precisely what the outcomes-based qualification model does:

> Learning outcomes in the NVQ sense, however, purport to act – be this inadequately and impossibly – as a surrogate both for aims of education and for standards, as a statement of the knowledge, skills, attitudes and understanding that a student is expected to have reached at the end of a vocational programme or when he/she has attained a particular level of certification. (Brockmann *et al.,* 2008, p. 104)

They argue that learning outcomes fail in the first sense—as aims of education—because they specify too narrowly, and fail in the second sense—as standards—because they do not provide a basis for assessing how *well* someone has met a standard, instead providing a binary target of competent/ not-yet-competent. One of the main problems, as they see it, is that to be an outcome of something a learning outcome would need to be linked to *that something*. Standards, criteria, outcomes, and aims can only be understood if they are embedded in a particular curriculum: "Just as standards can only be really understood in terms of the aims for which they provide a measure, so they also need to be understood in terms of the curricula that are designed for the aims to be achieved" (Brockmann *et al.,* 2008, p. 105). Standards, they go on to argue:

> ... face "upwards" towards aims and "downwards" towards curricula and

failure to refer them to one or the other is a recipe for confusion. Yet this is what "outcome" based approaches to education threaten to do, by detaching criteria of success from any meaningful educational context. (Brockmann *et al.*, 2008, p. 106)

They further elaborate:

any curriculum that is reasonably complex, which seeks to develop abilities, knowledge, understanding, attitudes and dispositions, is bound to be difficult to encapsulate in simple, very precise, statements related to highly particular behaviours. This, however, is precisely what is required of learning outcomes when these are referred to performance outputs.

None of the above discussion should be read as implying that that there is no role for aims or outcomes within curriculum design, or that discussing the outcomes of learning programmes can play no role in aligning qualifications. It is possible to have a syllabus which includes on the aims of a course, derived from the internal logic of the disciplinary or craft area. But the internal coherence and the substance of the learning programme would still have to be produced, in the main, by the logic of the knowledge area.

Aims would have to be articulated in relation to specific content; they would not be able to determine the content. And their appropriateness would have to be judged in relation to the specialized demands of the content that learners are being given access to (Shalem, Allais *et al.* 2004).

I am also not arguing that subjects and disciplines are static, 'given' bodies of knowledge, beyond questioning or changing. In the next chapter I discuss sociological theories of knowledge which provide a way of understanding that while knowledge is organized in specialized bodies, and in conceptual relationships which are often hierarchical, it is nonetheless socially developed, contingent, and open to constant change.

The focus of my argument in this chapter has been that, together with the focus on short-term and low-level employer needs discussed in the previous chapter, the spiral of specification means that the outcomes and competence-based model entrenches a narrow notion of skills. Curricula designed from narrow specifications of knowledge, in which knowledge becomes lists of information or task specifications, will not provide learners with the knowledge they need to progress to higher levels of learning. This trivialisation of knowledge may explain the low take-up of such qualifications in general, and particularly at higher levels. And as it leads to narrow qualifications without theoretical components, it is not only unappealing to learners, but also directly contradicts stated policy goals related to 'knowledge economies', as well as broader aims of raising the education levels of the workforce. Beck and Young (2005, p. 189) argue that relying on 'task specifications' and 'standards of performance' smacks of knowledge authoritarianism, for it denies trainees "access to the forms of knowledge which permit alternative possibilities to be thought" and thus will inevitably "negate the possibilities of understanding and criticism".

In a recent spat around curriculum reforms in the United Kingdom, respected education commentators Margaret Brown and John White criticized Michael Young's notion of 'powerful knowledge' as the starting point for curriculum design. Instead, they argued, there should be general aims for what the curriculum should achieve, which should then be broken down into sub-aims and sub-sub-aims, and what students learn should be chosen in relation to these (Brown & White, 2012). They argued that if, for example, 'responsible citizenship' was taken seriously as a curriculum aim, students would need to know something about the society in which they live, to understand something about the way in which its economy works, and have some sense of the scientific and technological basis of that economy. They argued that this could be the basis for deciding about which knowledge to include in the curriculum: in this case, aspects of physics, chemistry, ICT, and so on would be considered most relevant to understanding today's economy[5]. And, as discussed in Chapter 2, and is further discussed in Chapter 7, radical left-wing activists have suggested similar approaches, but with the starting point for curriculum design being the needs of the community and learners, rather than the economy.

However, this 'aims-based' curriculum also undermines the structured nature of bodies of knowledge. The idea that 'bits' of physics, chemistry, and other subjects can simply be selected and combined into a coherent curriculum ignores connections between concepts within bodies of knowledge, and the fact that certain concepts need to be mastered before others can be. It also ignores the value of bodies of knowledge, suggesting, much like outcomes-based approaches, that they derive their value from the practical aims they lead to. Sedunary (1996, p. 383) points out in relation to vocational education reforms in Australia:

> Competencies are thus increasingly accorded a foundational authority in curriculum design and practice. This trajectory certainly redraws, and promises to undermine, compulsory schooling's immanent capacity for a critical tension with the immediate conditions of life and work hitherto carried in the relatively detached school subjects.

Another fundamental problem, starkly demonstrated in the outcomes-based qualifications phenomenon, is that the idea that education can be, and should be, defined in terms of what learners, communities, parents, employers, and governments want it to be, results in education being seen as some kind of 'free-for-all'. Long wish-lists are inevitably produced, which frequently contain desires for schools to solve all the problems of society, including doing many things for which they are clearly not suited. As North American curriculum historian Herbert Kliebard (1975, p. 33) puts it:

> The missing ingredient in all this is some attention to the nature of the school.
> … the knowledge that is of the most worth may not be the kind of knowledge

that can be transmitted in a school context. ... if curriculum makers do not temper the question of what is most important to know with the question of what schools can accomplish, their claims for programs designed to reduce crime, improve human relations, prevent drunken driving, ensure economic independence, or remove sex inhibitions are unreliable.

Besides Kliebard's point that schools are unlikely to achieve success in preparing students for the specific goals that are seen as important by particular groups at particular moments in time, the idea that education is something that can be specified according to the needs of parents, communities, or industry has, as I discuss in detail in the following chapter, opened up education to extreme commodification.

ENDNOTES

[1] This does not necessarily mean that every institution which provides education designs its own syllabus—a syllabus for all schools could be designed within the state education system, for example.

[2] All unit standards were obtained from www.saqa.org.za during November 2005, except for those recommended by the South African Qualifications Authority as examples of good unit standards, which were obtained during November 2006, and have an asterisk after them.

[3] As mentioned in Chapter 4, the South African qualifications framework was originally divided into eight *levels* and twelve *fields*. Each field was broken into an unspecified number of *subfields*.

[4] I am grateful for personal correspondence with Christopher Winch in which he elaborated these ideas.

[5] This perspective is elaborated in Reiss and White (2013).

WHO IS RIGHT?

Learning Outcomes and Economics Imperialism

By capturing ideals of individual freedom and turning them against the interventionist and regulatory practices of the state, capitalist class interests could hope to protect and even restore their position. Neoliberalism was well suited to this ideological task. But it had to be backed up by a practical strategy that emphasized the liberty of consumer choice, not only with respect to particular products but also with respect to lifestyles, modes of expression, and a wide range of economic practices. Neoliberalization required both politically and economically the construction of a neoliberal market-based populist culture of differentiated consumerism and individual libertarianism. As such it proved more than a little compatible with that cultural impulse called 'post-modernism' which had long been lurking in the wings but could now emerge full-blown as both a cultural and an intellectual dominant. (Harvey, 2005, p. 42)

This chapter examines how narrow economic ideas about individuals freely making rational choices in markets have come to dominate education policy and much educational thought. It argues that this process has been facilitated by ideas about knowledge which have dominated much educational reform in the past, and which have resurfaced in outcomes-based qualifications frameworks.

Let me start by recapping the arguments presented thus far.

I have discussed in Chapter 2 how learning outcomes have a long history of hostility to the idea that subjects are the basis of the curriculum and a key purpose of education. I also discussed how the idea of learner-centredness has sometimes shared this hostility. Although this hostility is not entirely intrinsic to either, both ideas are supported by reformers who reject the idea of organized bodies of knowledge as the starting point of the curriculum.

I have shown in Chapter 3 how, with the rise of neoliberalism, learning outcomes and learner centredness were invoked in qualifications reforms that aimed to change the role of the state in the delivery of education both by forcing state providers into markets and by increasing the regulatory role of the state; to make curricula more directly linked to the perceived needs of employers and learners through the specification of learning outcomes; to ensure that learners and employers could make better 'choices' through clearly specified learning outcomes; and, through all these measures, to improve how education provided skills for the economy. This reform movement, which initially emerged in the United Kingdom, and then spread to Australia and New Zealand, arose in the context of neoliberal reforms to the state, but also drew on educational ideas that had been surfacing and re-surfacing for over a century—in particular, the idea that subjects as defined by teachers or disciplinary experts in universities are not the best starting point for curriculum design, and are a cause of a 'mismatch' between education and labour markets.

When these policies spread to poorer countries, one of the major problems which emerged was that the shift to a regulatory mode for the state, with reliance on a market of provision, simply meant little new provision, and the neglect of existing provision, as discussed in Chapter 4. Many new qualifications were developed but never offered, and the emphasis on a regulatory state 'quality assuring' different providers did not increase the quantity or quality of provision, and in some cases, notably South Africa, may have decreased it. In most instances, the main achievement was to develop paper qualifications that were never used, despite the involvement of industry and other stakeholders in their development. At the same time, this type of reform, heavily supported by donors and international agencies, diverted attention away from building and supporting the provision of education.

In both developed and developing countries, the idea of employer-specified competencies does not seem to have succeeded in improving education/labour market relationships, as discussed in Chapter 5. I have argued that outcomes-based qualifications frameworks and competence-based training reforms are more likely to be a *symptom of* than a *solution to* weak relationships between education and labour markets, which perhaps accounts for their popularity in developing countries dominated by informal labour markets. Trying to change the *relationship* between education systems and labour markets by only changing education, without changing the labour market and the economy, ignores the extent to which education, specifically vocational and professional education, is shaped by industrial relations, welfare systems, social policy, income distribution, and production strategies. Further, the claim that these reforms can improve labour market mobility rests on the assumption that learning outcomes are transparent—something not realizable in practice.

In Chapter 6 I discussed the epistemological stance behind outcomes-based qualification frameworks, which sees knowledge as little bits of information that can be selected and combined at will. This stance implicitly rejects the importance to the educational process of particular bodies of knowledge, and ignores the ways in which these bodies of knowledge are organized into conceptual relationships. The epistemological stance of outcomes-based frameworks resonates with the epistemological stance of educational reformers who are opposed to subjects. This explains why educational reformers in many countries support outcomes-based qualifications frameworks. I showed how outcomes-based qualifications lead to a spiral of narrowly specified bits of information, which make curriculum coherence impossible.

This chapter shows that when the acquisition of bodies of knowledge is not seen as one of the primary purposes of schooling and education more generally, education is increasingly seen as a kind of 'free-for-all' that can and should be defined simply in terms of what learners, communities, parents, employers, and governments want it to be. I point out that from this perspective, there is no longer understood to be anything intrinsic about education, except perhaps some kind of socialization function, which is seen as relative to the needs, desires, and traditions of specific communities or countries. I suggest that this has made education receptive to colonization by neoclassical economics.

The notion of 'economics imperialism' is useful in understanding how, even as neoliberalism has been at least partially discredited internationally, its basic tools of analysis continue to dominate ways of thinking about managing and improving education. I argue that we can only maintain a notion of education which is autonomous from its function as a narrow and commodified 'service' if we have a sense of what education intrinsically is. A good starting point for such a perspective is educational knowledge. Education, I argue, is a structured and social activity, based upon knowledge which is structured and developed socially, through human contact and interaction, which is why it requires specific types of institutions for its existence.

I start with a consideration of the idea of 'economics imperialism'. Fine and Milonakis (2009) discuss how, in many areas of study, the conceptual tools of neoclassical economics have come to dominate different disciplines. They characterize this 'economics imperialism' as "marked by the common property of attempting to reduce as much as possible of the non-economic or the social to the optimizing behaviour of individuals" (Fine & Milonakis, 2009, p. 66).

NEOCLASSICAL ECONOMICS AND ECONOMICS IMPERIALISM

In order to understand how and why economic concepts have been deployed outside their origin, we must first consider economics as a discipline, considering both its scope and methodology (Milonakis & Fine, 2009).

The scope and methodology of any discipline are open to contest. Milonakis and Fine discuss how the social, the historical, and also the methodological, have shifted in economic theory since classical political economy. Classical political economy drew on historical and social analysis and used inductive and deductive methods to analyze the functioning of markets and the nature of profit, with the economy considered as part of a wider social and historical milieu. Through thinkers such as Adam Smith, David Ricardo, Thomas Malthus, and John Stewart Mill, classical political economy had "great concern for the nature and causes of the wealth of nations and its distribution to different fractions of society (classes)" (Milonakis & Fine, 2009, p. 13). Despite different political outlooks, all were interested in long-term economic development. Disciplines as we know them today were not developed at this point, and political economy was an attempt to create a kind of unified social science, rather than simply a science of the economy. Methodologically, this implied giving primacy to the social whole, as opposed to individuals, without precluding analysis at the level of the individual. The whole was seen as more than the aggregation of individuals, and individuals were understood to be moulded and influenced by the nature of collectives and institutions. In other words, the starting point was collectives such as institutions, classes, national economies, and society at large, rather than individual actions.

All of these ideas have remained key to sociology, which evolved out of classical political economy. But economics evolved in the opposite direction, with an increasing focus on methodological individualism—the individual as the starting point of all analysis—making deductive analysis on the basis of assumptions about individual behaviour, rather than inductive analysis based on a study of history. The 'marginalist revolution' of the 1870s, so named because the concept of marginal utility was key to the debate, is usually seen as a watershed in the history of economic thought, marking the separation between the classical political economy of the nineteenth century and the neoclassical economics of the twentieth[1].

Milonakis and Fine (2009) describe the development of economics as a discipline as a process of triple reductionism. This reductionism applied to both the subject matter of economics, and to its methodology and analytical tools.

Firstly, as Fine (2001) shows, methodological individualism was adopted. Neoclassical economists started removing 'society' from their analysis, paring it down to individual free agents (*homines economici*) conducting sensible transactions with each other in their own self-interest. The key analytical building block of economics became the utility maximizing individual. Collective agents and structures, not least classes and institutions, were ignored or seen simply as collections of rational self-interested individuals. Thus the complex relationships between institutions, structures, and individual agents that history, sociology, psychology, political economy, and other disciplines explored were ignored (Chang, 2002, 2007; Fine & Milonakis, 2009; Fine, 2001, 2010; Milonakis & Fine, 2009). This method of analysis and explanation, whereby the whole is explained in terms of the properties of its most basic constituent units, is referred to as 'methodological individualism'.

Secondly, the economy was reduced to market supply and demand, without consideration for other 'non-economic' or social factors, as if market relations could prevail independently of broader social contexts. In other words, the economy was seen simply as the market. This idea became key to neoclassical economics, and neoclassical economics has become the mainstream of economics, although it does not dominate all economic thought, as there are other schools of thought within economics, such as institutionalist economists and traditional political economy, which regard the market as only one of the many institutions that make up the capitalist economic system (Chang, 2002, p. 546).

Thirdly, economic analysis came to be based on principles that were claimed to be universal across time and place. Economic thought adopted the notion that its analytical principles such as utility and production function were universal, rather than historically or conceptually rooted in time, place, activity, stage of development, and so on. This idea of universality was a huge intellectual compromise, for it meant that economics had to detach itself from other social sciences, confining its subject matter to the market. It became the science of the market, or the science of economic behaviour, instead of a unified science of society that included the economy. Fine (2010, p. 45) describes how economics established itself as the science of economic behaviour through attention to the technical details of utility optimization:

> In order to do this, everything else was stripped out to focus on rationality. This involved intellectual compromises at the time that were often acknowledged, both within economics and between economics and the other social sciences... Systemic economic properties and the impact of the non-economic upon the economic (and vice versa) were to be studied elsewhere. In short, the marginalist revolution and its aftermath witnessed the division of the social sciences into separate disciplines, with economics appropriating the study of economic rationality, together with the presumption that its scope of analysis was to be confined to individual optimisation directed towards or even within the market.

Although the scope of economics was thereby increased, there had to be a corresponding reduction in what these concepts meant. Even where neoclassical economists use terms that seem peculiarly capitalist—terms like 'profit' and 'wage'—the assumption is that these are the equivalent of reward systems in other societies. The claim or assumption that the basic concepts that constitute the discipline are universal has

> strengthened its commitment to falsifiability (or to close consistency with empirical evidence through statistical methods), to axiomatic deduction from abstract assumptions, to methodological individualism of a special type (utility maximisation), and to equilibrium (and efficiency) as an organising concept... As a result, economics has been marked by an almost exclusive reliance, at least in principle, upon abstract mathematical formalism married to statistical testing or estimation against given evidence i.e. data. Anything within the discipline that does not conform to these dictates is dismissed as lacking science and rigour (with the same attitude that has been imperiously adopted towards other social sciences). (Milonakis & Fine, 2009, p. 5)

Milonakis & Fine (2009, p. 3) point out that "as a discipline, economics tends to pride itself (inevitably erroneously) on being value-free and independent of external influence".

The technical apparatus of neoclassical economics, associated with an impressive and intimidating array of complex mathematical models, was developed on the basis of this triple reductionism. The result was the establishment of neoclassical orthodoxy as the dominant school of thought in economics and its separation from

175

other social sciences. Economics became intolerant of approaches other than its own mainstream, and

> dominated by the neoclassical approach, taught almost exclusively as a standard, often without reference either to irrefutable criticism or to alternative approaches that at most cling for survival upon its margins. Variously referred to as autistic, as monoeconomics, or as subject to Americanisation, homogeneity of thought and approach within the discipline has since the Second World War been strong, but it has also intensified over the past decade or so. (Fine & Milonakis, 2009, p. 4)

The technical apparatuses of neoclassical economics discussed above are the backbone of neoliberalism. Neoclassical economics and neoliberalism are not synonymous. Chang (2002) describes neoliberalism as an unholy alliance between neoclassical economics, which supplied the analytic tools, and the Austrian-libertarian tradition which provided the political and moral philosophy. Once "the technical apparatus had been established, and lay, as it continues to do, at the core of economics as a discipline, the potential boundaries attached to its scope of application are unlimited" (Fine, 2010, p. 45). This point is important: economics developed tools of analysis which claimed to be universally applicable to *markets*. This universality was achieved by extracting markets from their social and historical contexts and assuming that they existed in a vacuum, in order to examine them in principle. This was acknowledged by economists at the time to be a compromise, and a reduction in the scope of economics' subject matter. However, once the analytical tools developed from this move had been well established and accepted as universal, economists started to apply them to areas other than the market. In other words, having developed tools of analysis through the exclusion of much social reality, economics turned outwards to apply these 'universal' tools to those areas of society that their analysis had excluded (Fine & Milonakis, 2009). Economics came to define itself as 'the science which studies human behaviour as a relationship between means and scarce ends and which have alternative uses', and economists started arguing that its technical apparatus had a wider application than 'the market'. As mainstream economics became increasingly intolerant of dissent within its own discipline, it increasingly sought to 'colonize' other disciplines. Both proponents and critics of this 'colonization' have labelled the extension of economic analysis to subject matters beyond its traditional borders as 'economics imperialism'.

The borders between different subjects are always disputed, in principle as well as in practice. Economics imperialism uses this lack of clarity to claim ground from other disciplines, and to apply the tools of analysis of neoclassical economics to aspects of the social world which other disciplines have accounted for. Fine and Milonakis's account considers two major manifestations of the economics imperialism phenomenon over time, both of which are important for a consideration of education policy. In the first economics imperialism phase, the idea was propagated that the principles of rational self-interested choice in a free market could be applied to all areas of life. This, however, was clearly an extreme position, and in general its impact was limited, although it had some achievements in its own terms, notably in thinking about education. The second economics imperialist phase started by conceding that individuals do not always make rational choices, and that markets do not always work, and, with these concessions in place, economic analysis was extended to more areas of society than had previously been the case. I consider these two phases in turn below.

Capitalizable Humans

The first manifestation of economics imperialism is usually associated with self-proclaimed economics imperialist Gary Becker, who has explicitly attempted to apply the neoclassical technical apparatus to the social sphere and to treat all aspects of society as if they were markets[2]. Becker, an early proponent of the notion of 'human capital', argued that *everything* should be treated as far as possible as reducible to individuals optimizing given utility over given goods in an as-if-perfectly-working market (Fine, 2010, p. 171). Fine and Milonakis (2009) argue that, because Becker's general approach is so crude, it has been discarded and is seldom mentioned by the newer economics imperialists. Nonetheless, the notion of 'human capital' continues to dominate much educational thinking and policy.

This notion is so widely accepted currently that it is even used as a synonym for education in much current policy, and is used unquestioningly by many educationalists. Thus, Fine (2002a) argues that human capital theory is an example of economics imperialism, whereby mainstream economics "appropriates and transforms the language and concepts of social theory", because, instead of considering education through disciplines such as psychology, sociology, philosophy, and so on, which have traditionally informed both how education is understood as well as how it is located in understandings of individuals and society, education is suddenly seen as no more than something that can be acquired in one market place, and used for advantage in a different market place. Education is emptied of any other content, and the social context of human motivation is ignored, as are the constraints which face individuals in labour markets. Human capital theory takes a neoclassical economic abstraction—that rational individuals make rational choices about purchasing things in market places—and applies it to education, seeing it purely as a phenomenon that can be seen through this lens. In other words, human capital theory uses market concepts and metaphors to explain something that is far more complex than an abstracted market.

Human capital theory works within a *homo economicus* notion of rational choice. The *homo economicus* or 'rational, self-interested individual' is "a fantastic creature that aims exclusively at private gain, has no altruism and strictly calculates the necessary means to achieve the desired ends, but deploys neither power nor violence to achieve them" (Lapavitsas, 2005, p. 35). This theory assumes that simple financial and status incentives are all that are needed to motivate individuals to work.

The idea is that individuals make rational choices to acquire things in the market place, which they can then reinvest. Education is one such acquirable *thing*. Lin (2001, p. 12) explains: "From the perspective of human capital theory, however, investment in the acquisition of skills and knowledge is motivated by a cost-benefit calculus on the part of the laborers themselves. This calculus drives their investment in acquiring skills and knowledge. It reflects a rational choice, and the action taken is a purposive act consistent with the laborer's self-interest". This is seen as part of a win-win scenario:

> Human capital in the acquisition of skills and knowledge generates economic value, allowing laborers to become capitalists… as they enjoy the surplus value of their labor. Thus, there is a blurring of the two classes. Since laborers become capitalists by acquiring human capital or, at the minimum, since capital is conceived as being shared (however unequally) by the capitalist and the laborer in production and exchange, the worker's acquisition of human capital is now in the interest of both the capitalist and the laborer. (Lin, 2001, pp. 12–13)

The initial arguments of the proponents of human capital theory were based on the observed difference in earnings of people with higher levels of education, and an analysis of the fact that income in the United States had been increasing at a much higher rate than national resources (Schultz, 1961, p. 361). Many subsequent studies across a range of different countries have found that in general, more educated people receive higher earnings (for example, Ashton & Green, 1996, who also point out that the rate of higher earnings is very variable across countries and across research studies). This led analysts to argue that the skill differentials of labour needed to be incorporated into economic theory. Thus, instead of seeing labour as one homogenous category, what is supplied and demanded in the labour market is seen as composed of different characteristics 'owned' by workers. In turn, the productive capability, or the value of the labourer's work, is determined by the amount they have invested in income producing human capital investments (Carnoy, 1987, p. 10). The key idea is that education enhances individuals' productivity. Employers, it is assumed, are willing to pay higher wages to better-educated workers because they will be more productive than uneducated workers. The mechanism at work here is the productivity-enhancing competencies that students acquire through education (van de Werfhorst, 2011). While it was conceded that a major problem in measuring human capital was in distinguishing between investment and consumption, it was thought that investment could be measured by its yield—increased earnings—rather than by its cost.

Human capital theory focuses on individual worker's decisions. For example, the unemployed are seen as those who have not invested in the right amount or kind of education in order to enable them to join the ranks of the employed. Thus, unemployment is seen as the fault of the individual. Human capital theory posits the inadequacy of people as a more important cause of poverty than the inadequacy of the economic system (Bluestone, 1977). This idea fits in well with the idea of 'employability', and the notion that individuals are responsible if they fail to find employment. As Lin (2001, p. 13) argues, "It is the laborer, instead of the manager or capitalist, who is rewarded for or deprived of the price and value of labor power. If labor's value is low, for example, this is due to a lack of human capital rather than the expropriation of surplus value or capital by the capitalist". This focus on individual decisions could be a major factor in explaining the importance attached by governments to 'human capital' as a determining factor of economic success, and as a way of solving various social problems, including poverty: it is an ideological move. This in turn explains why the many critiques of the notion of human capital theory have had little impact on policy makers.

And the critiques, both from inside and outside of economics, have been many and severe. According to Fine and Milonakis (2009), even mainstream neoclassical economists initially provided substantial resistance to the idea of human capital. This was partly informed by the fact that, by the 1950s, economics had such a rigidly agreed subject matter and methodology that any expansion of its scope would provoke (at least initially) much criticism. Many studies have pointed to serious conceptual deficiencies in the notion of human capital, as well as severe difficulties in actually measuring the 'capital' obtained through education, and the rates of return obtained or obtainable from it (for example, Ashton & Green, 1996; Blackman, 1987; P. Brown & Lauder, 2001, 2006; Dunk, McBride, & Nelsen, 1996; Fine, 2001; Lapavitsas, 2005; Vaizey, 1972). Many researchers suggest that the premise of human capital theory is inherently tautological: "the fact that there is an education premium in wages in the labour market is enough for the human capitalist to assume that market forces choose workers with greater productivity and hence education must be the main causal factor behind the wage gap" (Baker, 2009, p. 164). Further, using wages as a measure of productivity—the idea that people whose human capital is more valuable are paid more—has been shown to be flawed. Salaries are not a simple function of the productivity of the trained individuals, and qualifications function in labour markets in many different ways than that assumed by human capital theory.

Whilst a correlation between education and lifetime earnings certainly exists, this does not in itself prove that a person's level of education determines their level of earnings. The statistical attempts to analyze this relationship have to sort out the independent effects of related variables, such as socio-economic background, race and sex, and many others, and are therefore, "far more complex than many economic studies have assumed[3]" (Vaizey, 1972, p. 49). Blackman (1987, p. 35) criticizes studies into the salaries of graduates relative to the salaries non-graduates, for ignoring the possibility that non-graduate incomes have declined, for hiding disparities in graduate incomes, and for assuming that past returns offer a good guide to future returns.

Another problem is that the 'inputs' to education—including teachers' labour; capital in the form of buildings, infrastructure, and learning materials; and the inputs made by the learners—are not easy to measure and define, compared with, say, the inputs to manufacturing. Vaizey argues that, in education, "[w]hat is terribly difficult is to value the inputs and outputs, and to ascribe shifts in the processes of learning and teaching to shifts in relative prices" (Vaizey, 1972, p. 214). Similarly, concepts such as capital, returns, and productivity seem not to have a clear and useful function in a discussion of education. The more the objectives of education are examined, the less easy they are to define and to measure. Vaizey also argues that because the consumption and investment effects of education are inseparable, the concept of human capital is not meaningful.

A further problem with human capital theory is how to define 'skill', and how to decide which jobs are skilled, and which are not. Skills are not objective phenomena that can be measured and accounted for, which individuals either do or do not possess. They are social constructs variable through time and space, and perceptions of skills are mediated by racial/ethnic and gender identity (Dunk *et al.*, 1996). As Charles Tilly (1988, pp. 452–3) famously argued:

> As a historical concept, skill is a thundercloud: solid and clearly bounded when seen from a distance, vaporous and full of shocks close up. The commonsense notion—that "skill" denotes a hierarchy of objective individual traits—will not stand up to historical scrutiny; skill is a social product, a negotiated identity. Although knowledge, experience, and cleverness all contribute to skill, ultimately skill lies not in characteristics of individual workers, but in relations between workers and employers; a skilled worker is one who is hard to replace or do without, an unskilled worker one who is easily substitutable or dispensable.

This relates to a broader critique of the overly technicist approach to the economy that human capital theory assumes. Seeing labour as a homogenous category assumes a technical notion of the economy as a simple machine. The human capital notion is a more nuanced version of this technicist approach, but instead of just inserting 'labour' as a general category into the machine of the economy, different kinds of labour are inserted (Fine, 2001). Ashton and Green (1996) suggest that it should be called 'capital human theory', instead of 'human capital theory', because of the way it ignores the social context of skill and of technology, and treats 'human capital' as a 'thing' to be acquired and utilized.

An alternative view of how qualifications operate in labour markets suggests that employers are uncertain about the marginal productivity of potential employees, and unable to clearly ascertain what knowledge and skills they bring, let alone how these enhance or otherwise affect productivity. What they do, therefore, is look for crude signals that differentiate applicants from *each other* (Spence, 1973). Educational qualifications are used as a screening device that gives broad information about individuals relative to each other. Lester Thurow (1976) posits a job competition model with two queues: one of vacancies for jobs, and one of applicants. The first queue is ordered by the complexity of the jobs available (itself a contested issue). The second is ordered by educational attainment of applicants. Selection in the labour market brings these two queues together, starting from the high paying, believed to be complex jobs, and highly educated applicants. Here education is a positional good; the key issue is one's position in the queue relative to others. One factor which is believed to be important to employers is an estimation of training costs, and more educated people are believed to be cheaper and easier to train. However, workers with experience are a known quantity, against a potentially risky decision. In models like this one, in which education is used to rank individuals, education can be a sorting device for characteristics that individuals had before entering education, as well as those that they obtained in or through education. Collini (2012) argues, for example, that employers have traditionally sought arts and humanities graduates for top jobs in the United Kingdom not because they necessarily gain 'useful' skills through these courses, but because these courses have historically attracted many of the brightest students. Of course other factors can explain one's relative position in the job queue. A key one in current labour markets around the world is work experience, which relegates young people to low positions in growing queues, even when they do have relatively good educational levels. This creates the perception of a 'youth' unemployment crisis, instead of just an unemployment crisis—and is usually interpreted as a problem originating in education systems! Thus, a serious problem with the notion of human capital is that the labour market "does not operate on a principle of free allocation which permits choice and equal access" and cannot "be considered as an ordinary commodity market because it is never insulated against the impact of organized structural discrimination" (Blackman, 1987, p. 35).

An important distinction between the productive skills or human capital approach, on the hand, and the positional good approach on the other, is that in the former the individual holding a job is seen as the key to the productivity of the job, whereas the latter sees productivity as primarily determined by jobs, and an individual's earnings depend on the job she acquires, and not her personal characteristics (van de Werfhorst, 2011) Both approaches, though, focus on the productive characteristics of qualifications, whether indirect or direct. Other theories suggest that qualifications have nothing to do with productive capacities or the 'trainability' indicated by levels of educational achievement, but rather, as a legitimized means for social inclusion and exclusion. Van de Werfhorst (2011) labels this the 'social closure' perspective, because more advantaged groups close off opportunities to less advantaged groups, and educational qualifications or credentials are a key means to doing so, particularly in democracies where overt forms of nepotism and favouritism are frowned upon or made illegal. By demanding formal qualifications for access to jobs, employers can control access to privileged positions. High earnings frequently do not reflect a "high contribution to the social product", but instead reflect scarcity relative to market demand, which is often manipulated (Vaizey, 1972, p. 42). This can be seen in the way in which various professional bodies limit the number of possible entrants into their field—keeping salaries high by keeping relative scarcity high. The dramatic difference between managerial salaries and workers' salaries across the world makes it implausible that this difference is based on any kind of objective valuation of workers' and managers' relative 'productivity' (Chang, 2010). Brown, Lauder, and Ashton (2011) provide one account of this mechanism at work in what they describe as a beauty contest between the world's top universities and top multinational companies. The latter describe themselves as in a 'war for talent' which Brown and colleagues argue is completely implausible because the qualities and qualifications they seek are in fact widely available (Brown *et al.,* 2011; Brown & Tannock, 2009). Rather, the authors suggest, the 'war for talent', and its current result of recruiting exclusively from a tiny handful of universities, is a way of eliminating most potential applicants, in an era of increasingly widely available higher qualifications. Other researchers who explore this perspective suggest that formal education and/or training is a kind of con (for example, Berg, 1970).

Another set of issues is raised by researchers who examine how education has changed work, instead of seeing education simply as the process of producing productive workers. While strongly arguing that the relationship between schooling and work is more complicated and less 'efficient' than proponents of human capital theory would desire, David Baker (2009, p. 179) points out that we cannot see the world of work as "mostly fixed in some preconceived 'natural' fashion" but must instead understand that it "expands and adapts given large-scale changes in the characteristics of the work force". Education, he argues, has transformed work, reconstituting the very foundations of society and the way work is organized, our understanding and expectations for peoples' capabilities, the nature of work, and even what is usable knowledge for economic value.

Human capital theory assumes that people with more education will earn more, and get better employment prospects than people with less education. This, though, is increasingly not the case, as more and more people get higher levels of qualifications. In many countries education provision has become relatively more equal, but income distribution has become more and more disparate; in others rapid growth in education has not led to equivalent growth in the economy (Lauder, Brown, & Tholen, 2012; Livingstone & Guile, 2012). Brown, Lauder, and Aston (2011) point out, for example, multi-national employers are increasingly off-shoring legal and information technology work, which has the effect that young people in developed countries who made educational investments, often at considerable personal expense, in the hope of achieving well-paying and rewarding jobs, are increasingly less likely to do so. Lauder, Brown, and Tholen (2012) present what they call the Global Auction model, which they suggest has more explanatory power than human capital theory with regard to graduate employment and incomes. The Global Auction is essentially a Dutch auction, where employers bid for the lowest possible wages, driving down the earning power of high levels of education. Brown and Tannock (2009, p. 377) argue that this 'global war for talent' is entrenching and promoting a narrow, market-based conception of education, skill, and talent, as well as an attempt to liberalize the global movement not just of capital and commodities, but also of highly skilled labour. The casualization of academic work in the United States demonstrates that it is relative power in labour markets, and not qualifications, skills, or knowledge, that determines how work is valued and rewarded (Newfield, 2010).

While educational expansion has changed society in many ways, much current qualification reform attempts to change the relationship between education systems and labour markets by changing aspects of education such as curriculum and assessment without changing the labour market and the economy. This ignores the extent to which developments in education will always be affected by, and so must be understood within, the context in which they exist. Differences in industrial relations, welfare systems and social policy, income distribution, and production strategies are major factors in determining the shape of this development, and are a major factor in accounting for differences between national systems of vocational education and training.

There is also research which fundamentally questions the relationships between education and labour markets. Collins (1979, 2013) suggests that educational expansion is not driven by technological requirements of work, but rather by the inability of labour markets to absorb labour. He argues that rising demand for education absorbs increasingly surplus labour by keeping more people out of the labour force; he suggests that in places where the welfare state is unpopular for ideological reasons, belief in the importance of education supports a hidden welfare state.

Despite the critiques mentioned above, as well as various other empirical and theoretical critiques, human capital theory has remained popular with politicians and education policymakers (Lauder *et al.,* 1999). Carol-Ann Spreen (2001) argues that the global proliferation of rhetoric about outcomes or competence-based education, decentralization, life-long learning, and effective schools, has emerged as part of the dominance of human capital logic. Jessup, the most famous advocate of learning outcomes in the United Kingdom, writes:

> Happily, the needs of individuals to realise their potential, to develop their skills and knowledge, to take on more responsible and fulfilling work and to earn more money, seem to be compatible with the current needs of the country and the economy, for a workforce of more competent, responsible, flexible and autonomous employees. (Jessup, 1991, p. 6)

Sally Tomlinson (2009, p. 6) suggests that human capital theory was rediscovered with 'Third Way' ideology and the general anti-welfare state politics of the 1990s, as governments wanted a theory which suggested that "improving people's skills and capabilities makes them act in new productive ways, and assumed that investment in education will improve the quality of the workforce". She goes on to argue that "[t]wo terms of New Labour government saw a relentless emphasis on the duties and responsibilities of individuals to retrain, reskill and engage in lifelong learning, although there was eventually a greater recognition that factors beyond government control made investing in one's own human capital a risky business" (Tomlinson, 2009, p. 7).

Human capital theory was accepted by many of the centre left, suggesting that they bought into the idea that 'there is no alternative', and that the 'Third Way' was the most plausible way forward. Also, the appeal to the left and to education policy formulators of human capital theory, is that, like the 'knowledge economy/society' and post-Fordism, it *appears* to provide an argument for state spending on education. Economic objectives are presented by policy makers as coinciding with individual objectives. So, for example, the Australian Labour Party, in its policy on early childhood education, argues that,

> Investing in human capital formation delivers significant benefits to individuals, society and the economy. International research demonstrates that earlier investment yields a higher rate of return. (Australian Labour Party 2001, p. 2, cited by Wheelahan, 2010, p. 109)

Originally, the notion of 'human capital' did not venture into the terrain of the curriculum, but increasingly its ideas of education as key to improving the economy have been used to mobilize new arguments for 'relevance'. As Dale *et al.* (1990, p. 31) put it: "The secret garden of the curriculum should be given over to the rapid production of cash crops".

A Brief Word on Capital and Other 'Capitals'

Different kinds of capital are increasingly emerging in social theory. Baron and Hannan (1994, p. 1124) argued some years ago that "... we are therefore somewhat baffled that sociologists have begun referring to virtually every feature of social life as a form of capital", and cite Dimaggio's (1979, p. 168) early warning: "... capital becomes less a potent and precise tool than a weak figure of speech".

Examples of this abound in educational literature. Rizvi and Lingard (2010) are critical of a curriculum that emphasizes human capital development at the expense of "other forms of capital, such as social and cultural capitals". Hargreaves and Fullan (2012, p. 1), arguing against a market-based, cost-cutting vision of educational reform, use the term 'professional capital', which they define as a combination of 'human', 'social', and 'decisional capital'. They write: "Capital relates to one's own or a group's worth, particularly concerning assets that can be leveraged to accomplish desired goals". Hargreaves and Fullan (2012, p. 3) argue that 'individual capital' must be distinguished from 'social capital', which they say, quoting Carrie Leana, a business professor at the University of Pittsburg, is the "well-known finding that patterns of interaction among teachers and between teachers and administrators that are focused on student learning make a large and measurable difference in student achievement and sustained improvement". Although frequently used in totally different ways, the term 'social capital' is particularly pervasive in the social sciences today.

Referring to any kind of resource as capital cedes conceptual ground to neoclassical economics, and digs us deeper and deeper into a conceptual morass[4].

This can be seen in Hargreaves and Fullan's analogies—for example, they argue that professional capital is an 'investment'. Fine's (2001, 2010) comprehensive and devastating critiques of the concept of 'social capital' demonstrate how it too, as a concept even more pervasive than human capital, is a product of economics imperialism, and that attempts to refer to any kind of resource as 'capital' are similarly products of economics imperialism. The term 'social capital' implies that there is some kind of capital that is not social, or that is asocial. But the concept of capital is an inherently social one, which makes no sense outside of a social analysis. It is "embroiled in social relations, social structures, in social reproduction involving social power and conflict, and is attached to definite economic and social tendencies" (Fine, 2001, p. 33).

Capital is a concept attached to a specific socio-economic system, capitalism, which has been dominant for the past 200 years of human history. When we refer to capital, social capital, or any other of the plethora of 'capitals' that are emerging in literature, "we ought to be conscious that we are taking capitalism as our point of historical, and hence analytical, departure" (Fine, 2001, p. 29). Capitalism depends on wage labour "able and willing to produce a surplus for capital" (p. 29). Capital is therefore embedded in a particular kind of social relation—class relations—whilst also containing many other social factors—such as patriarchy—which add to its social complexity and social character. Capital is attached to a definite economic structure which is primarily based on the production and sale of commodities. Fine (2001, p. 25) writes that "the notion of social capital is understood as a particularly intense form of commodity fetishism", and goes on to argue:

> Any use of the term social capital is an implicit acceptance of the stance of mainstream economics, in which capital is first and foremost a set of asocial endowments possessed by individuals, rather than, for example, an exploitative relation between classes and the broader social relations that sustain them. (Fine, 2001, p. 38).

The same applies to the various other concepts of 'capital', including Bourdieu's more nuanced notion of cultural capital (Bourdieu, 1973, 1984). By using the term to refer to social resources, trust, knowledge, networks, or any of the other aspects of society which have been labelled as a kind of 'capital', we are accepting an economistic re-writing of society as a whole.

Second Expanded Imperialist Phase

Despite the continuing, and apparently increasing, pervasiveness of the notion of human capital, early economics imperialism was criticized even from within economics for seriously over-extending the notion of rational choice and perfectly functioning markets[5]. More recently, however, economics imperialism has had more success. This is partly due to the fact that economics as a discipline has now accepted that markets are *imperfect* as a result of information asymmetries and transaction

185

costs. With this move, economics can now address society, institutions, and other structures that were previously excluded by its narrow focus on the economy as the market. Mainstream economics now understands social entities to be a result of, and a response to, the existence of market imperfections, especially informational ones. Thus, mainstream economics readdresses the social, allowing itself to appear more attractive to the other social sciences—institutions and history are seen to matter—whilst maintaining the same core ideas: the economy as supply and demand in the market, methodological individualism and marginal utility, as well as the universalistic nature of these concepts. The difference is that individuals are now seen as optimizing their utility in recognized conditions of historically evolved market and non-market imperfections. Thus behavioural economics acknowledges that choices are not always rational, and are frequently irrational, but rather than seeing this as a challenge to the tools and ideas which are built on the notion of the utility maximizing individual, it sees it as something to be added to it.

ECONOMICS IMPERIALISM AND QUALIFICATIONS FRAMEWORKS

We have seen in previous chapters how the trend towards a purely regulatory state has affected education policy. The idea of economics imperialism explains how ideas about education policy have been shaped by the tools of analysis, assumptions, and boundaries of possibility derived from neoclassical economics. In other words, as I suggested in the introductory chapter, not only is the primary function of education considered to be to serve the economy, but the economy is seen as a model for how education should function.

The 'outcomes and qualifications framework gospel' demonstrates what happens when education is rewritten according to this narrow economic script. The learner-centered education system becomes a market in which rational individual learners purchase 'bits' of learning, as and when they are required. However, inadequate information is a problem for buyers—both for learners who are purchasing 'human capital' in the education market, and for employers who are purchasing 'capitalized humans' in the labour market. Governments intervene, and, using the language of learning outcomes, try to increase the 'transparency' of educational qualifications, and, at the same time, try to break down a monopoly on provision, to create the possibility of contracting new suppliers, and to assist individuals in purchasing the required 'bits' of education. Governments may even intervene to provide individuals with vouchers or other funding mechanisms which fund individual learners instead of giving funding to education institutions based on the argument that this gives individuals 'choice'.

Central to neoliberalism is the idea that the "state cannot be assumed to be an impartial and omnipotent social guardian, but should rather been seen as an organization run by self-seeking politicians and bureaucrats who are limited in their ability to collect information and execute policies but are also under pressures from interest groups" (Chang, 2002, p. 540). Similarly, recent education policies suggest that self-interested lecturers and teachers run education institutions in their own interests, ignorant or ignoring the needs of industry and of individual learners. In both ideas what is assumed is that *homo economicus* will always try to do the least work possible for the most money, thus maximizing their individual utility. Thus, the argument is that forcing civil servants or educators to function either within markets or *as if* they were within a market will force them to be more efficient and responsive.

As discussed in Chapter 3, many of the education policies which have become prevalent globally over the past 30 years or so—quality assurance, outcomes-based qualifications, accreditation—can be seen as a series of mechanisms broadly aimed at creating and regulating markets in educational provision, underpinned by mistrust in state-run institutions, a belief that market-based institutions will perform better, and a belief that the state can best play a regulatory role in society. Governments have been trying to find ways of simultaneously controlling education institutions and educators, and opening markets or breaking 'monopolies' of provision. Learning outcomes, qualifications frameworks, and competence-based training models appear to provide the tools through which governments can become buyers of educational services, rather than managing and supporting education institutions. At the same time, they allow for a discourse which is, to a limited extent, critical of markets, pointing to their failure. The role of governments becomes simply the establishment of rules for purchasing training, and the regulation of the quality of services offered. Rather than building state provision, which is seen as inefficient, they are meant to improve the function of markets. Instead of managing institutions, governments establish rules for purchasing training, select bids, and control or regulate the quality of services offered. In other words, they create surrogate markets for services previously provided by the public sector, or, in the case of countries which have never had strong provision of education, they create surrogate markets for services which the public sector does not feel able to expand into. In both cases, learning outcomes and competences are seen as necessary for creating the possibility of contracting new suppliers. By providing more information to buyers and sellers about the 'commodity' in question (bits of knowledge and skills acquired for use in labour markets) they are supposed to improve how markets in education function.

Through relying on competition to improve efficiency, while the state simply creates the appropriate regulatory environment and mechanisms, learning outcomes, qualifications frameworks, and competence-based training *seem* to provide the tools to expand education provision and therefore lifelong learning without dramatically increasing state expenditure or creating new state education institutions[6].

The fact that neoclassical economics ignores institutions and society—or sees them simply as collections of self-interested individuals—has fundamentally affected the parameters of research as well as policy thinking. All of this leads to a confluence of self-reinforcing factors: education is seen as the key to individual and national competitiveness under a global neo-liberal regime; it is also seen as an investment that rational individuals make in order to acquire capital that they can re-invest; and markets are seen as the best way to deliver all goods and services, with governments reduced to playing a regulatory role, and supporting the creation of markets where none exist. In this context, it is not surprising that reforms including learning outcomes, competences, national qualifications frameworks, and lifelong learning have become 'magic concepts'[7] in education policy. They fit perfectly with the dominant discourse of the magic of the market and the ineptitude of the state, and re-describe education as a process of individual utility maximization. Like the concept of 'employability', this 'new learning paradigm' is set up to blame individuals who fail to 'take advantage of opportunities', fail to 'invest in themselves', and fail to climb the qualification ladder.

A final point, which is broader than education policy but which has considerable effect on it, is that, when economics narrowed its scope of study to consider only the market, and then, with these narrow tools of analysis, re-extended its scope to consider 'society', the idea developed that the needs of the economy were the same as the needs of employers and business.

In sum, neoliberalism has increasingly affected governments' economic and political policies and neoclassical economic ideas have increasingly affected policy thinking in a range of areas, including education. The essential tools of neoclassical economics are derived from the notion that everything starts from individual free agents conducting sensible transactions with each other in their own self-interest. These ideas also underpin outcomes-based qualifications frameworks, which assume that individuals will make rational choices, in order to purchase education which will help them to get employed, and that institutions will perform better when forced to compete with each other.

LEFT-WING SUPPORT FOR LEARNING OUTCOMES AND QUALIFICATIONS FRAMEWORKS

In many of the examples of frameworks and competence-based qualifications discussed in this book, there was support from educational reformers and researchers who associated themselves with left-wing politics. Some progressive educationalists supported the National Vocational Qualifications in the United Kingdom (Wolf, 2002; Young, 2008, 2009b). Trade unions in Australia and South Africa were major champions of competence-based education and of the outcomes-based qualifications framework respectively (Allais, 2003, 2007c; Cooper, 1998; Wheelahan, 2010). Phillips (1998) argues that although the New Zealand qualifications framework was embedded in New Public Management and neoliberal public sector reform, it was also associated with democratic ideals and equity. Why was this the case? Why do these policies, or at least the broad policy approach, have support from progressive educators, who are presumably not primarily concerned with economic efficiency? Why are they described in the language of empowerment and social justice?

Outcomes-based qualifications frameworks appear to address the concerns both of reformers who are principally concerned with social justice and of reformers who are principally concerned with economic efficiency, apparently enabling a successful marrying of left and right, *à la* the 'third way' politics discussed above. (Keevy *et al.,* 2011, p. 9, my emphasis), writing in support of the growth of international qualifications frameworks, argue:

> With increased demand for trans-disciplinary and multi-skilled workers in the globalised environment at the end of the 20th century, *the formal education system was viewed as limited and complicit in sustaining educational and social inequalities* (Higgs & Keevy, 2009). It is at this juncture that the search for a more visionary or progressive approach to education and training led to the idea of a national qualifications framework. Strong influences at the time included a call for the removal of the strong academic and vocational divisions between school and non-school knowledge (Mukora, 2006) and a move towards a competency-based vocational training model that advocated that 'qualifications could (and should) be expressed in terms of outcomes without prescribing learning pathway or programme' (Young, 2005, p. 5).

The curriculum reforms which outcomes-based qualifications frameworks claim to achieve resonate with the traditional concerns of many left-wing educational reformers: emphasis on skills rather than prescribed content; opposition or indifference to subjects and subject divisions; and relevance to learners as essential to learner motivation. Industry-based advocates of competence-based training seem to share the same concerns, although the relevance they are interested in is relevance to the workplace, rather than to the interests of individual learners. Despite this difference, both movements aim to move away from the traditional subject-based curriculum, and both suggest curriculum design should instead start from *activities* in the world—whether in work, or in the citizenry, or family—and attempt to design education backwards from these activities, selecting knowledge on the basis that it will support people to be successful in these activities. There is also, in the claims made about outcomes-based qualifications frameworks, much emphasis on active pedagogy, which resonates with both progressive educationalists and industrial reformers. So, educational concerns which have traditionally been espoused by radical or progressive educational reformers are now also espoused by mainstream or pro-free market institutions (for example, OECD, 2007).

There are various possible reasons for why educators, and in particular progressive educators, have supported this type of reform. One is that they believe that outcomes-based qualifications frameworks are potentially liberatory, even though these policies can be, and sometimes are, co-opted by a right-wing agenda. Another is that the centre left has conceded so much conceptual ground to the right that there are few fundamental differences between them. A third is that the epistemological ideas traditionally favoured by many left-wing educationalists in fact weaken education, by leaving it with no intrinsic criteria or sense of specificity, which has opened it up to being redescribed in economic language.

Co-option or 'rearticulation' is a long-standing complaint of education reformers: that their radical ideas get watered down, perverted, or distorted[8]. This idea is implicit in much critical discourse analysis of education policy, which describes how terms get 'captured' (for example, Rizvi & Lingard, 2010). The co-option argument is either based on an assumption that qualifications frameworks and outcomes-based qualifications represent a project that can be driven in different directions; as one researcher put it to me, a knife which could be used to cut food or to stab someone. In other words, a policy to be wrestled over, to ensure it is used in a good way. In South Africa, for example, most early critical texts focused on what were described as 'competing discourses' that shaped its development. Commentators argued that, on the one hand, the South African qualifications framework was driven by the goals of social justice, egalitarianism, redress, and empowerment, and on the other hand, by concepts of flexibility, mobility, and re-trainability (for example, Cooper, 1997). This is echoed in later texts (e.g. French, 2009), which maintain the argument that the qualifications framework contained within it the potential for a conservative, bureaucratic system, as well as for an emancipatory one.

The cooption argument enables left-wing critics to distance themselves from specific instances of outcomes-based reform, without distancing themselves from the idea of outcomes-based qualifications. For example, Hyland (1994) presents the case that the competence-based movement co-opted ideas from progressive educationalists. Arguing that learner-centredness in the National Vocational Qualifications was a myth, he describes it as "a popular slogan which, along with notions of open access, the accreditation of prior learning (APL), individualized learning contracts, action plans, records of achievement and student-centredness, has been appropriated by the industrial-training lobby from the progressive tradition" (p. 13), and goes on to argue that flexible and open learning has instead been adopted "to cope with structural under-employment and the rapid rate of technological change in post-Fordist economies" (p. 14). Hyland suggests that the relationship between the epistemological model of the National Vocational Qualifications and the broader neoliberal project of which they were a part lies in the behaviourism that underpins competence-based approaches: "… the notions of behaviourism, consumerism and pre-specified outcomes can be seen to come together and complement each other in ensuring a perfect fit between the NVQs and the social-market model of education and training" (Hyland, 1994, p. 135). In this line of thought, progressivist approaches to education are invoked as necessary to save education from this type of behaviourism.

I argue that the co-option or 'rearticulation' argument is insufficient, and can be dangerous because it avoids analysis of the underlying weaknesses of some of the positions traditionally occupied by left-wing educationalists. I suggest that there are substantial *overlaps* between the ideas that many left-wing educationalists see as progressive, and the competence-based or outcomes-based reforms that they distance themselves from. Sedunary (1996), in her analysis of the relationship between progressive educational reforms and new vocationalism in Australia, suggests that these ideas are less at odds with each other than many people think, and that in fact they have similar, contiguous agendas. She argues that there is a need for a historical analysis "that registers and theorizes the existence of a fundamental concurrence between these two complex and ostensibly contradictory events" (Sedunary, 1996, p. 384). Young and Muller (2010) suggest that the increasingly instrumental focus of education policy, which is much criticized by left-wing commentators, has many affinities with social constructivist and postmodernist views of knowledge and truth, which are often (although with many exceptions) championed by left-wing educationalists.

The argument that mainstream left-wing thinking and right-wing thinking (as represented, for example, by centre-left and centre-right political parties) are increasingly similar is persuasive. Many of the left have come to believe that 'there is no alterative', and so buy in to the notion of a 'third way', of 'capitalism with a human face'. Ideas such as 'post-Fordism' seemed to offer a more desirable and equitable form of capitalism, if only all individuals could acquire higher levels of education and training. The previously left-wing parties that embraced the idea of a 'third way' also embraced the idea of 'market failure', thereby creating the impression that their support for the market was not uncritical, but 'practical' and 'realistic'. This move conceded a key philosophical position of the left—that public interest is not the same as an aggregation of private interests. With this concession, it is accepted that individual preferences can be the basis for social decisions.

Individuality and individual welfare are of concern to many in society, including many left-wing reformers, which may explain why ideas underpinned by methodological individualism have gained popular purchase. As David Harvey describes below, emphasis on individual rights in opposition to purportedly oppressive states facilitated the broad appeal of neoliberal ideas:

> For almost everyone involved in the movement of '68, the intrusive state was the enemy and it had to be reformed.... But capitalist corporations, business, and the market system were also seen as primary enemies requiring redress if not revolutionary transformation: hence the threat to capitalist class power. By capturing the ideals of individual freedom and turning them against the interventionist and regulatory practices of the state, capitalist class interests could hope to protect and even restore their position. (Harvey, 2005, p. 42)

In education in many instances, this rejection of an interventionist state shared by neoliberals and progressives, translates also into an attack on teachers and educational institutions, which are also seen as opposing individual freedoms—such as the freedom to choose what to learn when. Qualifications frameworks and learning outcomes resonate with the ideas about knowledge held by many left-wing reformers. I argue that outcomes and competence-based qualifications reveal a fundamental weakness with the epistemological positions that have been embraced by educational reformers: the emphasis on recreating the everyday world in the curriculum, the equation of what is learnt in everyday life with what is learnt in educational institutions, and the position that education should not be about teaching bodies of knowledge, have led to an abandoning of the specificity of education, leaving education open to be 'rewritten' by the powerful and imperialist ideas of neoclassical economics.

'Love to Hate It': Drawing on a Long Established Tradition

The rejection of the value of organized bodies of knowledge is common to many left approaches to education. Support for a subject-based curriculum is often associated with a conservative political and economic agenda, and presented as backward looking (Muller, 2001). Why is this the case?

Educationalists have tended to have a love-hate relationship with formal education, and, in particular, although not only, with educational knowledge. Over the past century and even further back, many progressive educators have positioned themselves in opposition to the subject-based curriculum, although there are significant exceptions to this, some of which are discussed below. As discussed in Chapter 2, since Jean-Jacques Rousseau (1712-1778), whose educational ideas were taken up by the revolutionaries in France, progressive[9] reformers have criticized the subject-based curriculum and argued that learners must follow paths of their own choosing (Darling, 1994). The progressive tradition has in many instances emphasized the "cultivation of individuality, free activity as opposed to external discipline, learning from experience rather than from texts and teachers, acquiring skills that are deemed relevant to the individual at the present time rather than preparing for some unknown future, and becoming acquainted with the world rather than learning static aims and old materials" (Stout 2000, pp. 76-77).

Many educationalists have argued that the knowledge that constitutes the curriculum is essentially arbitrary—the boundaries between subjects are arbitrary, the selection of particular subjects is arbitrary, and the knowledge that is taught within subjects is arbitrary. Darling, for example, argues:

> ... in their thinking about the curriculum, child-centred educationalists advocate some form of curriculum integration and attach great importance to the maintenance of interest in children. These two ideas are often seen as interrelated: children's drive to find out about the world leads their minds to range widely; the kind of question they are interested in recognizes *no subject boundary*. It is sometimes further suggested that the differences between traditional divisions of knowledge have been *overdrawn*: the techniques involved in these disciplines need to be demystified and seen as *minor variations of a general skill of enquiry*. (Darling, 1994, p. 82, my emphasis)

This idea contains an implicit assumption that complexity, structure, and organization in bodies of knowledge don't matter, either in deciding which bodies of knowledge to teach, or in designing the curriculum, and ignores the role of structured of bodies of knowledge in enabling deeper understanding.

Dewey (1897), whose philosophy of knowledge was based on the idea of pragmatism, writes: "True education comes through the stimulation of the child's powers by the demand of the social situations in which he finds himself". He argues that educational activity should be organized as "intelligently directed development of the possibilities inherent in ordinary experience" (Dewey, 1963, p. 89). The pragmatic tradition emphasized the value of application in practice. Ideas were seen as valuable to the extent that they were useful (Novack, 1975). Nell Noddings (1983), in Flinders and Thornton (2004, p. 169), invokes Dewey to argue:

> Any subject freely undertaken as an occupation—as a set of tasks requiring goal-setting, means-end analysis, choice of appropriate tools and materials, exercise of skills, living through the consequences, and evaluating the results—is educative. Cooking can be approached with high intelligence and elegant cultural interests or it can deteriorate to baking brownies and cleaning ovens; similarly, mathematics can be taught so as to require deep reflective and intuitive thinking or it can be taught as a mindless bag of tricks. It is not the subjects offered that make a curriculum properly part of education but how those subjects are taught, how they connect to the personal interests and talent of the students who study them, and how skillfully they are laid out against the whole continuum of human experience.

Dewey makes a similar point in his comparison between teaching zoology and teaching about laundry work, arguing that both could either be narrow and confining, or could give understanding and illumination—the former of natural life, the latter of social facts and relationships (Dewey, 1931, p. 21). While it is no doubt true that one aspect of his point holds—anything can be taught either in a narrow or a more critical manner—his argument elides the difference between zoology as a structured body of knowledge and laundry work as a practice in everyday life.

Later educational reformers have also rejected what is seen as a traditional curriculum. This rejection is informed by a different motivation, as well as a different notion of knowledge from that held in the progressivist position. Whilst progressivists are primarily concerned with individual interest and success, and so argue that educational processes should start with the interests of the learner, more recently educationalists have been more concerned that traditional educational knowledge sustains social inequality. Let us consider this position further.

On the one hand, education and the acquisition of knowledge is viewed as a potential route out of individual and collective problems, empowering, important, and a right for everyone. On the other hand, it is viewed as the cause of many social problems, and a major mechanism in the reproduction of class inequalities. The standard narrative about the role of education in the reproduction of inequality is well mapped out by Hirtt (2009): education initially reproduced ruling elites; it was expanded in the late 18th and early 19th centuries in the 'developed' world in order to ensure social control; in both the developed and developing world it now focuses on creating national cohesion and identity and reproducing a compliant workforce. Sociologists have demonstrated that education does not rupture social inequalities, and frequently concluded that it therefore should be seen as reproducing current unequal social orders (Bowles & Gintis, 1976). Others, such as Bourdieu (1973, 1984), have argued that education provides certain people with access to social resources such as networks, the right accent, and knowledge of high culture, all of which mark the bearers as members of the elite, and thereby perpetuate an unequal social order. And other left-wing critiques of education recruit Foucault's ideas about the oppressive nature of institutions, with some radicals in the 1960s and 70s such as Everett Reimer, Ivan Illich, and Paul Goodman opposing the institution of the school in its entirety, as discussed in Chapter 2.

There is a range of ways in which schools could play a role in reproducing the ideas of dominant groups and socially unequal societies. These ideas could be perpetuated not only through the curriculum, but also through the 'hidden curriculum'—the way in which schools are organized. For example, Diane Ravitch (2010) describes how billionaire 'philanthropists' in the United States are aggressively supporting reforms to school governance and management which mirror their ideological perspective, increasing competition, choice, deregulation, incentives, and other market-based approaches. She uses this example to show how the ways in which schools are managed and organized have an influence on the prevailing ideas in society, and *vice versa*. As Marx famously wrote, the ruling ideas in any society are the ideas of the ruling class:

> The class which has the means of material production at its disposal, has control at the same time over the means of mental production, so that thereby, generally speaking, the ideas of those who lack the means of mental production are subject to it. The ruling ideas are nothing more than the ideal expression of the dominant material relationships, the dominant material relationships grasped as ideas; hence of the relationships which make the one class the ruling one, therefore, the ideas of its dominance. (Marx, 1932, p. 64)

Marx is not talking about knowledge *per se* here, but about the dominant or hegemonic ideas of a particular period—he gives the examples of ideas such as honour, loyalty, freedom, and equality:

> The individuals composing the ruling class possess among other things consciousness, and therefore think. Insofar, therefore, as they rule as a class and determine the extent and compass of an epoch, it is self-evident that they do this in its whole range, hence among other things rule also as thinkers, as producers of ideas, and regulate the production and distribution of the ideas of their age: thus their ideas are the ruling ideas of the epoch. For instance, in an age and in a country where royal power, aristocracy, and bourgeoisie are contending for mastery and where, therefore, mastery is shared, the doctrine of the separation of powers proves to be the dominant idea and is expressed as an "eternal law." (Marx, 1932, p. 65)

Clearly the dominant ideology in society plays a role in the selection of curriculum knowledge, as well as in the development of knowledge—as seen today in the dominance of notions such as 'entrepreneurialism' in schools, and the narrow content of economics curricula at universities. However, accepting that education institutions, like any other institution in society, play a role in the perpetuation of ideology, and accepting that ideology can and does influence the curriculum, is not the same as accepting that the traditional curriculum is *nothing more than* the knowledge of the ruling class, or the knowledge of the powerful; that there is no difference between knowledge and ideology. Louis Althusser, in support of the latter position, famously argues that the school

> ...takes children from every class at infant-school age, and then for years, the years in which the child is most 'vulnerable', squeezed between the family State apparatus and the educational State apparatus, it drums into them, whether it uses new or old methods, a certain amount of 'know-how' wrapped in the ruling ideology (French, arithmetic, natural history, the sciences, literature) or simply the ruling ideology in its pure state (ethics, civic instruction, philosophy). (Althusser, 1971, p. 155)

He goes on to argue:

> ... it is by an apprenticeship in a variety of know-how wrapped up in the massive inculcation of the ideology of the ruling class that the *relations of production* in a capitalist social formation, i.e. the relations of exploited to exploiters and exploiters to exploited, are largely reproduced. (Althusser, 1971, p. 156)

The idea that the subjects and disciplines which constitute the curriculum of education institutions are nothing but ideas that express the interests of the ruling class is a conflation of knowledge and ideology. This conflation is popular in much educational thinking, influenced by the notion of the social construction of knowledge, sometimes referred to as social constructionism. The term 'constructionism' or 'social constructionism' (sometimes 'constructivism') has different uses in different disciplines and fields of educational enquiry. As a theory of knowledge, the term is often used to refer to the idea that our knowledge of the world comes from daily interactions in the course of social life, which, according to scholar of social constructionism Vivien Burr (2003, p. 6), implies that "there can be no such thing as an objective fact. All knowledge is derived from looking at the world from some perspective or other, and is in the service of some interests rather than others". For, she argues: "If we accept the possibility of many different realities constructed within different historical and cultural contexts, we have no way of asserting that one of these is the right one" (Burr, 2003, p. 81).

As a theory of pedagogy, constructionism is principally concerned with how learners learn or acquire knowledge, and not the status of knowledge *qua* knowledge, although, particularly where the term 'constructionism' is appropriated by policy makers, there can be a slippage between the two ideas, with learning described as the 'construction' of knowledge. In the political sciences and international relations, constructionism deals with the "role of human consciousness and the embeddedness of actors in their social context", and is based on the assumption that interests and preferences are social constructions, and are not objectively given, with a focus on non-state actors (Verger, 2010, p. 124). Despite these apparent variations in the use of the term, Burr suggests that there are commonalities:

> Social constructionism can be thought of as a theoretical orientation which to a greater or lesser degree underpins all these newer approaches ['critical psychology', 'discursive psychology', 'discourse analysis', 'deconstruction', and 'poststructuralism'], which are currently offering radical and critical alternatives in psychology and social psychology, as well as in other disciplines in the social sciences and humanities. (Burr, 2003, p. 2)

Not all uses of the term 'social constructionism' can be united in the way Burr argues. Randall Collins (1998, p. 858), for example, argues that "social constructivism is sociological realism"; it is *because* knowledge is socially constructed that it approaches objectivity, improves our insight and understanding of both the natural and social world, and achieves the status of truth. He argues that truth can only arise in social networks:

> Truth characterizes statements. Reality is that which makes statements true, but reality itself is neither true nor false; it simply is. Statements are inevitably human; truth, when it exists, is inevitably a phenomenon of the human world. The abstract truths we are concerned with, found in the statements of intellectuals, arise in the specialized discourse of social networks. (Collins, 1998, p. 877)

To distinguish between these two very different uses of the term 'social constructionism' (or 'social constructivism'), as well as to separate its use in discussions of epistemology from its use in other areas of the social sciences, I will use the term 'epistemological constructionism' to refer to the position that knowledge is inevitably and inextricably bound to the interests and standpoints of the individuals and groups producing it *because* it is socially constructed. Epistemological constructionism can be seen as part of postmodernism, which is a prominent trend in critical theory, influenced by and associated with philosophers such as Derrida, Lyotard, Baudrillard, and Foucault (Appleby, Covington, Hoyt *et al.* 1996). Postmodernist writers are concerned with meaning, language, and signs, and the relationship between language, text, and reality. The contingency of meaning inherent in all symbolic systems is seen to problematize the relationship between language and reality (Lopez and Potter 2001). Put more simply, language is understood to be self-referential, rather than describing a neutral, extra-linguistic reality.

Simpson (1995) demonstrates how the terms, vocabulary, and, indeed, the general method of postmodernism, come principally from literature and literary criticism, with a focus on storytelling, and a celebration of localism, autobiography, and anecdote; this is sometimes referred to as a 'narrative turn' in contemporary theory. Literary theory's traditional means of operation, Simpson argues, have been intuition and imprecision, as against theory. Postmodernism is seen as having introduced a weakening or even undoing of boundaries between writing literature and writing about literature, and between literature, philosophy and science.

Postmodernism is not exactly a theory or body of knowledge, because it does not claim to have any consistent arguments. Instead, it incorporates an eclectic set of work united under the belief that it is impossible to "aspire to any unified representation of the world, or picture it as a totality full of connections and differentiations rather than as perpetually shifting fragments" (Harvey, 1990, p. 52). The everyday is celebrated, and so sport, fashion, hairstyles, shopping, and games become a focus of study (Connor 1989). Anecdotes and individual instances of things are studied and celebrated. Postmodernists are generally opposed to what they call 'grand narratives'—theories that claim to offer explanations across space and time. Theories are seen as being over-determined, mustering data to support them rather than being able to provide meaningful accounts of the world; for every set of data there are argued to be infinitely many mutually incompatible theories that are compatible with those data (Bricmont 2001). This rejection of grand narratives can, as many critics have pointed out, be seen as rejecting all grand narratives other than its own. As Eagleton (2003, p. 45) puts it: "From one end of a diseased planet to the other, there were calls to abandon planetary thinking". Simpson (1995, p. 29) similarly argues,

> we would be foolish to pretend that little narratives are true alternatives to grand ones, rather than chips off a larger block whose shape we no longer see because we are not looking. What, we might wonder, is the grand narrative behind the compulsive appeal of little stories?

For the purpose of thinking about educational knowledge, what is of significance are the ideas that meaning cannot correspond to reality, that reality cannot be known, that all knowledge is a *text*. These ideas have all lent weight to a notion that all knowledge claims are equal, that no forms of knowledge or methods of attempting to understand reality can claim precedence over others. From this point of view, there is no such thing as 'objective' knowledge, there are only competing ways of looking at things and knowing about things (Jones 2003). The truth or falsity of a statement is seen as relative to an individual or social group—what's true for me may not be true for you (Bricmont 2001). From this perspective, scientific knowledge is not powerful because it is true, it is 'true' (thought to be true) because it is powerful (Jones 2003). Knowledge is understood "in terms of the standpoints, experiences, and interests held to be those of the groups constructing the knowledge", in other words, "in terms of external interests and power relations" (Moore, 2009, p. 2).

When considering education, the relationship between knowledge and power is seen to be doubly problematic, because first knowledge is produced or constructed by the powerful in their own interests, and then a curriculum is constructed from this constructed knowledge—a 'double' construction.

The ideas of postmodernism have been particularly pervasive in the sociology of education from the eighties to the present, but can also be seen right across the humanities and social sciences. Paul Boghossian (2007, p. 2), for example, argues:

> Especially within the academy, but also and inevitably to some extent outside of it, the idea that there are 'many equally valid ways of knowing the world,' with science being just one of them, has taken very deep root. In vast stretches of the humanities and social sciences, this sort of 'postmodernist relativism' about knowledge has achieved the status of orthodoxy.

What informs this pervasiveness? One reason may be that postmodernist or epistemological constructionist approaches to knowledge have often been associated with left-wing thinking, and tend to be presented as new, forward-looking, revolutionary, anti-authoritarian, and against established interests, which is frequently a popular stance in the social sciences (Moore, 2009). Advocates often define their positions in relation to positivism, and suggest that anti-positivist positions are empowering. Zajda and Zajda (2005), for example, argue:

> The major paradigm shift of the early 1970s between positivism (empirical/ quantitative research) and anti-positivism (non-empirical/qualitative research) began to question the very construct of 'value-free' empirical research and the scientific dominance of empiricism. This paradigm shift reached its heights in the 1980s, as illustrated by post-structuralist and post-modernist education and policy articles. Described as a 'postmodernist revolt' (Mitter, 1997) against the dominating theories of the Enlightenment and modernity, such a paradigm shift in policy directions challenged the meta-narratives in education and policy, the 'regime of truth', the disciplinary society, and promised to empower the learner, by re-affirming the centrality of the learner in the curriculum, and the diversity of learner needs (Zajda, 2002; Zajda, 2003b).

The epistemological stance, Moore (2004, p. 155) argues, is appealing because it

> apparently 'unmasks' false claims to universalism and disinterestedness on the part of the knowledge of dominant groups ... what is important is not only what is said, but who says it; the former can only be understood in terms of the standpoint of the latter.

Educational sociology has been predominantly concerned with educational differentiation, social opportunities, and social inequalities. The relationship between educational and social inequalities and opportunities is

> ...one of the most fundamental issues in the sociology of education, uniting its core theoretical concerns and research interests and its broader uses in public debate and policymaking. (Moore, 2004, p. 1)

Drawing on the epistemological stance described above, many educationalists have argued that the curriculum, and the knowledge which is transmitted through it, plays a role in the reproduction of social inequalities (Moore, 2009). Epistemological constructionism perhaps appeals to educational reformers because it *appears* to offer a solution to the elite control of education. It *appears* to provide a basis for the dismantling of the traditional curriculum, and for taking power away from elitist educational institutions, by stressing that no one piece of knowledge or kind of knowledge can make better claims to truth than any other knowledge, and that arguments in favour of particular bodies of knowledge are nothing more than arguments made in the interests of certain groups in society:

> By arguing that all knowledge derives from partial and potentially self-interested standpoints, relativism can be seen as a superficially powerful basis for challenging what are assumed to be the repressive and dominant knowledge forms of the existing curriculum. Relativists attack the claims to objectivity of dominant forms of knowledge and by implication defend the "voices" that are denied or hidden. (Moore and Young 2004, p. 243)

The thinking behind much educational reform has been that, because knowledge expresses the interests of the dominant social group, radically changing the knowledge taught in education should radically change its social effects (Young, 1971). The 'New Sociology of Education' in the United Kingdom, an influential movement in educational sociology largely emanating from the Institute of Education at the University of London, crystallized these ideas in their debates about the curriculum in the 1970s. Educational sociologists who were attempting to account for the unchanged class differentials in British education, and the fact that widely available secondary education had not produced the expected results in terms of increased social mobility and equality, came to argue that *what* pupils were taught affected how they learnt and their relative levels of attainment. They argued that while previous educational researchers had pointed to the relationships between education and inequality, they had not questioned the role of knowledge in perpetuating inequality (Young, 1971). For example, the ruling class in apartheid South Africa taught that Jan Van Riebeck discovered South Africa because this knowledge served their project of remaining in power. From the point of view of the white elite, this 'knowledge' was 'true', because Jan Van Riebeck was the first white person to officially sail to the tip of Africa and bring news of this back to Europe, much as Christopher Columbus was said to have 'discovered' America. Thus the New Sociology of Education represented a clearly articulated and influential notion of a causal relationship between the organization of knowledge in education and the reproduction of the *status quo* in society.

The progressivist tradition discussed previously, and the epistemological constructionist tradition introduced here, are not the same. The former is primarily concerned with the idea that knowledge should be based on the interests of learners, in order to increase learners' success in education. As I argued above, this often implicitly rejects the idea that there is an intrinsic value to organized bodies of knowledge and clearly contradicts the argument that, in the development of the curriculum, the organization of bodies of knowledge should override learners' immediate interests. The progressivist position is sometimes seen as a relativist one. Novack (1975, p. 181), for example, argues that relativism is inherent in the pragmatism of Dewey: "He himself [Dewey] was an unrestricted relativist. This viewpoint molded his theory of knowledge and his conception of the nature of truth. He regarded truth as relative through and through; it did not possess any objective quality." Novack (1975, p. 56) also argues: "The pragmatists defined truth and error not as correspondence or lack of it with independent and prior material conditions, but as a quality which was acquired by ideas solely through their application in practice". However, progressivism is not necessarily relativist, as the idea that knowledge can represent truth is not necessarily inconsistent with the idea that learners' interests should dominate either pedagogy or curriculum.

The epistemological constructionist position in education is generally associated with the position that school knowledge is the knowledge of the ruling class. The epistemological constructionist position sometimes holds that because subjects represent knowledge of other groups—ruling classes and elites, colonial rulers, Western or male elites—it is not of interest to learners, or, it is alienating to them. It does not necessarily reject the idea that bodies of knowledge are structured. And contesting the way in which knowledge is selected within the curriculum is not necessarily inconsistent with holding the view that bodies of knowledge are important. However, in holding that theoretical and everyday knowledge are both products of social practice, epistemological constructionism can lead, as progressivism sometimes does, to a collapsing of the two types of knowledge. Moore (2004, p. 177) writes:

> It is strange that the sociology of *education* should, from phenomenology to post-modernism, have such a predeliction for skeptical, epistemologically weak perspectives. But then, this same predeliction has also, in varieties of *progressivism*, been powerfully influential in educational discourse. The two field orientations, positivism/ constructionism and traditionalism/ progressivism, run parallel, and to a considerable extent the constructionist position in sociology has serviced (rather than problematized) the progressive position in education.

The primary commonality between progressivism and epistemological constructionism is their frequent opposition to subjects as the starting point for curriculum design, and for thinking about education.

Weak Epistemologies and Economics Imperialism

Many critiques of outcomes-based approaches, such as much of that levelled at the National Vocational Qualifications in the United Kingdom, centre around attempts to show that the outcomes-based approach is at odds with its claimed progressive heritage. In some cases, critics argue that although the ideas of learning outcomes are in keeping with the progressive heritage, they are wrongly implemented, and so lead to a behaviourist approach no longer in keeping with that heritage (French, 2009; Hyland, 1994). I make a different case. I suggest that the problems of outcomes-based qualifications reveal weaknesses in progressive educational thought itself.

I use the term 'weak epistemologies' to include postmodernist and constructionist approaches which deny realism and account for knowledge solely in terms of the standpoints of the groups constructing the knowledge, as well as progressivist approaches in educational reform which do not account for the internal structure and importance of organized bodies of knowledge. How do these epistemological stances relate to economistic thinking about education?

Below I discuss two ways in which weak epistemologies have facilitated the colonization of the social sciences by neoclassical economic ideas. The first is that by not concerning itself with the economy, postmodernism out leaves any material analysis of economic conditions affecting society out. The second is that by overemphasizing the individual, weak epistemologies facilitate the tools of analysis brought to bear by neoclassical economics, which is based, as described above, on methodological individualism.

Fine (2001, 2002) argues that an important reason for the co-existence of neoliberalism and postmodernism is that they both respect one another's territory in a double sense—conforming where they overlap, but not engaging where they are inconsistent with one another. They are both heavily concentrated on individual subjectivity (neo-liberalism emphasizing consumer and entrepreneurial sovereignty, and postmodernism emphasizing the construction of identity). The state is perceived negatively by both—as an instrument of inefficiency and oppression respectively, although they reach this conclusion from very different perspectives. On the other hand, Fine argues that neo-liberalism, especially in its academic version, is entirely unconcerned with the meaning of things—for example, with the nature of the consumer and the consumed—in complete contrast to postmodernism, which is exclusively preoccupied with meanings. I would add to Fine's list, that both of them perceive educational institutions negatively, as backward and monopolistic.

Fine (2001; 2002a) further argues that because social theory, under the influence of postmodernism, distanced itself from the economic to focus on culture and identity issues, while at the same time arguing that reality cannot be known and that all knowledge is relative, economics has been able to increasingly influence areas of social theory. Thus, he argues that the rise of postmodernism facilitated 'economism' in social theory, or what he calls 'economics imperialism': postmodernist approaches to cultural and political theory "essentially abandoned the economic, and the material more generally, thereby giving free rein to neo-liberalism and the triumph of the economists" (Fine 2002a, p. 1). The result of the de-emphasis on the role of the economy, as Harvey (1990, p. 117) argues, is that it denies

> the kind of meta-theory which can grasp the political—economic processes
> (money flows, international divisions of labour, financial markets, and the like)

201

that are becoming ever more universalizing in their depth, intensity, reach and power over daily life... It avoids confronting the realities of political economy and the circumstances of global power.

Eagleton (2003, p. 7) describes the relationship between postmodernism and neoliberalism when he says:

Over the dreary decades of post-1970s conservatism, the historical sense had grown increasingly blunted, as it suited those in power that we should be able to imagine no alternative to the present.

Eagleton (2003, p. 29) further argues

Both postmodernists and neo-liberals are suspicious of public norms, inherent values, given hierarchies, authoritative standards, consensual codes and traditional practices. It is just that neo-liberals admit that they reject all this in the name of the market. Radical postmodernists, by contrast, combine these aversions with a somewhat sheepish chariness of commercialism. The neo-liberals, at least, have the virtue of consistency here, whatever their plentiful vices elsewhere.

The weak epistemologies which I have discussed above emphasize the role of the individual: individual choice, and the individual constructing their own knowledge. The progressivist roots of an over-emphasis on individualism can perhaps be found in the ideas of the early pragmatists. Certainly Novack makes this critique of them, arguing:

William James [a pragmatist who influenced Dewey] had construed the practical in highly individual terms. Dewey, following Peirce, gave a broader scope to the concept, identifying it with social habits and the repeatable experimental procedure of the community of scientists. Nonetheless he continued to regard the will of the individual, rather than the practice of the collective or the class, as the ultimate agency of social change. (Novack, 1975, p. 193)

Elsewhere Novack argues that James set out from "the assumption of an abstract isolated human individual as the norm" (p. 71), and that although Dewey combatted the "one-sided and egotistic individualism" by which the rich and powerful sought to justify their privileges, he never gave up the notion that the individual was the decisive force in social life (p. 31). Similarly, as discussed above, within some postmodernist or epistemological constructionist thinking there is an argument that individual identity and knowledge reflects the standpoint of individuals. Given that the individual is the key analytical unit of neoclassical economics, this creates a useful common ground. Another conceptual similarity is a de-emphasis on structure. This includes the structure of knowledge (particularly in progressivism), as well as the structure of educational institutions, with a particular distaste for hierarchy.

The prevalence of these ideas about knowledge and the curriculum leave education open to colonization by neoclassical economics because they disown any real or meaningful claims to specificity: they empty education of content by both abandoning a notion of the acquisition of bodies of knowledge as the main purpose of education, and the notion that bodies of knowledge needs specific institutional structures for its development and acquisition.

As discussed above, weak epistemologies appeal to progressives because they *appear* to dethrone elites who use their knowledge to perpetuate power and deny the knowledge of others, by rejecting the idea that any forms of knowledge can claim superiority over any others. They also provide ways of thinking about educational knowledge that *appear* to support the democratization of both knowledge and educational institutions, because they emphasize the way in which knowledge is implicated in power relations. By drawing on these ideas, the outcomes-based approach claims to remove the privileged position of educational institutions as the creators and transmitters of knowledge, by recognizing that knowledge is transmitted in a variety of contexts. People who are not specialists in educational institutions can have knowledge which is at least as relevant and important as those who are, and can therefore be involved in specifying outcomes. The suspicion of specialists and the desire to sidestep them in educational reform ties in with the idea that anyone with any interest in education can be involved in setting educational standards.

In the previous chapter I demonstrated that the learning outcomes approach has an implicit epistemological stance, which, firstly, does not see any bodies of knowledge as intrinsically valuable, and secondly, does not see bodies of knowledge as internally structured, meaning that any piece of them can be selected for any particular programme. Many documents advocating learning outcomes explicitly advocate constructionism, although frequently with some degree of confusion about whether they are talking about pedagogy or curriculum (Moll, 2002). This resonates with ideas about knowledge that have been supported by progressive education reformers, who, as discussed above, have frequently argued that subjects are either arbitrary or simply vehicles to express the knowledge of the elite, and who instead promote the idea of the individual learner selecting and acquiring the knowledge that interests them. Thus the notion of learner centredness which is invoked in much documentation associated with outcomes-based qualifications has a precedent in this educational thinking, and so the advocates of outcomes-based qualifications appear to claim a progressive heritage.

The implicit epistemology that is invoked when learning outcomes are seen as the starting point of curriculum design abandons the notion that certain types of knowledge are central to education, and by implication, the notion that certain types of institutions are required to produce and transmit knowledge. This fits in well with the neoliberal ideas described above, because it allows education to be redefined as just another good or service to be purchased by rational individuals on an open market. The outcomes-based approach provides, therefore, what *looks like* an educational rationale for treating educational institutions as generic 'service providers' rather than specialist and specific institutions. The notion of undifferentiated learning and undifferentiated knowledge resonates with marketization, and the attempt to break what was described in the United Kingdom, as discussed in Chapter 3, as the 'provider capture' and consequent monopolization of the market, because as long as there is nothing distinctive about educational knowledge and therefore educational institutions, any 'provider' can offer them. The role of the state is reduced to fostering this competition, and setting performance statements against which providers can be measured.

Harris (1996, p. 3) describes the common ground between democratic reformers and neoliberal reformers in relation to the National Council for Vocational Qualifications in the United Kingdom as an overemphasis on the individual learner as a consumer, and an underemphasis on the role of institutions in educational provision: "The aim has […] been to move away from provider and curriculum dominated vocational education and towards a system that is employer and learner (consumer?) centered".

Thus, neoliberalism and weak epistemologies can be seen as supporting and reinforcing each other with regard to educational reform, which can be clearly seen in an outcomes-led qualifications framework model. This is why the cooption argument discussed above (that neoliberal policy is able to coopt outcomes-based qualifications frameworks which are essentially progressive and turn them to its purposes) is flawed. Rather than being 'coopted' by neoliberalism, weak epistemologies *support* neoliberal policy ideas. It is the withdrawal from a claim to knowledge, and from the notion of the acquisition of knowledge as a human activity at the heart of education, which leaves education open to be colonized by economics. For, if education is not about something specific, it can be defined by stakeholders or interest groups, or redefined as a generic 'service' to be contracted in. As Wheelahan (2010, p. 111) argues:

> The specification of outcomes in a marketized system where outcomes are exchanged through buying and selling gives purchasers greater control over the development of outcomes, because producers aim to please the customer. This shifts the locus for determining educational outcomes to 'stakeholders' outside education, and these outcomes are in turn used to derive learning programmes.

I have discussed, in Chapter 2, how subject-based approaches to education have tended to be supported by conservative educational reformers, and anti-subject based approaches have frequently appealed to left-wing reformers, although also pointing out that there is a strong left-wing voice that has supported a subject-based approach. John Lea (2008), in a finely argued and nuanced discussion of political correctness and the politics of higher education in the United Kingdom and United States, clearly articulates both the left and right-wing variants of subject-based approaches to education, and the left and right-wing *realist* approaches to epistemology. But he suggests that *relativist* approaches to knowledge, captured in particular as multi-cultural and learner-centred approaches to curricula, are exclusively associated with the left.

The objectives- and efficiency-movement in curriculum reform, with its narrow focus on 'useful' knowledge, as well as the new outcomes-based qualifications policies, offer a counter-argument. It is not only the left that criticizes the traditional subject-based curriculum. Politicians and industrialists have for over a century considered it to be associated with an out-of-touch aristocratic elite, and have argued, much like left-wing reformers, that education should be made more 'relevant' and practically useful (Callahan, 1962; Wolf, 2002). Neither do left-wing thinkers have a monopoly on being forward-looking—which is an idea often associated with outcomes-based qualifications frameworks in relation to curriculum and pedagogy reform. The original outcomes (or objectives) approaches were positioned as forward looking, and part of a modernization agenda, with subjects presented as backward, and supporters of the modern version of learning outcomes have similarly argued that subject-centred education is out of step with the needs of industry and the economy, as Dale *et al.* (1990) discuss. Both the traditional academic curriculum—dominated by requirements of university entrance—and the 'child-centred' curriculum—preoccupied with notions of 'self-expression' and "the realization of 'inner potential'"—have been criticized by modern advocates of learning outcomes as divorced from the practical activities of the 'modern world' (Dale *et al.*, 1990, p. 25).

Despite the popularity of subject-centred approaches among traditional conservatives, the relationship between neoliberal public sector reform and weak epistemologies in education reform explains why the learner-centred and constructionist approach has been able to reach a better settlement with modern capitalism—or neoconservatives—than the traditional approach. Neoconservatives are more concerned with free markets, competition, and the control of public spending than with ideas about tradition and hierarchy (although this does not mean that in practice neoliberal states are not hierarchical and authoritarian).

Moore (2004) argues that in the current sociology of education, 'progressivism' in education is seen as the only possible progressive position. He suggests that the left has effectively "ceded, in a remarkable post-Enlightenment reversal, epistemologically powerful, strong forms of rational knowledge to conservatism", and goes on to argue:

> There is no language whereby a knowledge-based curriculum can be supported for socially progressive purposes. The default settings of the field of educational discourse assume that the 'progressive' position must be associated with epistemologically weak modes of curriculum and pedagogy. Or, on the other hand, that epistemologically weak forms of *progressive* education represent the best educational interests of working class, ethnic minority and female pupils. This association has systematically encouraged teachers to approach such pupils in a therapeutic/ compensatory rather than an academic mode, as *victims*, and has thereby preserved the privileged access of the social elite to epistemologically powerful forms of knowledge. (Moore 2004, p. 178)

But the weak epistemological positions supported by many educationalists have enabled the redescription of education as a process whereby individuals are forced to constantly purchase their own retraining in order to attempt to be employed, and have enabled this redescription to be seen as empowering. Thus, we have the free market fantasy of individuals freely and rationally acquiring their chosen human capital, assisted by the state, which uses its regulatory power to ensure that the same information is available to all agents. And we have a new version of Illich's deschooling fantasy (Illich, 1970) in which learning is not constrained by institutions, and individuals are free to choose from a wide range of learning possibilities when and how it suits them. Neither of these fantasies take into account, firstly, the necessary conditions for the acquisition of knowledge, and secondly, how and why institutions would emerge to offer such learning, and how they could be sustained. Some of the very real consequences of this fantasy have been discussed: in many poor countries the result of outcomes-based qualifications frameworks has been a neglect of supporting and/or building educational institutions.

The outcomes-based qualifications approach emphasizes that the important aspect of education is the 'outcome' or 'competence' produced—the educational programme is not important, as long as the learner acquires the prescribed outcome. It also argues that the outcome provides a 'standard' against which any learner can be assessed, regardless of whether they have in fact been on an educational programme: 'prior learning' can be recognized against outcome statements. As suggested in the previous chapter, this type of approach provides a conceptual basis for a de-emphasis on educational institutions, which are expensive for a state to maintain. This is how the curriculum reform contained in the outcomes-based approach, and the delivery/ management of education reform come together: the denial of the specificity of knowledge is the basis for undermining educational institutions. The common error made by both educational reformers and neoliberal reformers is the underestimation of the specificity and structure of educational knowledge, and therefore of educational institutions.

While the outcomes-based qualifications frameworks *appear* to be concerned with democratization and empowerment, and *appear* to be designed to support the production of relevant skills for the labour market, my analysis suggests that, by denying the specificity of educational knowledge and education institutions, the outcomes-based movement supports economics imperialism by facilitating a redescription of education in economic terms while maintaining an appearance of concern with democracy and educational opportunities. This flawed idea supports a flawed policy that undermines educational institutions and educational knowledge.

As discussed in Chapters 3 and 4, there have been other unintended consequences of outcomes-based qualifications frameworks. In particular, the strong emphasis on recognition of prior learning that pervades documents on learning outcomes can have at least four pernicious effects. One is that it provides a basis for de-emphasizing the need for building and supporting education institutions: in other words, asserting the commensurability of different kinds of knowledge runs the risk of diminishing the importance of access to the academy and becoming an excuse for not providing formal education (Muller, 2000; Wheelahan, 2010). Anderson and Harris (2006) point out that although recognition of prior learning is generally associated with progressive educational ideas, it became popular with policy makers as a way of appearing to fast-track rising qualification levels of workforces.

A second potential danger is that outcomes-based qualifications advocates tend to over-emphasize formal entry requirements to education institutions as the major obstacle to accessing education, which deflects attention away from other important barriers to education, and implies that once prior learning has been officially recognized against learning outcomes, there will no longer be barriers. But even if outcomes could be used to demonstrate prior learning, this would not solve the problem of access to education. In South Africa, for example, the qualifications framework was introduced as a major policy intervention to increase access to education, by recognizing prior learning against learning outcomes. But, as was discussed in Chapter 4, it is not traditional entry requirements that prevent many South Africans from accessing education institutions. It is because they do not have money to pay fees; because workplaces do not want to offer training to their staff or give them time-off to attend courses; because children head households where parents have died from AIDS-related diseases; because children do not have enough to eat; because there is no safe, efficient, and reasonably-priced public transport in South Africa; and the list goes on. When South Africans do gain access to education, in many instances they find schools which are ill-equipped, teachers who are poorly trained and motivated, university lecturers who never publish research and so on. And when learners leave educational institutions, jobs are not readily available, except for a small minority of highly-skilled professionals. Increasing the number of formal credentials available will not address any of these problems—and, as it is a costly and complex enterprise, may be at the cost actually addressing them.

A third potential danger is suggested by Young and Muller (2006), who warn that this type of policy could put people off the difficult work of learning, and engaging with formal education:

the more learners identify with the possibility of obtaining qualifications by credit accumulation and transfer, the less they are likely to be convinced of the value of sustained learning in a particular domain. So if credit transfer schemes did in fact work, it is possible that they would lead to unforeseen and undesirable consequences. For example, one possible consequence of placing less emphasis on what are sometimes referred to as "linear" learning pathways is that alternative routes to qualification via "credit transfer" may seem easier and fewer learners will opt for the pathways which provide the most likely basis for them to progress to higher levels. This could mean that in the longer term, employers find themselves worse off than before with regard to finding appropriately-qualified job applicants.

The fourth potential dangerous effect of over-emphasising the commensurability of different kinds of knowledge is that this can end up devaluing all of them. Wheelahan (2010) argues that both theoretical knowledge and tacit and contextual knowledge are necessary in vocational education, and both are impoverished by collapsing the distinction between them. Knowledge is not the same as experience. Both are valuable. It is precisely the explicit structure of knowledge, and hence its potential to be shared, that distinguishes it from experience and why we have specialized institutions such as schools, colleges, and universities for teaching it.

I am not suggesting that there is never a case for recognizing prior learning. As is discussed in Anderson and Harris (2006), recognition of prior learning is a complex and often contradictory set of practices operating at the interface between formal education and everyday experience. There may well be the need in many countries for more openness in terms of formal requirements for educational programmes, and policies to support the recognition of prior learning could assist in this regard. As Young (2008) argues, if recognition of prior learning forces institutions to be more transparent about their entry criteria, then that is a good thing. But, as I have demonstrated above, an over-emphasis on the 'sameness' of knowledge that is learnt within and outside of education is not a progressive move.

There is also little empirical evidence that this is a viable way for large numbers of people to earn qualifications, or that qualifications thus earned are really valued. Even advocates recognize that in most countries achievements in this area have been very limited (Blom *et al.*, 2007; European Union, 2011). The evidence from our study was that while in all instances there was a lot of rhetoric about learning outside of formal institutions, no countries had strong data that reflected large-scale awards of qualifications for this type of learning.

ESCAPING THE PENDULUM?

Outcomes-based qualifications frameworks demonstrate how weak epistemologies have opened education up to economics imperialism and commodification, ultimately undermining the provision of education, particularly to poor people, people in poor countries, and people in weaker parts of education systems such as vocational education. Economics imperialism within the academy, and the dominance of narrow economic concepts within policy, such as the general acceptance of the terrain of market failure, have undermined our ability to make arguments based on what has been learnt across other disciplines. Economics imperialism leaves us with very empty ideas about education, and no basis with which to develop policy or think about education. This is why there is a need to develop a clear sense of the specificity of education.

I have mentioned above how critical analysts both decry the domination of traditional subjects in the curriculum, and lament their absence. Similarly, while some, such as Boghossian cited above, see post-modernist, social constructionist, and relativist epistemological stances as dominant in the academy, others see positivism and empiricism as dominant, as extensively documented by Moore (2009). This duality or paradox perhaps becomes more understandable if we take on board Moore's explanation that positivism and the standpoint epistemologies usually associated with social constructionism or postmodernism are two sides of the same coin. Moore, drawing on Abbott, Gellner, Fay and Niiniluoto, as well as Bourdieu and Popper, argues that constructionism and positivism are both based on 'foundationalism'.

Moore defines 'foundationalism' as the idea that true beliefs are built on "certain foundational terms or propositions that do not in turn derive their own justification from any other terms or propositions" (Moore 2004, p. 157). 'Foundationalists', according to Moore, believe that it is only such knowledge that is non-social, and therefore true. He argues that both positivists and epistemological constructionists are foundationalists, for both suggest that knowledge must be based on these foundations in order to make truth claims, but while the former believe that such absolute foundations are possible, the latter believe they are not possible. As Moore and Young (2002, 2008) explain:

> Only positivists and their post-modernist critics insist that for knowledge to be knowledge it must be outside history, though of course they then draw precisely the opposite conclusions as to its actual possibility.

Epistemological constructionists take the position that because knowledge cannot be based on a firm and absolute foundation, no knowledge can claim precedence over any other knowledge: "All beliefs are cognitively equal, because none can claim the *necessary* epistemological privilege of *not* being socially constructed" (Young, 2008).

Moore suggests that the 20th century has been dominated by positivism and reactions to it because they share the same premise, and therefore cannot escape from each other. This insight may assist in understanding the seemingly unresolved war in educational reform, as well as finding a way of stepping back from it. The tug-of-war between the two main ways of thinking about the curriculum, and the history of swings between one and the other, as well as the attempts to form compromises between them, are partly based on the inadequacy of each of them in their own right, and partly based on something that they hold in common: the false idea that knowledge requires foundational terms or propositions that do not receive justification from other terms or propositions.

Young and Muller (2010) describe the traditional approach to curriculum development as a 'taken-for-granted' approach to knowledge, because subjects are not justified through appeals to specific criteria, but primarily through appeals to tradition, although implicit in this is the idea that the curriculum contains unquestionable knowledge which has been established by experts, and therefore does not need debate; they suggest that this 'taken-for-granted' approach is rooted in logical positivism and its empiricist parallels in the social sciences, in which knowledge is seen as sets of verifiable propositions and the methods for testing them. What these different approaches have in common is what Young and Muller (2010) describe as an 'under-socialized' notion of knowledge, so called because the social production of knowledge, in particular its historical and social contexts, and the boundaries of particular disciplines, is taken for granted. Because it does not acknowledge relationships between knowledge and power, because many students do not succeed in school, and because of lack of clear criteria for the selection of subjects and knowledge within subjects, critics over-emphasize individual learners and relationships between knowledge and power, resulting in swings towards epistemological constructionism, the child/learner centred tradition, and outcomes, aims, and objectives-based approaches which reject formal bodies of knowledge.

Young and Muller refer to perspectives on the curriculum which emphasize learners' interests as '*over*-socialized' because the propositional character of knowledge—its potential to get closer to the truth, and its structured nature— is downplayed or denied, and the social constructedness of knowledge and its relationships to power are over-emphasized (Young & Muller, 2010). Epistemology is reduced to the question 'who knows?'

It is not sufficient to invoke tradition. But it is also problematic to simply invoke the needs of the child or the employer. The outcomes-based movement is one manifestation of the latter approach, and of course differs substantially from other manifestations of it. But what it demonstrates is the weakness of thinking about the purpose of education without starting from areas of knowledge, and the weakness of thinking about education as something defined by stakeholders, divided into bits of knowledge that can be selected or rejected by learners. If education is not seen as an activity that has very specific purposes and possibilities, it is open to being seen as simply another commodity or generic service that anyone can provide. And there is danger that curriculum coherence within subjects will suffer if, rather than taking the intrinsic qualities and structure of a subject as the starting point, we begin from outcomes extraneous to subjects. While learner-centred curricula and epistemological constructionist ideas about knowledge may well have progressive origins, and are still popularly associated with progressive politics, their consequences are anything but progressive: they have facilitated a conquest of education by economics, whereby the tools of neoclassical economics have been used to redescribe how education is thought about in policy internationally.

If we are to avoid this, we need to think more coherently about what education can and should do. We need a coherent way of thinking about education and knowledge, which acknowledges and analyzes the social ways in which knowledge is developed, but also takes seriously the idea of knowledge as a structured and differentiated organization of symbolic ways of thinking about the world (Moore, 2009; Muller, 2000; Young, 2008). Thinking sociologically about knowledge includes thinking about the different actors involved in knowledge creation, and their standpoints, experiences, interests, and relationships, as well as the labour process of knowledge development. It also involves thinking about the intrinsic properties of knowledge, and how bodies of knowledge interact with each other, how ideas shape each other, how knowledge areas are structured, which tools, assumptions, key ideas, and key subject matters are the focus of different areas, where the boundaries lie, and how and when they shift (Moore, 2009).

Explicitly taking account of the social construction of knowledge is important, because clearly the development of knowledge is influenced by power, evidenced, for example, in the dominance of neoclassical ideas that lend 'scientific' support to policies which empower rich elites in economics courses, or in the amount of money that is spent on researching cosmetic surgery as opposed to diseases that kill millions in poor countries, as well as the examples cited above of the respective 'discoveries' of South Africa and North America.

Further, as a product of human society, it is the social constructedness of knowledge that enables it to get closer towards objectivity, or to develop better—in the sense of more accurate, more insightful, capable of explaining more—accounts of the social and natural world. It is because many people are involved in the development of knowledge, arguing, testing, developing contrary positions, and so on, that bodies of knowledge are developed which transcend individual points of view (Collins, 1998; Young, 2008). The fact that knowledge is socially developed underpins its robustness; enables its specialization and differentiation; and allows us to gradually contest ideological biases that have been accepted as knowledge. Young (2012) argues that the distinctiveness of disciplinary communities is the unique value they place on the development of knowledge: it is their primary reason for existence. As a result, disciplinary communities, while open to manipulation of various kinds, particularly when they are, as they are in most instances, vulnerable to funding requirements, nonetheless have their own rules, codes, traditions, and core values that have been developed over time, and are thus able to some extent to resist ideological manipulation, and to provide tools to contest bias and ideology.

School subjects are not a source of new knowledge, but are created by drawing on disciplinary concepts, and organizing, sequencing, and selecting from them in ways that enable learners to acquire their key concepts. As discussed above, this process, as much as the development of knowledge, is influenced by, and embedded in, power relations. But the disciplines and the subjects themselves are not reducible to power relations. Taking explicit account of these power relations is necessary in order to meaningfully contest the curriculum. But instead of arguing that schools should dispense with subjects to focus on learners' immediate interests and every day contexts, or the projected utility of bits of knowledge in the workplace, a left-wing approach to the curriculum should support subjects but contest which subjects are selected, and which knowledge is selected within subjects.

Such an approach has a left-wing heritage, despite the frequent association of a subject-based curriculum with right-wing politics. Lenin, for example, argued that education must focus on ensuring that young people acquire "what human knowledge has accumulated" (Lenin (1943), pp. 467-8, cited in Entwistle, 1979, p. 43). Italian revolutionary and major social philosopher Antonio Gramsci believed that in order to achieve a more egalitarian society, the working classes must be given a classical education. He emphasized the mastery of history, science and the national language as well as reading the 'classics' (Gramsci, 1986). Gramsci argued history was vital to give people an understanding that the society that they find themselves in is not god-given or inevitable, but a product of contingent circumstances as well as human struggles (Gramsci, 1971). Education, he believed, must involve discipline and the memorization of facts; examinations were necessary and useful (Edinburgh Letters, no CXXII, cited in Entwistle (1979)). While the study of ideology and its maintenance by the ruling class was central to much of his work, he did not see educational knowledge as ideology. Gramsci suggested that some thought systems were cognitively and logically superior to others, and that while local knowledge, common sense, or folklore had some value, it was often superstitious, fossilized, and anachronistic. Furthermore, he argued that teachers and professors should and did have authority, based not on inherent social power, but on intellectual criteria (Gramsci, 1986).

Critical of the progressive educational reforms of the Fascist government in Italy, Gramsci pointed out that a focus on the emotional disposition of the young above knowledge and facts, and a campaign against the memory of the past or information about contemporary social and cultural alternatives, works well for political authoritarians. Entwistle (1979, pp. 83–84) characterizes Gramsci's position thus:

> It is not too much to claim that a political system which, thus, denies access to information is well served by an educational ideology whose polemic constantly derides the acquisition of information and which elevates the experience of the immature above 'knowledge to be acquired and facts to be stored'. The political authoritarian who would form the young with an emotional disposition in favour of his own ideology does well to canvass the merit of ignorance, the value of not having a memory of the past or information about contemporary social and cultural alternatives. His ally is not the schoolmaster functioning as authority and requiring the learning of the facts of history, geography, or science, but the anonymous teacher encouraging spontaneity and 'autodidactism'
>
> [....]
>
> It should not strain credulity at all to argue that democracy, above all, is dependent on the well-informed citizen, and ill-served by schooling which eschews the disciplined transmission of information in favour of the alternative of leaving children to follow their own spontaneous dispositions. It is difficult to see the point of emphasising the value of freedom of thought without also stressing the need to learn the cognitive repertoires which liberate thought, or of a concept of freedom of action without there being knowledge of the manifold alternatives which confront the human agent in a modern society.

Entwistle, writing in the late 1970s, was arguing against what he saw as the pernicious effects of the New Sociology of Education discussed above. His conclusion is that the proposed 'radical' alternatives seem "utterly conservative in their implications, more likely to keep the working class in its traditional chains than to be liberating and counter-hegemonic in outcome" (Entwistle, 1979, p. 179). He suggested that Gramsci's argument—that a thoroughgoing, child-centred progressivist curriculum is friendly to political authoritarianism—was a prophetic insight in terms of the debates of the day. It can be seen as equally prophetic in relation to the outcomes-based movement. Many critics of the outcomes- and competence-based movement agree: Wheelahan, (2010, p. 116) for example, argues that "'Wishing away' the distinction between academic knowledge and knowledge of the excluded leaves them exactly where they started, as excluded."

KNOWLEDGE IS NOT JUST BITS AND SOCIETY IS NOT JUST INDIVIDUALS

I have argued above that it is possible and necessary to take account of ways in which knowledge is socially developed, without doing away with the idea of the acquisition of bodies of knowledge as a key purpose of education. We need criteria for deciding which knowledge is most worthwhile, to avoid the notion that we can simply rely on tradition to determine what should be taught, thus undermining our ability to challenge the abuse of power in the development and transmission of knowledge. But at the same time we must avoid seeing knowledge and truth as merely relative to the socio-historical context in which they were developed, and must also avoid conflating everyday knowledge and disciplinary knowledge. We must think about education as a way of enabling students to move beyond the particularities of their everyday experience, rather than remaining trapped inside it.

It is also necessary to reestablish in educational thinking a notion of society. One of the major insights of sociology is that while society is made up of individuals, it is not explicable simply in terms of individuals; "what may appear to be rational for an individual acting in isolation is often not what would be rational for a society acting in concert" (Collini, 2010). The problems with the idea that individuals purchasing commodities in their own interests will ultimately lead to the collective good are clear in the world today. Karl Polanyi, writing about the first period of international market liberalism, argued:

> All societies are limited by economic factors. Nineteenth-century civilization alone was economic in a different and distinctive sense, for it chose to base itself on a motive only rarely acknowledged as valid in the history of human societies, and certainly never before raised to the level of a justification of action and behaviour in everyday life, namely, gain. The self-regulating market was uniquely derived from this principle. (Polanyi, 1944, p. 31)

Polanyi demonstrated that the idea of individual interest has not been a dominant human trait, or used as the basis for organizing society, for most of the history of humanity:

> The outstanding discovery of recent historical and anthropological research is that man's economy, as a rule, is submerged in his social relationships. He does

213

not act so as to safeguard his individual interest in the possession of material goods; he acts so as to safeguard his social standing, his social claims, his social assets. He values material goods only in so far as they serve this end. (Polanyi, 1944, p. 48)

Polanyi was writing this in response to the first major period of experimentation in market-led social policy in the 19th century, drawing attention to its anomalous character within history, in the hope that humanity would not revert to this system of organizing and thinking about society again. However, this hope was not realized, and since the 1970s this economic thinking has again dominated economic policy internationally, and extended further than the first time, both in terms of geographical reach and in terms of how much societies have been pushed to operate on market principles. In the logic of much social policy today, society has changed from being something which markets were a part of, to being an adjunct to markets.

Sociology emerged as a discipline precisely as economics was divorced from society and history, and the separation was complete by the end of World War II. Based on Vilfredo Pareto's distinction between economic behaviour as rational and non-economic behaviour as non-rational (Milonakis & Fine, 2009), economics was seen as the science of rational action, and sociology as the discipline of non-rational action. Over the course of its development, the great sociological thinkers have demonstrated that society is not just a group of individuals, but something substantively different, something that exists in its own right; that groups are different from individuals; and that the ways in which groups are organized and structured in society affect and constrain how individuals behave and what they believe. Social facts are explained by supra-individual causes. Emile Durkeim showed how the most individual of acts, suicide, occurs differently depending on the degree of social integration in a given society. He explained why the rules that people enforce on each other, the forms of institutions within which people act, and even the ideas that they hold, cannot be explained by examining an individual and multiplying the result. Marx showed how the economy—the material conditions in which the production of goods and services is organized in a society—affects and constrains social life, political processes, and spiritual beliefs. Weber explored social organizational form, and how bureaucratic rationality affected the human spirit. Building on, revising, and adding to these traditions, sociological research has shown that society is a ritual order, a collective conscience founded on the emotional rhythms of human interaction (Collins & Makowsky, 1993). It is comprised of groups with shared cultures and moralities, and not individuals.

Society cannot be explained in terms of the motivations of individuals, anymore than individuals can be seen to be basically rational:

We know that the patterns of rationality lie on the surface of appearances, and that in order for people to be rational they have to operate within certain socially given limits. We know that much of what shape's people's behaviour lies beyond the lighted circle of our focused consciousness, in the penumbra of the taken-for-granted. (Collins, 1982, pp. 186–187)

Our basis, our essence, is social. "Individuals", argues Collins (1998, p. 71), do not stand apart from society as if they are whatever they are without ever having interacted with anyone else". It is physical interaction in groups which creates energy, group bonds, identity, and solidarity. People can do things in groups that they could not do as individuals—even individual acts, like the individual acts of bravery of soldiers fighting together for a cause. As Marx argues in his 6th Thesis on Feuerbach[10], social relationships constitute the essence of human beings. Even, as Collins (2004) demonstrates, our modern idea about individuals is a product of our socialness. Different societies have different notions of individuals, and it is only relatively recently that we have developed a conception of individuals as having an inner self. Goffman (1959, 1967) demonstrated how this conception of self is created through social interaction.

The social nature of humans, and the fact that society is more than the sum of individuals, is key both to understanding the problems of neoliberal economic policy and the nature and essence of knowledge and education. Human societies—people in interaction with each other—have developed bodies of knowledge that further our understanding of both the natural and social world. These bodies of knowledge are not acquired through everyday experience, and they are very seldom acquired by individuals alone. This is why societies bring young people together in institutions which can provide structured and social learning experiences: to acquire the heritage of humanity. This is a heritage that outcomes-based qualifications frameworks disregard.

The following chapter explores whether there are different or better ways of doing qualifications frameworks and learning outcomes.

ENDNOTES

[1] As Milonakis and Fine demonstrate, this was not a hard barrier, and there were also continuities: some aspects of political economy had prepared the way for the new ideas, and the more traditional ideas of political economy also continued to hold sway in various ways.
[2] For example, Becker (1976); also see www.acton.org/pub/religion-liberty/volume-3-number-2/economic-imperialism
[3] Of course economics has advanced since Vaizey was writing, and Ashton and Green (1996) describe some of the complex equations that have been developed more recently to perform some of these calculations. Nonetheless, they still point out that this type of calculation can only be applied in fixed contexts and with a range of assumptions.
[4] This is similar to how the use of the term 'market failure' cedes ground to an approach which suggests that the market is the best ideal mechanism, even if it does not always work perfectly, and so accepts the underlying assumption that the sum of individual choices constitutes the best outcome for society.
[5] However, a remnant of the early colonization of the social sciences by economics can arguably still be seen in the continued (although contested) presence of rational choice theory within sociology.
[6] Although, as discussed in the previous chapter, these types of policies do in fact often lead to new state regulatory institutions.

7   In Chapter 1 I mentioned Novoa's (2002, p. 135) notion of the spread of 'banalities' around the world, which become universally accepted as truth, and are then transformed into 'magic concepts' which provide solutions. I suggest that they are not so much 'banalities' as economistic ways of thinking about education.

8   For example, Paul Goodman (1964) decries how progressivist ideas are distorted in the schooling system.

9   As briefly discussed in Chapter 2, 'progressivism' in education is by no means a clear and homogenous school of thought. Some strands of it deal with pedagogical aspects of education, and have been associated with 'child-centeredness', focusing on the individual's learning experiences rather than on traditional subjects. Others have emphasized the role that schools should play in society, and how new research in psychology and the social sciences could be used to make schools more efficient.

10 http://www.marxists.org/archive/marx/works/1845/theses/theses.htm accessed 8th September 2013

CHAPTER 8

WHERE IS IT GOING?

Are There Different and/or Better Ways to do Qualifications Frameworks and Learning Outcomes?

This short chapter returns to a discussion of empirical research into qualifications frameworks, to consider what seem to be some of the more successful qualifications frameworks, in light of the criticisms raised in the previous chapters. I consider the possibility that while there are problems with the competency-based training model and outcomes-based qualifications frameworks, there are other successful ways of designing qualifications frameworks. I argue that while some frameworks do *seem* to have achieved relative success, this is mainly because they do not attempt to achieve the kinds of claims made by the advocates of qualifications frameworks, or, at most, attempt to make very modest contributions to achieving these claims. Either qualifications frameworks are radical reform mechanisms to change curricula, pedagogy, and assessment; the delivery of education; and the relationships between education systems and labour markets, or, they are modest reforms which describe the qualifications available in a country, and try to make the relationships between these qualifications a bit more explicit. While there are some hybrid models, such as that described in Mauritius, in practice the different components of the frameworks tend to operate within one of the two approaches; in the Mauritian example, the vocational qualifications were competence-based and attempted to introduce substantial reform, and the rest of the framework focused more on documenting and to some extent comparing existing qualifications. Whilst there is some evidence that the latter, modest approach can be successful, there is very little evidence of success in the former approach. Unfortunately the two are frequently conflated or confused in policy documents and in policy borrowing processes. At the end of the chapter I briefly consider where the trajectory of qualifications frameworks seems to be going, as more and more countries try to develop them. I suggest that while it could be the case that the former, modest reform is what is mainly being developed, this is not consistent with the hype which surrounds qualifications frameworks. If the latter model of outcomes-based qualifications frameworks is being implemented, it is likely to be indicative of the growing liberalization of labour markets and economies.

THE STORY SO FAR

Let's briefly consider some of the key points of this story. Learning outcomes made an early appearance in educational reform in the first decade of the twentieth

217

century, under the name 'objectives', and were directly linked to attempts to make education more relevant to industry and more efficient. This was largely at odds with another major current in educational reform that has an even longer history, that of emphasizing the importance of basing education on the perceived interests of children. However, there was some underlying similarity in the epistemological stances of both, as neither started from a position which valued bodies of knowledge for their own sake, or saw bodies of knowledge as having intrinsic properties and particular structures that needed to be transmitted and developed in particular ways. The objectives movement ended up collapsing due largely to the large and unwieldy number of objectives that were developed, and the impossibility of turning them into a curriculum. The child-centred or progressivist reform trajectory was implemented patchily, and succeeded in some objectives, in some places, but was pushed back in others.

Learning outcomes re-surfaced in the 1940s and 50s. By then they were supported by some progressive educational reformers, who were concerned with helping all children to succeed in education. In this way, the idea of learning outcomes started to develop more common ground with reform trajectories under the broad banners of child-centredness and progressivism, which made gains and suffered setbacks in turn, so that some aspects of their ideas became 'taken-for-granted' in education. The issue that remained unresolved was the role of knowledge in the curriculum. Many, but not all, advocates of outcomes or objectives argued that skills, cognitive processes, and abilities could be specified outside of the context of specific bodies of knowledge. Many but not all advocates of learner-centredness argued that education should start from learners' knowledge and interests, and were against rigid boundaries between subjects, or sometimes against having any subjects at all (as mentioned in Chapter 2, some advocates of learner-centredness see it as primarily a pedagogical matter of interesting learners in subjects).

In the 1970s in the United States, outcomes became seen as a central mechanism for the reform of both the curriculum and the delivery and management of teacher education, mainly for primary and vocational teachers. Learning outcomes were then taken up in the 1980s in the reform of vocational education in the United Kingdom, through the National Vocational Qualifications in England, Northern Ireland, and Wales, and the 16+ Action Plan in Scotland. Outcomes, and the National Vocational Qualifications, were described as 'standards of a new kind'. In the context of neoliberal economic policies and public sector reform, outcomes-based qualifications were introduced with a focus on both curriculum reform and the reform of the management and delivery of education, in the name of improving economic performance through 'better' education. The main idea of curriculum reform was to make education relevant to what industry wanted, with an assumption that this could be easily ascertained. Industry was supposed to drive the process of developing the outcomes that would be the basis of the qualifications. The main idea of the reform of the management and delivery of education was to marketize provision, using learning outcomes as a target against which the government could measure providers, thereby treating state providers the same as private providers, forcing competition, and, it was hoped, enabling the entrance of new players into the market of educational provision. There was also an argument that specifying outcomes in qualifications would provide a mechanism through which institutions could award certificates to learners for outcomes that they had achieved before entering the institution.

The National Vocational Qualifications in the United Kingdom had many problems, and achieved few of their specified aims, with only some successes in a few sectors. One of the key problems was that the specification of learning outcomes in qualifications led to highly detailed over-specified qualifications, often for trivial or low-level outcomes. Because outcomes were seen as the starting point, and because knowledge was selected in so far as it 'led to' or 'underpinned' a specific outcome, curricula were not developed from bodies of knowledge, at least where the official rules were being followed. Many of the qualifications designed in this way end up at a very low level, with very little theoretical knowledge being taught. Many qualifications were never used. Despite the enormous problems in the United Kingdom, the model was adopted in the reform of vocational education in Australia, under the banner of competency-based training. As in the United Kingdom, there was a dual focus of making curricula more relevant and marketizing provision. At the same time, the idea of outcomes-based education was taken up by reformers of the school curriculum, who also drew on the North American models, which in turn had drawn on older versions of outcomes/objectives. Both the competency-based training model for vocational education and the outcomes-based curriculum in schooling in Australia were the subject of enormous debate and contestation. Clear evidence of successes and failures is hard to come by, but sharp contestation and fierce criticism did not prevent the model from spreading to other countries. First of all it spread to a comprehensive qualifications framework in New Zealand, where the approach was attempted in the reform of all levels and sectors of the education system; after problems were experienced, the model was dramatically modified.

The English National Vocational Qualifications model was taken up in Latin American and Caribbean countries in the late 1990s and early 2000s, as well as in some African and Asian countries, mainly in the reform of vocational education. Again, the problem of over-specification, low-level qualifications, and unused qualifications could be seen, as well as the development of new state agencies and systems for the regulation of very weak systems of provision. One of the starkest differences between the experiments in the United Kingdom, Australia, and New Zealand and these countries, was that the latter, poorer, countries did not have a strong base of educational provision to start with, particularly in vocational education. The outcomes-based qualification model assumes a regulatory state, as opposed to a state delivering education, but there were few providers ready to step into the gap. The waste of time and resources mattered the most here.

From about 2005, qualifications frameworks were developed in many countries in the Asia-Pacific region, particularly for vocational education.

The creation of the European Union led to an effort to bring the educational traditions of different European countries into some kind of alignment with each other, and in the late 1990s the 'Bologna process' introduced the ideas of levels and outcomes to higher education reform in Europe. In 2008, the European Union adopted the European Qualifications Framework. This led to most and, according to Cedefof (2009), *all* European countries committing themselves to developing qualifications frameworks, and a dramatic increase in the number of countries close to Europe, or with close ties to Europe, developing qualifications frameworks. The European Training Foundation assisted in developing qualifications frameworks in many countries surrounding Europe or with a wish to join Europe, and the European Council provided financial resources further afield to help design frameworks for vocational education reform, in countries such as Bangladesh, India, and Somaliland.

In nearly all of the developments described above, the idea of using outcomes-based qualifications as a driver of reform was limited to, or ended up being focused on, vocational education. During the last two decades, competency-based training has increasingly become the only game in town for the reform of vocational education, and qualifications frameworks are being developed for vocational education in every region of the world.

DIFFERENT MODELS?

In discussions that I have had with colleagues at international conferences and seminars on qualifications frameworks, three statements have repeatedly struck me. One is a sympathetic utterance like, "Yes, you South Africans really messed it up, but we are doing things differently." Another is something like, "Qualifications frameworks are not the same as NVQs! We are not making the same mistakes as the British made". And perhaps reflecting a perspective that underlies both of the previous statements, people say, "There is a middle ground, learning outcomes and qualifications frameworks can play a useful role if not taken to an extreme".

I have demonstrated some of the problems with the idea that employer-specified competencies can improve the relevance and quality of curricula, and improve the relationships that education and training systems have with labour markets. I have demonstrated problems with the idea that learning outcomes can 'translate' across different types of learning and different sectors or different countries, as well as problems with the idea of specifying learning outcomes separately from bodies of knowledge.

Do these problems manifest in the same way in the frameworks which have not suffered extreme difficulties, and which are perceived to be relatively successful?

Let's start by considering the Scottish framework. The qualifications framework in Scotland, as well as its outcomes-based qualifications and use of outcomes in its curriculum, did not receive the type of widespread criticism seen in the rest of the United Kingdom, or in other countries such as New Zealand and Australia. Raffe (2009b) suggests that this is because in Scotland outcomes and inputs are both considered in qualification design. Knowledge is not seen as implied in outcomes, but is separately specified. Given the increasing dominance of the idea of qualifications frameworks and learning outcomes, and given the serious problems with the notions of competences or outcomes as used in the National Vocational Qualifications-type model, it is important to consider whether the Scottish model suggests that outcomes-based qualifications frameworks could work if they were implemented differently.

The idea of learning outcomes emerged explicitly in Scotland in 1984, in a reform known as the *16+ Action Plan*. This laid the basis for a series of reforms which used the idea of learning outcomes to introduce more flexibility to the ways in which qualifications for learners over the age of 16 could be acquired, and the ways in which different qualifications related to each other. David Raffe (2003, 2007, 2009a, 2009b) tells the story of a series of reforms spanning over a decade, which followed the *16+ Action Plan*. Various policy changes were implemented which focused on or affected qualifications and curriculum policy for post-compulsory education. There were different attempts to introduce the idea of learning outcomes and criterion-referenced assessment into qualifications, with varying and in many instances loose interpretations of outcomes. Qualifications were 'unitized', which in this context means broken into smaller bits that learners could accumulate separately. The concept of accumulating 'credit' towards qualifications was introduced. The idea of a comprehensive framework of qualifications which indicated levels of achievement emerged in the mid-1990s. By this time, most mainstream qualifications belonged to one of three relatively distinct 'families': the Scottish Qualification Authority's National Qualifications, which included school qualifications and many of the qualifications offered in colleges; higher education qualifications; and Scottish Vocational Qualifications, which were somewhat similar to the English National Vocational Qualifications. The Scottish Credit and Qualifications Framework was launched in 2001 to incorporate them into one single framework. The different 'families' of qualifications became seen as 'sub-frameworks' of this larger framework. This umbrella framework was intended neither to establish new qualifications nor to overhaul existing ones. Instead, it was the culmination of a series of reforms which had taken steps towards incorporating the ideas of outcomes, levels, and credit accumulation into the different qualifications *already* available.

Raffe (2009b) discusses three aspects of the context of Scottish educational policy-making that he believes are relevant to the development of the qualifications framework in that country. The first is scale: the Scottish policy community is relatively small, and where consensus does not already exist, it is easy to pursue it through face-to-face discussion. The second is institutional uniformity: there is a relatively small number of institutions with organization and standards tending to be consistent among institutions of different types. This reduces the number of conflicting interests that have to be consulted, and so contributes to the ability to reach national consensus: for example, school-college collaboration can more easily be discussed at national level in Scotland than in larger countries with more diverse systems. Thirdly, in Scotland there is a tradition of public provision: there is a strong expectation that education should be provided free of charge, for all citizens, and in the public interest.

This context is different from the context in the rest of the United Kingdom. The Scottish reforms were different in other ways as well. Instead of being aimed at reducing the power of education institutions, the qualification framework was driven by education institutions, or at least, by a body which represented higher education institutions, although Raffe (2009b) describes how some of the earlier reforms were forced on education institutions, particularly colleges. Instead of being imposed by government, it was led by a partnership of organizations involved in education which had all chosen to be part of it. This partnership was initially comprised of two higher education bodies, the Scottish Qualifications Authority (the main awarding body for school and college qualifications), and the Scottish government. Later it included the colleges, which are multi-purpose institutions which, along with the universities, are responsible for most public, institution-based, vocational and general post-school education. This, then, was not a process driven by policy makers in the name of employers but by the education institutions themselves.

The framework is described as outcomes-based. Outcomes in the Scottish reforms were initially seen as a mechanism through which educational institutions could communicate with each other and develop shared understandings of each other's programmes (Raffe, 2003). As Lassnigg (2012) points out, much advocacy documentation uses the metaphor of 'language' to describe the role of learning outcomes and qualifications frameworks, and indeed this term is explicitly invoked in documentation on the Scottish framework. There is a considerable difference, however, between a lengthy process in which a small group of stakeholders get together, develop a shared understanding of each other's learning programmes, and develop level descriptors that attempt to capture what the various qualifications have in common, and the idea that simply by specifying learning outcomes, learning programmes across sectors and contexts will be comparable to each other. Some research in Scotland argues that learning outcomes have aided expert judgements about qualifications and learning programmes (Raffe, 2009b). But it would be difficult to prove one way or the other the extent to which this is the result of the specification of learning outcomes, and the extent to which it is the result of a lengthy process of building up common understandings of different learning programmes and qualifications.

While evidence is limited on the *direct* impact of objectives, for example in increased access and transfer, the Scottish framework is described as *associated with* positive developments in access, progression, and transfer, and is seen to have contributed to a more transparent, flexible system (Raffe, 2009b). These associations, Raffe (2009b, p. 31) argues, have enabled the Scottish framework to assume "an almost moral authority among NQFs and to become a source of lessons to others".

The Scottish qualifications that most resemble the English National Vocational Qualifications are the Scottish Vocational Qualifications, a sub-framework of outcomes-based vocational qualifications. These, Raffe (2009b) suggests, have not been that easy to fit into the other Scottish qualifications, and have strong links with their equivalent qualifications in the rest of the United Kingdom. Raffe suggests Scotland had a history of developing curricula and qualifications which were meant to be more relevant to the labour market, but also points out that, as in the rest of the United Kingdom, employer engagement "has been a continuing challenge" (Raffe, 2009b, p. 36).

As pointed out above, there is a stark contrast between the general reception of the Scottish Credit and Qualifications Framework and of the English National Vocational Qualifications. Whereas the English National Vocational Qualifications, the South African and New Zealand qualifications frameworks, and competence-based training in Australia, triggered fierce and robust research pointing out many flaws, most research on the Scottish framework has been measured, but broadly supportive. There has been no flurry of negative evidence, or arguments against it. This may be because, as Raffe (2009b) suggests, it has retained the support of all sectors of education and training. It could also be because it has not changed much, something Lassnigg (2012) argues to apply to many qualifications frameworks in Europe.

This general acceptance cannot be said to be the case for outcomes-based reforms in general: the recently introduced school curriculum in Scotland, organized around capabilities and learning outcomes, has been the subject of much debate and fierce criticism (for example, Paterson, 2009, 2012).

A qualifications framework was also introduced in Ireland to help different sectors of the education system define standards and operations within their own sectors, without directing how they did so (Granville, 2003). Gary Granville argues that the Irish framework was an attempt to codify existing practice with regard to qualifications, although Raffe (2009c) suggests that it has started to play a greater role in changing the education and training system in various ways, for example by "filling gaps in provision or increasing accountability" (Raffe, 2009c, p. 25). Unlike the Scottish framework, which is voluntary, the Irish framework is statutory and has a regulatory role.

France has a long established and complicated system of classifying qualifications, which explicitly makes links between job requirements and qualifications. Recently there have been moves to simplify the classification system into a catalogue of qualifications, with stronger emphasis on the links and equivalence between different qualifications. A national grid of existing vocational qualifications—the *Répertoire National* or national qualifications register—was created in 2002 by the National Qualification Commission, which brought together different groups involved in technical and vocational education, including awarding bodies, employer organizations, and trade unions. Bouder (2003) speculated in 2003 that this could be a move towards a framework type system, and indeed, subsequent to the creation of the European Qualifications Framework and the requirement for all European countries to benchmark their frameworks against it, the French system is now officially described as a qualifications framework. There are some similarities with the English model, including, for example, the French system's increasing emphasis on modularity, and its use of competence terms to describe modules. However, the differences between reform attempts in France and the English-type frameworks are many, including, for example, no attempt to unitize, and no expectation that learners will provide evidence of competence against separate items. France's national qualification register differs substantially in its underlying principles from both the English model and the European Qualifications Framework (Méhaut, 2011). For example, the methodology for designing qualifications uses studies and research to define occupations, work activities, and the labour market outlook, instead of simply relying on stakeholders' inputs. In France, a curriculum is developed by teachers and specialists, and there are specifications in terms of content as well as required time of study for qualifications; this is different to the outcomes/ competence-based model whereby only learning outcomes are specified, each teacher is expected to develop their own curriculum against them, and there are no specifications for the time the process should take. Perhaps most importantly, like the Scottish framework, the changes introduced in France were not dramatic. It was a reform which worked within the logic of the existing systems and policies, even though it is now associated with the new terminology of 'national qualifications frameworks'.

It is also worth noting that the term *'qualification'* in France has different connotations to the equivalent English term: Méhaut (2011) argues that although the French term more heavily implies a labour market component, it also suggests something that has been negotiated, and that describes a social relationship, rather than an objective and measurable quality.

Lassnigg (2012, p. 312) argues that the emerging qualifications framework in Austria is an example of a reform which suggests movement at the political level, without the intention of changing much at the level of practice:

> … we should not expect much change in terms of learning and bridging – rather it might bring about the illusion of better learning and bridging. As a result, the actors at both levels, the educational and the political, might be content with the policy, as the practices of the former are not so much affected, and the latter can legitimise their activities by pointing to the superficial changes in structures.

Austria has a proposed framework based on learning outcomes that includes vocational and higher education. University representatives argued against a single overarching framework, and convinced the government to split higher education and vocational education into two frameworks with overlapping levels. The Austrian education system is not based on learning outcomes, and so an interim strategy proposes relating current programmes to a provisional qualifications framework without using learning outcomes. Lassnigg (2012) describes another provisional measure whereby vocational programmes could be related to the levels of the European Qualifications Framework without using learning outcomes. Assessment and recognition of prior experiential learning has also been postponed. As Lassnigg points out, this means that in practice initial education and training will provide the benchmarks against which other forms of learning will be measured. As I have argued in the previous chapter, using formal education and training as the benchmark for evaluating is inevitable in any system that recognizes prior learning, but doing so goes against the stated claims about outcomes-based qualifications framework, as they are supposed to provide an independent benchmark in the form of learning outcomes.

Thus the Austrian framework is currently an attempt to make more explicit a "partly implicit and partly explicit hierarchical structure" of qualifications which predates any attempt to create a national qualifications framework (Lassnigg, 2012, p. 322). Lassnigg argues that any substantial change or reform to the Austrian system has been postponed. Instead the Austrian framework has created: an explicit and formal hierarchy of programmes according to the eight levels of the European Qualifications Framework; more attention to the idea of learning outcomes; debate about programmes which had not previously been effectively included in the qualification system; and attention to the way in which non-formal and informal learning were incorporated.

In many other cases it is too early to make clear judgments about the frameworks emerging in Europe, and in many instances it is difficult even to gain insight into the processes, as very little research has yet been done, and official documentation is often difficult to penetrate. However, from the preliminary evidence found in our study (Allais, 2010b), the patterns seem to conform: either outcomes-based qualifications frameworks are expected to play major roles in reforming education and training, in the ways described in Chapter 1, or they are an attempt to make relationships between existing qualifications a bit more explicit. Sometimes, as pointed out above, the two different patterns can be found within the same country, in different parts of the qualifications framework, muddying how the picture is perceived. In the case of the latter, qualifications frameworks are used to *describe* existing systems of education, and so unsurprisingly, there is evidence to show that they have often succeeded in this narrow task. In the case of the former, there is as yet no evidence of positive achievements, and some of the patterns described in earlier chapters seem to be emerging, similar to the developments described in Chapter 4 in poorer countries.

For example, in Lithuania a qualifications framework was seen as a mechanism to build trust in institutions and social partners, a trust which was lacking due to a legacy of weak trade unions, weak networks of employers, suspicion of public institutions, and a historical absence of civil society institutions. This legacy stems from the context of a highly centralized education system, a command economy, and little social dialogue, so the participation and partnerships necessary to make the qualifications framework work were missing for historical reasons. At the time of our study the process of developing a qualifications framework was viewed with suspicion by educationalists, who saw it as top-down and highly regulatory. In general there was weak participation from both education institutions and employers, the two parties who are supposed to be brought together by qualifications frameworks.

Experiences in Russia seemed to echo the complexity of processes and structures which were described in some of the developing countries in Chapter 4, particularly Mexico and South Africa. At the time of our research in 2009, Russia had various processes underway, largely not coordinated with each other, which were meant to lead towards the development of a qualifications framework. The Federal Institute of the Development of Education, working with the Russian Union of Industralists and Entrepreneurs, created educational and occupational standards which were correlated with international standards. At the same time, the Centre for Development of Occupational Qualifications of the Higher School for Economics created a framework of occupational qualifications called a 'Unified System of Classification of Occupational Qualifications'. It is supposed to conform to a framework for classifying occupations, called the 'Unified System of Occupational Classifications and Information Coding'. This is intended to coordinate *three* other classification systems: the Russian Classification of Workers' and Employees' Occupations and Wage Grades, the Russian Classification of Occupations, and the Single Qualifications Reference Book. This 'Unified System' falls under the jurisdiction of the Ministry of Health and Social Development. At the same time, there is a Russian Classification of Professions, which deals with educational qualifications. This is the jurisdiction of the Ministry of Education and Science. The Institute of Labour and Social Insurance was working, at the time our case study was written, with the Ministry of Health and Social Development to develop new elements in the system of occupational qualifications, including occupational standards. These processes appeared to be somewhat at odds with each other. An ongoing problem was a lack of working relations between the Ministry of Education and Science, and the Ministry of Health and Social Development.

One of the aims of the qualifications framework process in the Russian case is to try to bring these various sets of documents and issues together. The hope seems to be that a qualifications framework with a set of level descriptors will enable the rationalization of the various classification systems, and make the relationships between them more clear. But so far this process has proved difficult and complex. For example, bachelor and master level qualifications have been introduced to the educational classification system for occupational qualifications, but they are not in the classification of labour qualifications. In addition, despite the many criticisms made about the old systems, such as that they are outdated and inappropriate, the various old classification systems and documents continued to be used, and are constantly being developed in their own right, so that any attempt to align them is working with shifting systems.

Russia is also a good example of the way in which qualifications frameworks can clash with deeply entrenched cultures. Our case study showed that there was a strong culture of valuing formal education and a history of regulatory systems that specified that qualifications must be linked to formal education and training. This conflicted with the trend towards recognition of prior learning.

SUCCESSES AND FAILURES

In previous chapters, I have presented a detailed discussion of the lack of achievements of qualifications frameworks against claims made about them, as well as difficulties experienced in implementing qualifications frameworks in the first countries in which they were developed, as well as in various developing countries.

The initial evidence from Europe does not counteract these findings. It suggests that if qualifications frameworks are seen as modest policy reforms which do not make grand claims about reforming curricula, education-labour market relationships or educational delivery, but simply claim to *describe* the existing education system, to improve somewhat the coherence between the qualifications on offer, and to make relationships between them a bit more explicit, then they are more likely to succeed. This may account for the relative success of the Scottish framework. However, by 'success' here I simply mean that it has been accepted and not dismantled. There is no evidence so far that the *strong* claims made for outcomes-based qualifications frameworks, in relation to improving transparency, relevance, and the quality of education, and improving education/ labour market relationships, have been or will be met, and there is considerable evidence of extreme difficulties with them, supported by strong theoretical arguments concerning their inherent limitations. 'Successful' qualifications frameworks often seem to acquire their reputation for 'success' (understood either in the sense of lack of contestation, or in the sense of actual concrete achievements) by virtue of not trying to change too much in the education and training system. The problem with much literature on qualifications frameworks internationally is that it does not distinguish this minor 'success' from the stronger claims made for qualifications frameworks. In other words, it starts with claims made about qualifications frameworks, and then goes on to point out examples of countries in which qualifications frameworks have been implemented and are still in place. But it does not recognize that in most instances, the success stories do not achieve the strong claims made about learning outcomes, and do not even try to.

It could be argued that qualifications frameworks are good and necessary policies, but cannot change things in the absence of other reforms. Raffe (2009a) suggests that qualifications frameworks are more likely to be successful if, while attempting to implement the intrinsic logic of the new reforms, they recognize the institutional logics that already exist; the implication is that either the framework works with these logics, and perhaps changes very little, or that these logics need to be changed through other reforms. Our Malaysian case study (Keating, 2010) shows that qualifications frameworks are inherently dependent on established institutions, and that by drawing on the strengths of institutions, qualifications frameworks are more likely to succeed. As education, training, and labour market relations are deeply embedded in institutional, social, and economic realities, new policies for qualifications seldom succeed in changing them.

There are a few other difficulties which were experienced in various countries in our study. One is that the various aims of qualifications frameworks could be in tension with each other. In Malaysia, for example, representatives of industry tended to be happy with the skills qualifications, but policy makers felt that learners need pathways to higher levels of skills, and that the current qualifications set-up did not allow this. Improving pathways between vocational education and higher education may be in conflict with improving pathways between education and training systems and the labour market. This also emerged in some of the European cases. For example, in Scotland, as Higher National Diplomas became more accepted as a route to a degree, they started to lose their character as an exit qualification leading into employment. This is a tension that many countries have to face. Improving the possibilities for progression from vocational education to higher education is often seen as a major way of improving the esteem with which vocational education is held in society. It is believed that learners will be more likely to enrol for vocational education and training programmes if they have the possibility of progressing to higher education, both in countries where vocational education was previously not well regarded, and in countries which already have highly respected systems of vocational education and training. However, equally important to improving the esteem in which vocational education is held, or perhaps more important, is changing the conditions, remuneration, and career paths from vocational education into the working world.

The desire to promote short courses and greater responsiveness on the part of providers is in tension with the desire for more regulation, standardization, and better quality. While unit standards or competency standards are supposed to lead to flexibility, in some cases they are seen as rigid. The desire to make educational programmes shorter in order to meet the short-term requirements of the labour market (described variously in different countries by names such as 'cost-effective', 'quick start', 'accelerated short-term employment-oriented training activities' for identified priority jobs) seems to conflict with the idea of improving quality, and makes it less likely that learners who complete qualifications will acquire a sufficient basis to move up the education and training system. This seems to be in contradiction with the idea of a 'knowledge economy' and 'knowledge workers', and seems more related to deskilling and subcontracting than the outcomes and qualifications framework rhetoric of improving skills levels.

In many instances, the way in which educational institutions and systems are governed and managed is affected by qualifications frameworks, and, at times, these existing governance structures conflict with qualifications frameworks. Our case studies showed instances of strong support from governments, instances in which governments appeared to be taking a back seat, and instances where different government bodies were at odds with each other. There were also countries in which bodies representing employers supported a qualifications framework, and countries where they did not. There were instances in which trade unions had strong aspirations for what qualifications frameworks could do for workers, and countries where trade unions were not involved, or were disillusioned with qualifications frameworks. Lastly, many education and training institutions seemed to have reservations about qualifications frameworks, although instances of support were found.

Across the countries, our study revealed several difficulties with achieving social dialogue and stakeholder involvement. It was not only often difficult to involve industry in the process of developing frameworks, but also difficult to involve trade unions, particularly in countries where trade unions were weak. If employees' interests are going to be addressed in qualifications frameworks or other education and training policies, clearly there needs to be more effort to build and support the involvement of trade unions. The role of education and training institutions was also a point of concern in the study, as in many instances they appeared to be critical of qualifications frameworks and related reforms. Our study also suggested that the increasingly influential role of qualifications authorities in the design and implementation of qualifications frameworks, and in broader education and training policies, should be a focus for future research, because once these bodies have been created, they become influential stakeholders in education and training systems, with a vested interest in maintaining their own survival.

The financing of qualifications frameworks is another issue in many countries. Some countries seem to see qualifications frameworks as ways of getting employers to contribute to the financing of training, assessment, and certification. However, this is not easy. There is often a lack of employer involvement as well as a lack of take up of qualifications and competency standards by learners. These problems with employer involvement might partly be explained by the fact that employers often see qualifications frameworks as a way of getting governments to publicly fund assessment systems for the workforce, something that clearly contradicts the idea of education funded by industry. Another contradiction with regards to financing is that while qualifications frameworks are argued to be necessary to increase access to education and training, they are often associated with the introduction of user fees, both for training and for assessment and certification.

It is also important to ensure that learners can afford to access education and training, not just in terms of fees, but in terms of lost income. Thus future research could usefully focus on finding viable mechanisms and systems to evaluate the quality of provision, as well as mechanisms for ensuring that access is equitable. The English National Vocational Qualifications experience, as well as the problems experienced in Botswana and Mauritius, shows that even when this approach was confined to vocational education and training it experienced difficulties. As mentioned in Chapter 3, reviews of the competence-based training system in Australia have argued that training packages are too detailed and lengthy, are not user friendly to educators, and have outlived their usefulness. The Labour Competence Framework in Chile and Mexico has also experienced difficulties, despite having a limited aim of enabling the recognition of existing skills in the workforce. And the Australian and Botswana studies suggest that if this approach is used in vocational education and not in the rest of the system, it will introduce a new division between schooling and vocational education and between vocational education and higher education, which could further accentuate the low status of vocational qualifications.

WHERE IS IT GOING?

What it is that makes specific policies apparently resilient in the face of dismal failures and critique? Qualifications frameworks seem to work neither in theory nor in practice. Advocates acknowledge their problems, and absorb them in a piecemeal fashion, without allowing them to disturb their fundamental assumptions, and without revising their claims about what qualifications frameworks can achieve. Dissent is sometimes addressed by 'clarification' of definitions, particularly definitions of outcomes and competences. Much literature tries to redeem the concepts such as learning outcomes, along the lines of: it has been misused, but could be really useful if only we understood it properly.

In vocational education, competency-based training seems to be firmly entrenched, despite being the subject of extensive conceptual and empirical criticism, and having little empirical evidence in its favour. As discussed in previous chapters, initially qualifications frameworks were focused on vocational education. But recently there is a trend in Europe towards developing frameworks that include higher and vocational education. Few countries, with the notable exceptions of South Africa and New Zealand, have attempted to include school qualifications in their qualifications frameworks. But reforming vocational education through qualifications frameworks or competences could be seen as a first step to reforming entire education systems, or, could be seen as a way of sidestepping or providing an alternative to what is seen as a flawed education system. Dale argues that technical and vocational education reform was introduced in the United Kingdom to initiate reform in the education system as a whole, without intervening in the existing curriculum mechanisms:

> Vocational education is called on in the Great Debate and Green Paper to save a system with an inappropriate curriculum bias, low standards, and insufficient and ineffective links with industry. Hence vocational education comes to be associated with three quite distinct purposes, making pupils more able to get jobs, making them better performers in jobs, and making them more aware of the world of work and of the workings of the economy which await them. (Dale, 1989, p. 152)

Hyland (1994) suggests that the competency-based training model which was developed through the National Vocational Qualifications has extended its influence downwards into British schools and upwards into teacher education, higher education, and professional studies. This seems to be now extending across other countries: one of the things that struck me when looking at policy developments in Europe and some surrounding countries (such as accession countries and North African countries) was the way in which flawed ideas from vocational education were being recycled as part of attempts to reform education in general—both in school curricula and in higher education—despite the fact that this model has not worked in vocational education, which continues to have a low status, particularly in the Anglophone world.

Brockman *et al.* (2011, p. 19) argue that the "emphasis on learning outcomes and the discounting of educational knowledge have been, to a considerable extent, adopted as design features of the EQF, reflecting the influence of 'Anglo-Saxon' conceptions of practical knowledge beyond British shores." They also suggest (Brockmann, Clarke, Winch, *et al.,* 2011, p. 6) that "... valuable elements of the VET systems of some countries are neglected to the benefit of dubious ones originating in some others". Whilst strong education systems might be able to appear to adopt these systems without actually adopting them in practice—thus retaining their current education system— weaker countries, and weaker parts of education systems, are less likely to be able to resist their practical influence.

Where learning outcomes have been least controversial is where they have been based in strong professional associations and strong education institutions. The relatively successful Scottish framework was led by educational institutions and awarding bodies, and while it uses learning outcomes, it has a flexible approach to how they are created and used. David Raffe (2009c) refers to 'outcomes-referenced' national qualifications frameworks, which use outcomes together with various 'input' factors—meaning, for example, that content could be specified, or other factors such as time required to complete a qualification. As I discussed in Chapter 6, there is a conceptual confusion with using 'outcomes' and 'inputs' in this manner, as specifications in qualification documentation never represent actual outcomes of learning, but only desired outcomes. Further, it is clear that specifications about qualifications which include the content covered in order to obtain a qualification, as well as other specifications such as those suggested by Brockmann *et al.* above, will enable better judgements to be made when comparing qualifications across countries, and it could be useful to have such information centrally stored somewhere. But keeping it up-to-date would be a major undertaking, and it is not clear who would use it. Our study revealed the inherent tension between the desire to classify and describe all competences and all qualifications and the desire for simplicity and transparency. Some frameworks end up with thousands of qualifications, each stipulated in detail, leading to very long and cumbersome documentation.

The vocationalization of schooling and higher education, as well as the development of vocational education, seems to be more on the agenda than ever before. After a long history of opposing it, the World Bank is now supporting technical and vocational education and training (TVET) projects around the world. Many international agencies are involved in similar projects, from Save the Children to the ILO. Understanding what is really driving this 'turn to TVET' is something that requires additional research. One possibility is that it is a way of channeling taxpayers' money into the private sector, through schemes in which public funds are given to employers to 'incentivize' them to train their workers. Dale (1989) argues that a major function of vocational education is to keep the reserve army of workers ready for employment, to ensure there is 'vocational preparation' even when there are no jobs for them. However, many commentators (for example, Sennet, 2012; Wolf, 2002) argue that, on the contrary, where jobs are less stable, *general education* is increasingly important because, they suggest, a worker with more general knowledge is able to move with more ease from one occupation to another.

It is not easy to foresee where the current hype around qualifications frameworks, competence-based training, and general reform of vocational education is leading. But certainly, much will depend on the broader political and economic choices made by countries, as well as on the extent of the changes they make to their education and training systems through learning outcomes and qualifications frameworks.

Qualifications are grounded in both curricula and labour markets, and while both are different in different countries, labour market regulation is particularly distinctive to national traditions and economic systems. While in many continental European countries education and labour markets have for a long time had a strong relationship, in liberal market economies there has been little or no historical relationship between the labour market and education, which is why, as discussed in Chapter 5, there are two major different approaches to vocational education in the developed world: one in which substantive education programmes prepare for long-term employment in regulated occupations, and another in which competences are used to regulate the provision of programmes which individuals are expected to select to improve their employability in shifting employment conditions. The European Qualifications Framework *could* bridge the gap between these two systems, or, it could put more emphasis on one than the other. If the latter, if the framework logically works better or implicitly supports one or the other of the two systems, this would either necessitate changes to the system less preferred by the European framework, or the practical rejection of this framework in countries with the less preferred approach.

In developed countries, the most hopeful possibility is that qualifications frameworks will be adopted only to describe existing education systems, without further changes. However, the increasing liberalization of the economy and of labour markets within Europe (although of course accompanied by tightening immigration controls to protect European workers from the rest of the word), means that more European countries are starting to resemble Anglo-American capitalism. It is likely, then, that linkages between education systems and labour markets will start to break down, and that these countries will increasingly adopt the education policies of the more liberal market economies. The spread of the qualifications framework phenomenon in Europe could be another indication of the spread of the Anglo-model of economic liberalization.

Méhaut and Winch (2011) suggest that an unstated objective of the European Qualifications Framework is to tilt the balance of power away from education institutions, and towards the labour market. In fact, this objective is made explicit. Bjornavold and Coles (2007, p. 231), advocates for qualifications frameworks, argue that

> Introducing NQFs based on learning outcomes alters the point of equilibrium of governance in education and training systems. Additionally we propose there are general shifts of position of the key actors where consumers of qualifications, mainly individuals and businesses are likely to be empowered at the cost of providers.

Thus continental European countries could be attracted by the outcomes-based qualifications model as a result of the liberalization of their economies, and the consequent pressure to roll back the welfare state; they are likely to end up with less regulated labour markets, more insecure work, and less state support for education institutions, all of which are the conditions which qualifications frameworks were initially a response to.

In poor countries, qualifications frameworks are likely to continue to be developed. Qualifications frameworks appeal to these countries for a number of reasons: the learner-centred rhetoric as well as the anti-subject stance appear to offer the possibility of freedom from curricula dominated by the interests of Western elites; the certification of existing skills seems to offer possibilities for individual advancement in the workplace, particularly for those who have been disadvantaged by education and training systems; they seem to give the opportunity to improve the levels of skills in the workforce, thereby increasing economic competitiveness; they seem not to require government funding; it is something that the rich and successful countries at least appear to be doing; and so on. And if we add to these reasons the fact that outcomes-based qualifications are being promoted by richer countries through 'aid' projects, then it seems likely that time and resources will continue to be focussed on this type of reform within developing countries.

Governments have largely implemented these frameworks without any regard for empirical evidence. The *relatively* successful frameworks, such as the Scottish framework, have been used to invoke support for the idea of qualifications frameworks in general, rather than for a specific model. Its relative success (or at least lack of obvious failures) make it a useful example for governments or policy makers wanting to argue in favour of implementing a qualifications framework. As Raffe (2009c) points out, a qualifications framework is not something that can be 'plugged in and switched on'. Examining what qualifications frameworks look like on paper cannot tell us much about how they are being implemented in practice, or what they are being used for, which is why the research presented in this book is important. The evidence suggests that qualifications frameworks have either been a failed attempt to completely change the delivery of education, the way in which education relates to labour markets, and the way in which the curriculum is determined, or modest reforms that make qualifications systems a bit more explicit.

CHAPTER 9

LESSONS AND ALTERNATIVE DIRECTIONS

Outcomes-Based Qualifications Frameworks as a Failed
but Instructive Fad

SUMMARY OF ARGUMENTS

This book is concerned with the relationships between education and the economy. It has looked at three main aspects of these relationships: first, how education has been positioned as a solution to economic problems; second, how neoliberal public sector reform has affected the delivery of education; and third, how the economy, and specifically the market, has come to be used as a model for thinking about education. I have argued that the goals claimed for education in much policy rhetoric today are misguided and unrealistic, and reflect a lack of willingness to tackle structural economic and political problems. The reforms made in the name of that goal have considerable negative consequences for individuals and education systems. I have also argued that neglecting or opposing the acquisition of bodies of knowledge in the form of subjects and disciplines as a key purpose of education and as a starting point of curriculum design facilitates policies which attempt to deepen the marketization of the provision of education, by emptying education of its specificity, and allowing it to be viewed as something open to redefinition by different stakeholders. Further, it leads to curricula which undermine our individual and collective abilities to analyze, criticize, and change the circumstances of our lives.

My study of outcomes-based qualifications frameworks reveals the problems caused by thinking about education from a narrow economistic perspective, which ignore broader insights into the structure of society, institutions, and knowledge. It also illuminates the problem of thinking about education as something that can be endlessly redefined and shaped at will. I briefly elaborate these arguments below.

Whilst education is positioned as the only way out of poverty, the rolling back of welfare states in the developed world and the pressure upon poor countries not to build welfare states has decreased public provision of education worldwide. At the same time, unemployment has been positioned by policy makers as an individual problem, and education is seen as part of individual responsibility for their own welfare. In this context outcomes- and competence-based education and training seem to be the perfect policy reform: they are claimed to ensure that education will meet the needs of employers; to facilitate more competitive delivery of education; to assist individuals to acquire the appropriate skills, allowing them to get better jobs or perform better in their current jobs; and, as a result, to assist societies to grow more prosperous.

Neoliberalism has had a dramatic effect not only on how countries manage economic policy but also on how they manage social policy. As described in Fine's and Milonakis' (2009) account of economics imperialism, the basic tools of analysis of neoclassical economics have been extended beyond the boundaries of economic analysis, and have been applied within other disciplines that affect social policy. The idea of individual free agents conducting transactions with each other in their own self-interest now holds sway in many areas of social policy. Neoliberal social public sector reform drives towards increasing profit and commodifying as many aspects of society as possible, including education. Underpinned by competition, it favours contracting out social services to private providers. Even when there is no contracting out it treats units of the state as private contractors to be evaluated against outputs. Neoliberalism, as it has been implemented in economic and social policy in many countries around the world, does not ignore the idea of market failure. As evidenced in the 'post-Washington Consensus' (which, as I discussed in Chapter 3, is sometimes presented as a softening of neoliberal ideology), neoliberal policy has recognized market failure, but, instead of questioning the basic philosophy that the market is the best way of distributing goods and services, it argues that the role of the state is to make markets work better, whilst continuing to expand them to as many areas as possible.

Outcomes-based qualifications frameworks are described within a rhetoric of empowering individuals, improving education, and contributing to economic development. In some instances, they have been explicitly advanced as tools to marketize education, while in others they have been described or viewed as progressive interventions. Either way, their logic fits well within the neoliberal ideology described above. Their advocates often draw on or refer to ideas about education which are supported by many educationalists. I have shown that the vision of empowerment through education presented by advocates of outcomes-based qualifications frameworks is at heart the *power of the consumer*: the learning outcomes specified in qualifications are intended to assist individuals to make better choices about the productive skills that they can invest in, as the learning outcomes in the qualifications specify what it is one is getting when one purchases education. They are also intended to assist employers to make informed choices when hiring prospective workers. By improving the information available to both learners and employers, they can be seen as tools which attempt to improve the functioning of markets. Further, education institutions are supplied with the competences required by employers so that they can 'manufacture' according to standard, and do so in a competitive environment. Governments are supposed to use the qualifications as targets against which to judge the outputs of education institutions, enabling them to regulate provision, hold their own institutions to account, and break down a monopoly on provision, creating the possibility of contracting out to new suppliers. This is based on the assumption that forcing civil servants or educators to function either within markets or *as if* they were within a market will make them more efficient and responsive; if they are not forced to compete, self-interested teachers, ignorant or careless about the needs of industry and individual learners, tend to teach and run education institutions in their own interests, and try to do the least work possible for the most money, to maximize their individual utility. In contrast, the learner-centered education system proposed through outcomes-based qualifications frameworks becomes a market in which individual learners control what is taught to them by purchasing 'bits' of learning as and when they are required. Governments believe they are improving the functioning of labour markets by ensuring that all individuals who have the right skills, and not only those who have purchased them from suppliers, get recognition for this, thus improving the ability of 'sellers' to find 'buyers'.

Outcomes-based qualifications frameworks could be seen as the ultimate policy instrument of Third Way politics: they are supposed to help individuals to attain appropriate skills to improve economies, while assisting governments to improve the functioning of markets and market-like behaviour in the provision of skills, and ensuring that employers can purchase the skills that they require in labour markets.

But there is no clear evidence that qualifications frameworks have improved relationships between education systems and labour markets. The mechanisms by which they claim to do this—by making it clearer to employers what the bearers of qualifications can do, and by making it clearer to education institutions what employers need their graduates to be able to do—do not work. I have shown that competence-based training and outcomes-based qualifications frameworks originally emerged in countries with weak education/ labour market relationships, and have argued that they are more likely to be a symptom of this problem than a solution to it.

I have shown that the epistemology behind this policy intervention is one that sees knowledge as more or less the same as information: something that is of value to the extent that it leads to a particular competence, and which can be derived from the specification of a competence, or measured against such a specification; something that can be, and is likely to be, acquired anywhere. The nature of knowledge, and the importance of the organization of bodies of knowledge with their own internal structure, is ignored or underestimated.

I have demonstrated that the specifics of outcomes-based qualifications as a policy mechanism—the claims that outcomes will be understood in the same way by employers, learners, and educators across countries, sectors, and other boundaries—lead inevitably to over-specification, in a vain attempt to create learning outcomes which refer to a clearly identifiable competence that everyone understands in the same way. This over-specification reinforces the tendency for knowledge to be confused with information, as it leads to narrow specification of bits of knowledge. Knowledge is seen as a commodity comprised of isolatable and measurable discrete objects that can be picked up or dropped at will, as opposed to holistic, connected, and structured bodies of knowledge which are located in structured social relationships.

I have argued that this approach to knowledge—underestimating the value of bodies of knowledge and their importance in curriculum design—resonates with and finds support from ideas about knowledge and education which have in the past been championed by many left-wing reformers. Specifically, much educational thinking has opposed the idea of the acquisition of bodies of knowledge as one of the main purposes of education and of subjects as the starting point of curriculum design. Many educationalists have argued that the curriculum should be driven by the needs and interests of learners, and not by subjects as organized bodies of knowledge. Others have argued that the subjects which comprise the curriculum are a representation of the ideas of the ruling class; they are alienating and oppressive for many learners. Others have argued that starting with bodies of knowledge leads to a focus on facts and memorization, and that curriculum design should instead start with a sense of the broader aims of education.

In all of these ideas, the importance of bodies of knowledge, their claims to reliable insight into the social and natural world, and their internal structure and organization, are ignored or underestimated. This has led educationalists to empty education of content; to render it as something vacuous and open to be shaped by relevant interest groups, whether these are government policy makers, community groups, parents, or industry. Learners can choose what they should learn, as can employers, parents, or other groups. Education becomes a malleable activity, a kind of 'free-for-all' that can and should simply be defined by in terms of what interest groups want it to be. This, I suggest, has opened education up to colonization by neo-classical economics, and made it easy for policy makers to believe that they can redefine education to fit the needs of the moment, whether these are solving economic problems, reducing road accidents and teen pregnancy, or improving citizens.

Many people who champion qualifications frameworks are not trying to support neoliberal policy. Nor are they neoclassical economists. But the logic of policy instruments derives from ideas which are not apparent on the surface. My analysis derives from a detailed tracking of attempts to implement outcomes-based qualifications frameworks, located in an analytical framework that draws on political economy as well as the sociology of knowledge.

The ideas of learning outcomes and learner centredness, both of which have a long educational history, were readily taken up by policy makers wanting to implement neoliberal public sector reform, because they could fit within the idea of a contractualized state, with an emphasis on individuals and individual responsibility, and would enable policy makers to avoid building and sustaining education institutions.

Neoliberalism is certainly less hegemonic than it was. Many countries have state-led industrial development and others have increased state-led welfare provision and provision of social services, both of which go against the tenets of neoliberalism, particularly China with regard to the former, and many countries in Latin America with regard to the latter. It is widely accepted, even by former proponents, that neoliberalism has not even delivered on its own terms (for example, Sainsbury, 2013). The primary claim made by its adherents was that it would lead to economic growth, and that this would be worth the increased inequality that would also result. While inequality has been spectacularly achieved, economic growth has not. Kurt Bayer (2009) argues that governments increasingly accept that neoliberalism causes more problems than it solves, and are aware that successful economic development in countries like China took place because neoliberal policies were *not* implemented. He suggests that the international financial institutions and the governments of powerful states are changing their strategies, resulting in a more pragmatic approach to development.

Nonetheless, neoliberalism remains highly influential. Crouch argues that although the 2008 economic crisis has led many to suggest that it is now "in tatters" (2011, p. 163), in fact what remains of neoliberalism after the financial crisis is "virtually everything" (2011, p. 179). Similarly, Harvey (2010, p. 218) writes that:

> The existence of cracks in the ideological edifice does not mean it is utterly broken. Nor does it follow that because something is clearly hollow, people will immediately recognize it as such. ... While there is anger at bankers' duplicity and populist outrage over their bonuses, there seems to be no movement in North America or Europe to embrace radical and far-reaching changes. In the global south, Latin America in particular, the story is rather different. How the politics will play out in China and the rest of Asia, where growth continues and politics turns on different axes, is uncertain.

Whether or not neoliberalism is being, or will be, abandoned by more governments as an approach to economic policy remains to be seen. However, the policies which have been developed under the influence of neoliberalism, in particular the marketization of much social policy, will be difficult to reverse. Inequalities of wealth lead to inequalities of power, and neoliberalism has led to extreme inequalities of wealth. This fundamentally undermines democracy and collective decision-making about social and economic policy, which is aggravated by the tendency for collective spending on public goods to be replaced by private donations, enormously increasing the power of rich individuals over what is prioritized in society. For example, as Ravitch (2010) describes, Bill Gates has become a major influence on education policy in the United States through considerable funds given to the Charter schools movement, to the detriment of public schools. By the same token, because wealth is seen as a measure of success and because of the ability of individuals to donate wealth to specific causes, wealthy individuals have been appointed to influential positions in governments. This means that there remains a strongly inbuilt tendency for perspectives that favour the wealthy to hold sway, and for decisions to be taken which are not in the interests of the majority of the world's population, and even less in the interests of the population still to be born (Crouch, 2011).

Polanyi (1944, p. 60) demonstrated that liberalism subordinated society to the logic of the market, instead of the historically typical pattern of subordinating the economy to society:

> ... the control of the economic system by the market is of overwhelming consequence to the whole organization of society: it means no less than the running of society as an adjunct to the market. Instead of economy being embedded in social relations, social relations are embedded in the economic system.

Neoliberalism has extended this. As such, it has been very effective as a hegemonic ideology, infiltrating and changing how many different aspects of society are thought about, and the kinds of policies which are believed to be appropriate. The notion of 'economics imperialism' is useful for understanding how, even as neoliberalism has been at least partially discredited internationally, its basic tools of analysis—methodological individualism and utility maximization—continue to dominate ways of thinking about managing and improving education.

Crouch (2011) points out, for example, that neoliberalism placed all institutions in society under an obligation to behave 'efficiently', as if they were business corporations, with 'efficiency' defined as organizing all activities around the goal of profit maximization. Organizations that, by virtue of their nature, had multiple goals, and many goals that conflicted with profit maximization, were defined as 'failing'. Judging organizations by their ability to make a profit has become so dominant in social policy that it has become almost common sense. Thus, education has come to be seen by many as something individuals must purchase and sell, and as an investment for individuals.

While neoliberalism as a theory of economic growth has lost plausibility since the economic crisis of 2008, the goals of neoliberalism—competition, profit, commodification of as many aspects of society as possible—have become deeply embedded in the logic of how many policy mechanisms have been developed. Outcomes-based qualifications frameworks are just one example of this; others include the privatization of utilities and public services as well as state owned enterprises, the introduction of user fees for services even when they are provided by public companies, and the expectation that public services should make a profit. Even as the failures of neoliberalism are increasingly well understood internationally, and even as many countries are forging alternative paths, this aspect of neoliberal public policy looks set to continue.

Qualifications frameworks are likely to be abandoned. Like many education reforms, they are likely to be a candle that burns out fast. Given their poor track record, governments are likely to quickly grow disillusioned with them—although once qualifications authorities are created, they have tended to develop a life of their own, irrespective of success or failure. If future qualifications frameworks are anything like those already developed, then countries will set them up, their advocates will claim victory merely on the grounds that they have been established, their claims won't be achieved, and reformers will move on to the next fad, perhaps leaving the framework intact as a not very important addition to the education policy landscape, perhaps having undermined or damaged the provision of education in the process of the attempted implementation.

In this book, I have discussed the lack of evidence that outcomes-based qualifications frameworks have achieved the grandiose claims made for them. I have also shown that outcomes-based qualifications frameworks have had seriously damaging side effects, and represent a significant waste of time and money, which has particularly tragic effects in poor countries. I have also demonstrated that when the logic of learning outcomes and qualifications frameworks is unpacked, it is clear that they are inherently unable to achieve the goals stated for them. I have suggested that the difficulties that countries have had in implementing qualifications frameworks are caused by the way their logic clashes with the logic of education, the logic of labour markets, and the logic of economies and societies. At best, qualifications frameworks are a modest policy mechanism that can play a small role in improving communication between education institutions.

Unfortunately, when education policy reforms fail—often due to the unrealistic expectations made of education, and the conflicting aims which are set for it—many people blame education institutions, and begin to feel that nothing that is done to them will make them work.

In order to defend education institutions from these criticisms, it is important to understand the inherent logic that led to, or will in the future lead to, the failure of outcomes-based qualifications frameworks. It is also important to understand why they became popular in the first place, and the ways in which their logic will have a lasting effect on the education system, even once the frameworks themselves have burnt out. These two points have been explored in detail in this book. But I am frequently told by policy makers and their advisors that I can't criticize this policy mechanism unless I have an alternative, and am frequently asked despairingly by government representatives what they should do instead. The simple answer to this is that there is *no* policy mechanism that can simultaneously improve provision, enable evaluation of quality, improve curricula, teaching and assessment, and improve the relationships between education and the economy. There is no magic bullet. And while there may be *some* alternative policy interventions for *some* of the goals of outcomes-based qualifications frameworks, in many cases it is the goals themselves that are wrong. What is needed is not so much alternatives to achieve the goals that qualifications frameworks have failed to achieve, but alternative ways of thinking about the role, and so the goals, of education in society. I turn briefly to some ideas about this task.

EDUCATION AND WORK

One of the goals of outcomes based qualifications frameworks is to certify as many qualities of individuals as possible—in the hope that this will improve their chances of accessing lifelong learning and getting a job, and improve their productivity at work. I have shown that, in the main, qualifications frameworks have not achieved the first, direct goal of facilitating lifelong learning by certifying existing skills. Instead, if governments want to improve access to lifelong learning, then they should support education institutions that offer learning programmes to people already in workplaces, and build more where these don't exist. This would involve assessing individuals, deciding on their existing skills base, and offering the appropriate further education. To ensure that people could access education, institutions would have to offer programmes on flexible time frames, and/or employers would have to give their employees time off work. Financial support would be required, particularly for unemployed workers or people in badly paid work. This would all, of course, be costly. The more individual attention an education institution provides to learners, the more expensive it is. But this is what real lifelong learning would require. Inadequate provision of education, lack of time, and lack of funds are far more significant barriers to lifelong learning than the fact that individuals don't have certificates for the skills they have obtained in the course of life and work.

Lifelong learning is desirable: people who want to learn should be able to learn, and retraining when jobs become obsolete is useful for the economy, and access to lifelong learning could be improved by increasing provision of education and decreasing the cost for individuals, as well as increasing the time available to them to access it. But the indirect goal of improving individuals' life chances as well as improving economic productivity through lifelong learning is not realistic, even if governments support policies which make access to lifelong learning more realistic. Equally unrealistic is the goal of improving individual life chances as well as general economic productivity by making education more relevant, another claim made for outcomes-based qualifications frameworks. Today more than ever we hear constantly how ill-equipped graduates are for workplaces. But it is surely not plausible that, with most countries having dramatically higher education levels than a generation ago, people can on average be dramatically less prepared for work? As Livingstone and Guile (2012, p. xx) argue:

> There is a large contradiction between the widespread assumption in this discourse of skill deficits of current labour forces and their consequent need for lifelong learning and, conversely, the social facts of unprecedented levels of participation in higher education and adult education.

The idea that the labour force has skills deficits at which education policy must be directed does not hold water. Youth unemployment is not an educational phenomenon. It is an economic and political phenomenon. The problem is fewer jobs, more precarious jobs, and less and less collective social support. Today's young people are expected to work for free in 'internships' in order to gain experience that their parents were paid to gain, not because they have fewer skills than their parents had, or are less 'work ready', but because there are more people and fewer jobs.

Of course it would be great if education institutions had more capacity to offer programmes to individuals who were out of work or people who wanted to learn something new. And it would also be great if education institutions could be supported financially to develop better capacity to assess individuals and advise them on appropriate learning programmes. But even if this were the case, education could not provide the way out of structural economic problems—except, perhaps, in the sense predicted by Randall Collins (2013), who argues that the expansion of education will continue because it is the only way of absorbing excess middle class workers as more and more middle class jobs are eradicated, both by delaying their entry into the labour force through long periods as students, and by employing them as teachers.

The assumption behind outcomes-based qualifications frameworks is not only that a deficit of *skills* prevents general economic development and individual advancement, implausible, as I have discussed above, but that a lack of *formal recognition* of existing skills both prevents individuals from getting employment, and prevents them from accessing further education. There is also little evidence that this is the case. There may well be instances where education institutions are very rigid in their entrance criteria, but this is usually as a result of institutions having more applicants than places. Demonstrating that individuals who have gained skills and knowledge at work have the same skills and knowledge as those who have been on formal training programmes will not increase the ratio of places to applicants. And as long as there are more places than applicants, education institutions will accept those whom they believe are most likely to succeed, which are likely to be those who have had formal education. Although in isolated instances it may be correct that it is a lack of certification, and not a lack of appropriate knowledge and skills, that causes individuals to not get jobs, in the main this argument is based on a simplistic idea of how qualifications function in labour markets. It does not take into account the fact that in many instances employers don't use qualifications to provide an indication of the skills that an individual has, but only to judge individuals' attainment *relative* to other individuals—levels of education attained are seen to indicate something about potential, which is also seen as an indicator of their 'trainability' as discussed in Chapter 7. An extreme example of this is Brown *et al.*'s (2011) description of the 'war for talent' mentioned in that chapter, in which top multinational companies say they fiercely compete for the 'best' talent. Brown and colleagues argue that the notion that there is only a tiny handful of individuals who could fulfill the roles which these companies are trying to fill is completely implausible, given how many people have the requisite qualifications and knowledge (Brown *et al.*, 2011; Brown & Tannock, 2009). They argue that the 'war for talent' is simply a justification for recruiting exclusively from a tiny handful of universities, and eliminating most potential applicants.

Qualification inflation is one of many indicators that there are problems with the ways in which education qualifications are used in labour markets. Qualification inflation has a negative effect on individuals when students have to go into debt to fund their studies—leading to what some researchers describe as a new class of indentured labourers in countries like the United States. Qualification inflation also aggravates the perception that education is inappropriate for the needs of work, because when people have to obtain ever-higher qualifications just to get into the queue for possible jobs, they inevitably end up acquiring qualifications that have no relationship to the work that they will do. The clearer specification of the competences of the bearer of a qualification could not solve this problem, even if the problem of how to specify competences in such a way that everyone would understand them could be solved. There is little, maybe nothing, that can be done within education systems to address qualification inflation, because it is not caused by anything internal to education institutions or education programmes.

If stable well-paid jobs with reasonably short working hours were available, with more-or-less full employment, with collective support for individuals during periods in which they were out of work for whatever reason, qualification inflation would stop being a problem. If jobs were balanced, with a mixture of rewarding, autonomous, and interesting aspects, as well as tedious or onerous aspects, and if those with more of the latter qualities were better rewarded in compensation, qualification inflation would in all likelihood disappear, as the intense competition for certain types of jobs would disappear. People would still need to develop specialist knowledge, and proof of having acquired it would still be necessary to work in many kinds of jobs. Because those areas of work for which expert knowledge was required would be in the public benefit, and because people in specialist work would not be rewarded more than other people, and maybe even less, as unpleasant work should be better compensated than pleasant work, the training required for such areas of work would be undertaken by those with a genuine interest in it.

This is obviously utopian. Although there are countries which have managed to achieve some aspects of what I have described above, there are far more which have not, even more that have not even tried. In general most countries are moving away from this type of vision, towards making work less secure, hence aggravating competition for remaining secure areas of professional work, with all the consequent distorting effects on education systems which are used to sort people for work. It may be asserted that, in the absence of the utopia described above, education is the only way that most individuals can gain some kind of social mobility. However, due to decreasing numbers of jobs and subsequent credential inflation, this also appears increasingly utopian.

The relationships between education systems and labour markets cannot be improved by simply changing education, without changing the labour market and the economy too. To try to do so would be to ignore the extent to which education, specifically vocational and professional education, is shaped by industrial relations, income distribution, production strategies, welfare systems, and social policy. Education reform cannot allow us to short cut history or sidestep structural patterns in economies. I have argued that one of the reasons that vocational and technical education tends to be weak in countries with more liberal labour markets, is that they tend to have more short-term employment, particularly in 'mid-level' occupations. It's easy to blame education institutions for producing graduates with 'irrelevant' knowledge and skills, but any education programme takes time to develop. There is thus a limit to how responsive formal education can be to short-term skills needs. Improving relationships between education and the labour market is complex, and there is certainly no one solution, or even one problem that needs to be solved.

Furthermore, although preparation for work may sometimes be a positive by-product of general education, it is a wrong goal—general education should not be aimed at preparation for work. Even vocational and professional education should not be about narrow preparation for specific jobs. This does not mean that nothing can and should be done to improve education programmes which are specifically focussed on preparing people for the world of work—a point I will return to in the discussion about the curriculum below. For now, the point is that changes to the functioning of labour markets, and changes in social policy, could improve relationships between education and labour markets. Technical and vocational qualifications will be more likely to be high quality if the needs and conditions of specific sectors and industries are considered; long-term funding for education and training institutions is ensured; education and training institutions are built and sustained over time in such a way that they have a stable core of staff who, on top of offering a stable core of substantial programmes, can respond to short-term needs for certain courses where this becomes necessary; there is funding for general education to ensure that everyone can access education from a young age; and there is reasonably stable and well paid work available. They are also more likely to succeed in the presence of strong professional bodies, strong labour market research, and strong trade unions, and countries could consider policies to support all of these.

Outcomes-based qualifications frameworks implicitly, and sometimes explicitly, see qualifications as devices to regulate life and work, as opposed to devices to signify educational achievement. The central logic of outcomes-based qualifications is that certificates matter, education does not. Outcomes-based qualifications assume that learning can happen anywhere. There is no doubt that in some instances, people without educational qualifications have at least some of the same skills as those with them.

But what would it mean in practice to delink qualifications from learning in education institutions? Let's perform a thought-experiment, and imagine what the alternative could be to the current practice whereby qualifications signify what people have learnt and are awarded by education institutions. In this alternative system, everyone would be able to be tested, and if found competent, given certificates of competence, for the knowledge, skills, and abilities that they have achieved, regardless of how and where they were achieved. There would have to be independent agencies or institutions that issued certificates—perhaps the way drivers' licenses are issued. These bodies, or other independent agencies, would have to be able to conduct assessment against various specified competencies. Perhaps professional bodies could play this kind of role. In some cases they already do license individuals to practice in certain areas of work. However, professional bodies are usually very strongly linked to universities, and their licensing requirements are based on workplace experience and tests conducted after university study. Is it viable to create such bodies in every area of practice and work? They would need to have a substantial body of expertise. Where would this be obtained? In education institutions? Or in the workplace? What kinds of agencies or institutions would these bodies be, and on what basis would they make their judgements? They could be state testing bureaucracies, assessing people on their team-work and critical thinking abilities. Or they could be contracted out—which seems in fact to be the direction in some of the countries we have studied. But there is no plausible reason to believe that either of these alternatives will provide better information about individuals' knowledge

245

and skills than education institutions offer, and no reason to believe that they will be able to make meaningful judgements about areas that education institutions haven't, according to advocates of qualifications frameworks, made good judgements about. Educational assessments are already imprecise and contested. Imagine how much more contested they would be if they had to test people's ability to work in teams, their temperament, their initiative taking, and so on.

Manuel Souto-Otero (2012) points out that if the claim made for learning outcomes—that the same outcomes can be acquired anywhere—are true, then education institutions would only be able to be saved from complete redundancy if they were able to produce the same competences more efficiently than they are produced naturally in the course of life and work. But education institutions do not, cannot, and should not try to develop every conceivable 'useful' competence in individuals. What educational institutions can do well is impart bodies of knowledge: specialist knowledge, disciplinary knowledge, and the kinds of knowledge that are very unlikely to be picked up in the course of everyday life. One of the reasons that educational qualifications are seen as proxies for competence is that, in many areas of work, specialist knowledge is required. It is in education institutions, and not in the course of everyday life, that this specialist knowledge can be acquired. What educational institutions certify is that individuals have obtained this specialist knowledge. This does not mean that the individuals are competent in every aspect of the work—hence, for example, medical graduates have long practical internship periods. It simply means that they have acquired specialist knowledge. This knowledge is the basis of judgements that they will make later. It is essential, it requires educational institutions, but it does not and should not claim to capture every aspect of competence. When specialist knowledge is taken as the basis for judgement and action in the workplace, and this specialist knowledge has been assessed, it is far easier and more efficient to make judgements about competent practice. Because education can do this, and because this is useful, it does not follow that education can and should be expected to produce any skill that is seen to be useful in labour markets.

In terms of establishing equivalence of qualifications across countries, again, there are no easy solutions. Given that official recognition of qualifications between countries is usually largely dominated by political interests, it seems unlikely that official lists of achieved competences will assist the individual bearers of qualifications from other countries, even if the problem of mutual understanding of the lists of competences could be solved. The labour market currency of qualifications in their country of origin is far more likely to be key in this regard than official descriptions of qualifications. Building relationships between professional bodies, or between education institutions, can also facilitate the movement of students. But even if this were done far better than it is at present, it is not plausible that lack of recognition of qualifications is a primary reason for lack of labour market mobility.

None of the above discussion means that we do not need to improve education. Clearly, at all levels of education, we need improvements.

CURRICULUM

We need better insights into professional and occupational knowledge, and how knowledge is developed and used in work. With some notable exceptions, inadequate attention has been paid to this in the past. There is burgeoning interest in this field for good reasons, and it is likely to yield insights which will enable improvements in curriculum development in vocational, occupational, and professional education. But this is different to the idea contained in outcomes-based qualifications that learning outcomes will improve curricula by indicating to education institutions what employers need, or the knowledge, skills, and capabilities that learners should learn.

Any work that requires autonomy and application requires a broad education that teaches bodies of knowledge that allow people to reflect on and critique the world of work, to see it at a distance and in a context. This is why it is important to hold onto the idea of education as separate from everyday experience; where, as argued by Bernard Charlot (2009), the world is treated as an *object* and not as an *environment* or *place of experience*. Charlot explains that it is through the process of distancing and systematization that an epistemic Self[1] emerges, which is able to see the world as an object of thought. The bodies of knowledge which have been developed over the course of human history, and which continue to be developed, enable us to disengage from everyday belief, question taken-for-granted assumptions, and achieve some degree of estrangement from the common and the familiar. This enables us to view our immediate experience with a critical perspective, which is how education can enable individuals and societies to challenge power. This can only be achieved through holistic and in-depth learning that stands back from the immediacy of everyday life.

This idea is equally important at all levels of education. It is the acquisition of bodies of knowledge—not lists of facts—which allows us to move intellectually across different everyday contexts. The acquisition of bodies of knowledge in which concepts, principles, and facts are organized in structured relationships with each other enable us to step in and out of situations, reflect on them, compare them, and analyze them.

I have shown that the outcomes-based qualifications approach does not enable such an approach to curriculum because it implicitly rejects the idea of structured bodies of knowledge. I have discussed the idea of 'functional analysis', which has been associated with many outcomes-based qualifications frameworks and competence-based training, and shown how it begins curriculum design from tasks or activities in the real world and then selects 'bits' of knowledge to fit into these activities, rather than seeing knowledge as the starting point. The same critique applies to attempts by some progressivists to design curricula based on what are seen as socially desirable aims. Bodies of knowledge contain facts and concepts which take us beyond everyday experience. These concepts are part of bodies of knowledge, and derive their existence and meaning from them. Approaches to

247

knowledge which do not differentiate 'information' from subject or disciplinary knowledge do not reveal concepts or enable people to learn them. This is why the idea of learner-centredness in which education is based on the desires of the learner rather than bodies of knowledge leads to vacuous and superficial curricula, because they are devoid of the concepts and conceptual relationships that exist in bodies of knowledge.

Foregrounding the role of bodies of knowledge in the curriculum also necessarily entails a return to something like the 'traditional' curriculum. However, the idea of 'tradition', that 'it's always been done that way,' is not a clear criterion for the selection of knowledge. We need criteria both for the selection of bodies of knowledge, as well as for the selection and recontextualization of that knowledge into curricula.

If we start from the approach which accepts and values the fact that knowledge is socially constructed, but argues that some forms of knowledge have intrinsic value for study, we have a starting point for both processes of selection. Moore (2004) argues that decisions about educational knowledge must be concerned with "the relative reliability of the *different* ways in which we produce knowledge" (Moore, p. 164). Young (2008) invokes the idea of 'powerful knowledge', as opposed to the idea discussed in Chapter 7 of 'knowledge of the powerful', as the starting point for thinking about the curriculum. Knowledge is powerful, he suggests, if it can contribute to freeing those who have access to it to envisage alternative and new possibilities. Science and mathematics enable people to transform, predict, and control aspects of the natural world, although they need the social sciences to understand the social impact of such transformations (Young & Muller, 2013). Gramsci argued that learning history and geography is fundamentally empowering because both subjects teach individuals about other places, ways of life, and courses of events (Entwistle, 1979). Literature is also a powerful way of enabling learners to see beyond their own environments, and experience other epochs, countries, and ways of life. Literature and poetry are not only 'powerful' insofar as they enable us to experience the lives of other people, but in that they enable new insights into our own lives. They stimulate the imagination and emotional awareness, allow us to infer meaning, to explore unusual uses of language, and to develop a heightened awareness and command of language (Gillian, 1993). Young and Muller (2013) cite Rosen (2012) to make a similar case for the power of the arts, which provide access to an essentially contemplative aesthetic standpoint. The arts, they argue, speak to the universal, and can enable people to feel part of a larger humanity, allowing the possibility, in Bernstein's (2000) language, of 'thinking the un-thinkable' and the 'not yet thought'.

Organized bodies of knowledge provide insights into the natural world, the social world, and our humanness, and they provide the means to improve our insights into these. One criterion for the selection of bodies of knowledge is that a balance should be attained, especially in the lower levels of education systems and general education, between these different areas of the world; in other words, the traditional balance between some social science, some natural science, some language, and some art subjects. This does not mean it will be straightforward to determine which subjects should be taught in which kinds of educational institutions. There are constraints of time and resources, and the bodies of knowledge which can be acquired by a given body of learners will depend on what they already know on entering a learning programme. In the early years of schooling, there are also other questions which must inform the curriculum—such as the developmental needs of young learners. At higher levels, particularly in vocational and professional education, the way in which work is organized, and the relationships between the body of knowledge and its application, must be taken into consideration. But in every case, decisions about which bodies of knowledge (packaged into subjects) to teach, and what content to select from them, is a key starting point. This is partly because of the intrinsic logic and organization of disciplines—motor mechanics students will never be able to understand the physics of engines without being introduced to more basic physics first. It might be argued that motor mechanics don't need to understand the physics of engines in order to fix them. In some instances this type of argument is valid—there are many things one can do without understanding how they work. In many cases it is not true. But anyway, education is not just about helping people to survive, but about learning what other humans have learnt about ourselves and the world in which we find ourselves. Vocational education should enable learners to develop insight into what they are doing, but also to distance themselves from the world of work, reflect on it, and critique it. For this, they need to be given the opportunity to acquire some disciplinary knowledge, and not just 'bits' of knowledge isolated from the system of meaning in which those bits of knowledge were originally embedded (Wheelahan, 2010).

If we start from the idea that schools should teach some of the bodies of knowledge developed by humanity, and select these based on achieving a balance between those which provide insight into the natural world, the social world, and human culture, then we are likely to end up with a curriculum which has some similarities with traditional curricula. The traditional school subjects—such as mathematics, science, biology, history, geography, music, art, and literature and language—are drawn from disciplines that provide insight into key aspects of the world. We do not have to resort to the conservative ideas that support these subjects in order to see that there is much of value in them. Traditional subjects were used to groom elites and would-be elites precisely because they provided 'powerful knowledge' to these elites. While, as I discuss below, there are aspects of these subjects that we should challenge—such as the perspectives from which history is taught—rather than dismissing subjects and the powerful knowledge they contain as the knowledge of elites, we should aim to make this powerful knowledge no longer elite.

A key difference between the approach that I am advocating and the 'traditional' curriculum is that the latter is insufficiently sociological; it does not pay enough attention to the way in which knowledge is developed. A sociological approach to analyzing the development of knowledge[2] insists that we recognize and analyze not only the internal structure of bodies of knowledge, but also their social construction. This means that we should always be aware of the role of power in the development

249

of bodies of knowledge and in their reconstruction into curricula. We should never ignore instances in which ideology is presented as fact. This is a departure from the interpretation of the traditional curriculum as completely objective, and enables us to question the 'facts' it presents—such as that Europe is at the centre of history or that colonialism was a good thing.

Now we move from the question of which subjects should be studied in general, towards the question of how knowledge from broader discipline areas should be selected for curricula within specific subjects at particular levels in particular institutions. As discussed in previous chapters, this process is also located in power struggles and questions of ideology, although some subjects are more open to ideological contestation than others. Rather than suggesting that we don't need a knowledge-based curriculum at all, educationalists should challenge the substance of the bodies of knowledge selected in the curriculum, debate about which knowledge to include in it, and, where possible, draw learners' attention to how knowledge is developed and these major debates and differences. Curriculum development is always difficult. Even without ideological contestation, there is always contestation amongst disciplinary experts about the relative importance of particular concepts. Acknowledging that knowledge is constructed and that it changes and develops adds to this complexity, but also ensures that the role of power is taken seriously, and that it is contested and drawn to learners attention where necessary.

As mentioned in the previous chapter, a common critique of traditional subject-based curricula is that they lead to the memorization of inert facts, instead of the mastery of concepts. This is less likely to happen if we take seriously the structure of knowledge, the ways in which concepts are related to each other, when designing curricula. Winch (2012) argues that curriculum design requires

> introducing novices into the conceptual field that distinguishes the subject. This conceptual field can itself be seen in hierarchical terms with central organising and methodological concepts at its core and derivative concepts at the periphery. It follows that one cannot be introduced in a serious way into a subject unless one starts to acquire at least some grasp of these central concepts.

Winch goes on to argue that systematic knowledge is organised both in terms of the classification of and relationships between its various conceptual elements and also in terms of the procedures required to gain and to validate knowledge. In order to acquire such knowledge, instruction in abstract concepts, description of empirical examples, and acquaintance through experiments may all be pedagogically necessary. It may also be necessary for a teacher to draw to pupils' attention the relatedness of different concepts, in order to develop their inferential abilities, but also to develop an understanding of concepts in relationships with each other. This is why it is important to take explicit account of how bodies of knowledge are structured, as well as how they are developed, when selecting subjects and designing curricula for subjects.

We also need to take seriously the idea of epistemological access—how individuals actually acquire knowledge. This is something the traditional approach to the curriculum has largely ignored. Morrow (2007) reminds us that access to schools does not necessarily mean access to education, and Crain Soudien (2007) describes the tragedy of schools in South Africa, in which the *form* of school is retained, but no real learning happens. The solutions to providing epistemological access lie neither in a return to tradition, nor in attempts to make education more 'relevant' or learner-centred. They lie instead in serious attempts at developing curricula that help learners acquire bodies of knowledge. They also lie in improving society and people's economic circumstances, to make it viable for them to attend and learn at school.

In short, if education is about the acquisition of bodies of knowledge and if these are to be meaningfully delivered to children and young people, it is essential to have a well designed curriculum that carefully considers the structures of the discipline and makes difficult but clear choices about which content should be selected, and how it should be sequenced. This will only happen with strong education institutions. Learning happens everywhere, but the acquisition of bodies of knowledge requires education institutions.

BUILDING EDUCATION INSTITUTIONS

One consistent finding in our research, across most of the 16 countries that we studied, was that educational institutions were seen as 'offering resistance', 'failing to comply', or otherwise not supporting the move towards outcomes-based qualifications. In many instances, stakeholders interviewed, and even some of our researchers blamed this on the 'inherent conservativism' of education institutions. Ironically, however, (as discussed in Chapter 6) in many instances employers felt that the outcomes-based approach was something 'imposed on them', and often believed it was being imposed on them by the very education institutions who felt it was an imposition on themselves!

We also found that the more 'successful' qualifications frameworks seemed to be those which worked with the qualification systems of education institutions. They described and aligned existing qualifications, making relationships which were previously implicit more explicit, and sometimes opening up the space for debate and dialogue about these relationships. They were not seen as systems through which new qualifications were to be designed, or which would inform institutions on the basis for curriculum design.

Where outcomes-based qualifications frameworks are introduced as mechanisms for governments to regulate provision, *à la* neoliberal public sector reform, the state focuses on outcomes and outputs, and is not interested in inputs, rules, and processes. It contracts out for the delivery of outcomes wherever possible, and, where not possible, it treats parts of the state like contractors, operating within their logic. This focus on outputs is supposed to enable flexibility and dynamism within the state, and to address the problem of the inflexibility of bureaucracies, as well as their alleged tendency to be self-serving. In general—not just in education—this places more weight on outcomes, outputs, or targets than they can bear. Because contractors or parts of the state are evaluated in terms of numbers, they end up 'gaming' to reach targets: to meet the target of fewer queues, patients are shifted around hospitals; to build as many houses as possible, poor quality houses are built; to increase the numbers of qualifications, one three-year qualification is changed into three one-year qualifications; and so on. What's more, competences, like other outcome statements, are not transparent. Much as a 'house' can be interpreted to mean a palace or a hut, competences can also be interpreted strongly or weakly. Thus sharkish providers can claim to have taught a competence in a weekend. And whereas the size of a house, and to some extent the quality of a house, is fairly easy to see, the state has to have incredibly extensive regulatory capacity to catch out those providing weak curricula. This leads to a large regulatory state. But institutions, both regulatory and providing, take time and effort to develop. As Raymond Callahan (1962, p. 264) argued over 50 years ago in his critique of the efficiency movement in education: "We must face the fact that there is no cheap, easy way to educate a human being and that a free society cannot endure without educated men".

Not only do qualifications frameworks not provide a basis for building and supporting education institutions, and, in fact, support or facilitate funding models that make it difficult to build institutions because funding is linked to short-term course delivery, they also cause other difficulties for education institutions. Designing curricula against learning outcomes is tedious and restrictive, unless providers comply with the outcomes only cosmetically. Even then, as has been seen in higher education in South Africa, it adds an unnecessary administrative burden to people designing courses. This is a particular problem in poor countries where institutions are few and weak, and in weaker parts of education systems, such as vocational education. The South African case demonstrates how weaker providers, more dependent on short-term funds, with fewer professional educators, and weaker traditions and institutionalized systems, are most likely to attempt to voluntarily comply with the outcomes model. They are also more vulnerable to being forced to design their curricula against learning outcomes by regulatory agencies. The South African example also shows that strong providers such as universities and school systems with either strong central curricula or highly trained professional teachers are more likely to ignore learning outcomes, or comply with them only superficially. It also shows that where provision is weak, such as in vocational education, the end result of a system focused on developing outcomes-based qualifications and institutions to regulate provision against these qualifications is huge regulatory system with a tiny provision system.

Poor countries should instead focus on developing their education systems—building, equipping, and supporting their providing institutions. Policies that would support the success of education systems include giving teachers good quality education and training, and paying them well. Educating teachers in their discipline, in the pedagogy of their subject, as well as in the sociology and philosophy of education, will build their sense of professional and moral purpose, and enable, as I have been arguing above, an empowered sense of judgement that does not leave them trapped in their day-to-day experiences. They need autonomy over key aspects of their practice, particularly pedagogy, and need to be able to contribute to the curriculum. They need to be able to freely join professional associations, including unions.

If education is to be a common good, delivery cannot be left to the market. It cannot be seen as a simple service that can be bought or contracted for. The only people who would benefit from such a system are the elites who have access to the huge resources necessary to attend the top private schools. Educational systems will always fail to provide a quality education for all if they are judged as profit-making businesses, or judged in terms of their contribution towards the economy.

COLLECTIVITY

Building strong education institutions which are accessible to all, not only those who can pay, implies the need for collective politics, and to return to the state as the representative of the collective, and as the central authority for educational delivery. This does not mean that there are no problems with reliance on the state. For a start, states can fail, or be made up of extractive elites captured by business interests, whose interests lie in removing wealth from the country in question for personal gain, instead of building wealth within the country. As I write this, the South African government is being taken to court for its failure to ensure delivery of textbooks to schools. 20 years after liberation, children are still learning in mud schools, under trees, and without toilets. Many African states are considered to have failed to deliver education, which has meant that many people have turned to private provision, giving further ammunition to the proponents of marketization and of charter schools and vouchers-type systems whereby governments allocate funds to individuals and let them select which institution to attend or enrol their children in. This book is not the place for addressing the problem with voucher systems and charter schools (see Ravitch, 2010 for a detailed discussion of the problems they have caused in the United States). But I will briefly note two problems with the idea of privately run schools as the solution to the problems experienced with public provision. Firstly, it is based on the assumption that it is easy to set up a private school that will succeed in poor communities. This book presents some insights into why this is not the case: institutions require long-term investment which is unlikely to be achieved for poor people in market-based systems which tend to be short-term in their orientation. Further, it is well established that poverty makes it very difficult for learners to achieve in education, which is a major reason for the failure of public provision, and will only be aggravated if education is harder to afford. Secondly, even if the state isn't providing education, if it is funding it through vouchers or other mechanisms that follow individuals and don't support institutions, there still have to be some checks on schools and regulation of what learners learn, which governments are funding. This is the conundrum of a regulatory state, as opposed to both a welfare-based state and an extreme neoliberal state in which the market is simply allowed to function on its own. Either the regulatory function will be outsourced, potentially leading to a future in which children are taught only what is in the immediate interests of the businesses doing the checks and regulation, or we will have to rely on states to do this—the same states that are considered to have 'failed' to deliver education. Furthermore, actually investigating and evaluating education institutions is very costly and difficult, and so, whether the regulation is done through private providers or through the state, it is most likely to be carried out through the cheaper and simpler method of assessments. This will lead to an increase in the use of tests in schools. The problems of over-dependence on tests are well documented in the United States (Hyslop-Margison & Sears, 2006; Ravitch, 2010), where schools have to spend most of their time prepping for multiple choice tests, resulting in an incredible narrowing of the curriculum.

Nonetheless, relying on the state for provision of education is a complicated matter. The modern state arose in conjunction with capitalism, and has become more and more entwined with it; "... the state, seen for so long by the left as the source of countervailing power against markets and corporations, is today likely to be the committed ally of giant corporations, whatever the ideological origins of the parties governing the state" (Crouch, 2011, p. 145). However, the achievements of welfare states show us that social good can be achieved through the state. And, as discussed in Chapter 7, human beings are more than just buyers and sellers in markets; as social creatures, our lives are entwined, and we are "enmeshed in our needs for collective and public goods" (Crouch, 2011, p. 180). Education is a quintessentially collective good. Collectively, societies make it possible for their young people to acquire some of the knowledge about the social and natural world that humanity has developed over the course of history, in institutions dedicated to this purpose, through social interaction with those who have acquired various bodies of knowledge.

Harvey (2010, p. 197) points out that

> ... states are produced out of social relations and through technologies of governance. To the degree, for example, that states are reifications of mental conceptions, so theories of state formation must pay careful attention to what it is that people were and are thinking that the state should be in relation to them. [...] The neoliberal movement that began in the 1970s, for example, constituted a radical ideological assault upon what the state should be about. To the degree that it was successful (and often it was not) it led to wide-ranging state-sponsored changes in daily life (the promotion of individualism and an ethic of personal responsibility against the background of diminishing state provision), as well as in the dynamics of capital accumulation.

The neoliberal conception of the state is not inevitable, and can and has been challenged. A major reason why I have argued that outcomes-based qualifications frameworks are a negative phenomenon is because they operate within and reinforce a neoliberal notion of the state and society, and an approach to governance that promotes individualism and personal responsibility instead of collective welfare and state provision of public services. If we want all people to be educated, we need governments that build and support education institutions which are made accessible to all, and we need to collectively fund and support this endeavour.

This means ongoing struggles to make states democratic and accountable, and to rebuild a sense of collective responsibility. It means not only depending on the state, but also building a strong progressive civil society—those areas of life in which people organize and interact which are separate in various ways from the state. For example, one way in which we could counteract the vested interest of the rich within state would be to ensure a stronger role for professional bodies. For, while the professions are to various degrees influenced by the market and concerned with profit, as well as controlled by the state and dominated by bureaucratic rules, there is, as I discussed in Chapter 5, a logic to professional work which is different to both the state and market. Professional work is based on judgements rooted in specialized knowledge. This knowledge base enables, to varying degrees, professionals to control their own labour, and protect themselves from the dictates of both consumers and managers. That does not mean that professional bodies are exempt from being coopted or dominated, but that they are areas of society which have the potential for a degree of autonomy. Their relationship to bodies of knowledge, as well as this relative degree of separation from the state and the market, could be used to strengthen education systems. Professional bodies of teachers could play a strong role in education systems, and other professional bodies could contribute to thinking about curricula in areas related to their work. Universities have traditionally been involved in conceptualizing the school curriculum; this is an example of how professionals can play a constructive role in education systems, and, although it is not without difficulties, it is useful for the curricula of subjects taught at schools to be designed at least in part by experts in particular bodies of knowledge, in addition to expert teachers who have insight into the abilities of children. These two examples both demonstrate how individuals who have expert knowledge, and who are organized in professional bodies, and who have some autonomy from both the state and the market, can contribute to building education systems.

REALISTIC AIMS

Society needs to be equalized if all children are to succeed at education. But this equalization cannot be done through education itself. If work is decreasingly a source of security for most people, then welfarist policies must be adopted to support individuals (Barchiesi, 2011; Marais, 2011; Standing, 2011). Short-term policies will succeed in tackling inequality if they attack it head-on through social income grants. Longer-term solutions lie in a fundamental rethinking of the organization of countries, economies, and international organizations. Inequalities are reproduced and deepened by capitalist economies, which education cannot remove. Pretending that it can do so only means that what education really is or could be will continue to be eroded.

Education reform will fare better with far more limited goals. Rather than hurriedly rushing from one faddish revamp to the next, education reform should be based on what education actually is, what education institutions can plausibly do, and how they can be supported. The outcomes-based approach, which starts from the idea of defining things that people do or need to be able to do in the world of work, and the aims-based approach favoured by some progressive educationalists, as discussed in Chapter 6, both start from thinking about what we want people to do in society, and supplying the relevant goals to education systems. From here they move to defining the various social and economic problems which education should solve.

This is not only unrealistic, but results in education being blamed for economic and social problems. In response to this perceived failure, institutions have their funding cut, are marketized or privatized, educators criticized and targeted for various performance-improvement policies, and so on. The ever-growing list of expectations for education, particularly for vocational education, can only contribute to the ever-growing list of criticisms of education, educational institutions, and educators. Much as we want more money given to education, we should be realistic in our claims about its importance to society. David Labaree (2012, p. 156) writes:

> Schools are able to do some things well, so it pays to focus on these kinds of efforts. They can provide students with a broad set of basic skills (reading, writing, calculating, analysing, reasoning) and a broad understanding of major aspects of the natural and social world, the kinds of broad capacities we tend to consider part of a liberal education.

His point, also made by many other educationalists, is that, by accepting that education can play only a limited role, we will increase its chances of success. Egan (2002, 135–6) makes the same argument:

> Schools can be quite good institutions when they concentrate sensibly on intellectual education, but they are less good at developing the whole person or producing good citizens or ensuring parenting skills. [...] That so many problems that the young face today are urgent and desperate still doesn't make the school an adequate institution to deal with them, but in trying to deal with them, however ineffectually, schools guarantee that they will not accomplish the traditional academic job adequately either.

Clearly there are all sorts of important roles that education plays in society and the economy, from the basics of ensuring that people are literate and numerate, to the development of research and innovation. However, and apparently paradoxically, it is more likely that education will be able to play these and other important roles in society and the economy if it is valued not for playing these roles but *in itself* as education. The acquisition of bodies of knowledge is the basis for the integrity and intelligibility of education: this knowledge has its own internal justification separate from the economy and the short-term needs of society, and exists at the core of our common humanity.

ENDNOTES

[1]   This does not imply the detached, asocial, disembodied epistemic agent which is the target of post-modernists, but simply the self as engaged in the act of thinking and learning about the world as an object through sets of concepts which have been developed to make sense of this world.

[2]   As developed, for example, in the works of Gamble (2004a, 2004b, 2011), Moore (2004, 2009, 2011), Muller (2000, 2009), Young (2008, 2009a), and Wheelahan (2010).

AFTERWORD: AFRICA, 2025

Clerk Ndovu sighed, looking at the ragged line of people in front of him. After the closure of the last remaining sociology department in the last public university in the Republic of Kanzanda, he had been lucky to get a job as a first level verifier at the Centre for Accreditation, Recognition, and Validation (We Make Your Learning Visible). Some had been luckier, and got jobs in the gated corporation Learning Centres, but they were generally biologists or accountants, with a direct relationship to the bottom line. Verifiying whether the moderators and assessors had correctly interpreted the outcome statements was a tedious business. And he knew that although most of these people would leave with an official Human Capital Certificate containing a long list of competencies, skills, capabilities, and knowledge areas, (electronic, the lists were far too long for paper), none of them would be accepted by Nu Start, the company with the monopoly on emigration rights. None of them would make it to the high lands of northern Eurasia, North America, or China, despite the fact that their certificates were officially compatible with the Competencies, Capabilities, Skills, Knowledge, Outcomes, Attributes, and Personal Values of the Northern Globe Qualifications Framework, and although the republic used the prescribed Total Quality Management System. The certificates were also a legal requirement here at home, but they could hardly get you a job when there were no jobs to be had, and employers in the informal sector could not be bothered to trawl through the long lists.

Not that he really missed the university. In the last days, no one really wanted to work there. The pay was terrible, and the customers seemed to make ever increasing and conflicting demands of the Learning Advisors, and to have ever-decreasing knowledge. And most of his time working in the Self-Directed Learner-Centred Learning Centres had been spent completing forms for the Quality Assurance and Customer Happiness Unit. When the national university had finally closed down, he had not been sad to leave. The Centre for Accreditation, Recognition, and Validation had survived because of a massive grant from the International Development Agency, who had told the government that certifying people for what they already knew would increase skills levels. In the early days they had accredited educational providers, but it was becoming obvious, even then, that educational institutions were a dwindling group. Now, instead, they accredited assessment institutions, who accredited individuals to conduct assessment. Initially they had accredited the moderators and verifiers as well, but now even the Centre for Accreditation, Recognition, and Validation was having funds cut, and they did the moderation and verification themselves.

He looked up at a dilapidated sign which had once read 'Indigenous Knowledge for the Knowledge Economy'. The line of ragged, weary people, clutching their massive portfolio documents slightly blocked his view of it, so that it looked to him as if it read 'Indigent for the Knowledge Economy. He looked up at the first in line, tried to force a smile, and asked, "How can I validate you today?"

259

REFERENCES

Adam, S. (2008). Learning Outcomes Current Developments in Europe: Update on the issues and applications of learning outcomes associated with the Bologna process. In *Bologna Seminar: Learning outcomes based higher education: The Scottish experience 21 - 22 February 2008*. Edinburgh, Scotland: Heriot-Watt University.

Allais, S. (2003). The National Qualifications Framework in South Africa: A democratic project trapped in a neo-liberal paradigm. *Journal of Education and Work, 16*(3), 305–324.

Allais, S. (2006). *Apples and Oranges? A comparison of school and college subjects*. Pretoria: Umalusi.

Allais, S. (2007a). Education service delivery: The disastrous case of outcomes-based qualifications frameworks. *Progress in Development Studies, 7*(1), 65–78.

Allais, S. (2007b). *Learning from Africa: Umalusi's research comparing syllabuses and examinations in South Africa with those in Ghana, Kenya, and Zambia*. Pretoria: Umalusi.

Allais, S. (2007c). *The rise and fall of the NQF: A critical analysis of the South African National Qualifications Framework* (Doctoral thesis). University of the Witwatersrand.

Allais, S. (2010a). Outcomes-based education: Understanding what went wrong. In Y. Shalem & S. Pendlebury (Eds.), *Retrieving Teaching: Critical Issues in Curriculum, Pedagogy and Learning*. Cape Town: Juta.

Allais, S. (2010b). *The Implementation and Impact of Qualifications Frameworks: Report of a Study in 16 Countries*. Geneva: International Labour Office.

Allais, S. (2012a). Claims versus practicalities: Lessons about using learning outcomes. *Journal of Education and Work, 25*(3), 331–334.

Allais, S. (2012b). Why solving on-going problems with the NQF matters. In H. Perold, N. Cloete, & J. Papier (Eds.), *Shaping the Future of South Africa's Youth: Rethinking post-school education and skills training* (pp. 9–28). Cape Town: African Minds.

Allais, S., King, M., Bowie, L., & Marock, C. (2007). *The "f" word: The quality of the "fundamental" component of qualifications in general and further education and training*. Pretoria: Umalusi.

Althusser, L. (1971). Ideology and ideological state apparatuses (Notes towards an Investigation). In B. Brewster (Trans.), *Lenin and Philosophy and other essays*. New York, NY: Monthly Review Press.

Amsden, A. (2010). Say's law, poverty persistence, and employment neglect. *Journal of Human Development and Capabilities, 11*(1), 57–66.

Anderson, L. W., & Krathwohl, D. (2001). *A Taxonomy for Learning, Teaching, and Assessing: A Revision of Bloom's Taxonomy of Educational Objectives*. New York, NY: Longman.

Anderson, P., & Harris, J. (2006). *Re-theorising the Recognition of Prior Learning*. Leicester: NIACE.

APEC Human Resources Development Working Group. (2009). *Mapping Qualifications Frameworks across APEC Economies*. Signapore: APEC.

Arnold, M. (1993). Culture and anarchy. An essay in political and social criticism. In S. Collini (Ed.), *Culture and Anarchy and Other Writings* (pp. 53–187). Cambridge: Cambridge University Press.

Ashton, D., & Green, F. (1996). *Education, Training and the Global Economy*. Cheltenham: Edward Elgar.

Badroodien, A., & McGrath, S. (2005). *International influences on the evolution of South Africa's national skills development strategy, 1989–2004*. Eschborn: GTZ, Economic Development & Employment Division Technical & Vocational Education & Training Section.

Baker, D. P. (2009). The educational transformation of work: towards a new synthesis. *Journal of Education and Work, 22*(3), 163–191.

Ball, S. J. (2007). Big policies/small world. An introduction to international perspectives in education policy. In B. Lingard & J. Ozga (Eds.), *The Routledge Falmer Reader in Education Policy and Politics*. London, UK, and New York, NY: Routledge.

Barchiesi, F. (2011). *Precarious Liberation. Workers, the State, and Contested Social Citizenship in Postapartheid South Africa*. Albany and Scotsville: Suny and UKZN Press.

Baron, J. N., & Hannan, M. T. (1994). The impact of economics on contemporary sociology. *Journal of Economic Literature, 32*(3).

261

REFERENCES

Barrow, R. (1978). *Radical Education: A Critique of Freeschooling and Deschooling*. London, UK: Martin Robertson.

Bayer, K. (2009). Neoliberalism and development policy – Dogma or progress? *Development Dialogue, 51*, 89–102.

Beck, J., & Young, M. (2005). The assault on the professions and the restructuring of academic and professional identities: a Bernsteinian analysis. *British Journal of Sociology of Education, 26*(2), 183–197.

Becker, G. (1976). *The Economic Approach to Human Behavior*. Chicago, IL: University of Chicago Press.

Bell, D. (1973). *The Coming of Post Industrial Society*. New York, NY: Basic Books.

Berg, I. (1970). *Education and Jobs - The Great Training Robbery*. New York, NY: Praeger Publishers.

Bernstein, B. (1971). On the classification and framing of educational knowledge. In M. Young (Ed.), *Knowledge and Control*. London, UK: Collier-Macmillan.

Bernstein, B. (2000). *Pedagogy, Symbolic Control and Identity: Theory, Research, Critique* (Rev. ed.). London, UK: Taylor Francis.

Bills, D. B. (2004). *The Sociology of Education and Work*. Oxford: Blackwell Publishing.

Bird, A. (1992). Cosatu unions take initiatives in training. *South African Labour Bulletin, 16*(6), 46–51.

Bjornavold, J., & Coles, M. (2007). Governing education and training; The case of qualifications frameworks. *European Journal of Vocational Training*, (42/43), 203–235.

Blackman, S. (1987). The labour market in school: New vocationalism and issues of socially ascribed discrimination. In P. Brown & D. Ashton (Eds.), *Education, Unemployment and Labour Markets*.

Blom, R., Parker, B., & Keevy, J. (2007). *The Recognition of Non-Formal and Informal Learning in South Africa: Country Background Report Prepared for the OECD Thematic Review on Recognition of Non-Formal and Informal Learning*. Pretoria: SAQA.

Bloom, B., Engelhart, M., Furst, E., Hill, W., & Krathwohl, D. (1956). *Taxonomy of Educational Objectives. The Classification of Educational Goals*. London, UK: Longmans, Green and Co Ltd.

Bluestone, B. (1977). Economic theory and the fate of the poor. In J. Karabel & A. H. Halsey (Eds.), *Power and Ideology in Education*. New York, NY: Oxford University Press.

Bobbit, F. (1913a). *The Supervision of City Schools: Some General Principles of Management Applied to the Problems of City-School Systems, Twelfth Yearbook of the National Society for the Study of Education, Part I*. Bloomington, IL: National Society for the Study of Education.

Bobbit, F. (1913b). *Twelfth Yearbook of the National Society for the Study of Education, Part I The Supervision of City Schools*. Bloomington, IL: University of Chicago Press.

Bobbit, F. (1918). *The Curriculum*. Cambridge, MA: The Riverside Press.

Boghossian, P. (2007). *Fear of Knowledge: Against relativism and constructivism*. Oxford: Oxford University Press.

Bohlinger, S. (2007). Competences as the core element of the European qualifications framework. *European Journal of Vocational Training, 2007/3 - 2008/1*(42/43), 96–112.

Bohlinger, S. (2012). Qualifications frameworks and learning outcomes: Challenges for Europe's lifelong learning area. *Journal of Education and Work, 25*(3), 279–297.

Bosch, G., & Charest, J. (Eds.). (2010). *Vocational Training. International perspectives*. London, UK, and New York, NY: Routledge.

Bourdieu, P. (1973). Cultural reproduction and social reproduction. In J. Karabel & A. H. Halsey (Eds.), *Power and Ideology in Education*. New York, NY: Oxford University Press.

Bourdieu, P. (1984). *Distinction. A social critique of the judgement of taste*. London, UK: Routledge & Kegan Paul.

Bowles, S., & Gintis, H. (1976). *Schooling in Capitalist America. Educational reform and the contradictions of economic life*. New York, NY: Basic Books.

Breier, M. (2009). Doctors. In J. Erasmus & M. Breier (Eds.), *Skills Shortages in South Africa. Case studies of key professions*. (pp. 113–131). Cape Town: HSRC Press.

Brenner, N., Peck, J., & Theodore, N. (2010). After neoliberalization? *Globalizations, 7*(3), 327–245.

Brockmann, M. (2011). Higher education qualifications: Convergence and divergence in software engineering and nursing. In M. Brockmann, L. Clarke, & C. Winch (Eds.), *Knowledge, Skills and*

Competence in the European Labour Market. What's in a vocational qualification? (pp. 120–135). Abingdon and New York, NY: Routledge.

Brockmann, M., Clarke, L., & Winch, C. (2008). Can performance-related learning outcomes have standards? *Journal of European Industrial Training, 32*(2/3), 99–113.

Brockmann, M., Clarke, L., & Winch, C. (Eds.). (2011). *Knowledge, Skills and Competence in the European Labour Market. What's in a vocational qualification?* Abingdon and New York, NY: Routledge.

Brockmann, M., Clarke, L., Winch, C., Hanf, G., Méhaut, P., & Westerhuis, A. (2011). Introduction: Cross-national equivalence of skills and qualifications accross Europe? In *Knowledge, Skills and Competence in the European Labour Market. What's in a vocational qualification?* (pp. 1–21). Abingdon and New York, NY: Routledge.

Brown, M., & White, J. (2012). *An unstable framework - Critical perspectives on the framework for the national curriculum* (Paper formally endorsed by the New Visions for Education Group at its meeting on 28 March 2012). Retrieved June 29, 2012, from New Visions for Education Group: http://www. newvisionsforeducation.org.uk/2012/04/05/an-unstable-framework/

Brown, P. (1999). Globalisation and the political economy of high skills. *Journal of Education and Work, 12*(3), 233–251.

Brown, P. (2006). The opportunity trap. In H. Lauder, P. Brown, J. Dillabough, & A. H. Halsey (Eds.), *Education, Globalization, and Social Change* (pp. 295–307). Oxford: Oxford University Press.

Brown, P., & Ashton, D. (1987). *Education, Unemployment and Labour Markets.* London, UK: The Falmer Press.

Brown, P., Green, A., & Lauder, H. (2001). *High Skills.* Oxford: Oxford University Press.

Brown, P., & Lauder, H. (1992). *Education for Economic Survival: From Fordism to post-Fordism?* London, UK and New York, NY: Routledge.

Brown, P., & Lauder, H. (2001). *Capitalism and Social Progress. The future of society in a global economy.* Basingstoke: Palgrave Macmillan.

Brown, P., & Lauder, H. (2006). Globalization, knowledge and the myth of the magnet economy. In H. Lauder, P. Brown, J. Dillabough, & A. H. Halsey (Eds.), *Education, Globalization, and Social Change* (pp. 295–307). Oxford: Oxford University Press.

Brown, P., Lauder, H., & Ashton, D. (2008). *Education, Globalisation and the Knowledge Economy.* London, UK: Teaching and Learning Research Programme.

Brown, P., Lauder, H., & David Ashton. (2011). *The Global Auction. The broken promises of education, jobs, and incomes.* Oxford: Oxford University Press.

Brown, P., & Tannock, S. (2009). Education, meritocracy and the global war for talent. *Journal of Education Policy, 24*(4), 377–392.

Burr, V. (2003). *Social Constructionism* (Second Edition.). London, UK and New York, NY: Routledge.

Byron, J. (2003). Overview of the Australian qualifications framework. In G. Donn & T. Davies (Eds.), *Promises and Problems for Commonwealth qualifications frameworks.* London and Wellington: Commonwealth Secretariat and NZQA.

Cabrera, A. M. (2010). *Background case study on Chile.* Geneva: Skills and Employability Department, ILO.

Callahan, R. (1962). *Education and the Cult of Efficiency. A study of the social forces that have shaped the administration of the public schools.* Chicago, IL and London, UK: University of Chicago Press.

Callinicos, A. (2001). *Against the Third Way.* Cambridge: Polity Press.

Carlaw, K., Oxley, L., Walker, P., Thorns, D., & Nuth, M. (2012). Beyond the Hype. Intellectual property and the knowledge society/knowledge economy. In D. W. Livingstone & D. Guile (Eds.), *The Knowledge Economy and Lifelong Learning. A critical reader.* Rotterdam, NL: Sense.

Carnoy, M. (1987). *Higher Education and Graduate Employment in India.* Paris: International Institute for Educational Planning.

Cedefop. (2008). *The Shift to Learning Outcomes: Conceptual, political and practical developments in Europe.* Luxembourg: Office for Official Publications of the European Communities.

Cedefop. (2009). *The Development of National Qualifications Frameworks in Europe.* Luxembourg: Publications Office of the European Union.

REFERENCES

Cedefop. (2010). *The Development of National Qualifications Frameworks in Europe* (Working Paper No 8). Luxembourg: Publications Office of the European Union.

Chang, H.-J. (2002). Breaking the mould: An institutionalist political economy alternative to the neo-liberal theory of the market and the state. *Cambridge Journal of Economics, 26*, 539–559.

Chang, H.-J. (Ed.). (2003). *Rethinking Development Economics*. London, UK: Anthem Press.

Chang, H.-J. (2007). *Bad Samaritans: Rich nations, poor policies and the threat to the developing world.* London, UK: Random House.

Chang, H.-J. (2010). *23 Things They Don't Tell You About Capitalism.* London, UK: Allen Lane.

Charlot, B. (2009). School and the pupils' work. In *Sísifo. Educational Sciences Journal, 10*, 87–94.

Chisholm, L. (2007). Diffusion of the National Qualifications Framework and outcomes-based education in southern and eastern Africa. *Comparative Education, 43*(2), 295–309.

Clarke, L. (2011). Trade? Job? Or occupation? The development of occupational labour markets for Bricklaying and Lorry driving. In M. Brockmann, L. Clarke, & C. Winch (Eds.), *Knowledge, Skills and Competence in the European Labour Market. What's in a vocational qualification?* (pp. 102–119). Abingdon and New York, NY: Routledge.

Clarke, L., & Westerhuis, A. (2011). Establishing equivalence through zones of mutual trust. In M. Brockmann, L. Clarke, & C. Winch (Eds.), *Knowledge, Skills and Competence in the European Labour Market. What's in a vocational qualification?* (pp. 136–148). Abingdon and New York, NY: Routledge.

Clarke, S. (2005). The neoliberal theory of society. In A. Saad-Filho & D. Johnston (Eds.), *Neoliberalism: A Critical Reader*. London: Pluto Press.

Colas, A. (2005). Neoliberalism, globalisation and international relations. In A. Saad-Filho & D. Johnston (Eds.), *Neoliberalism: A Critical Reader*. London, UK: Pluto Press.

Coles, M. (2006). *A Review of International and National Developments in the Use of Qualifications Frameworks*. ETF.

Coles, M. (2007, June 3–5). *Qualifications frameworks in Europe: Platforms for collaboration, integration and reform*. Presented at the Making the European Learning Area a Reality, Munich.

Collini, S. (2010, April 8). Blahspeak. *London Review of Books, 32*(7), 29–34.

Collini, S. (2012). *What Are Universities For?* London, UK: Penguin.

Collins, R. (1979). *The Credential Society*. New York, NY: Academic Press.

Collins, R. (1982). *Sociological Insight. An introduction to non-obvious sociology*. New York and Oxford: Oxford University Press.

Collins, R. (1998). *The Sociology of Philosophies. A global theory of intellectual change*. Cambridge, MA and London, UK: The Belknap Press of Harvard University Press.

Collins, R. (2004). *Interaction Ritual Chains*. Princeton and Oxford: Princeton University Press.

Collins, R. (2013). The end of middle-class work: No more escapes. In I. Wallerstein, R. Collins, M. Mann, G. Derluguian, & C. Calhoun (Eds.), *Does Capitalism Have a Future?* Oxford University Press.

Collins, R., & Makowsky, M. (1993). *The Discovery of Society*. New York, NY: McGraw-Hill Inc.

Commonwealth of Learning and SAQA. (2008). *Transnational qualifications framework for the virtual university for the small states of the commonwealth. Concept document.* Vancouver and Pretoria: Commonwealth of Learning and SAQA.

Cooper, L. (1997). The implications of the national qualifications framework for emancipatory education in South Africa. In K. Pampallis (Ed.), *Reconstruction, Development and the National Qualifications Framework.* Johannesburg: Centre for Education Policy Development, Evaluation, and Management.

Cooper, L. (1998). From "Rolling Mass Action" to "RPL": the changing discourse of experience and learning in the South African labour movement. *Studies in Continuing Education, 20*(2), 143–157.

Crawford, L. (2003). Reviewing current national qualifications frameworks and regional qualifications initiatives in Australia. In E. French (Ed.), *Qualifications and standards: Harmonization and articulation initiatives* (pp. 85–98). Pretoria: SAQA.

Crouch, C. (2011). *The Strange Non-Death of Neoliberalism*. Cambridge: Polity.

Curriculum 2005 Review Committee. (2000). *A South African curriculum for the twenty-first century. Report of the review committee on curriculum 2005. (Under the coordination of Linda Chisholm).* Pretoria: Presented to the Minister of Education, May 2000.

Dale, R. (1989). *The State and Education Policy*. Milton Keynes: The Open University Press.

264

Dale, R., Bowe, R., Harris, D., Loveys, M., Moore, R., Shilling, C., Sikes, P., Trevitt, J., & Valsecchi, V. (1990). *The TVEI Story: Policy, practice and preparation for the work force.* Milton Keynes: Open University Press.

Darling, J. (1994). *Child-centered education and its critics.* London, UK: Paul Chapman Publishing Ltd.

De Anda, M. L. (2010). *Background case study on Mexico.* Geneva: Skills and Employability Department, ILO.

De Moura Castro, C. (2000). *Vocational Training at the Turn of the Century.* Frankfurt: Peter Lang.

Deissinger, T., & Hellwig, S. (2005). *Structures and Functions of Competence-based Education and Training (CBET): A comparative perspective.* Mannheim: InWEnt - Capacity Building International, Germany.

Departments of Education and Labour. (2002). *Report of the Study Team on the Implementation of the National Qualifications Framework.* Pretoria: Departments of Education and Labour, South Africa.

Departments of Education and Labour. (2003). *An Interdependent National Qualifications Framework System: Consultative Document.* Pretoria: Departments of Education and Labour.

Desaubin, F. (2002). *Politics and strategy of the labour movement in South Africa: A crisis of "strategic" and "social" unionism* (Doctoral thesis). Australia National University.

Dewey, J. (1897). *My Pedagogic Creed.* New York, NY & Chicago, IL: E.L. Kellogg.

Dewey, J. (1931). *The Way Out of Educational Confusion.* Cambridge, MA: Harvard University Press.

Dewey, J. (1956). *The Child and the Curriculum. The school and society.* Chicago, IL and London, UK: University of Chicago Press.

Dewey, J. (1963). *Experience and Education.* New York, NY: Collier Books.

DHET. (2012). *Green paper for the post-school system.* Pretoria: Department of Higher Education and Training.

Dimaggio, P. (1979). Review essay: On Pierre Bourdieu. *American Journal of Sociology, 86*(6), 1460–1474.

Donnelly, K. (2005). *Benchmarking Australian primary school curricula.* Canberra: Australian Government: Department of Education, Science and Training.

Dore, R. (1976). *The Diploma Disease: Education, qualifications and development.* London, UK: Allen and Unwin.

Drucker, P. (1969). *The Age of Discontinuity: Guidelines to our changing society.* London, UK: Heinemann.

Dunk, T., McBride, S., & Nelsen, R. (1996). *The Training Trap: Ideology, training, and the labour market.* Winnipeg/Halifax: Fernwoon Publishing.

Egan, K. (2002). *Getting it WRONG from the Beginning. Our progressivist Inheritance from Herbert Spencer, John Dewey, and Jean Piaget.* New Haven and London, UK: Yale University Press.

Egan, K. (2008). *The Future of Education: Reimagining our schools from the ground up.* New Haven and London, UK: Yale University Press.

Eisner, E. (1967). Educational objectives: Help or hindrance? *American Journal of Education, 91*(4), 549–560.

Enders, J. (2010). Political science and educational research. Windows of opportunity for a neglected relationship. In A. A. Jakobi, K. Martens, & K. D. Wolf (Eds.), *Education in Political Science. Discovering a neglected field* (pp. 205–217). Routledge/ECPR Studies in European Political Science.

Ensor, P. (2003). The National Qualifications Framework and higher education in South Africa: some epistemological issues. *Journal of Education and Work, 16*(3), 325–346.

Entwistle, H. (1970). *Child-centred Education.* London, UK: Methuen and Co Ltd.

Entwistle, H. (1979). *Antonio Gramsci. Conservative schooling for radical politics.* London, UK: Routledge & Kegan Paul.

European Commission. (2008). *The European Qualifications Framework for Lifelong Learning (EQF).* Luxembourg: Office for Official Publications of the European Communities.

European Union. (2011). *Using Learning Outcomes* (European Qualification Framework Series: Note 4). Luxembourg: Publications Office of the European Union.

Fine, B. (2001). *Social Capital Versus Social Theory: Political economy and social science at the turn of the millennium.* (J. Mitchie, Ed.). London, UK and New York, NY: Routledge.

Fine, B. (2002). Globalization and development: The imperative of political economy. In *Towards a New Political Economy of Development: Globalization and governance.* Sheffield.

REFERENCES

Fine, B. (2010). *Theories of Social Capital: Researchers Behaving Badly.* London, UK: Pluto Press.
Fine, B., & Milonakis, D. (2009). *From Economics Imperialism to Freakonomics. The shifting boundaries between economics and other social sciences.* London, UK and New York, NY: Routledge.
Flinders, D. J., & Thornton, S. J. (Eds.). (2004). *The Curriculum Studies Reader* (2nd ed.). London, UK and New York, NY: RoutledgeFalmer.
Foley, G. (1994). Adult Education and capitalist reorganisation. *Studies in the Education of Adults, 26*(2), 121–143.
Freidson, E. (2001). *Professionalism, the Third Logic.* Oxford: Polity Press.
Freire, P. (1974). *Pedagogy of the Oppressed.* New York, NY: Seabury.
French, E. (2009). *The NQF and its Worlds.* Pretoria: SAQA.
Furedi, F. (2009). *Wasted. Why education isn't educating.* London, UK and New York, NY: Continuum.
Gajaweera, G. A. K. (2010). *Background case study on Sri Lanka.* Geneva: Skills and Employability Department, ILO.
Gamble, J. (2002). Teaching without words: tacit knowledge in apprenticeship. *Journal of Education,* (28), 63–82.
Gamble, J. (2004a). *A knowledge perspective on the vocational curriculum.* Paper presented at the Human Sciences Research Council Colloquium on the FET Curriculum knowledge, Pretoria.
Gamble, J. (2004b). *Tacit knowledge in craft pedagogy: a sociological analysis* (Doctoral thesis). University of Cape Town.
Gamble, J. (2005). Working for the bosses: Moral education in the vocational curriculum. Paper presented at *Kenton at Mpekweni: (In) equality, democracy and quality.* Mpekweni Beach Resort.
Gamble, J. (2011). *Why improved formal teaching and learning are important in vocational education and training (TVET).* Draft background paper for forthcoming UNESCO World Report on TVET. Unesco.
Gay, G. (2003). The importance of multicultural education. *Educational Leadership, 61*(4), 30–35.
Giddens, A. (1998). *The Third Way.* Cambridge: Polity Press.
Gillian, L. (1993). *Literature and language teaching: A guide for teachers and trainers.* Cambridge University Press.
Glasser, W. (1969). *Schools Without Failure.* New York, NY: Harper and Row.
Goffman, E. (1959). *The Presentation of Self in Everyday Life.* New York, NY: Doubleday.
Goffman, E. (1967). *Interaction Ritual.* New York, NY: Doubleday.
Goodson, I. (1994). *Studying Curriculum. Cases and methods.* Buckingham: Open University Press.
Gramsci, A. (1971). On education. In Q. Hoare & G. N. Smith (Eds.), *Selections from the Prison Notebooks.* New York, NY: International Prisoners.
Gramsci, A. (1986). *Selections from the Prison Notebooks.* London, UK: Lawrence and Wishart.
Granville, G. (2003). "Stop making sense": Chaos and coherence in the formulation of the Irish qualifications framework. *Journal of Education and Work, 16*(3), 259–270.
Grubb, N., & Lazerson, M. (2004). *The Education Gospel: The economic power of schooling.* Cambridge, MA: Harvard University Press.
Grubb, N., & Lazerson, M. (2006). The globalization of rhetoric and practice: The education gospel and vocationalism. In H. Lauder, P. Brown, J. Dillabough, & A. H. Halsey (Eds.), *Education, Globalization, and Social Change* (pp. 295–307). Oxford: Oxford University Press.
Guthrie, H. (2009). *Competence and competency based training: What the literature says.* Adelaide: NCVER.
Hall, C., & Woodhouse, D. (1999). Accreditation and approval in New Zealand: Major surgery for the National Qualifications Framework? In M. Fourie, A. H. Strydom, & J. Setar (Eds.), *Reconsidering Quality Assurance in Higher Education: Perspectives on programme assessment and accreditation* (pp. 190–226). Bloemfontein: The University of the Orange Free State.
Hall, P. A., & Soskice, D. (Eds.). (2001). *Varieties of Capitalism: The institutional foundations of comparative advantage.* Oxford: Oxford University Press.
Hallendorff, E., Richardson, B., & Wood, B. (1999). *Standards writer course.* Johannesburg and Pretoria: The Learning Network.
Hanf, G. (2011). The changing relevance of the Beruf. In M. Brockmann, L. Clarke, & C. Winch (Eds.), *Knowledge, Skills and Competence in the European Labour Market. What's in a vocational qualification?* (pp. 50–67). Abingdon and New York, NY: Routledge.

266

Hargreaves, A., & Fullan, M. (2012). *Professional Capital. Transforming teaching in every school.* New York, NY: Teachers College Press.

Hart, G. (2006). Beyond Neoliberalism? Post-apartheid developments in historical and comparative perspective. In V. Padayachee (Ed.), *The Development Decade? Economic and social change in South Africa, 1994–2004* (pp. 13–32). Cape Town: HSRC Press.

Hart, J. (2009). *Cross-referencing qualifications frameworks* (CES Briefing No. 49). Edinburgh: Centre for Educational Sociology.

Harvey, D. (1990). *The Condition of Postmodernity: An enquiry into the origins of cultural change.* Cambridge, MA and Oxford, UK: Blackwell.

Harvey, D. (2005). *A Brief History of Neoliberalism.* Oxford, UK and New York, NY: Oxford University Press.

Harvey, D. (2010). *The Enigma of Capital and the Crises of Capitalism.* London, UK: Profile Books.

Higgs, P., & Keevy, J. (2009). Qualifications frameworks in Africa: A critical reflection. *South African Journal of Higher Education, 23*(4), 690–702.

Hirtt, N. (2009). Markets and education in the era of globalized capitalism. In D. Hill & R. Kumar (Eds.), *Global Neoliberalism and Education and Its Consequences* (pp. 208–226). London, UK and New York, NY: Routledge.

Hodgson, A., Spours, K., Isaacs, T., & Grainger, P. (2013). *A National Qualifications Framework for Qatar: Final report* (Report). London, UK: Centre for Post-14 Research and Innovation, Institute of Education, University of London.

Hoeckel, K., Field, S., Justesen, T. R., & Kim, M. (2008). *Learning for jobs. OECD reviews of vocational education and training. Australia.* Organization for Economic Co-operation and Development (OECD). Retrieved August 26, 2010, from http://www.oecd.org/dataoecd/27/11/41631383.pdf

Hofmeyr, J. M. (1982). *An examination of the influence of Christian National Education on the principles underlying white and black education in South Africa: 1948–1982* (MA dissertation). University of the Witwatersrand.

Holmes, K. (2003). Qualifications frameworks: Issues, problems and possibilities for small states. In G. Donn & T. Davies (Eds.), *Promises and Problems for Commonwealth Qualifications Frameworks.* London, UK and Wellington: Commonwealth Secretariat and NZQA.

Hood, C. (1995). The "New Public Management" in the 1980s: Variations on a theme. *Accounting, Organizations and Society, 20*(2/3), 93–109.

HSRC. (1995). *Ways of Seeing the NQF.* Pretoria: HSRC.

Hudson, C. (2010). Transforming the educative state in the Nordic countries. In A. A. Jakobi, K. Martens, & K. D. Wolf (Eds.), *Education in Political science. Discovering a neglected field* (pp. 56–70). Routledge/ECPR Studies in European Political Science.

Hyland, T. (1994). *Competence, Education and NVQs. Dissenting Perspectives.* London, UK: Cassel.

Hyland, T. (1998). Exporting Failure: the strange case of NVQs and overseas markets. *Educational Studies, 24*(3), 369–380.

Hyslop, J. (1993). A destruction coming in: Bantu education as response to social crisis. In P. Bonner, P. Delius, & D. Posel (Eds.), *Apartheid's Genesis: 1935–1962* (pp. 393–410). Braamfontein: Raven Press and Wits University Press.

Hyslop-Margison, E. J., & Sears, A. M. (2006). *Neo-Liberalism, Globalization and Human Capital Learning. Reclaiming education for democratic citizenship.* Dordrecht: Springer.

Illich, I. (1970). *Deschooling Society.* London, UK: Methuen.

ILO. (2004). R195 Human resource development recommendation. In *92 ILO Conference.* Geneva: ILO.

Isaacs, S. (2009, April 5–6). *Insights from the South African National Qualifications Framework.* Gulf Co-operation Council Qualifications Going Global Conference, Abu Dhabi.

Iverson, T., & Stephens, J. D. (2008). Partisan politics, the welfare state, and three worlds of human capital formation. *Comparative Political Studies, 45*(4/5), 600–637.

Jakobi, A. A., Martens, K., & Wolf, K. D. (Eds.). (2010). *Education in Political Science. Discovering a neglected field.* Routledge/ECPR Studies in European Political Science.

Jansen, J. (2001). Explaining non-change in Education. In Y. Sayed & J. Jansen (Eds.), *Implementing Education Policies: The South African experience.* Cape Town: UCT Press.

REFERENCES

Jansen, J. (2002). A very noisy OBE: The implementation of OBE in Grade 1 classrooms. In J. Gultig, U. Hoadley, & J. Jansen (Eds.), *Curriculum: From plans to practices*. Cape Town: SAIDE/OUP.

Jessup, B. (2012). A cultural political economy of competitiveness and its implications for higher education. In D. W. Livingstone & D. Guile (Eds.), *The Knowledge Economy and Lifelong Learning. A critical reader.* (pp. 77–83). Rotterdam, NL: Sense.

Jessup, G. (1991). *Outcomes. NVQs and the Emerging Model of Education and Training*. London, UK: The Falmer Press.

Kallaway, P. (1984). An introduction to the study of education for blacks in South Africa. In P. Kallaway (Ed.), *Apartheid and Education: The education of black South Africans*. Johannesburg: Raven Press.

Keating, J. (2003). Qualifications frameworks in Australia. *Journal of Education and Work, 16*(3), 271–288.

Keating, J. (2010). *Background case study on Malaysia*. Geneva: Skills and Employability Department, ILO.

Keep, E. (2005). Reflections on the curious absence of employers, labour market incentives and labour market regulation in English 14–19 policy: First signs of a change in direction? *Journal of Education Policy, 20*(5), 533–553.

Keevy, J., Chakroun, B., & Deij, A. (2011). *Transnational Qualifications Frameworks*. Turin: European Training Foundation.

Kennedy, P. (2012). The knowledge economy. Education, work, and the struggle to (Re-) Regulate the distinction between "Necessary" and "Free" Labour Time. In D. W. Livingstone & D. Guile (Eds.), *The Knowledge Economy and Lifelong Learning. A critical reader.* (pp. 163–183). Rotterdam, NL: Sense.

Killen, R. (n.d.). *William Spady: A paradigm pioneer*. Retrieved from http://www.learningtolearn.sa.edu.au/Colleagues/files/links/Spady_ParadigmPioneer.pdf

Killen, R. (2007). *Teaching Strategies for Outcomes-based Education* (2nd ed.). Cape Town: Juta.

King, K. (2012). The geopolitics and meanings of India's massive skills development ambitions. *International Journal for Educational Development*.

Klapp, C. J. (2003). National Qualifications Framework initiatives in Mexico. In E. French (Ed.), *Qualifications and standards: Harmonization and articulation initiatives* (pp. 123–124). Pretoria: SAQA.

Kliebard, H. (1975). The rise of scientific curriculum-making and its aftermath. *Curriculum Theory Network, 5*(1), 27–38.

Kliebard, H. (2004). *The Struggle for the American Curriculum* (3rd ed.). New York, NY: RoutledgeFalmer.

Knight, P. (2001). Complexity and curriculum: A process approach to curriculum-making. *Teaching in Higher Education, 6*(3), 369–381.

Labaree, D. F. (2012). School syndrome: Understanding the USA's magical belief that schooling can somehow improve society, promote access, and preserve advantage. *Journal of Curriculum Studies, 44*(2), 143–163.

Lapavitsas, C. (2005). Mainstream economics in the Neoliberal Era. In A. Saad-Filho & D. Johnston (Eds.), *Neoliberalism: A Critical Reader*. London, UK: Pluto Press.

Lassnigg, L. (2012). Lost in translation: Learning outcomes and the governance of education. *Journal of Education and Work, 25*(3), 299–330.

Lauder, H. (1997). Education, democracy, and the economy. In A. H. Halsey, H. Lauder, P. Brown, & A. Stuart Wells (Eds.), *Education: Culture, Economy and Society*. Oxford: Oxford University Press.

Lauder, H., & Brown, P. (2009). Economic globalization, skill formation and the consequences for higher education. In M. W. Apple, S. J. Ball, & L. A. Gandin (Eds.), *The Routledge International Handbook of the Sociology of Education*. London, UK: Routledge.

Lauder, H., Brown, P., & Tholen, G. (2012). The global auction model, skill bias theory and graduate incomes. Reflections on methodology. In H. Lauder, M. Young, H. Daniels, M. Balarin, & J. Lowe (Eds.), *Educating for the Knowledge Economy? Critical Perspectives* (pp. 43–65). Abingdon and New York, NY: Routledge.

Lauder, H., Hughes, D., Watson, S., Waslander, S., Thrupp, M., Strathdee, R., … Hamlin, J. (1999). *Trading in Futures: Why markets in education don't work*. Buckingham: Open University Press.

Lea, J. (2008). *Political Correctness and Higher Education: British and American perspectives* (1st ed.). New York, NY: Routledge.

Leney, T. (2009). *Qualifications that Count: Strengthening the recognition of qualifications in the Mediterranean region.* MEDA-ETD Project Team, European Training Foundation.

Lewis, L., Snow, K., Farris, E., & Levin, D. (2000). *Distance Education at Postsecondary Education Institutions: 1997–1998.* (Statistical analysis report NCES 2000-013.). Washington, DC: National Center for Educational Statistics.

Lin, N. (2001). *Social Capital: A theory of social structure and action.* Cambridge, MA: Cambridge University Press.

Lister, I. (1974). The challenge of deschooling. In I. Lister (Ed.), *Deschooling.* Cambridge, MA: Cambridge University Press.

Little, A. (1997). *Assessment in Education: Principles, policy & practice. Special Issue: The Diploma Disease Twenty Years On, 4*(1).

Little, A. (2000). Globalisation, qualifications and livelihoods: Towards a research agenda. *Assessment in Education: Principles, Policy, and Practice, 7*(3).

Livingstone, D. W. (2012). Debunking the "knowledge economy". The limits of human capital theory. In D. W. Livingstone & D. Guile (Eds.), *The Knowledge Economy and Lifelong Learning. A critical reader.* (pp. 85–116). Rotterdam, NL: Sense.

Livingstone, D. W., & Guile, D. (2012). *The Knowledge Economy and Lifelong Learning. A critical reader.* Rotterdam, NL: Sense.

Loose, G. (2008). Can we link and match training in the Duel System with Competency-Based Education and Training (CBET)? In G. Loose, G. Spottl, & Y. Sahir (Eds.), *Re-Engineering Dual training - The Malaysian experience* (pp. 75–78). Frankfurt: Peter Lang.

Lowry, S. (1995). A critique of the history curriculum in South Africa. *Perspectives in Education, 16*(1), 105–129.

Lugg, R. (2007). *Making different equal? Social practices of policy-making and the national qualifications framework in South Africa between 1985 and 2003.* University of London.

Lythe, D. (2008). *Qualifications frameworks in Asia and the Pacific.* Geneva: ILO Regional Skills and Employability, Programme for Asia and the Pacific, Supporting Skills Development in Asia and the Pacific.

Malan, S. (2000). The new paradigm of outcomes-based education in perspective. *Journal of Family Ecology and Consumer Sciences, 28,* 22–28.

Marais, H. (2011). *South Africa Pushed to the Limit. The political economy of change.* Cape Town: UCT Press.

Markowitsch, J., & Luomi-Messerer, K. (2008). Development and interpretation of descriptors of the European Qualifications Framework. *European Journal of Vocational Training, 42/43,* 33–58.

Marock, C. (2010). *Background case study on Mauritius.* Geneva: Skills and Employability Department, ILO.

Marock, C. (2011). *Considering key themes relating to the objectives of the NQF and the post-school objectives.* Johannesburg: Centre for Education Policy Development.

Marshall, J. D. (1997). The new vocationalism. In M. Olssen & K. M. Mathews (Eds.), *Education Policy in New Zealand: The 1990s and Beyond.* Palmerston North: The Dunmore Press Ltd.

Marx, K. (1932). In C. J. Arthur (Ed.), *The German ideology. Part One with selections from Parts Two and Three and supplementary texts.* New York, NY: International Publishers.

Masschelein, J., & Simons, M. (2013). In J. McMartin (Trans.), *In Defence of the School. A public issue.* Leuven: Education, Culture & Society Publishers.

McGrath, S. (2010). Beyond aid effectiveness: The development of the South African further and training college sector, 1994–2009. *International Journal for Educational Development, 30,* 525–534.

Méhaut, P. (2011). Savoir - The organizing principle of French VET. In M. Brockmann, L. Clarke, & C. Winch (Eds.), *Knowledge, Skills and Competence in the European Labour Market. What's in a vocational qualification?* (pp. 36–49). Abingdon and New York, NY: Routledge.

Méhaut, P., & Winch, C. (2011). *EU initiatives in cross-national recognition of skills and qualifications.* In M. Brockmann, L. Clarke, & C. Winch (Eds.), *Knowledge, Skills and Competence in the European Labour Market. What's in a vocational qualification?* (pp. 22–35). Abingdon and New York, NY: Routledge.

Mehl, M. C. (2004). The National Qualifications Framework: Quo Vadis? *SAQA Bulletin, 5*(1), 21–46.

REFERENCES

Mia, A. (2010). *Background case study on Bangladesh*. Skills and Employability Department, ILO.
Milonakis, D., & Fine, B. (2009). *From Political Economy to Economics. Method, the social and the historical in the evolution of economic theory*. London, UK and New York, NY: Routledge.
Mokhobo-Nomvete, S. (1999, January). Assessment in an outcomes-based education and training system: An overview. *SAQA Bulletin, 2*(3).
Moll, I. (2002). Clarifying constructivism in a context of curriculum change. *Journal of Education*, (27), 5–32.
Moore, R. (2004). *Education and Society: Issues and explorations in the sociology of education*. Cambridge: Polity.
Moore, R. (2009). *Towards the Sociology of Truth*. London, UK: Continuum.
Moore, R. (2011). Making the break: Disciplines and interdisciplinarity. In K. Maton & F. Christie (Eds.), *Disciplinarity: Functional linguistic and sociological perspectives* (1st ed., pp. 87–105). London, UK and New York, NY: Continuum.
Moore, R., & Ozga, J. (Eds.). (1991). *Curriculum Policy*. Oxford: Pergamon Press.
Morrow, W. (2001). Scriptures and practices. *Perspectives in Education, 19*(1), 87–106.
Morrow, W. (2007). *Learning to Teach in South Africa*. Cape Town: HSRC.
Mukora, J. (2006). *Social justice goals or economic rationality? The South African qualifications framework considered in the light of local and global experiences*. University of Edinburgh.
Muller, J. (2000). In P. Wexler & I. Goodson, Eds.), *Reclaiming Knowledge*. London, UK and New York, NY: RoutledgeFalmer.
Muller, J. (2001). Progressivism redux: Ethos, policy, pathos. In A. Kraak & M. Young (Eds.), *Education in Retrospect: Policy and implementation since 1990*. Johannesburg and London, UK: HSRC and Institute of Education.
Muller, J. (2008). *In search of coherence: A conceptual guide to curriculum planning for comprehensive universities* (Report prepared for the SANTED Project). Johannesburg: Centre for Education Policy Development.
Muller, J. (2009). Forms of knowledge and curriculum coherence. *Journal of Education and Work, 22*(3), 205–226.
Munck, R. (2005). Neoliberalism and politics, and the politics of neoliberalism. In A. Saad-Filho & D. Johnston (Eds.), *Neoliberalism: A critical reader*. London, UK: Pluto Press.
Murgatroyd, S. (2010). Wicked problems and the work of the school. *European Journal of Education, 45*(2, Part 1), 259–279.
National Centre for Vocational Education Research. (1999). *Competency based training in Australia* (Research at a Glance) (pp. 1–8). NCVER.
Newfield, C. (2010). The structure and silence of the cognitariat. *Edu-factory web journal*, 10–26.
Noddings, N. (1983). The false promise of the Paideia: A critical review of the Paideia proposal. *Journal of Thought, 18*(4), 81–91.
Norris, N. (1991). The trouble with competence. *Cambridge Journal of Education, 21*(3), 331–341.
Novack, G. (1975). *Pragmatism versus Marxism: An appraisal of John Dewey's philosophy*. New York, NY: Pathfinder Press, Inc.
Novoa, A. (2002). Ways of thinking about education in Europe. In A. Novoa & M. Lawn (Eds.), *Fabricating Europe: The formation of an education space*. Dordrecht: Kluwer Academic Publishers.
OECD. (2007). *Qualifications Systems: Bridges to lifelong learning*. OECD.
OECD. (2010). *The High Cost of Low Educational Performance: The long run economic impact of achieving PISA outcomes*. Paris: Programme for Improving Student Assessment, OECD.
Palma, G. (2003). Latin America During the Second Half of the 20th Century: From the Age of ISI to the Age of The End of History. In H.-J. Chang (Ed.), *Rethinking Development Economics* (pp. 125–152). London, UK and New York, NY: Anthem Press.
Paterson, L. (2009, September). *Assessment and the curriculum for excellence*. Lecture given by Lindsay Paterson to SQA Masterclass series, 22, Glasgow.
Paterson, L. (2012). *Lindsay Paterson: Have we excellent curriculum or not? - Comment* Retrieved July 10, 2012, from Scotsman.com: http://www.scotsman.com/the-scotsman/opinion/comment/lindsay-paterson-have-we-excellent-curriculum-or-not-1-2191644

Pestalozzi, J. H. (1894). In L. E. Holland & F. C. Turner (Trans.), *How Gertrude Teaches her Children: A attempt to help mothers to teach their own children and an account of the method.* London, UK: S. Sonneschein.

Phillips, D. (1998). *The switchment of history: The development of a unitary qualifications framework.* (Doctoral thesis). University of Wellington.

Polanyi, K. (1944). *The Great Transformation. The political and economic origins of our time.* New York, NY: Beacon Press.

Pollit, C. (1998). Managerialism revisited. In B. Guy Peters & D. Savoie (Eds.), *Taking Stock: Assessing public sector reforms.* Montreal: Canadian Centre for Management Development.

Popham, W. J. (1972). *An Evaluation Guidebook: A set of practical guidelines for the educational evaluator.* Los Angeles, CA: The Instructional Objectives Exchange.

Postman, N., & Weingartner, C. (1971). *Teaching as a Subversive Activity.* Harmondsworth, UK: Penguin Education.

Pring, R. (1976). *Knowledge and Schooling.* London, UK: Open Books.

Raffe, D. (2003). Simplicity itself: The creation of the Scottish credit and qualifications framework. *Journal of Education and Work, 16*(3), 239–258.

Raffe, D. (2007). Making haste slowly: The evolution of a unified qualifications framework in Scotland. *European Journal of Education, 42*(4), 485–502.

Raffe, D. (2009a). The action plan, Scotland and the making of the modern educational world: The First Quarter Century. *Scottish Educational Review, 41*(4), 22–35.

Raffe, D. (2009b). The Scottish credit and qualifications framework: A case study of a very early starter. In S. Allais, D. Raffe, & M. Young (Eds.), *ILO Working Paper* (Vol. Employment Sector Working Paper No. 45, pp. 31–64). Geneva: ILO.

Raffe, D. (2009c). Towards a dynamic model of NQFs. In S. Allais, D. Raffe, & M. Young (Eds.), *Researching NQFs: Some conceptual issues* (Vol. Employment Sector Working Paper No. 44, pp. 22–43). Geneva: ILO.

Raggat, P. (1994). Implementing NVQs in colleges, progress, perceptions and issues. *Journal of Further and Higher Education, 18*(1), 59–74.

Raggat, P., & Williams, S. (1999). *Government, Markets and Vocational Qualifications. An anatomy of policy.* London, UK and New York, NY: Routledge.

Rata, E. (2012). *The Politics of Knowledge in Education.* London, UK and New York, NY: Routledge.

Rauner, F. (2007). Vocational education and training--A European perspective. In A. Brown, S. Kirpal, & F. Rauner (Eds.), *Identities at Work* (p. 115). Dordrecht: Springer.

Ravitch, D. (2001). *Left Back. A century of battles over school reform.* New York, NY: Touchstone.

Ravitch, D. (2010). *The Death and Life of the Great American School System. How testing and choice are undermining education.* New York, NY: Basic Books.

Reiss, M. J., & White, J. (2013). *An Aims-based Curriculum. The significance of human flourishing for schools.* London, UK: Institute of Education Press.

Republic of South Africa. (1998). *The Skills Development Act.* Pretoria.

Rizvi, F., & Lingard, B. (2010). *Globalizing Education Policy.* London, UK and New York, NY: Routledge.

Rosen, C. (2012). Freedom and art. *New York Review of Books.*

Sainsbury, D. (2013). *Progressive Capitalism: how to achieve economic growth, liberty and social justice.* London, UK: Biteback Publishing.

SAQA. (1997). *SAQA Bulletin, 1*(1).

SAQA. (2000a). *SGB Manual Part One.* Pretoria: SAQA.

SAQA. (2000b). *SGB Manual Part Two.* Pretoria: SAQA.

SAQA. (2000c). *The National Qualifications Framework and Curriculum Development.* Pretoria.

SAQA. (2000d). *The National Qualifications Framework and Quality Assurance.* Pretoria: The South African Qualifications Authority.

SAQA. (2000e). *The National Qualifications Framework and Standards Setting.* Pretoria: SAQA.

SAQA. (2001a). *Criteria and Guidelines for the Assessment of NQF Registered Unit Standards and Qualifications.* Pretoria: SAQA.

REFERENCES

SAQA. (2001b). *Criteria and Guidelines for the Registration of Assessors*. Pretoria: SAQA.
SAQA. (2003). *Qualifications and Standards: harmonization and articulation initiatives. Conference proceedings*. Pretoria: SAQA.
Schofield, K., & McDonald, R. (2004). *Moving on... Report of the high level review of training packages*. Brisbane: Australian National Training Authority (ANTA).
Schultz, T. (1961). Investment in Human Capital. In J. Karabel & A. H. Halsey (Eds.), *Power and Ideology in Education*. New York, NY: Oxford University Press.
Scott, D. (2008). *Critical Essays on Major Curriculum Theorists*. London, UK and New York, NY: Routledge.
Sedunary, E. (1996). Neither new nor alien to progressive thinking: Intepreting the convergence of radical education and the new vocationalism in Australia. *Journal of Curriculum Studies, 28*(4), 369–396.
Sellin, B. (2007). The proposal for a European qualifications framework. Making it a reality - possibilities and limitations. *European Journal of Vocational Training*, (42/43), 4–32.
Sennet, R. (2012). *This is not the kids' problem | Richard Sennett | Comment is free*. Retrieved July 10, 2012, from | The Guardian: http://www.guardian.co.uk/commentisfree/2012/jul/04/unemployment-not-kids-problem
Shalem, Y., Allais, S., & Steinberg, C. (2004). Outcomes-based quality assurance: What do we have to lose? *Journal of Education*, (34), 51–77.
Shields, E. (1996). Flexible work, labour market polarisation, and the politics of skills training and enhancement. In T. Dunk, S. McBride, & R. Nelsen (Eds.), *The Training Trap: Ideology, training, and the labour market*. Winnipeg/Halifax: Fernwoon Publishing.
Silber, K. (1965). *Pestalozzi: The man and his work* (2nd ed.). London, UK: Routledge and Kegan Paul.
Soudien, C. (2007). The A factor: Coming to terms with the question of legacy in South African education. *International Journal of Educational Development, 27*, 182–193.
Souto-Otero, M. (2012). Learning outcomes: good, irrelevant, bad or none of the above? *Journal of Education and Work, 25*(3), 249–258.
Spence, M. (1973). Job market signaling. *Quarterly Journal of Economics, 87*, 355–374.
Spreen, C. A. (2001). *Globalization and educational policy borrowing: Mapping outcomes-based education in South Africa* (Doctoral thesis). Columbia University.
Standing, G. (2011). *The Precariat. The new dangerous class*. New York, NY: Bloomsbury.
Stenhouse, L. (1975). *An Introduction to Curriculum Research and Development*. London, UK: Heinemann.
Stenhouse, L. (2002). A process model of curriculum. In J. Gultig, U. Hoadley, & J. Jansen (Eds.), *Curriculum: From plans to practices*. Cape Town: SAIDE/OUP.
Stewart, J. (2005). *Forward to: National Qualifications Frameworks: Their feasibility for effective implementation in developing countries*. Geneva: International Labour Organization.
Stewart, J., & Sambrook, S. (1995). The role of functional analysis in national vocational qualifications: A critical appraisal. *Journal of Education and Work, 8*(2), 93–106.
Strathdee, R. (2009). The implementation and impact of the New Zealand qualifications Framework. In S. Allais, D. Raffe, R. Strathdee, M. Young, & L. Wheelahan (Eds.), *Learning from the Early Starters* (Employment Sector Working Paper no. 45, pp. 65–89). Geneva: International Labour Organization.
Strathdee, R. (2011). The implementation, evolution and impact of New Zealand's national qualifications framework. *Journal of Education and Work, 24*(3-4), 303–321.
Tau, D., & Modesto, S. (2010). *Background case study on Botswana*. Geneva: Skills and Employability Department, ILO.
Taylor, N. (2000). Anything but knowledge: The case of the undisciplined curriculum. In *Designing Education for the Learning Society*. Enschede, Netherlands.
Thompson, L. (1990). *A History of South Africa*. New Haven and London, UK: Yale University Press.
Thurow, L. (1976). *Generating Inequality*. New York, NY: Basic Books.
Tilly, C. (1988). Solidary logics: Conclusions. *Theory and Society, 17*(3, Special Issue on Solidary Logics), 451–458.
Toffler, A. (1980). *The Third Wave*. London, UK: Collins.
Tomlinson, S. (2009). *Education in a Post-Welfare Society* (2nd ed.). Maidenhead: Open University Press.
Tyler, R. (1949). *Basic Principles of Curriculum and Instruction*. Chicago, IL: University of Chicago Press.

Vaizey, J. (1972). *The Political Economy of Education*. London, UK: Duckworth.

Van de Werfhorst, H. G. (2011). Skills, positional good or social closure? The role of education across structural–institutional labour market settings. *Journal of Education and Work*.

Van Rooyen, K. (2003). Policy and practice: Qualifications frameworks in New Zealand. In G. Donn & T. Davies (Eds.), *Promises and Problems for Commonwealth Qualifications Frameworks*. London, UK and Wellington: Commonwealth Secretariat and NZQA.

Vargas Zuñiga, F. (2005). *Key Competencies and Lifelong Learning*. Montevideo: CINTERFOR/ILO.

Verger, A. (2010). The role of ideas in GATS. Evidence from Argentina and Chile. In A. A. Jakobi, K. Martens, & K. D. Wolf (Eds.), *Education in Political Science. Discovering a neglected field* (pp. 123–139). Routledge/ECPR Studies in European Political Science.

Vidovich, L., & Slee, R. (2001). Bringing universities to account? Exploring some global and local policy tensions. *Journal of Education Policy, 17*(5), 431–453.

Vorwerk, C. (2004). Essential embedded knowledge - the forgotten dimension. *SAQA Bulletin, 6*(2), 67–86.

Wainwright, H. (1994). *Arguments for a New Left: Answering the free market right*. Oxford UK and Cambridge USA: Blackwell.

Werquin, P. (2012). The missing link to connect education and employment: Recognition of non-formal and informal learning outcomes. *Journal of Education and Work, 25*(3), 259–278.

Wheelahan, L. (2008). *Can learning outcomes be divorced from processes of learning? Or why training packages make very bad curriculum*. In 11th Annual Australian vocational education and training research association conference. Adelaide.

Wheelahan, L. (2009). From old to new: The Australian qualifications framework. In S. Allais, D. Raffe, R. Strathdee, M. Young, & L. Wheelahan (Eds.), *Learning from the Early Starters* (Employment Sector Working Paper no. 45, pp. 114–138). Geneva: ILO.

Wheelahan, L. (2010). *Why Knowledge Matters in Curriculum*. Abingdon and New York, NY: Routledge.

Wildschut, A., & Mgqolozana, T. (2009). Nurses. In J. Erasmus & M. Breier (Eds.), *Skills Shortages in South Africa. Case studies of key professions.* (pp. 132–151). Cape Town: HSRC Press.

Winch, C. (2011). Skill - A concept manufactured in England? In M. Brockmann, L. Clarke, & C. Winch (Eds.), *Knowledge, Skills and Competence in the European Labour Market. What's in a vocational qualification?* (pp. 85–101). Abingdon and New York, NY: Routledge.

Winch, C. (2012, February 23). *Curriculum design and epistemic ascent*. Paper presented at the seminar: Disciplines, Professional and School Knowledge. Final seminar of the Alternative Education Futures for a Knowledge Society project, London Knowledge Laboratory, Institute of Education, University of London.

Wolf, A. (1993). *Assessment Issues and Problems in a Criterion-based System*. London, UK: Further Education Unit, University of London.

Wolf, A. (1995). In H. Torrance (Ed.), *Competence-based Assessment.*. Buckingham: Open University Press.

Wolf, A. (2002). *Does Education Matter? Myths about education and economic growth*. London, UK: Penguin.

Wolf, K. D. (2010). Normative dimensions of reform in higher education. In A. A. Jakobi, K. Martens, & K. D. Wolf (Eds.), *Education in Political Science. Discovering a neglected field* (pp. 178–190). Abingdon and New York, NY: Routledge.

World Bank. (2002). *Constructing knowledge societies: New challenges for tertiary education. A World Bank report*. Washington DC: World Bank.

Young, M. (Ed.). (1971). *Knowledge and Control: New directions in the sociology of education*. Basingstoke: Macmillan.

Young, M. (1996). The outcomes approach to education and training: Theoretical grounding and an international perspective. In T. Coombe (Ed.), *IMWG conference on the National qualifications framework. Proceedings* (pp. 22–40). Johannesburg: Technikon SA Conference Centre: HSRC on behalf of the Inter-Ministerial Working Group on Education and Training.

Young, M. (2003). National Qualifications Frameworks as a global phenomenon. In G. Donn & T. Davies (Eds.), *Promises and Problems for Commonwealth Qualifications Frameworks*. London and Wellington: Commonwealth Secretariat and NZQA.

REFERENCES

Young, M. (2005). *National Qualifications Frameworks: Their feasibility for effective implementation in developing countries*. Geneva: International Labour Organization.

Young, M. (2007). Qualifications frameworks: Some conceptual issues. *European Journal of Education, 42*(4), 445–458.

Young, M. (2008). *Bringing Knowledge Back In: From social constructivism to social realism in the sociology of knowledge*. London, UK and New York, NY: Routledge.

Young, M. (2009a). Education, globalisation, and the voice of knowledge. *Journal of Education and Work, 22*(3), 193–204.

Young, M. (2009b). NVQs in the UK: Their origins and legacy. In S. Allais, D. Raffe, R. Strathdee, M. Young, & L. Wheelahan (Eds.), *Learning from the Early Starters*. Employment Sector Working Paper no. 45, pp. 5–29). Geneva: ILO.

Young, M. (2010). Alternative educational futures for a knowledge society. *European Educational Research Journal, 9*(1), 1–12.

Young, M. (2012). *The curriculum - An entitlement to powerful knowledge: A response to John White* (Paper offered to the New Visions Group for Education in response to An Unstable Framework - Critical Perspectives on The Framework for the National Curriculum.). New Visions for Education Group. Retrieved June 29, 2012, from http://www.newvisionsforeducation.org.uk/2012/05/03/the-curriculum-%E2%80%98an-entitlement-to-powerful-knowledge%E2%80%99-a-response-to-john-white/

Young, M., & Allais, S. (2009). Conceptualizing the role of qualifications in education reform. In S. Allais, M. Young, & D. Raffe (Eds.), *Researching Qualifications Frameworks: Some conceptual issues*. (Employment Sector Working Paper Number 44, pp. 5–22).

Young, M., & Allais, S. (Eds.). (2013). *Implementing National Qualifications Frameworks across Five Continents*. London, UK and New York, NY: Routledge.

Young, M., & Muller, J. (2010). Three educational scenarios for the future: Lessons from the sociology of knowledge. *European Journal of Education, 45*(1), 11–27.

Young, M., & Muller, J. (2013, April 9–11). *On the Powers of Powerful Knowledge*. Presented at the The Second Inernational Social Realism Symposium, Cambridge.

Zajda, J., & Zajda, J. (2005). Globalisation, education and policy: Changing paradigms. In *International Handbook on Globalisation, Education and Policy Research* (pp. 1–22). Dordrecht: Springer.

Lightning Source UK Ltd.
Milton Keynes UK
UKOW04f2334090614

233133UK00005B/161/P